# FOR REFERENCE

### Do Not Take From This Room

# Opening Science

Sönke Bartling · Sascha Friesike
Editors

# Opening Science

The Evolving Guide on How the Internet
is Changing Research, Collaboration
and Scholarly Publishing

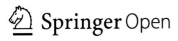 Springer Open

*Editors*
Sönke Bartling
German Cancer Research Center
Heidelberg
Germany

and

Institute for Clinical Radiology
   and Nuclear Medicine
Mannheim University Medical Center
Heidelberg University
Mannheim
Germany

Sascha Friesike
Alexander von Humboldt Institute
   for Internet and Society
Berlin
Germany

Opening science

ISBN 978-3-319-00025-1     ISBN 978-3-319-00026-8   (eBook)
DOI 10.1007/978-3-319-00026-8
Springer Cham Heidelberg New York Dordrecht London

Library of Congress Control Number: 2013953226

Printed on acid-free paper

Springer is part of Springer Science+Business Media (www.springer.com)

# Preface

Initially the Internet was designed for research purposes—so was the World Wide Web. Yet, society deviated from this intended use and as such many aspects of our daily lives have changed drastically over the past 20 years. The Internet has changed our ways of communicating, watching movies, interacting, shopping, and travelling. Many tools offered by the Internet have become second nature to us. At first, the net was designed as a plain data transfer network for researchers, yet it has since morphed into a vivid, transforming, living network. The evolution of the Internet came with barely foreseeable cultural changes, affecting core elements of our society, such as collaboration, government, participation, intellectual property, content, and information as a whole.

Novel online research tools pop up constantly and they are slowly but surely finding their way into research culture. A culture that grew after the first scientific revolution some 300 years ago and that has brought humanity quite far is on the verge of its second profound metamorphosis. It is likely that the way that researchers publish, assesses impact, communicate, and collaborate will change more within the next 20 years than it did in the past 200 years.

This book will give researchers, scientists, decision makers, politicians, and stakeholders an overview on the *basics*, the *tools*, and the *vision* behind the current changes we see in the field of knowledge creation. It is meant as a starting point for readers to become an active part in the future of research and to become an informed party during the transition phase. This is pivotal, since research, as a sensitive, complex process with many facets and millions of participants, hierarchies, personal networks, and structures, needs informed participants.

Many words are used to describe the future of research: 'Science 2.0', 'Cyberscience 2.0', 'Open Research', 'Open Science', 'Digital Humanities', 'eScience', 'Mode 2', etc. … They may trigger feelings of buzzwordism, yet at the same time the struggle for precise definitions highlights the current uncertainty regarding these and shows the many possible outcomes the current changes in research might bring.

It seems contradictory in itself to publish a 'traditional' book on this topic—why don't we simply go online? The book is and will be an important medium in research, just as papers and abstracts, and most importantly human interactions, will continue to be. However, all will be supplemented by novel tools, and accordingly so is this book. You can find, download, and even edit the entire book online at www.openingscience.org. It is published under the Creative Commons license, and everyone is invited to contribute to it and adopt and reuse its content. The book was created using a collaborative authoring tool, which saved us many meetings and tedious synchronizations of texts among authors. We made this book a living example of the communication culture research can have—not only in the future—but already today.

We thank all authors; their contributions and invested efforts are highly appreciated. The authors participated in the review process of the book. Besides our authors, many thanks go to our discussion partners and reviewers of our work, and to those who have not (yet) contributed a particular text, who are Annalies Gartz, Ayca-Nina Zuch, Joeseph Hennawi, Prof. Fabian Kiessling, Christine Kiefer, Thomas Rodt, Kersten Peldschus, Daniel Schimpfoessl, Simon Curt Harlinghausen, Prof. Wolfhard Semmler, Clemens Kaiser, Michael Grasruck, Carin Knoop, Martin Nissen, Jan Kuntz, Alexander Johannes Edmonds, Aljona Bondarenko, Prof. Marc Kachelrieß, Radko Krissak, Johannes Budjan, Prof. Henrik Michaely, Thomas Henzler, Prof. Christian Fink, Prof. Stefan O. Schönberg, Tillmann Bartling, Rajiv Gupta, and many others ...

Heidelberg                                                        Sönke Bartling
Berlin                                                           Sascha Friesike

# Contents

**Part III   Vision**

**Part IV   Cases, Recipes and How-Tos**

# Part I
# Basics/Background

# Towards Another Scientific Revolution

**Sönke Bartling and Sascha Friesike**

*But even within those limits, the openness I am advocating
would be a giant cultural shift in how science is done, a second
Open Science revolution extending and completing the first
Open Science revolution, of the 17th and 18th centuries.*
—Michael Nielsen

**Abstract** In this introductory chapter we establish a common understanding of
what are and what drives current changes in research and science. The concepts of
Science 2.0 and Open Science will be introduced. As such we provide a short
introduction to the history of science and knowledge dissemination. We explain
the origins of our scientific culture which evolved around publication methods.
Interdependencies of current concepts will be elucidated and it will be stated that
the transition towards Open Science is a complex cultural change. Reasons as to
why the change is slow are discussed and the main obstacles are identified. Next,
we explain the recent changes in scientific workflows and how these cause changes
in the system as a whole. Furthermore, we provide an overview on the entire book
and explain what can be found in each chapter.

Nicole Forster's goal as a researcher is to enhance cancer treatment. That is why
she and her colleagues in the laboratory of Leif W. Ellisen at Massachusetts
General Hospital Cancer Center in Boston, Massachusetts, study tumors on individual levels and search for cancer causes. In March 2012 Forster was trying to
isolate ribonucleic acid (RNA)—the genetic blueprint for proteins within the
cell—within mouse cells. To prepare the cells for her experiment she mixed them
with a special gel that provided them with all the nutrients to grow and proliferate,
even outside the body, for a short period of time. Yet in the following step, she had
to get rid of the gel to get to the information she needed: the RNA. And therein lay

S. Bartling (✉)
German Cancer Research Center, Heidelberg, Germany
e-mail: soenkebartling@gmx.de

S. Bartling
Institute for Clinical Radiology and Nuclear Medicine, Mannheim University
Medical Center, Heidelberg University, Mannheim, Germany

S. Friesike
Alexander von Humboldt Institute for Internet and Society, Berlin, Germany
e-mail: friesike@hiig.de

S. Bartling and S. Friesike (eds.), *Opening Science*,
DOI: 10.1007/978-3-319-00026-8_1, © The Author(s) 2014

her problem. She had never done that specific isolation before and hence did not know how to do it. Her colleagues did not know, either. *No one in my lab or even on my floor of the Cancer Center was doing such experiments,* said Forster. She was stuck. Then Forster thought of turning to the community of ResearchGate. ResearchGate is a social network (Boyd & Ellison 2007) for scientists to exchange ideas, publications, and to discuss research. Forster had first signed up to ResearchGate in 2009. She had heard about the network at a conference in Boston and was intrigued: *I thought that sharing research experience and discussing topics that you always wanted to discuss with someone would be a great opportunity. I like that it is a professional network where you can help other people and be helped.* Since then she had answered multiple questions from fellow ResearchGate members and now it was her turn to ask the community for help. Within 24 h Forster had a solution. Two researchers replied to her post and suggested different methods. She tried one and it worked. *You don't have to search for the best approach* via *Google or go through all of these publications,* Forster says. A social network for scientists helped Forster to solve a problem that she had bugged colleagues about for several weeks within a single day. Forster's case is far from uncommon. Researchers all over the world use modern communication tools such as social networks, blogs, or *Wikipedia* to enhance their scientific expertise, meet experts, and discuss ideas with people that face similar challenges. They do not abandon classical means of scientific communication such as publications or conferences, but rather they complement them. Today we can see that these novel communication methods are becoming more and more established in the lives of researchers; we argue that they may become a significant part of the future of research. We undertook this book in order to highlight the different developments that are currently arising in the world of knowledge creation. We do not know whether all of these developments will prevail, yet we are certain that institutional knowledge creation will change drastically over the next decade. Naturally, anyone involved in research does well to inform themselves about these developments. There is no perfect way by which research will be carried out in the future. Every researcher has to decide for themselves which technologies and methods they will include in their work. This, however,—as anything in research—starts with informing oneself about what is already out there; it is our goal to provide that information with this book.

## Knowledge Creation and Dissemination: A Brief History

In an early draft-version of this book, the present section was called 'A Brief History of Science'. Yet, we ran into several problems with this heading. *Firstly,* there is a singularity in the English language that differentiates between knowledge creation that is concerned with the rules of the natural world (science) and knowledge creation that is concerned with the human condition (humanities). Throughout the preparation of this book we constantly ran into this dilemma and we would like to take the opportunity to tell you that whenever we talk about science we mean any organized form of knowledge creation (see chapter Open Science and the Three Cultures: Expanding Open Science to all Domains of Knowledge Creation). *Secondly*, science is often understood as the product created by a scientists. And a scientists is understood as someone with a full-time job at a university or a research institute. Yet, new forms of collaboration reach far beyond our institutional understanding of doing research, which brings us to certain dissent.

As such we labeled the section 'Knowledge Creation and Dissemination'. Knowledge creation and its dissemination are two sides of the same coin—knowledge does not impact on society if it is unable to disseminate (Merton 1993). Throughout history we can see that breakthroughs in knowledge creation went hand in hand with breakthroughs in its dissemination. In turn, dissemination is not only bound to technological changes but also societal changes such as freedom of speech or the Renaissance. In large, the present book is a compendium that presents current changes that we see in knowledge creation and dissemination. Actually, many chapters of this book challenge our traditional understanding of how scientific knowledge should be disseminated. Moreover, as of today, researchers' views on how knowledge creation is changing differ drastically in many aspects. And it is likely that our understanding differs from your understanding. As such, all we want to offer in this book is a comprehensive overview on what is changing in the world of knowledge creation, which foundations are being laid today, and what might become essential in the future.

The history of human knowledge is closely linked to the history of civilization—one could even argue that the history of civilization is in large parts based on knowledge creation and its dissemination. In prehistoric times, knowledge was passed from one generation to the next one orally or by showing certain techniques. This mainly applied to basic everyday tasks such as hunting, fire making, manufacturing clothes, or gathering nutritious foods. The creation of this knowledge was not yet structured and it was not recorded, except for occasional drawings like cave paintings. The drastic change in knowledge creation was the invention of a writing system. Roughly at the same time, agriculture came to life. These two inventions combined laid the groundwork for what we today consider civilization. Civilization allowed for the division of labor and hence individuals began to specialize—knowledge creation accelerated. The researcher as a profession concerned with the creation of knowledge made his debut in ancient Greece. Scientists like Plato, Aristotle, Pythagoras, Socrates, or Archimedes wrote their observations down, taught others, and created knowledge that is still relevant roughly 2,500 years later. Disciplines as we know them today formed many centuries later and as such ancient scientists were usually philosophers, mathematicians, and physicists in one. Similar developments were noticeable in other societies as well. In China for instance thinkers like Confucius, Laozi, or Sun Tzu were concerned with question similar to those raised in ancient Greece.

During the following centuries, religion played a major role in the development of knowledge creation. Beliefs about certain essential questions such as *how was*

*the earth created? where do diseases come from?* or *what happens after death?*
impeded scientific advances in many fields and as such slowed down overall
knowledge creation. Not very surprisingly, the middle Ages are often considered
to be a dark age, in which rational thinking was prohibited. With the invention of
the printing press and the beginning of the Renaissance in the 17th century,
research slowly emancipated itself from religion. Slowly meaning that it took the
church until 1992 to rehabilitate Galileo for his outrageous claim that the sun
might be the center of our universe.

During the Renaissance, considerable amounts of knowledge were created by a
few polymaths—more or less a small group of outstanding thinkers involved in all
kinds of questions ranging from biology, to art, to engineering—hence the label
'Renaissance man'. Da Vinci, for instance, developed machines related to today's
helicopters, analyzed water, clouds, and rain, painted some of the most important
paintings of mankind, and did considerable research on anatomy. Goethe wrote,
did research in botany, and was in dispute with Newton over questions concerning
optics and color.

What we consider modern science came to life in the 17th century when
knowledge creation was both, professionalized and institutionalized. The number
of scientists started to skyrocket—from a few polymath during the renaissance to
over a million scientists in 1850. This growth did not slow down over the following 150 years and today we can globally count roughly 100 million people
involved in science. More and more disciplines formed and scientists became
professional specialists in tiny fields rather than experts in general knowledge.

## Professionalization of Knowledge Creation: The First Scientific Revolution

The professionalization of knowledge creation is often called the first scientific
revolution. Indeed it is this revolution that laid the groundwork for many principles
that guide scientific work today. Academic disciplines as we today know them
formed during the first scientific revolution, as did our publishing system. The
professionalization of knowledge creation required means of assessing the value of
a contribution, so that incentives for successful research could be provided.
Lacking a sufficient system for these incentives, 17th century researchers were
secretive in their discoveries. Without a scientific publication system they claimed
inventorship by sending out anagrams to fellow researchers that did not make
sense without knowledge of the discovery.[1] This method prevented other scientists
from claiming inventorship, and was still a form of publishing. When the
knowledge in question began to spread and the anagrams could be made sense of,
future research funding was hopefully already secured. Today, this sounds

---

[1] http://www.mathpages.com/home/kmath151/kmath151.htm

downright preposterous, as we all agree upon the notion that research is always based upon other research and as such that research results should be available to those interested in them.

It was the development of a journal publication system that drastically changed publishing in research and gave appropriate credits to researchers. The first journal purely dedicated to science was *Philosophical Transactions* which has been published ever since [e.g. one of the first scientific articles (Hook 1665)]. Publishing scientific journal articles became a pivotal building block of modern science. Researchers developed a common understanding that it is in the common interest for research results to be openly available to all other researchers (David 2004). This understanding of the necessity for openness in science ... *led to the modern journal system, a system that is perhaps the most open system for the transmission of knowledge that could be built with seventeenth-century media* (Nielsen 2011). Based on this core concept of publishing, myriads of partially institutionalized, partially commercialized structures grew. These structures developed constitute the cultural, political, and fundamental background in which academic knowledge creation works till today. The entire system is inherently based upon journals printed on paper. Almost every scientific publication we see today is created as if it is meant to be printed. Articles come in very predefined forms and are usually downloaded as printout-like PDFs. There is no fundamental reason to stick to this principle—other than our scientific heritage.

Currently, we can see a transition in knowledge dissemination set off by the Internet that enables scientists to publish in forms unimaginable only a few years ago. In all kinds of disciplines these new methods pop up, be it in the humanities under the term 'digital humanities', from a Web 2.0 angle under the term 'Science 2.0', or from those fighting for free knowledge under the term 'open research' and 'Open Science'. The Internet offers new answers to many challenges which the first scientific revolution overcame hundreds of years ago. And it is the task of today's researchers to assess and evaluate those newly created options, to bridge the legacy gap, and to lay a path towards the second scientific revolution.

## Legacy Gap: The Background of the Second Scientific Revolution

The journal system developed at a time when written or printed letters and a few books were the only means of transferring knowledge. Before printing and disseminating a piece of knowledge, it had to be in a *complete* and *correct* form, otherwise it was not worth paying for the costly publication process (Fig. 1). Publishers derived control over scientific content by controlling the printing and dissemination of scientific results. Accordingly, the assessment of scientific impact developed around the journal system.

However, paper is no longer the only media of choice. Publishing costs diminished and from a technical viewpoint preliminary results or idea snippets

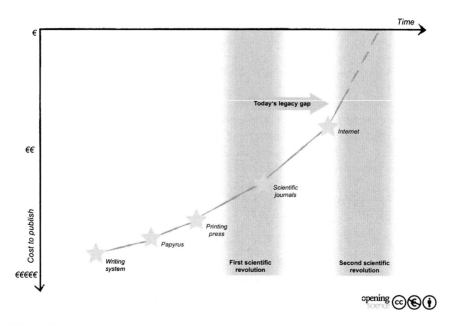

**Fig. 1** The first scientific revolution happened when the publishing of scientific papers became the prevailing means of disseminating scientific knowledge. Our scientific culture developed around this. Today the Internet provides novel means of publishing and we are in the 'legacy gap' between the availability of these tools and their profound integration into the scientific culture (second scientific revolution)

could be published, edited, and commented on. Yet, research as a whole is affected by the culture it has developed; it is affected by a the journal system created when results simply had to be printed on paper. We are currently in a "legacy gap" (Fig. 1) and everything points to the fact that we are on the brink of a new scientific revolution. Yet, how this revolution actually will be played out remains one of the most interesting questions in modern science.

## The Second Scientific Revolution

Picture a situation in which scientists would be able to publish all their thoughts, results, conclusions, data, and such as they occur, openly and widely available to everybody. The Internet already provides tools that could make this possible (microblogs, blogs, wikis, etc.). Moreover, picture a scientific culture in which researchers could be in the situation of doing so with the assurance that they will be credited appropriately. Imagine the potential for interactions between researchers. Knowledge could flow quickly, regardless of institutions and personal networks. Research results could be published as they occur. There would be no need to wait until results are complete enough to support a full paper. Similarly, if

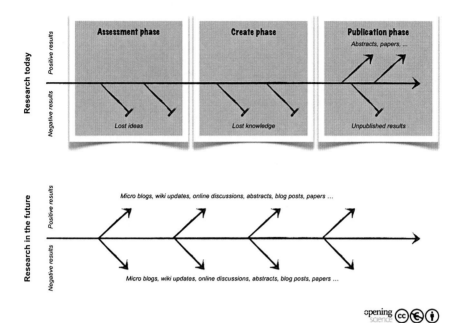

**Fig. 2** Today, research projects are conducted until results justify a full-blown paper. In the future, scientists might openly share ideas, preliminary results, and negative results at much earlier stages of their research using the novel publication methods that became available with the Internet

projects were to be stopped, negative or small findings could be published in blog posts or other low threshold publications. These findings could therefore still contribute to the scientific knowledge process. Today, negative results are often dismissed and thus the entire knowledge created in such a research project is not available to others. Someone else might start a similar project running into the same problem that stopped the first project simply because the first project never published an explanation of its failure (Fig. 2).

The advantages of such a scientific culture are multifaceted. We would see faster knowledge exchange, prevention of unnecessarily repeated experiments, and a more vivid discussion (Fig. 3). However, in order to use these novel publication formats, they must be appropriately credited by other scientists and—maybe more importantly—by granting authorities, which is not yet the case.

# Naming the New: Science 2.0, Open Science, eScience, Mode2, Open Research

Terms like Science 2.0, Open Science, Digital Humanities, eScience, Mode2, or Open Research are all umbrella terms that formed over the past few years and that emphasize various aspects of the second scientific revolution.

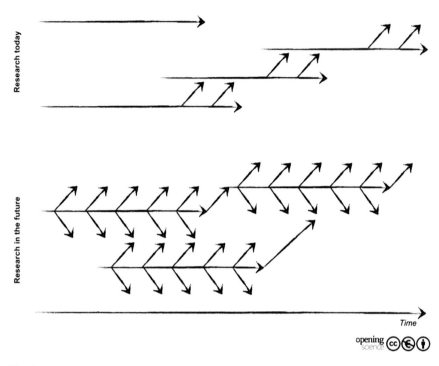

**Fig. 3** The research culture of the future possibly supports an open and wide communication beyond institutes and personal networks by providing novel, credited means of disseminating knowledge between researchers. Negative as well as positive findings will contribute to other research projects much sooner after the findings occur

All of these umbrella terms struggle to find a clear definition and people often use them interchangeably when talking about current changes in scientific pursuits. We sought after defining each and every one of these terms in order to establish a coherent picture of how the change in knowledge creation is seen from different angles. Yet, what each of the terms means and how exactly it differs from the others is often unclear. If you ask five people how Mode 2 and Science 2.0 are associated you can be certain to get five different and possibly contradictory answers. All terms are somewhat born of the necessity that a term for the present changes was needed. Knowledge creation is a wide field and thus several terms emerged, whereof we would like to define only two—mainly in order to use them in the discussions contained within this book.

- **Science 2.0** refers to all scientific culture, incl. scientific communication, which employs features enabled by Web 2.0 and the Internet (in contrast to Science 1.0 which represents a scientific culture that does not take advantage of the Internet).
- **Open Science** refers to a scientific culture that is characterized by its openness. Scientists share results almost immediately and with a very wide audience.

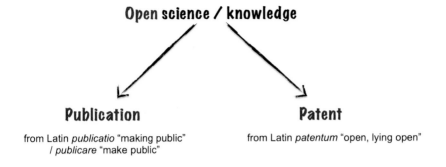

**Open science / knowledge**

**Publication**

from Latin *publicatio* "making public"
/ *publicare* "make public"

**Patent**

from Latin *patentum* "open, lying open"

**Fig. 4** Since the first scientific revolution, science and knowledge creation was open—as open as the methods of the seventeenth century allowed it to be. The Internet has brought about novel methods, thus allowing science to be more open

Strictly speaking, since the first scientific revolution, science has been open (Fig. 4). Through the Internet and Web 2.0 science can become '*more* Open Science', meaning that researchers share results, ideas, and data much earlier and much more extensively to the public than they do at the moment.

Science 2.0 enables Open Science, but Science 2.0 does not necessarily have to happen in an Open Science fashion, since scientists can still employ features of the Internet, but stay very much put in terms of publishing their results. This might be due to cultural and legal restrictions.

## The Second Scientific Revolution: Road to a Great New Future?

Many stakeholders serve the current scientific culture. They brought research, and with it society, quite far. Yet now, we have to face the challenges that come with all the novel developments and with the second scientific revolution. History shows that knowledge creation has always adopted new opportunities. In turn, it certainly will do so this time, too. Yet the question remains as to who will be the drivers and the stakeholders of tomorrow. In the best case, the biggest benefactor will be the scientific knowledge generating process—and with it research itself.

Many researchers show considerable concern in respect to the novel concepts of the second scientific revolution. From these concerns vivid discussions should arise and useful conclusions should be found that steer the second scientific revolution in the right direction. This is especially true since significant input should come from within the active research community itself.

Another question is whether future *openness* and *onlineness* will set optimal incentives for the creation of knowledge. Many wrong paths could be picked and may result in dead-ends. It is important that stakeholders are flexible and honest enough to be able to leave dead-end streets.

Some voices discuss the current transition of research as a revolutionizing process that might overcome current shortcomings in scientific conduct. Shortcomings are among many others: questionable proof generating means (such as wrongly applied statistics (Ioannidis 2005; Sterne 2001), intolerance against uncommon theses and approaches, citation-based 'truth generation', and inflexible cultures of scientific approaches within disciplines. Furthermore, publication-bias through rejection of negative results or rejection of non-confirming studies (Turner et al. 2008; Begley & Ellis 2012) and questionable incentives that are set by the current methods to assess scientific quality (see chapter Excellence by Nonsense: The Competition for Publications in Modern Science) are also factors. The transition towards the second scientific revolution can help to solve these problems, but it does not necessarily have to. It can be a way to make science more open, liberal, and fair, but it can also result in the opposite.

To conclude, much will depend upon whether researchers become the leading force within this transition, or whether they play a passive role driven by other stakeholders of the research process. In order to prevent the latter, researchers should be deeply involved in this process and they should be aware of the potential consequences. *This book is meant to support scientists in becoming a constructing factor in the designing process of the second scientific revolution.*

## The Second Scientific Revolution is Based on Many Novel Aspects and Tools

Despite their separation, the key aspects of the second scientific revolution are interconnected (Fig. 5). Open Access (see chapter Open Access: A State of the Art), for instance, needs new forms of copyright concepts (see Creative Commons Licences). Reference managers (see Reference Management) are a great addition to social networks for scientists (see chapter Academia Goes Facebook? The Potential of Social Network Sites in the Scholarly Realm). Assessing the scientific impact of novel publications such as blog posts (see (Micro)Blogging Science? Notes on Potentials and Constraints of New Forms of Scholarly Communication) needs novel impact measurement factors—altmetrics (see chapter Altmetrics and Other Novel Measures for Scientific Impact), which might be based on unambiguous researcher IDs (see chapter Unique Identifiers for Researchers). Altmetrics, at the same time, can be integrated into social networks. There is no single most important factor: it is more a multitude of facets that jointly change how research works.

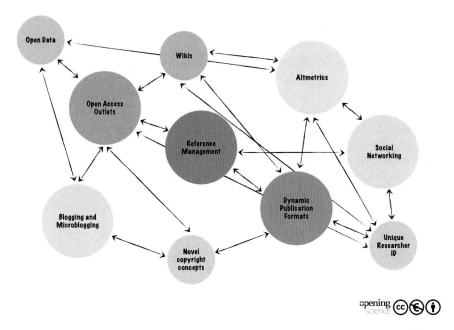

**Fig. 5** It is important to understand that many tools of the second scientific revolution will only make sense if others are also implemented. For example, alternative impact measurement systems such as altmetrics only make sense if researchers can be uniquely identified—either with a Unique Researcher ID or within a social network

## How This Book Works: Artificially Dissecting the Second Scientific Revolution

This book brings together the enabling concepts that shape the current discussion on our changing research environment. We divided the book into three parts in order to make its content easily accessible.

- The first part of the book is called **Basics**; here we cover topics that highlight the overall shift in scientific thinking. It begins with the chapter "Open Science: One Term, Five Schools of Thought" in which *Benedikt Fecher* and editor *Sascha Friesike* explain the many meanings which have been given to the term Open Science. This is followed by *Mathias Binswanger's* "Excellence by Nonsense: The Competition for Publications in Modern Science" in which he highlights some of the downsides in today publication driven scientific environments. *Alexander Gerber's* article titled "Science Caught Flat-footed: How Academia Struggles with Open Science Communication" follows; here the author explains why social media are adopted quite slowly by the research community, especially in Europe. The last article in the section was written by *Michelle Sidler* and is entitled "Open Science and the Three Cultures:

Expanding Open Science to All Domains of Knowledge Creation"; in it the author highlights a core weakness that the terms Open Science and Science 2.0 share: the fact that all of the implied concepts are valid for researchers outside the sciences as well, yet the name might scare them away.

- The second part of the book is called **Tools** and deals with implementations that already work today. *Cornelius Puschmann* starts the section with his piece on blogging and microblogging among researches called "(Micro) blogging Science? Notes on Potentials and Constraints of New Forms of Scholarly Communication". He is followed by *Michael Nentwich* and *René König's* article "Academia Goes Facebook? The Potential of Social Network Sites in the Scholarly Realm". "Reference Management" by *Martin Fenner, Kaja Scheliga*, and editor *Sönke Bartling* is the next chapter. It is succeeded by "Open Access: A State of the Art" by *Dagmar Sitek* and *Roland Bertelmann*, and *James MacGregor, Kevin Stranack*, and *John Willinsky's* "The Public Knowledge Project: Open Source Tools for Open Access to Scholarly Communication".
- The third part named **Vision** takes a more long term view on the issue and thus explains how single aspects of research might develop over the next decade or two. The section begins with an article by *Martin Fenner* named "Altmetrics and Other Novel Measures for Scientific Impact" and an article by *Lambert Heller, Ronald The,* and *Sönke Bartling* called "Dynamic Publication Formats and Collaborative Authoring". It follows "Open Research Data: From Vision to Practice" by *Heinz Pampel* and *Sünje Dallmeier-Tiessen*, and "Intellectual Property and Computational Science" by *Victoria Stodden.* The next chapter is called "Research Funding in Science 2.0" and was written by *Jörg Eisfeld-Reschke, Ulrich Herb,* and *Karsten Wenzlaff.* The last chapter of the book was written by *ThomasSchildhauer* and *Hilger Voss* and is entitled "Open Innovation and Crowdsourcing in the Sciences".
- The book closes with a collection of cases which highlight in a rather brief manner some aspects of the Open Science movement. Here the authors focus on specific aspects and projects, give advice, or present their experience

# References

Begley, C. G., & Ellis, L. M. (2012). Drug development: raise standards for preclinical cancer research. *Nature, 483*(7391), 531–533. doi:10.1038/483531a.

Boyd, D. M., & Ellison, N. B. (2007). Social network sites: definition, history, and scholarship. *J. Comput.-Mediated Commun., 13*(1), 210–230. doi:10.1111/j.1083-6101.2007.00393.x.

David, P. A. (2004). Understanding the emergence of "Open Science" institutions: functionalist economics in historical context. *Ind. Corporate Change, 13*(4), 571–589. doi:10.1093/icc/dth023.

Hook, M. (1665). Some observations lately made at London concerning the planet Jupiter. *Philosophical transactions of the royal society of London, 1*(1–22), pp. 245–247. doi:10.1098/rstl.1665.0103.

Ioannidis, J.P.A. (2005). Why most published research findings are false. *PLoS Medicine, 2*(8), p. e124. doi:10.1371/journal.pmed.0020124.

Merton, R.K. (1993). *On the shoulders of giants: a Shandean postscript* Post-Italianate ed., Chicago: University of Chicago Press.

Nielsen, M. (2011). *Reinventing discovery: the new era of networked science.* New Jersey: Princeton University Press.

Sterne, J. A. C. (2001). Sifting the evidence—what's wrong with significance tests? Another comment on the role of statistical methods. *BMJ, 322*(7280), 226–231. doi:10.1136/bmj.322.7280.226.

Turner, E. H., Matthews, A. M., Linardatos, E., & Tell, R. A. (2008). Selective publication of antidepressant trials and its influence on apparent efficacy. *New England J. Med., 358*(3), 252–260. doi:10.1056/NEJMsa065779.

# Open Science: One Term, Five Schools of Thought

Benedikt Fecher and Sascha Friesike

**Abstract** Open Science is an umbrella term encompassing a multitude of assumptions about the future of knowledge creation and dissemination. Based on a literature review, this chapter aims at structuring the overall discourse by proposing five Open Science schools of thought: The *infrastructure school* (which is concerned with the technological architecture), the *public school* (which is concerned with the accessibility of knowledge creation), the *measurement school* (which is concerned with alternative impact measurement), the *democratic school* (which is concerned with access to knowledge) and the *pragmatic school* (which is concerned with collaborative research).

There is scarcely a scientist who has not stumbled upon the term 'Open Science' of late and there is hardly a scientific conference where the word and its meaning are not discussed in some form or other. 'Open Science' is one of the buzzwords of the scientific community. Moreover, it is accompanied by a vivid discourse that apparently encompasses any kind of change in relation to the future of scientific knowledge creation and dissemination; a discourse whose lowest common denominator is perhaps that science in the near future somehow needs to open up more. In fact, the very same term evokes quite different understandings and opens a multitude of battlefields, ranging from the democratic right to access publicly funded knowledge (e.g. Open Access to publications) or the demand for a better bridging of the divide between research and society (e.g. citizen science) to the development of freely available tools for collaboration (e.g. social media platforms

B. Fecher
German Institute for Economic Research, Mohrenstraße 58, Berlin 10117, Germany

S. Friesike (✉)
Alexander von Humboldt Institute for Internet and Society, Berlin, Germany
e-mail: friesike@hiig.de

S. Bartling and S. Friesike (eds.), *Opening Science*,
DOI: 10.1007/978-3-319-00026-8_2, © The Author(s) 2014

for scientists). From this vantage point, openness could refer to pretty much anything: The process of knowledge creation, its result, the researching individual him- or herself, or the relationship between research and the rest of society.

The diversity, and perhaps ambiguity, of the discourse is, however, understandable considering the diversity of stakeholders that are directly affected by a changing scientific environment. These are in the first place: Researchers from all fields, policy makers, platform programmers and operators, publishers, and the interested public. It appears that each peer group discussing the term has a different understanding of the meaning and application of Open Science. As such the whole discourse can come across as somewhat confusing. By structuring the Open Science discourse on the basis of existing literature, we would like to offer an overview of the multiple directions of development of this still young discourse, its main arguments, and common catchphrases. Furthermore, we intend to indicate issues that in our eyes still require closer attention.

Looking at the relevant literature on Open Science, one can in fact recognize iterative motives and patterns of argumentation that, in our opinion, form more or less distinct streams. Referring to the diversity of these streams, we allowed ourselves to call them schools of thought. After dutifully combing through the literature on Open Science, we identified five distinct schools of thought. We do not claim a consistently clear-cut distinction between these schools (in fact some share certain ontological principles). We do, however, believe that our compilation can give a comprehensible overview of the predominant thought patterns in the current Open Science discourse and point towards new directions in research regarding Open Science. In terms of a literature review, we furthermore hope that this chapter identifies some of the leading scholars and thinkers within the five schools.

The following table (Table 1) comprises the five identified schools together with their central assumptions, the involved stakeholder groups, their aims, and the tools and methods used to achieve and promote these aims.

It must be noted that our review is not solely built upon traditional scholarly publications but, due to the nature of the topic, also includes scientific blogs and newspaper articles. It is our aim in this chapter to present a concise picture of the ongoing discussion rather than a complete list of peer-reviewed articles on the topic. In the following, we will describe the five schools in more detail and provide references to relevant literature for each.

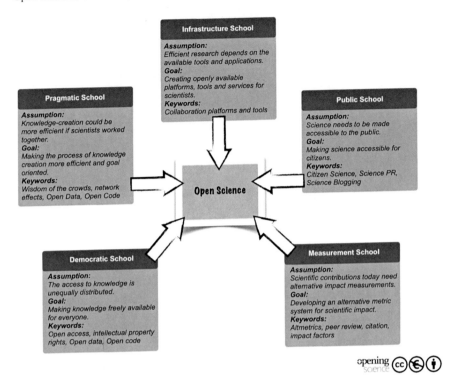

## Public School: The Obligation to Make Science Accessible to the Public

In a nutshell, advocates of the public school argue that science needs to be accessible for a wider audience. The basic assumption herein is that the social web and Web 2.0 technologies allow scientists, on the one hand, to open up the research process and, on the other, to prepare the product of their research for interested non-experts (see Table 2).

Accordingly, we recognize two different streams within the public school: The first is concerned with the accessibility of the research process (the production), the second with the comprehensibility of the research result (the product). Both streams involve the relationship between scientists and the public and define openness as a form of devotion to a wider audience. In the following section we will elaborate more on both streams in reference to relevant literature.

### *Accessibility to the Research Process: Can Anyone be a Scientist?*

To view the issue as a formerly hidden research process becoming transparent and accessible to the common man seems a decidedly romantic image of doing science.

**Table 1** Five Open Science schools of thought

| School of thought | Central assumption | Involved groups | Central Aim | Tools & Methods |
|---|---|---|---|---|
| Democratic | The access to knowledge is unequally distributed. | Scientists, politicians, citizens | Making knowledge freely available for everyone. | Open Access, intellectual property rights, Open data, Open code |
| Pragmatic | Knowledge-creation could be more efficient if scientists worked together. | Scientists | Opening up the process of knowledge creation. | Wisdom of the crowds, network effects, Open Data, Open Code |
| Infrastructure | Efficient research depends on the available tools and applications. | Scientists & platform providers | Creating openly available platforms, tools and services for scientists. | Collaboration platforms and tools |
| Public | Science needs to be made accessible to the public. | Scientists & citizens | Making science accessible for citizens. | Citizen Science, Science PR, Science Blogging |
| Measurement | Scientific contributions today need alternative impact measurements. | Scientists & politicians | Developing an alternative metric system for scientific impact. | Altmetrics, peer review, citation, impact factors |

**Table 2** Public School

| Author (Year) Type of Publication | Title | Content |
|---|---|---|
| Puschmann (2012) Book chapter | (Micro)blogging Science? Notes on Potentials and Constraints of New Forms of Scholarly Communication | Scientists today need to make their research accessible to a wider audience by using (micro)blogs. "Scientists must be able to explain what they do to a broader public to garner political support and funding for endeavors whose outcomes are unclear at best and dangerous at worst, a difficulty that is magnified by the complexity of scientific issues." (P. XX) |
| Cribb & Sari (2010) Monograph | Open Science—Sharing Knowledge in the digital age | The accessibility of scientific knowledge is a matter of its presentation. "Science is by nature complicated, making it all the more important that good science writing should be simple, clean and clear." (p. 15) |
| Grand et al. (2012) Journal Article | Open Science: A New "Trust Technology"? | Scientists can raise public trust by using Web 2.0 tools. "As mainstream science—and comment on science—follows the pioneers into the realm of Web 2.0, to be able to navigate the currents of the information flow in this relatively unmapped territory, scientists and members of the public will all need reliable and robust tools." (p. 685) |
| Morris & Mietchen (2010) Proceedings | Collaborative Structuring of Knowledge by Experts and the Public | Using Web 2.0 tools to make knowledge production accessible for the public. "(...) there is still plenty of opportunities for reinventing and experimenting with new ways to render and collaborate on knowledge production and to see if we can build a more stable, sustainable and collegial atmosphere (...) for experts and the public to work together." (p. 32) |
| Tacke (2012) Blog entry | Raus aus dem Elfenbeinturm: Open Science | The Web 2.0 gives scientists new opportunities to spread scientific knowledge to a wider public. "Im einfachsten Fall können Wissenschaftler etwa in Blogs über Themen aus ihrem Fachgebiet berichten und Fragen von interessierten dazu beantworten." (p. 2) |

(continued)

**Table 2** (continued)

| Author (Year) Type of Publication | Title | Content |
|---|---|---|
| Irwin (2006) Monograph | The politics of talk | Due to modern technology, citizens can participate in scientific knowledge creation. "(...) this book is committed both to an improved understanding of 'science, technology and citizenship' and to better social practice in this area (...)" (p. 8) |
| Hand (2010) Article | Citizen science: People power | Citizens possess valuable knowledge from which science can benefit. "By harnessing human brains for problem solving, Foldit takes BOINC's distributed-computing concept to a whole new level." (p. 2) |
| Ebner & Maurer (2009) Article | Can microblogs and weblogs change traditional scientific writing? | Blogs can contribute to make research more accessible to the public. Yet they cannot replace articles and essays in scholarly communication. "Weblogs and microblogs can enhance lectures by bringing the resources of the WorldWideWeb to the course and making them discussable. Both new technologies, however, cannot replace writing essays and articles, because of their different nature." |
| Catlin-Groves (2012) Review article | The Citizen Science Landscape: From Volunteers to Citizen Sensors and Beyond | Citizens can help monitoring on a large scale. "The areas in which it [citizen science] has, and most probably will continue to have, the greatest impact and potential are that of monitoring ecology or biodiversity at large geographic scales." |
| Powell & Colin (2009) Article | Participatory paradoxes: Facilitating citizen engagement in science and technology from the Top-Down? | Citizen science projects are often short-lived. "Most participatory exercises do not engage citizens beyond an event or a few weeks/months, and they do not build citizens' participatory skills in ways that would help them engage with scientists or policy makers independently." (p. 327) |

Yet, coming from the assumptions that communication technology not only allows the constant documentation of research, but also the inclusion of dispersed external individuals (as supposed in the pragmatic school), an obvious inference is that the formerly excluded public can now play a more active role in research. A pervasive catchphrase in this relationship is the concept of so-called citizen science which, put simply, describes the participation of non-scientists and amateurs in research. Admittedly, the term, as well as the idea, have already existed for a long time. In 1978, well before the digital age, the biochemist Erwin Chargaff already used this term to espouse a form of science that is dominated by dedicated amateurs. The meaning of the term has not changed; it merely experiences a new magnitude in the light of modern communication technology.

Hand (2010) refers, for instance, to Rosetta@Home, a distributed-computing project in which volunteer users provide their computing power (while it is not in use) to virtually fold proteins. The necessary software for this also allowed users to watch how their computer tugged and twisted the protein in search of a suitable configuration (ibid., p.2). By observing this, numerous users came up with suggestions to speed up the otherwise slow process. Reacting to the unexpected user involvement, the research team applied a new interface to the program that allowed users to assist in the folding in form of an online game called Foldit. Hand states: *"By harnessing human brains for problem solving, Foldit takes BOINC's distributed-computing concept to a whole new level"* (ibid., p. 2). In this specific case, the inclusion of citizens leads to a faster research process on a large public scale. Citizen science is in this regard a promising tool to 'harness' a volunteer workforce. However, one can arguably question the actual quality of the influence of amateurs upon the analytical part of the research research. Catlin-Groves (2012) takes the same line as the Rosetta@Home project. She expects citizen science's greatest potential in the monitoring of ecology or biodiversity at a large scale (ibid., p. 2). The specific fields possibly issue from the author's area of research (Natural Sciences) and the journal in which the review article was published (International Journal of Zoology). Nonetheless, in respect to the two fields, it becomes apparent that citizens can rather be considered a mass volunteer workforce instead of actual scientists.

Indeed, most citizen science projects follow a top-down logic in which professional scientists give impetuses, take on leading roles in the process and analysis, and use amateurs not as partners, but rather as a free workforce. Irwin (2006) even claims that most citizen science projects are not likely to provide amateurs with the skills and capacities to significantly affect research in meaningful ways. Powell and Colin (2009) also criticize the lack of a meaningful impact for non-experts in the research: *"Most participatory exercises do not engage citizens beyond an event or a few weeks/months, and they do not build citizens' participatory skills in ways that would help them engage with scientists or policy makers independently"* (ibid., p. 327).

The authors further present their own citizen science project, the Nanoscale Science and Engineering Center (NSEC), which at first also started as a onetime event. After the project was finished, however, the University engaged a citizen scientist group which is in frequent dialogue with field experts. The authors do not lay out in detail how citizens can actually influence research policies, rather present a perspective for a bottom-up relationship between interested amateurs and professionals. There is still a lack of research when it comes to models of active involvement of citizens in the research process beyond feeder services. Future research could therefore focus on new areas of citizen participation (e.g. citizen science in 'soft sciences') or alternative organizational models for citizen science (e.g. how much top-down organization is necessary?).

Another, also yet to explored, aspect that can be associated with citizen science is the crowdfunding of science. Crowdfunding is a financing principle that is already well established in the creative industries. Via online platforms, single Internet users can contribute money to project proposals of their choice and, if the project receives enough funding, enable their realization. Contributions are often rewarded with non-monetary benefits for the benefactors. A similar model is conceivable for science: The public finances research proposals directly through monetary contributions and in return receives a benefit of some description (for instance: access to the results). Crowdfunding of science allows direct public influence on the very outskirts of the research (a kind of civic scientific agenda setting) yet hardly at all during the process. Nonetheless, it possibly constitutes a new decisive force in the pursuit of research interests besides the "classica" of institutional and private funding. There is still, at least to the authors' knowledge, no research regarding this topic. Future research could for instance cover factors of success for project pitches or the actual potential of crowdfunding for science.

## *Comprehensibility of the Research Result: Making Science Understandable*

The second stream of the public school refers to the comprehensibility of science for a wider audience, that is mainly science communication. Whereas, for instance, citizen science concerns the public influence on the research, this sub-stream concerns the scientists' obligation to make research understandable for a wider audience—a demand that Tacke (2012), in an entry on his blog, provocatively entitled *"Come out of the ivory tower!"*.

In this regard, Cribb and Sari demand a change in the scientific writing style: *"Science is by nature complicated, making it all the more important that good science writing should be simple, clean and clear"* (2010, p. 15). The authors' credo is that as the scientific audience becomes broader and the topics more specific, the academic dissemination of knowledge needs to adapt.

On a perhaps more applied level, numerous authors suggest specific tools for science communication. Weller and Puschmann (2011), for instance, describe the microblogging service Twitter as a suitable tool to direct users to, for example, relevant literature and as a source for alternative impact factors (as expressed in the measurement school). In this volume (see chapter Micro(blogging) Science? Notes on Potentials and Constraints of New Forms of Scholarly Communication), Puschmann furthermore dwells on the role of the scientist today and his need to communicate: "*Scientists must be able to explain what they do to a broader public to garner political support and funding for endeavors whose outcomes are unclear at best and dangerous at worst, a difficulty that is magnified by the complexity of scientific issues*". As adequate tools for the new form of scholarly public justification, the author refers to scientific blogging or Twitter during conferences. In the same line of reasoning, Grand et al. (2012) argues that by using Web 2.0 tools and committing to public interaction, a researcher can become a public figure and honest broker of his or her information (ibid., p. 684).

While numerous researchers already focus on the new tools and formats of science communication and the audience's expectations, there is still a need for research on the changing role of a researcher in a digital society, that is, for instance, the dealings with a new form of public pressure to justify the need for instant communication and the ability to format one's research for the public. A tenable question is thus also if a researcher can actually meet the challenge to, on the one hand, carry out research on highly complex issues and, on the other, prepare these in easily digestible bits of information. Or is there rather an emerging market for brokers and mediators of academic knowledge? Besides, what are the dangers of preparing research results in easily digestible formats?

## Democratic School: Making Research Products Available

The democratic school is concerned with the concept of access to knowledge. Unlike the public school, which promotes accessibility in terms of participation to research and its comprehensibility, advocates of the democratic school focus on the principal access to the products of research. This mostly relates to research publications and scientific data, but also to source materials, digital representations of pictorial and graphical materials, or multimedia material (as Sitek and Bertelmann describe it their chapter).

Put simply, they argue that any research product should be freely available. The reason we refer to the discourse about free access to research products as the democratic school issues from its inherent rationale that everyone should have the equal right to access knowledge, especially when it is state-funded.

In the following, we will focus on two central streams of the democratic school, namely Open Access to research publications and Open Data. We assume that both represent a wider set of arguments that accompanies discussion on free access to research products.

## Open Data

Regarding Open Data in science, Murray-Rust (2008, p. 52) relates the meaning of the prefix 'open' to the common definition of open source software. In that understanding, the right of usage of scientific data does not demise to an academic journal but remains in the scientific community: *"I felt strongly that data of this sort should by right belong to the community and not to the publisher and started to draw attention to the problem"* (ibid., p. 54). According to Murray-Rust, it is obstructive that journals claim copyright for supporting information (often data) of an article and thereby prevent the potential reuse of the data. He argues that *"(it) is important to realize that SI is almost always completely produced by the original authors and, in many cases, is a direct output from a computer. The reviewers may use the data for assessing the validity of the science in the publication but I know of no cases where an editor has required the editing of (supporting information)"* (ibid., p. 53). The author endorses that text, data or meta-data can be re-used for whatever purpose without further explicit permission from a journal (see Table 3). He assumes that, other than validating research, journals have no use for claiming possession over supporting information—other researchers, however, do.

According to Murray-Rust's understanding, data should not be 'free' (as in free beer), but open for re-use in studies foreseen or unforeseen by the original creator. The rationale behind Open Data in science is in this case researcher-centric; it is a conjuncture that fosters meaningful data mining and aggregation of data from multiple papers. Put more simply, Open Data allows research synergies and prevents duplication in the collection of data. In this regard, Murray-Rust does not only criticize the current journal system and the withholding of supporting information but also intimates at the productive potential of Open Data. It has to be said, though, that the synergy potentials that Murray-Rust describes mostly apply to natural sciences (or at least research fields in which data is more or less standardized) or at least fields in which an intermediate research product (e.g. data) can be of productive use for others.

Similar to Murray-Rust, Molloy (2011) criticises the current journal system which, according to the author, works against the maximum dissemination of scientific data that underlies publications. She elaborates on the barriers inherent in the current journal system thus: *"Barriers include inability to access data, restrictions on usage applied by publishers or data providers, and publication of data that is difficult to reuse, for example, because it is poorly annotated or 'hidden' in unmodifiable tables like PDF documents"* (ibid., p. 1). She suggests a dealing with data that follows the Open Knowledge Foundation's definition of openness, meaning that the data in question should be available as a whole, at no more than a reasonable reproduction cost (preferably through download), and in a convenient and modifiable form.

Other than Murray-Rust (2008) and Molloy (2011), Vision (2010), and Boulton et al. (2011) firstly hold the researchers liable for practicing Open Data. Vision refers to a study by Campbell et al. (2002), in which it is shown that only one

**Table 3** Democratic School—Open data

| Author (Year) | Type of Publication | Title | Content |
|---|---|---|---|
| Murray-Rust (2008) | Proceedings | Open data in science | Open data depends on a change of the journal practice regarding the withholding of supporting information. "The general realization of the value of reuse will create strong pressure for more and better data. If publishers do not gladly accept this challenge, then scientists will rapidly find other ways of publishing data, probably through institutional, departmental, national or international subject repositories. In any case the community will rapidly move to Open Data and publishers resisting this will be seen as a problem to be circumvented." (p. 64) |
| Vision (2010) | Journal Article | Open Data and the Social Contract of Scientific Publishing | Data is a commodity. The sharing of data enables benefits other researchers. "Data are a classic example of a public good, in that shared data do not diminish in value. To the contrary, shared data can serve as a benchmark that allows others to study and refine methods of analysis, and once collected, they can be creatively repurposed by many hands and in many ways, indefinitely." (p. 330) |
| Boulton et al. (2011) | Comment | Science as a public enterprise: the case for open data | Data needs to be prepared in a usable format. "Conventional peer-reviewed publications generally provide summaries of the available data, but not effective access to data in a usable format." (p. 1634) |
| Molloy (2011) | Open Access Article | The open knowledge foundation: Open data means better science | Data should be free to reuse and redistribute without restrictions. "The definition of "open", crystallised in the OKD, means the freedom to use, reuse, and redistribute without restrictions beyond a requirement for attribution and share-alike. Any further restrictions make an item closed knowledge." (p. 1) |
| Auer et al. (2007) | | DBpedia: A nucleus for a web of open data the semantic web | Open Data is a major challenge for computer scientists in future. "It is now almost universally acknowledged that stitching together the world's structured information and knowledge to answer semantically rich queries is one of the key challenges of computer science, and one that is likely to have tremendous impact on the world as a whole." (p. 1) |

(continued)

**Table 3** (continued)

| Author (Year) Type of Publication | Title | Content |
|---|---|---|
| Löh & Hinze (2006) | *Open Data types and open functions* | The problem of supporting the modular extensibility of both data and functions in one programming language (known as expression problem) "*The intended semantics is as follows: the program should behave as if the data types and functions were closed, defined in one place.*" (p. 1) |
| Miller et al. (2008) | *Open Data Commons, A Licence for Open Data* | Practicing open data is a question of appropriate licencing of data. "*Instead, licenses are required that make explicit the terms under which data can be used. By explicitly granting permissions, the grantor reassures those who may wish to use their data, and takes a conscious step to increase the pool of Open Data available to the web.*" (p. 1) |

quarter of scientists share their research data—even upon request. According to the study, the most common reason for denying requests was the amount of effort required for compliance. Vision presents disciplinary data repositories that are maintained by the data creators themselves as an appropriate solution to the problem. This way, scientists would only need to upload their data once instead of complying with requests. Although Vision emphasizes the necessity to minimize the submission burden for the author, he does not suggest concrete inducements for scientists to upload their data (for instance forms of community recognition or other material rewards). In an empirical study about the sharing behavior among scientists, Haeussler found out that the sharing of data is indeed closely related to a form of counter-value (Haeussler 2011, p. 8).

Who is to blame for the fact that Open Data has not yet achieved its break-through despite its potential? Is it the journal system and its supporting information practice? Researchers and their reluctance to share? Missing incentive systems? Or overcomplicated data repositories? The apparent divergence regarding the impediments of Open Data demonstrates the need for further empirical research on this issue. Future studies could address the reluctance of researchers to practice Open Data, the role of journals and supporting material, or the design of an appropriate online data repository or meta-data structures for research data. The implied multitude of obstacles for practicing Open Data also illustrates that research on this issue needs to be holistic.

## Open Access to Research Publication

When it comes the Open Access of research publications, the argument is often less researcher-centric. Cribb and Sari (2010) make the case for the Open Access to scientific knowledge as a human right (see Table 4). According to them, there is a gap between the creation and the sharing of knowledge: While scientific knowledge doubles every 5 years, the access to this knowledge remains limited—leaving parts of the world in the dark: *"As humanity progresses through the 21st century (…) many scholars point to the emergence of a disturbing trend: the world is dividing into those with ready access to knowledge and its fruit, and those without."* (ibid., p. 3). For them, free access to knowledge is a necessity for human development. In a study on Open Access in library and information science, Rufai et al. (2012) take the same line. They assume that countries *"falling in the low-income economic zones have to come on Open Access canvas"* (ibid., 2011, p. 225). In times of financial crises, open journal systems and consequently equal access to knowledge could be an appropriate solution. Additionally, Phelps et al. (2012) regard Open Access to research publications as a catalyst for development, whereas limited access to a small subset of people with subscription is a hindrance to development. Consistently, they define Open Access as *"the widest possible dissemination of information"* (ibid., p. 1).

**Table 4** Democratic School—Open Access to publications

| Author (Year) Type of Publication | Title | Content |
|---|---|---|
| Cribb & Sari (2010) Monograph | Open Science - Sharing Knowledge in the Global Century | Open Access to knowledge is a tool for development.<br>"As humanity progresses the 21st century (...) many scholars point to the emergence of a disturbing trend: the world is dividing into those with ready access to knowledge and its fruit, and those without." (p. 3) |
| Rufai et al. (2012) Journal Article | Open Access Journals in Library and Information Science: The Story so Far | Open Access helps underdeveloped countries to bridge the gap between them and developed countries.<br>"The sustainability of Open Access journals in the field of LIS is evident from the study. Countries falling in the low-income economic zones have to come on Open Access canvas." (p. 225) |
| Phelps, Fox & Marincola (2012) Journal Article | Supporting the advancement of science: Open Access publishing and the role of mandates | Open Access increases the dissemination of a scholar's work.<br>"Maybe one of the reasons that Open Access is an increasingly popular choice for society journals is that it fits well with many society missions to encourage the advancement of knowledge by providing the widest possible dissemination with no barriers to access." (p. 3) |
| Carrol (2011) Journal Article | Why full Open Access matters | Open Access helps overcoming the inefficiency of traditional peer-review journals.<br>"Pricing of traditional, subscription-financed scientific journals is highly inefficient. The growth in digital technologies and in digital networks should be driving down the price of access to the scholarly journal literature, but instead prices have increased at a rate greatly in excess of inflation." (p. 1) |
| Harnad & Brody (2004) | Comparing the Impact of Open Access (OA) vs. Non-OA Articles in the Same Journals | Open Access can increase the number of citations and helps skirting the high access tolls of journals.<br>"Access is not a sufficient condition for citation, but it is a necessary one. OA dramatically increases the number of potential users of any given article by adding those users who would otherwise have been unable to access it because their institution could not afford the access-tolls of the journal in which it appeared; therefore, it stands to reason that OA can only increase both usage and impact." |

(continued)

**Table 4** (continued)

| Author (Year) Type of Publication | Title | Content |
|---|---|---|
| Harnad et al. (2004) | *The Access/Impact Problem and the Green and Gold Roads to Open Access* | Only 5% of journals are gold, but over 90% are already green (i.e., they have given their authors the green light to self-archive); yet only about 10-20% of articles have been self-archived. *"Along with the substantial recent rise in OA consciousness worldwide, there has also been an unfortunate tendency to equate OA exclusively with OA journal publishing (i.e., the golden road to OA) and to overlook the faster, surer, and already more heavily traveled green road of OA self-archiving."* (p. 314) |
| Antelmann (2004) | *Do Open-Access Articles Have a Greater Research Impact?* | Open Access articles have a higher research impact than not freely available articles. *"This study indicates that, across a variety of disciplines, Open-Access articles have a greater research impact than articles that are not freely available."* (p. 379) |

Apart from the developmental justification, Phelps et al. (2012) mention another, quite common, logic for Open Access to research publications: *"It is argued (...) that research funded by tax-payers should be made available to the public free of charge so that the tax-payer does not in effect pay twice for the research (...)"* (ibid., p.1). 'Paying twice for research' refers to the fact that citizens do not only indirectly finance government-funded research but also the subsequent acquisition of publications from public libraries.

Carroll (2011) also criticizes the inefficiency of traditional, subscription-financed scientific journals in times of growth in digital technologies and networks. He argues that prices should have dropped considerably in the light of the Internet—instead they have increased drastically. He further argues that the Open Access model would shift the balance of power in journal publishing and greatly enhance the efficiency and efficacy of scientific communication (ibid., p. 1). By shifting the financing away from subscriptions, the Open Access model re-aligns copyright and enables broad reuse of publications while at the same time assuring authors and publishers that they receive credit for their effort (e.g. through open licensing).

## Pragmatic School: Making Research More Efficient

Advocates of the pragmatic school regard Open Science as a method to make research and knowledge dissemination more efficient. It thereby considers science as a process that can be optimized by, for instance, modularizing the process of knowledge creation, opening the scientific value chain, including external knowledge and allowing collaboration through online tools. The notion of 'open' follows in this regard very much the disclosed production process known from open innovation concepts (see Table 5).

Tacke (2010) for instance builds upon the connection between open innovation and Open Science. Similar to open innovation, the author applies the outside-in (including external knowledge to the production process) and inside-out (spill-overs from the formerly closed production process) principles to science. He regards Web 2.0 in this regard as a fertile ground for practicing collaborative research (ibid., p. 41) and emphasizes the 'wisdom of the crowds' as a necessity in solving today's scientific problems: *"Taking a closer look at science reveals a similar situation: problems have become more complex and often require a joint effort in order to find a solution"* (ibid., p. 37).

Tacke refers to Hunter and Leahey (2008) who examined trends in collaboration over a 70 years period. They found out that between 1935 and 1940 only 11 % of the observed articles were co-authored, whereas between 2000 and 2005 almost 50 % were coauthored—a significant increase that according to Tacke issues from the increasing complexity of research problems over time; research problems that apparently can only be solved through multi-expert consideration. Indeed, Bozeman and Corley (2004) found out in an empirical study on researcher

**Table 5** Pragmatic school

| Author (Year) Type of Publication | Title | Content |
|---|---|---|
| Tacke (2010) Proceedings | Open Science 2.0: How research and education can benefit from open innovation and Web 2.0 | Complex situations can be better judged by the collective wisdom of the crowds. "However, several critics emphasize that one person can never possess enough knowledge in order to judge complex situations expediently, and that it may more appropriate to use the collective wisdom of crowds." (p. 37) |
| Haeussler (2011) Journal Article | Information-sharing, social capital, Open Science | Scientists expect a benefit from sharing information. "My study showed that factors related to social capital influence the impact of the competitive value of the requested information on a scientist's decision to share or withhold information." (p. 117) |
| Neylon & Wu (2009) Symposium Workshop | Open Science: tools, approaches, and implications | Open Science tools need to fit to the scientific practice of researchers. "Tools whether they be social networking sites, electronic laboratory notebooks, or controlled vocabularies, must be built to help scientists do what they are already doing, not what the tool designer feels they should be doing." (p. 543) |
| Nielsen (2012) Monograph | Reinventing Discovery: The New Era of Networked Science | "We need to imagine a world where the construction of the scientific information commons has come to fruition. This is a world where all scientific knowledge has been made available online, and is expressed in a way that can be understood by computers." (ibid., p. 111) |
| Weiss (2005) | The Power of Collective Intelligence | Participation in collective knowledge-creation depends on the tools and services available. "With ever more sophisticated APIs and Web services being shared, attracting a critical mass of developers to build tools on those services, and a critical mass of users contributing to the services' value by aggregating shared knowledge and content, we have the makings of a truly collaborative, self-organizing platform." (p. 4) |

(continued)

**Table 5** (continued)

| Author (Year) | Type of Publication | Title | Content |
|---|---|---|---|
| Arazy et al. (2006) | | *Wisdom of the Crowds: Decentralized Knowledge Construction in Wikipedia* | Participation in the co-creation of knowledge depends on the entry barriers. "*To entice participation, organizations using wikis should strive to eliminate barriers (e.g. allow users to post anonymously) and provide incentives for contributions.*" |
| Gowers & Nielsen (2009) | | *Massively Collaborative Mathematics* | Natural sciences can profit from collaboration of researchers. "*But open sharing of experimental data does at least allow open data analysis. The widespread adoption of such open-source techniques will require significant cultural changes in science, as well as the development of new online tools. We believe that this will lead to the widespread use of mass collaboration in many fields of science, and that mass collaboration will extend the limits of human problem-solving ability.*" (p. 881) |

collaboration that some of the most frequent reasons for collaborative research are access to expertise, aggregation of different kinds of knowledge, and productivity. Apart from the assumed increasing complexity of today's research problems and the researcher's pursuit of productivity, Tacke also points out the technical progress that enables and fosters collaboration in the first place. The Web 2.0 allows virtually anyone to participate in the process of knowledge creation (ibid., p. 4). It is thus tenable to consider, besides the strive for productivity and the increasing complexity of research process, also the emerging communication and collaboration technology as a solid reason for collaborative research.

Nielsen (2012) argues accordingly. He proceeds from the assumption that openness indicates a pivotal shift in the scientific practice in the near future—namely from closed to collaborative. Through reference to numerous examples of collective intelligence, such as the Polymath Project (in which Tim Gower posted a mathematical problem on his blog that was then solved by a few experts) or the Galaxy Zoo Project (an online astronomy project which amateurs can join to assist morphological classification), he emphasizes the crucial role of online tools in this development: *"Superficially, the idea that online tools can make us collectively smarter contradicts the idea, currently fashionable in some circles, that the Internet is reducing our intelligence"* (ibid., p. 26).

Nielsen's presentation of examples for collaborative knowledge discoveries permits conjecture on the wide variety of collaborative research when it comes to scale and quality—be it a rather-small scale expert collaboration as in the Polymath project or large-scale amateur collaboration as in the Galaxy Zoo project. Nielsen also points towards the importance of Open Data (ibid., p. 101) and promotes comprehensive scientific commons: *"We need to imagine a world where the construction of the scientific information commons has come to fruition. This is a world where all scientific knowledge has been made available online, and is expressed in a way that can be understood by computers"* (ibid., p. 111). It becomes obvious that Nielsen's vision of Open Science is based on vesting conditions like the enhanced use of online platforms, the inclusion of non-experts in the discovery process and, not least, the willingness to share on the part of scientists; all of which show that Nielsen's notion of collective research is also bound to numerous profound changes in the scientific practice—not to mention the technological ability to understand all formats of knowledge by computers.

Haeussler (2011) addresses the sharing behaviour of researchers in an empirical study among scientists. She uses arguments from social capital theory in order to explain why individuals share information even at (temporary) personal cost. Her notion of Open Science is thereby strongly bound to the free sharing of information (similar to one of Nielsen's core requirements for Open Science). One of Haeussler's results concerns the competitive value of information. She concludes: *"My study showed that factors related to social capital influence the impact of the competitive value of the requested information on a scientist's decision to share or withhold information."* (ibid., p. 117). If academic scientists expect the inquirer to be able to return the favor, they are much more likely to share information. Haeussler's study shows that the scientist's sharing behaviour is not altruistic per se—which is often taken for granted in texts on Open Science. Instead, it is rather built on an, even non-monetary, system of return. The findings raise the question as to how the sharing of information and thus, at least according to Nielsen and Haeussler, a basic requirement for Open Science could be expedited. It implies that a change in scientific practice comes with fundamental changes in the culture of science; in this case the incentives to share information.

Neylon and Wu (2009), in a general text on the requirements for Open Science, elaborate more on Web 2.0 tools that facilitate and accelerate scientific discovery. According to them, tools *"whether they be social networking sites, electronic laboratory notebooks, or controlled vocabularies, must be built to help scientists do what they are already doing, not what the tool designer feels they should be doing"* (ibid., p. 543). The authors thereby regard the implementation of Web 2.0 tools in close relation to the existing scientific practice. Following this, scientific tools can only foster scientific discovery if they tie in with the research practice. The most obvious target, according to the authors, is in this regard *"tools that make it easier to capture the research record so that it can be incorporated into and linked from papers"* (ibid., p. 543). Unfortunately, the authors do not further elaborate on how potential tools could be integrated in the researchers' work flows. Nonetheless, they take a new point of view when it comes to the role of Web 2.0 tools and the necessity to integrate these into an existing research practice. In this regard, they differ from what we subsume as the infrastructure school.

The authors mentioned in this chapter reveal visionary perspectives on scientific practice in the age of Web 2.0. Nonetheless, we assume that further research must focus on the structural requirements of Open Science, the potential incentives for scientists to share information, or the potential inclusion of software tools in the existing practice. In other words: The assumed coherence in regard to Open Science still lacks empirical research.

## Infrastructure School: Architecture Matters Most

The infrastructure school is concerned with the technical infrastructure that enables emerging research practices on the Internet, for the most part software tools and applications, as well as computing networks. In a nutshell, the infrastructure school regards Open Science as a technological challenge (see Table 6). Literature on this matter is therefore often practice-oriented and case-specific; it focuses on the technological requirements that facilitate particular research practices (e.g. the Open Science Grid).

In 2003, Nentwich (2003, p. 1) coined the term cyberscience to describe the trend of applying information and communication technologies to scientific research—a development that has prospered since then. The authors locate cyberscience in a Web 2.0 context, alluding not only to the technical progress that fosters collaboration and interaction among scientists, but also to a cultural change similar to the open source development. Most Open Science practices described in

**Table 6** Infrastructure school

| Author (Year)/Type of Publication | Title | Content |
|---|---|---|
| Altunay et al. (2010) Article | A Science Driven Production Cyberinfrastructure—the Open Science Grid | Science grid can be used for high-throughput research projects. "This article describes the Open Science Grid, a large distributed computational infrastructure in the United States which supports many different high-throughput scientific applications (...) to form multi-domain integrated distributed systems for science." (p. 201) |
| De Roure et al. (2008) Conference Paper | Towards Open Science: the myExperiment approach | "myExperiment is the first repository of methods which majors on the social dimension, and we have demonstrated that an online community and workflow collection has been established and is now growing around it." (p. 2350) |
| Foster (2002) Journal Article | The grid: A new infrastructure for 21st century science | Computation is a major challenge for scientific collaboration in future. "Driven by increasingly complex problems and by advances in understanding and technique, and powered by the emergence of the Internet (...), today's science is as much based on computation, data analysis, and collaboration as on the efforts of individual experimentalists and theorists." (p. 52) |
| De Roure et al. (2003) Book Chapter | The Semantic Grid: A Future e-Science Infrastructure | Knowledge layer services are necessary for seamlessly automating a significant range of actions. "While there are still many open problems concerned with managing massively distributed computations in an efficient manner and in accessing and sharing information from heterogenous sources (...), we believe the full potential of Grid computing can only be realised by fully exploiting the functionality and capabilities provided by knowledge layer services." (p. 432) |
| Hey & Trefethen (2005) Article | Cyberinfrastructure for e-Science | Service-oriented science has the potential to increase individual and collective scientific productivity by making powerful information tools available to all, and thus enabling the widespread automation of data analysis and computation. "Although there is currently much focus in the Grid community on the lowlevel middleware, there are substantial research challenges for computer scientists to develop high-level intelligent middleware services that genuinely support the needs of scientists and allow them to routinely construct secure VOs and manage the veritable deluge of scientific data that will be generated in the next few years." (p. 820) |

the previously discussed schools have to be very much understood as a part of an interplay between individuals and the tools at hand. The technical infrastructure is in this regard a cyclic element for almost all identified schools in this chapter; imagine Open Data without online data repositories or collaborative writing without web-based real-time editors. In one way or another it is the new techno-logical possibilities that change established scientific practices or even constitute new ones, as in the case of altmetrics or scientific blogging.

Still, we decided to include the infrastructure school as a separate and super-ordinate school of thought due to discernible infrastructure trends in the context of Open Science; trends that in our eyes enable research on a different scale. We will therefore not list the multitude of Open Science projects and their technological infrastructure but instead dwell on two infrastructure trends and selected examples. It has to be said that these trends are not mutually exclusive but often interwoven. The trends are:

- Distributed computing: Using the computing power of many users for research
- Social and collaboration networks for scientists: Enabling researcher interaction and collaboration

## *Distributed Computing*

A striking example for distributed computing in science is the Open Science Grid, *"a large distributed computational infrastructure in the United States, which supports many different high-throughput scientific applications (...) to form multi-domain integrated distributed systems for science."* (Altunay et al. 2010, p. 201). Put simply, the Open Science Grid enables large-scale, data-intensive research projects by connecting multiple computers to a high-performance computer net-work. Autonomous computers are interconnected in order to achieve high-throughput research goals. The Open Science Grid provides a collaborative research environment for communities of scientists and researchers to work together on distributed computing problems (ibid., p. 202).

It is thus not completely accurate to confine the Open Science Grid to its computational power alone as it also provides access to storage resources, offers a software stack, and uses common operational services. Nonetheless, its core strength resides in the computational power of many single computers, allowing scientists to realize data-intensive research projects, high throughput processing and shared storage. Typical projects that use the Open Science Grid are therefore CPU-intensive, comprise a large number of independent jobs, demand a significant amount of database-access, and/or implicate large input and output data from remote servers.

Foster encapsulates the increasing importance of grids as an essential com-puting infrastructure: *"Driven by increasingly complex problems and by advances in understanding and technique, and powered by the emergence of the Internet (...), today's science is as much based on computation, data analysis, and collaboration as on the efforts of individual experimentalists and theorists."* (2003, p. 52). Foster (ibid.) further emphasizes the potential to enable large-scale sharing of resources within distributed, often loosely coordinated and virtual groups—an idea that according to the author is not all new. He refers to a case from 1968, when designers of the Multics operating system envisioned a computer facility operating as a utility (ibid., p. 52). What is new though, according to Foster, is the performance of such network utilities in the light of technological progress (ibid., p. 53).

Distributed computing allows scientists to realize research almost independently from the individual computing resources. It is thereby an opportunity to untie a researcher from locally available resources by providing a highly efficient computer network. Considering the importance of big data, scientific computing will be an essential research infrastructure in the near future. One could say that the objective of scientific computing is the increase of performance by interconnecting many autonomous and dispersed computers.

## Social and Collaboration Networks

A second, more researcher-centric, infrastructure trend focuses on platforms that foster interaction between locally dispersed individuals and allow collaboration by implementing Web 2.0 tools. Drawing on the example of myExperiment, De Roure et al. (2008) propose four key capabilities of what they consider a Social Virtual Research Environment (SVRE):

- According to the authors, a SVRE should *firstly* facilitate the management and sharing of research objects. These can be any digital commodities that are used and reused by researchers (e.g. methods and data).
- *Secondly*, it should have incentives for researchers to make their research objects available.
- *Thirdly*, the environment should be open and extensible—meaning that software, tools and services can be easily integrated.
- *Fourthly*, it should provide a platform to action research. Actioning research is, in the authors' understanding, what makes a platform an actual research environment. Research objects are in this regard not just stored and exchanged but they are used in the conduct of research (De Roure et al. 2008, p. 182).

This depiction of a SVRE does of course not exclude mass computation (the third capability in fact endorses the integration of additional services)—it does, however, clearly focus on the interaction and collaboration between researchers. Furthermore, it becomes apparent that the authors' notion of 'virtual social research' involves a multitude of additional tools and services enabling collaborative research. It implies (directly or indirectly) the existence of integrated large-scale data repositories that allow researchers to make their data publicly available in the first place.

Nentwich and König (2012, p. 42), who are also featured in this book, point towards other social networks for scientists, such as ResearchGate, Mendeley, Nature Networks, Vivo, or Academia.edu. The authors state that present academic social networks are principally functional for scientists and do not (yet) feature a convergence towards one provider. They further point towards the use of multi-purpose social networks (such as Facebook, LinkedIN, or Xing) among scientists. These are used for thematic expert groups (not only scientists), self-marketing, or job exchange. In the chapter "Academia Goes Facebook?: The Potential of Social Network Sites in the Scholarly Realm", the authors elaborate more on the role of social networks for scientists—including tools for scientific collaboration such as collaborative writing environments.

## Measurement School: Finding Alternative Measurements for Scientific Output

The measurement school is concerned with alternative standards to ascertain scientific impact. Inarguably, the impact factor, which measures the average number of citations to an article in a journal, has a decisive influence on a researcher's reputation and thereby his or her funding and career opportunities. It is therefore hardly surprising that a discourse about Open Science and how science will be done in the future is accompanied by the crucial question as to how scientific impact can be measured in the digital age.

Advocates of the Open Science measurement school express the following concerns about the current impact factor:

- The peer review is time-consuming. (McVeigh 2004; Priem and Costello 2010)
- The impact is linked to a journal rather than directly to an article. (McVeigh 2004)
- New publishing formats (e.g. online Open Access journals, blogs) are seldom in a journal format to which an impact factor can be assigned to (Weller and Puschmann 2011; Priem et al. 2012; Yeong and Abdullah 2012)

Accordingly, this school argues the case for an alternative and faster impact measurement that includes other forms of publication and the social web coverage of a scientific contribution. The general credo is: As the scholarly workflow is migrates increasingly to the web, formerly hidden uses like reading, bookmarking, sharing, discussing, and rating are leaving traces online and offer a new basis by which to measure scientific impact. The umbrella term for these new impact measurements is altmetrics (See Table 7).

**Table 7** Measurement school

| Author (Year) | Title | Content |
|---|---|---|
| Priem & Light Costello (2010) Proceedings | How and why scholars cite on twitter | Tweets can be used as an alternative basis to measure scientific impact. "Twitter citations are much faster than traditional citations, with 40% occurring within one week of the cited resource's publication. Finally, while Twitter citations are different from traditional citations, our participants suggest that they still represent and transmit scholarly impact." |
| Weller & Puschmann (2011) Poster | Twitter for Scientific Communication: How Can Citations/References be Identified and Measured? | Scientific tweets can be identified in numerous ways. |
| Priem et al. (2012) Proceedings | Uncovering impacts: CitedIn and total-impact, two new tools for gathering altmetrics | CitedIn and total-impact are tools that can measure scientific impact. "CitedIn and total-impact are two tools in early development that aim to gather altmetrics. A test of these tools using a real-life dataset shows that they work, and that there is a meaningful amount of altmetrics data available." |
| McVeigh (2012) News paper article | Twitter, peer review and altmetrics: the future of research impact assessment | "So why is a revolution needed? Because long before the tools even existed to do anything about it, many in the research community have bemoaned the stranglehold the impact factor of a research paper has held over research funding, careers and reputations." |
| Priem & Hemminger (2012) Journal article | Decoupling the scholarly journal | "This tight coupling [of the journal system] makes it difficult to change any one aspect of the system, choking out innovation." |
| Yeong & Abdullah (2012) Position paper | Altmetrics: the right step forward | Altmetrics are an alternative metric for analysing and informing scholarship about impact. "Altmetrics rely on a wider set of measures [than webometrics] (...) are focused on the creation and study of new metrics based on the social web for analysing and informing scholarship." |

(continued)

**Table 7** (continued)

| Author (Year) | Title | Content |
|---|---|---|
| Björneborn & Ingwerson (2001)<br>Journal article | *Perspectives of webometrics* | The lack of metadata attached to web documents and links and the lack of search engines exploiting metadata affects filtering options, and thus knowledge discovery options, whereas field codes in traditional databases support KDD (Knowledge Discovery in Databases)<br>*"As stated above, the feasibility of using bibliometric methods on the Web is highly affected by the distributed, diverse and dynamical nature of the Web and by the deficiencies of search engines. That is the reason that so far the Web Impact Factor investigations based on secondary data from search engines cannot be carried out." (p. 78)* |

Yeong and Abdullah (2012) state that altmetrics differ from webometrics which are, as the authors argue, relatively slow, unstructured, and closed. Altmetrics instead rely upon a wider set of measures that includes tweets, blogs, discussions, and bookmarks (e.g. mendeley.com). Altmetrics measure different forms of significance and usage patterns by looking not just at the end publication, but also the process of research and collaboration (ibid., p. 2). Unfortunately, the authors do not further outline how a scientific process instead of a product could be evaluated. A possibility could be to measure the impact of emerging formats of research documentation in the social web (e.g. scientific blogs) or datasets (e.g. Open Data).

As a possible basis for altmetrics, Priem et al. (2011, p. 1) mention web pages, blogs, and downloads, but also social media like Twitter, or social reference managers like CiteULike, Mendeley, and Zotero. As a result of a case study with 214 articles, they present the two open-source online tools, CitedIn and Total Impact, as potential alternatives to measure scientific impact as they are based on a meaningful amount of data from more diverse academic publications. At the same time, they emphasize that there is still a need for research regarding the comparability of altmetrics, which is difficult due to the high dimensionality of altmetrics data.

While many authors already recognize the need for new metrics in the digital age and a more structured and rapid alternative to webometrics (Yeong and Abdullah 2012), research on this matter is still in its infancy. There is scarcely any research on the comparability of altmetrics and virtually no research on their potential manipulations and network effects. Furthermore, altmetrics are not yet broadly applied in the scientific community, raising the question as to what hinders their broad implementation. A possible reason is the tight coupling of the existing journal system and its essential functions of archiving, registration, dissemination, and certification of scholarly knowledge (Priem and Hemminger 2012). All the more, it appears that future research should also focus on the overall process of science, its transformative powers, and, likewise, constraints.

## Discussion

This chapter showed that "Open Science" is an umbrella term that encompasses almost any dispute about the future of knowledge creation and dissemination, a term that evokes quite different understandings depending on the viewpoint of its respective advocates and leads to many quarrels under the same flag—yet with varying inducements and targets. Even though the chapter implies a certain lack of conceptual clarity in the term Open Science, we do not promote a precisely defined concept. On the contrary, we assume that doing so could prevent fertile discussions from the very beginning. We therefore aimed at offering an overview of the leading discourses by suggesting five (more or less) distinct schools of thought, and their core aims and argumentations. We suggest that this classification can be a starting point for structuring the overall discourse and locating its common catchphrases and argumentations. In this respect the mindmap graphic below attempts to arrange the most common keywords in the Open Science discourse according to the aforegoing described schools.

Although Open Science covers in the broadest sense anything about the future of knowledge creation and dissemination, not necessarily all developments described in this chapter are novel. In fact, many demands and argumentations existed long before the dawn of the Internet and the digital age. Some would even argue that science is per definition open, since the aim of research is, after all, to publish its results, and as such *to make knowledge public*. Nonetheless, science certainly has experienced a new dynamic in the light of modern communication technology. Collaborative forms of research, the increasing number of co-authored scientific articles, new publication formats in the social web, the wide range of online research tools, and the emergence of Open Access journals all bear witness to what is entitled in this book 'the dawn of a new era'.

Science is doubtlessly faced with enormous challenges in the coming years. New approaches to knowledge creation and dissemination go hand in hand with profound systemic changes (e.g. when it comes to scientific impact), changes in the daily practice of researchers (e.g. when it comes to new tools and methods), changes in the publishing industry (e.g. when it comes to coping with alternative publication formats), and many more. In this regard, this chapter should not only provide insight into the wide range of developments in the different Open Science schools, but also point towards the complexity of the change, the intertwinedness of the developments, and thus the necessity for holistic approaches in research on the future of research. For example: How could one argue for extensive practicing of Open Data if there is no remuneration for those who do it? How could one expect a researcher to work collaboratively online if platforms are too complicated to use? Why should a researcher invest time and effort in writing a blog if it has no impact on his or her reputation?

The entirety of the outlined developments in this chapter marks a profound change of the scientific environment. Yet even if the most prominent accompaniments of this change (be it Open Access, Open Data, citizen science, or collaborative research) are possibly overdue for a knowledge industry in the digital age and welcomed by most people who work in it, they still depend upon comprehensive implementation. They depend upon elaborate research policies, convenient research tools, and, not least, the participation of the researchers themselves. In many instances Open Science appears to be somewhat like the proverbial electric car—an indeed sensible but expenseful thing which would do better to be parked in the neighbor's garage; an idea everybody agrees upon but urges others to take the first step for.

# References

Altunay, M., et al. (2010). A science driven production Cyberinfrastructure—the Open Science grid. *Journal of Grid Computing, 9*(2), 201–218. doi:10.1007/s10723-010-9176-6.

Antelmann, K. (2004). Do Open-Access articles have a greater research impact? *College & Research Libraries, 65*(5), 372–382.

Arazy, O., Morgan, W., & Patterson, R. (2006). Wisdom of the Crowds: Decentralized Knowledge Construction in Wikipedia. *SSRN Electronic Journal.* doi:10.2139/ssrn.1025624.

Auer, S., et al. (2007). DBpedia: a nucleus for a web of open data. In K. Aberer et al., (Eds.), *The Semantic Web* (pp. 722–735). Berlin, Heidelberg: Springer Berlin Heidelberg. Available at: http://www.springerlink.com/index/10.1007/978-3-540-76298-0_52.

Boulton, G., et al. (2011). Science as a public enterprise: the case for open data. *The Lancet, 377*(9778), 1633–1635. doi:10.1016/S0140-6736(11)60647-8.

Bozeman, B., & Corley, E. (2004). Scientists' collaboration strategies: implications for scientific and technical human capital. *Research Policy, 33*(4), 599–616. doi:10.1016/j.respol. 2004.01.008.

Campbell, E. G., et al. (2002). Data Withholding in Academic Genetics: evidence from a national survey. *JAMA, 287*(4), 473. doi:10.1001/jama.287.4.473.

Carroll, M. W. (2011). Why full Open Access matters. *PLoS Biology, 9*(11), p.e1001210. doi:10.1371/journal.pbio.1001210.

Catlin-Groves, C. L. (2012). The citizen science landscape: from volunteers to citizen sensors and beyond. *International Journal of Zoology, 2012*, 1–14. doi:10.1155/2012/349630.

Cribb, J., & Sari, T. (2010). *Open Science: sharing knowledge in the global century.* Collingwood: CSIRO Publishing.

De Roure, D., et al. (2008). myExperiment: defining the social virtual research environment. In IEEE (pp. 182–189). Available at: http://ieeexplore.ieee.org/lpdocs/epic03/wrapper. htm?arnumber=4736756.

De Roure, D., & Goble, C. (2009). Software design for empowering scientists. *IEEE Software, 26*(1), 88–95. doi:10.1109/MS.2009.22.

De Roure, D., Jennings, N.R., Shadbolt, N. R. (2003). The semantic grid: a future e-science infrastructure. In F. Berman, G. Fox, & T. Hey (Eds.), *Wiley Series in communications networking & Distributed Systems* (pp. 437–470). Chichester: John Wiley & Sons, Ltd.

Ebner, M., & Maurer, H. (2009). Can Weblogs and Microblogs change traditional scientific writing? *Future Internet, 1*(1), 47–58. doi:10.3390/fi1010047.

Foster, I. (2002). The grid: a new infrastructure for 21st century science. *Physics Today, 55*(2), 42. doi:10.1063/1.1461327.

Gowers, T., & Nielsen, M. (2009). Massively collaborative mathematics. *Nature, 461*(7266), 879–881. doi:10.1038/461879a.

Grand, A., et al. (2012). Open Science: a new "Trust Technology"? *Science Communication, 34*(5), 679–689. doi:10.1177/1075547012443021.

Haeussler, C. (2011). Information-sharing in academia and the industry: A comparative study. *Research Policy, 40*(1), 105–122. doi:10.1016/j.respol.2010.08.007.

Hand, E. (2010). Citizen science: people power. *Nature, 466*(7307), 685–687. doi:10.1038/ 466685a.

Harnad, S., et al. (2004). The access/impact problem and the green and gold roads to Open Access. *Serials Review, 30*(4), 310–314. doi:10.1016/j.serrev.2004.09.013.

Hey, T. (2005). Cyberinfrastructure for e-Science. *Science, 308*(5723), 817–821. doi:10.1126/ science.1110410.

Hunter, L., & Leahey, E. (2008). Collaborative research in sociology: trends and contributing factors. *The American Sociologist, 39*(4), 290–306.

Irwin, A. (1995). *Citizen science: a study of people, expertise, and sustainable development, London.* New York: Routledge.

Irwin, A. (2006). The politics of talk: coming to terms with the "New" scientific governance. *Social Studies of Science, 36*(2), 299–320. doi:10.1177/0306312706053350.

Löh, A., & Hinze, R. (2006). Open data types and open functions (p. 133.). In ACM Press, doi:10.1145/1140335.1140352.

McVeigh, M. E. (2004). Open Access journals in the ISI citation databases: analysis of impact factors and citation patterns. Citation Study. In Thomson Scientific. Available at: http://science.thomsonreuters.com/m/pdfs/openaccesscitations2.pdf.

Miller, P., Styles, R., Heath, T. (2008). Open data commons, a license for open data. In *Proceedings of the WWW 2008 Workshop on Linked Data on the Web.*

Molloy, J. C. (2011). The open knowledge foundation: open data means better science. *PLoS Biology, 9*(12), p.e1001195. doi:10.1371/journal.pbio.1001195.

Morris, T., & Mietchen, D. (2010). Collaborative structuring of knowledge by experts and the public. In *Proceedings of the 5th Open Knowledge Conference* (pp. 29–41). London, UK.

Murray-Rust, P. (2008). Open data in science. *Serials Review, 34*(1), 52–64. doi:10.1016/j.serrev.2008.01.001.

Nentwich, M. (2003). *Cyberscience: research in the age of the Internet.* Vienna: Austrian Academy of Sciences Press.

Nentwich, M., & König, R. (2012). *Cyberscience 2.0: research in the age of digital social networks.* Frankfurt; New York: Campus Verlag.

Neylon, C., & Wu, S. (2009). Open Science: tools, approaches, and implications. In *Pacific Symposium on Biocomputing. Pacific Symposium on Biocomputing* (pp. 540–544).

Nielsen, M. A. (2012). *Reinventing discovery: the new era of networked science.* Princeton: Princeton University Press.

Phelps, L., Fox, B. A., & Marincola, F. M. (2012). Supporting the advancement of science: Open Access publishing and the role of mandates. *Journal of Translational Medicine, 10*, 13. doi:10.1186/1479-5876-10-13.

Powell, M. C., & Colin, M. (2009). Participatory paradoxes: facilitating citizen engagement in science and technology from the top-down? *Bulletin of Science, Technology & Society, 29*(4), 325–342. doi:10.1177/0270467609336308.

Priem, J., et al. (2010). Altmetrics: a manifesto. *Altmetrics.* Available at: http://altmetrics.org/manifesto/.

Priem, J., et al. (2011). Uncovering impacts: CitedIn and total-impact, two new tools for gathering altmetrics (pp. 9–11). In iConference 2012. Available at: http://jasonpriem.org/self-archived/two-altmetrics-tools.pdf.

Priem, J., & Costello, K. L. (2010). How and why scholars cite on Twitter. *Proceedings of the American Society for Information Science and Technology, 47*(1), 1–4. doi:10.1002/meet.14504701201.

Priem, J., & Hemminger, B. M. (2012). Decoupling the scholarly journal. Frontiers in Computational Neuroscience, 6. doi:10.3389/fncom.2012.00019.

Priem, J., Piwowar, H., Hemminger, B. M. (2012). Altmetrics in the wild: using social media to explore scholarly impact. In ACM Web Science Conference 2012 Workshop. Evanston, IL, USA. Available at: http://altmetrics.org/altmetrics12/priem/.

Rufai, R., Gul, S., Shah, T. A. (2012). Open Access journals in library and information science: the story so far. *Trends in information management, 7*(2).

Tacke, O. (2010). Open Science 2.0: how research and education can benefit from open innovation and Web 2.0. In T. J. Bastiaens, U. Baumöl, & B. J. Krämer (Eds.), *On collective intelligence* (pp. 37–48). Berlin: Springer Berlin Heidelberg.

Tacke, O. (2012). Raus aus dem Elfenbeinturm: Open Science. *olivertacke.de.* Available at: http://www.olivertacke.de/2011/10/23/raus–aus–dem–elfenbeinturm–open–science/.

Vision, T. J. (2010). Open data and the social contract of scientific publishing. *BioScience, 60*(5), 330–331. doi:10.1525/bio.2010.60.5.2.

Weiss, A. (2005). The power of collective intelligence. *NetWorker, 9*(3), 16–23. doi:10.1145/1086762.1086763.

Weller, K., & Puschmann, C. (2011). Twitter for scientific communication: how can citations/
    references be identified and measured? In *Proceedings of the ACM WebSci'11* (pp. 1–4).
    Koblenz: ACM Publishers.
Yeong, C. H., & Abdullah, B. J. J. (2012). Altmetrics: the right step forward. *Biomedical Imaging
    and Intervention Journal, 8*(3), 1–2.

# Excellence by Nonsense: The Competition for Publications in Modern Science

**Mathias Binswanger**

> *Most scientific publications are utterly redundant, mere quantitative 'productivity'.*
>
> —Gerhard Fröhlich

**Abstract** In this chapter, Binswanger (a critic of the current scientific process) explains how artificially staged competitions affect science and how they result in nonsense. An economist himself, Binswanger provides examples from his field and shows how impact factors and publication pressure reduce the quality of scientific publications. Some might know his work and arguments from his book 'Sinnlose Wettbewerbe'.

## In Search of Excellence

Since the Age of Enlightenment, science has mostly taken place at universities and their respective institutes, where for a long time the ideal of uniting research and teaching was upheld. Since their re-establishment by Humboldt in 1810, German universities have been, also in terms of academic work, largely independent and the principle of academic freedom was applied.

The government merely determined that amount of money that was paid to universities and set the legal framework for science and teaching. In terms of research, the government did not impose specific research policies-with the exception of some inglorious episodes (e.g. the Nazi regime). Universities were trusted to know best what kind of research they were doing.

Generally, it was accepted not to tell a country's best academics what they should be interested in and what research they should be doing (Schatz 2001; Kohler 2007). Therefore, the academic practice of professors and other scientists

M. Binswanger (✉)
University of Applied Sciences of Northwestern Switzerland, Olten, Switzerland
e-mail: mathias.binswanger@fhnw.ch

M. Binswanger
University of St. Gallen, St. Gallen, Switzerland

S. Bartling and S. Friesike (eds.), *Opening Science*,
DOI: 10.1007/978-3-319-00026-8_3, © The Author(s) 2014

49

was hardly documented and assessed systematically, as it was assumed that academics would strive for excellence without having to be forced to do so.

Sometimes this was right and sometimes it was wrong. Huge differences in quality between individual scientists were the result. Scientific geniuses and lame ducks jointly populated universities, whereby even during the scientists' lifetimes it was not always discernible who was the lame duck and who the genius.

*The extraordinary is the rare result of average science and only broad quality, growing out from mediocrity, brings the great achievement at the end* says Jürgen Mittelstrass, philosopher of science (2007). Still in 1945, the then president of Harvard University wrote in a letter addressed to the New York Times (August, 13th, 1945): *There is only one method to guarantee progress in science. One has to find geniuses, support them and let them carry out their work independently.*

Meanwhile, the government has given up its reservations towards universities and formerly proud bastions of independent thinking have turned into servants of governmental programs and initiatives. Lenin's doctrine applies once again: trust is good, control is better.

To ensure the efficient use of scarce funds, the government forces universities and professors, together with their academic staff, to permanently take part in artificially staged competitions. This is happening on two fronts: universities have to prove themselves by competing, both in terms of education and scientific research, in order to stay ahead in the rankings. Yet how did this development occur? Why did successful and independent universities forget about their noble purpose of increasing knowledge and instead degenerated into "publication factories" and "project mills" which are only interested in their rankings?

To understand this, we have to take a closer look at the development of universities since the 1960s. Until then, people with a tertiary education made up a relatively small fraction of the population. Universities were relatively elitist institutions which remained out of reach for the majority of working class kids. Since the 1960s however, increasing access to tertiary education occurred, for which the term 'mass higher education' (Trow 1997) was coined.

From 1950, first-year student rates increased from an average of 5 % in the industrialized countries to up to 50 % at the beginning of the 21st century (Switzerland, with its 20 %, is an exception). Universities and politics, however, were not prepared to deal with this enormous increase. It was believed to be possible to carry on with 1,000 students in the same way as has been done with 50 students, by just increasing the number of universities and professors and by putting more money into administration.

The mass education at universities made a farce of Humboldt's old idea of unity of research and education. This had consequences for both education and research. There were more and more students and also more and more researchers who were employed at universities (and later on at universities of applied sciences), but most of them no longer had any time for research. In Germany, the number of students also grew disproportionately faster than the number of professors due to the very generous government support of students through BAFÖG (Federal Education and Trainings Assistance Act). Therefore, one professor had to supervise more and more students and postgraduates and there was no more time to seriously deal with them.

Dissertations became mass products, the majority of which added little or nothing to scientific advancement. An environment emerged that was neither stimulating for professors, nor for their assistants and doctoral students, which logically led to increasing mediocrity. German universities in particular have often been criticized along the following lines: studies last too long, the dropout rates are too high, the curricula are obsolete, and research performance is only average and rarely of value and relevance for industrial innovations.

A second phenomenon which did a lot of harm to the European universities, was the lasting glorification of the American higher education system. Many politicians, but also scientists themselves, see this system as a permanent source of excellence and success without—as US scientist Trow (1997) writes—getting the general picture of the American higher education system. Attention is directed exclusively at Harvard, Princeton, Yale, MIT, and other Ivy-League universities, which make up only a small percentage of the university landscape in the US. In this euphoria, it is intentionally overlooked that the majority of colleges and universities displays an intellectually modest standard and hardly contributes to academic progress. Much of what we celebrate as 'globalization' and 'adjustment to international standards' is in reality the adjustment to US-American provincialism (Fröhlich 2006).

In Europe, the idea became fashionable that imitating top US universities would magically create a new academic elite. Like small boys, all universities wanted to be the greatest, and politics started propagating sponsorship of Ivy-League universities, elite institutions, and elite scientists. Germany started an Excellence Initiative in order to boost its international competitiveness. Switzerland aimed to be one of the top 5 countries for innovation by supporting excellence, and the European Union, with the so-called Lisbon-strategy of 2000, hoped to turn the EU into the most dynamic knowledge-based economy by 2010.

Cutting-edge universities, top-institutes, and research clusters shot up everywhere, and everyone wanted to be even more excellent than their already-excellent competitors. Amongst this childish race for excellence, it was overlooked that not all can be more excellent than the rest. This fallacy of composition applies here as well. Instead, the term 'excellence' became a meaningless catchword. Philosopher Mittelstrass (2007) writes:

> Until now, no one took offence at the labeling of excellent cuisine, excellent performance, excellent academics or excellent scientists. [...] In the case of science this changed since science policy has occupied this term and talks about excellent research, excellent research establishments, clusters of excellence and Excellence Initiatives, in endless and almost unbearable repetitions.

Yet how do we actually know what excellence is and where it is worthwhile to foster a scientific elite? In reality, no one actually knows, least of all the politicians who enthusiastically launch such excellence initiatives. This is where the idea of artificially staged competition comes in. It is assumed that these competitions will automatically make the best rise to the top—without the need to care about neither content nor purpose of research. We may call this 'contest illusion'. This contest illusion was applied to science in England for the first time under the Thatcher government in the 1980s. Afterwards it was quickly copied in other countries. The Thatcher government, inspired by its belief in markets and competition, would have loved to privatize all institutions engaged in academic activities and to let markets decide which kind of science was needed, and which was not. However, this proved to be impossible. Basic research constitutes, for the most part, a common good which cannot be sold for profit at a market. Privatization would therefore completely wipe out basic research. Thus, artificially staged competitions were created, which were then termed markets (internal markets, pseudo-markets), even though this was false labeling.

Connected to the euphoria about markets and competition, there was also a deep mistrust towards independent research taking place within "ivory towers", the purpose of which politicians often do not understand. What does the search for knowledge bring apart from high costs? On these grounds, the former British minister of education Charles Clarke characterized "the medieval search for truth" as obsolete and unnecessary.[1] Modern universities should produce applicable knowledge, which can be transformed into growth of the gross domestic product, and additionally make it more sustainable. Universities should think "entrepreneurial" and adjust to economic needs (see Maasen and Weingart 2008). For this reason, governments in many countries, particularly in the EU, started to organize gigantic research programs. Instead of making research funds directly available to universities, they are now in competition with each other, so that only the "best" get a chance. This should ensure that above all practice-oriented and applicable knowledge is created and government funds are not wasted (e.g. for "unnecessary" basic research). Hence universities are forced to construct illusionary worlds of utility and pretend that all research serves an immediate purpose (Körner 2007).

How can you impress the research commissions responsible for the distribution of funds? This is mainly achieved by increasing measurable output such as publications, projects funded by third-party funds, and networks with other institutes and universities. In this way, "excellence" is demonstrated, in turn leading to easier access to further government research funds. Competitiveness has therefore become a priority for universities and their main goal is to perform as highly as possible in measurable indicators which play an important role in these artificially staged competitions. The underlying belief is that our knowledge increases proportionally to the amount of scientific projects, publications, and intensity of networking between research institutions, which in turn is supposed to lead to more progress and wealth. This naïve ton ideology is widespread among politicians and bureaucrats.

---

[1] BBC News. Clarke questions study as 'adornment': http://news.bbc.co.uk/2/hi/uk_news/education/3014423.stm

The modern university is only marginally concerned with gaining knowledge, even though the public from time to time is assured that this is still the major goal. Today's universities are, on the one hand, fundraising institutions, determined to receive as many research funds as possible. On the other hand, they are publication factories, trying to maximize their publication output. Hence, the ideal professor is a mixture of fundraiser, project manager, and mass publisher (either directly as author, or as co-author in publications written by employees of the institution), whose main concern is measurable contribution to scientific excellence, rather than increasing our knowledge. Moreover, in order to make professors deliver their contribution to excellence, faculty managers have been recruited for each department in addition to traditional deans. Nowadays, the principal is sort of a CEO who is supposed to implement new strategies for achieving more and more excellence. Research becomes a means in the battle for "market shares" of universities and research institutions (Münch 2009).

Universities which on the surface expose themselves as great temples of scientific excellence, are forced to participate in project- and publication-olympics, where instead of medals, winners are rewarded with the elite or excellence status, exemption from teaching duties, and sometimes also with higher salaries. This is how it goes, even though many of the projects and publications do not have the slightest importance for the rest of the population outside the academic system.

Two artificially staged competitions in particular incentivize the production of nonsense: the competition for the highest amount of publications and the competition for the highest amount of research funding. The resulting indicators for publications and third-party funds play a central role in today's research rankings, such as, for example the German CHE Research Ranking of German universities (see Berghoff et al. 2009).

The competition for the highest amount of publications will be analyzed below in more detail. On the basis of the competition for publications, it can be nicely demonstrated how perverse incentives emerge and what consequences this entails not only for research, but also generally for society and the economy.

## The Competition for Publications in Academic Journals: The Peer-Review Process

In almost every academic discipline, publications are the most important and often the only measurable output. Indeed, in some natural sciences and in engineering inventions or patents also play a certain role, yet this more concerns applied science. Basic research, however, always manifests itself in publications. What is more obvious than measuring a scientist or institute's output or productivity on the basis of publications? For is it not the case that many publications are the result of a lot of research, consequently increasing our relevant knowledge? Should not every scientist be driven to publish as much as possible in order to achieve maximum "scientific productivity"? Someone who has just a little knowledge of universities and academic life can immediately answers these questions with an overwhelming "no". Indeed, more publications increase the amount of printed sheets of paper, but this number does not say any more about the significance of a scientist or institute's research activity than the number of notes played says about the quality of a piece of music.

Of course, measurements of scientific output are not as primitive as counting every written page of scientific content as scientific activity. Relevant publications are in professional journals, where submitted work is subjected to a "rigorous" and "objective" selection method: the so-called "peer-review process". This should ensure that only "qualitatively superior" work is published, which then is regarded as a "real scientific publication". Thus, strictly speaking, the aim of the artificially staged competitions amongst scientists is to publish as many articles as possible in peer-reviewed scientific journals.

However, among scientific journals strict hierarchies also exist which are supposed to represent the average "quality" of the accepted papers. In almost every scientific discipline there are a few awe-inspiring top-journals (A-journals), and then there are various groups of less highly respected journals (B- and C-journals), where it is easier to place an article, but where the publication does not have the same significance as an A-journal article. Publishing one's work in an A-journal is therefore the most important and often also the only aim of modern scientists, thus allowing them to ascend to the "Champions' League" of their discipline. Belonging to this illustrious club makes it easier to publish further articles in A-journals, to secure more research funds, to conduct even more expensive experiments, and, therefore, to become even more excellent. The "Taste for Science", described by Merton (1973), which is based on intrinsic motivation and supposed to guide scientists was replaced by the extrinsically motivated "Taste for Publications."

But what is actually meant by the peer-review process? When a scientist wants to publish a paper in an accepted scientific journal, the paper has to be submitted to the journal's editors, who have established themselves as champions within their disciplines. These editors usually do not have the time to deal with the day-to-day business of "their journal" and thus there is a less accomplished Managing Editor, who is responsible for administrative tasks and receives manuscripts from the publishing-hungry scientists and then puts the peer-review process in motion. The Managing Editor gives the submitted manuscripts to one or several professors or other distinguished scientists (the so-called peers) who ideally work in the same field as the author and therefore should be able to assess the work's quality.

To ensure the "objectivity" of the expert judgments, the assessment is usually performed as a double-blind procedure. This means that the reviewers do not know who are the authors of the article to be reviewed, and the authors are not told by whom their paper is assessed. At the end of the peer review process, the reviewers inform the editor in writing whether they plead for acceptance (very rare), revision, or rejection (most common) of the article submitted to the journal in question. Quite a few top journals pride themselves on high rejection rates, supposedly reflecting the high quality of these journals (Fröhlich 2007). For such journals the rejection rates amount to approximately 95 %, which encourages the reviewers to reject manuscripts in almost all cases in order to defend this important "quality measure". Solely manuscripts that find favor with their reviewers get published, because although the final decision concerning publication rests with the editors, they generally follow the expert recommendations.

The peer-review process is thus a kind of insider procedure (also known as clan control, Ouchi 1980), which is not transparent for scientists outside the established circle of champions. The already-established scientists of a discipline evaluate each other, especially newcomers, and decide what is worthy to be published. Although the claim is made that scientific publications ultimately serve the general public, and thereby also serve people who are not active in research, the general public, who is actually supposed to stand behind the demand for scientific achievement, has no influence upon the publication process. The peers decide on behalf of the rest of mankind, since the public can hardly assess the scientific quality of a work.[2] Outside of the academic system, most people neither know what modern research is about, nor how to interpret the results and their potential importance to mankind. Although scientists often also do not know the latter, they are—in contrast to the layman—educated to conceal this lack of knowledge behind important sounding scientific jargon and formal models. In this way, even banalities and absurdities can be represented as A-journal worthy scientific excellence, a process laymen and politicians alike are not aware of. They are kept in the blissful belief that more competition in scientific publication leads to ever-increasing top performance and excellence.

Considering the development of the number of scientific publications, it seems that scientists are actually accomplishing more and more. Worldwide, the number of scientific articles, according to a count conducted by the Centre for Science and Technology Studies at the University of Leiden (SBF 2007) has increased enormously. The number of scientific publications in professional journals worldwide increased from approximately 686,000 in 1990 to about 1,260,000 in 2006, which corresponds to an increase of 84 %. The annual growth rate calculated on this basis was more than 5 %. The number of scientific publications grows faster than the global economy and significantly faster than the production of goods and services in industrial countries, from where the largest number of publications originates (OECD 2008).

By far the largest share of world production of scientific articles comes from the U.S. (25 %), followed by Britain with 6.9 %. Germany produces 6.3 %, Switzerland 1.5 %, and Austria 0.7 % (SBF 2007). However, calculating published articles per capita, Switzerland becomes the world's leading country,

---

[2] In the language of economics, this means that the information asymmetry between scientists and lay people is so large that "monitoring" by outsiders is no longer possible (Partha and David 1994, p. 505).

because there are 2.5 published scientific articles per 1,000 inhabitants, while in the U.S. there are 1.2 articles, and only one article in Germany (SBF 2007).[3] The same picture emerges if one applies the number of publications to the number of researchers. In this case, in Switzerland for each 1,000 researchers there are 725 publications while there are 295 in Germany and 240 in the United States. Thus, in no other country in the world are more research publications squeezed out of the average researcher than in Switzerland.

Once we begin to examine the background of this increasing flood of publications it quickly loses its appeal. This is to a large extent inherent in the peer-review process itself. This supposedly objective system for assessing the quality of articles in reality rather resembles a random process for many authors (Osterloh and Frey 2008). A critical investigation reveals a number of facts that fundamentally question the peer-review process as a quality assurance instrument (cf. Atkinson 2001; Osterloh and Frey 2008; Starbuck 2006). It generally appears that expert judgments are highly subjective, since the consensus of several expert judgments is usually low. One reason is that by no means do all peers, who are mostly preoccupied with their own publications, actually read, let alone understand, the articles to be evaluated. Time is far too short for this and usually it is not even worth it because there are much more interesting things to do. Hence, time after time reviewers pass on the articles to their assistants who, in the manner of their boss, draft the actual review as ghostwriters (Frey et al. 2009). No wonder that under such conditions important scientific contributions at hindsight are frequently rejected. Top journals repeatedly rejected articles that later on turned out to be scientific breakthroughs and even won the Nobel Prize. Conversely, however, plagiarism, fraud and deception are hardly ever discovered in the peer review process (Fröhlich 2007). In addition, unsurprisingly, reviewers assess those articles that are in accordance with their own work more favorably, and vice versa, they reject articles that contradict them (Lawrence 2003).

Due to the just-described peer-review process, the competition for publication in scientific journals results in a number of perverse incentives. To please the reviewers, a potential author undertakes everything conceivably possible. To describe this behavior Frey (2003) rightly coined the term "academic prostitution", which—in contrast to traditional prostitution—does not spring from natural demand, but is induced by artificially staged competition (cf. Giusta et al. 2007). In particular, the following perverse effects can be observed:

*Modes of perverse behavior caused by the peer-review process:*

---

[3] Nevertheless, the Neue Zürcher Zeitung already worried in an article from 2004 that the growth of publications in Switzerland compared to the average of OECD countries was below average. This thinking reveals once again a naive ton ideology, in which more scientific output is equated with more well-being.

- *Strategic citing and praising*[4]
  When submitting an article to a journal, the peer-review process induces authors to think about possible reviewers who have already published articles dealing with the same or similar topics. To flatter the reviewers, the author will preferably quote all of them or praise their work (as a seminal contribution, ingenious idea, etc.); An additional citation is useful for the potential reviewer because in turn it is improving his own standing as a scientist. Furthermore, editors often consult the bibliography at the end of an article while looking for possible reviewers, which makes strategic citing even more attractive.
  Conversely, an author will avoid criticizing the work of possible reviewers, as this is a sure road to rejection. Accordingly, this attitude prevents the criticism and questioning of existing approaches. Instead, the replication of established knowledge gets promoted through elaboration upon preexisting approaches through further model variations or additional empirical investigations.

- *No deviation from established theories*
  In any scientific discipline there are some eminent authorities who dominate their field and who often at the same time are the editors of top journals. This in turn allows them to prevent the appearance of approaches or theories that question their own research. Usually this is not difficult, since most authors try to adapt to the prevailing mainstream theories in their own interest. The majority of the authors simply wants to publish articles in top journals, and this makes them flexible in terms of content. They present traditional or fashionable approaches that evoke little protest (Osterloh and Frey 2008). In this way, some disciplines (e.g. economics) have degenerated into a kind of theology where heresy is no longer tolerated in established journals. Heresy takes place in only a few marginal journals specializing in divergent theories, but these publications rarely contribute to the reputation of a scientist. As Gerhard Fröhlich aptly writes: "In science as in the Catholic Church similar conditions prevail: censorship, opportunism and adaptation to the mainstream of research. As a result, a highly stylized technocratic rating- and hierarchy-system develops, which hinders real scientific progress."
  In empirical studies, the adherence to established theories can also be discovered by the results of statistical tests. To falsify an existing theory is linked to low chances of publication and thus there is an incentive to only publish successful tests and to conceal negative results (Osterloh and Frey 2008).

- *Form is more important than content*
  Since presenting original content usually lowers the chances of publication, novelty has shifted to the form how content is presented. Simple ideas are blown up into highly complex formal models which demonstrate the technical and mathematical expertise of the authors and signal importance to the reader. In many cases, the reviewers are not able to evaluate these models because they

---

[4] In the meantime, there are now so-called guides along the lines of "How to publish successfully?", which provide strategic advice to young scientists in the manner described herein.

have neither the time nor the inclination to deal with these models over several days. Since they cannot admit this, in a case of doubt formal brilliance is assessed positively because it usually supports prevailing theories. It helps to immunize the prevailing theories against criticism from outside, and all colleagues who are not working within the same research field just need to believe what was "proven to be right" in the existing model or experiment.

With this formalization, sciences increasingly move away from reality as false precision is more important than actual relevance. The biologist Körner writes (2007, p. 171): *The more precise the statement [of a model], the less it usually reflects the scale of the real conditions which are of interest to or available for the general public and which leads to scientific progress.*

The predominance of form over content (let us call this 'crowding-out' of form by content) does also attract other people to science. The old type of an often highly unconventional scientist who is motivated by intrinsic motivation is increasingly being replaced by formally gifted, streamlined men and women,[5] who in spite of their formal brilliance have hardly anything important to say.

- *Undermining of anonymity by expert networks*
  In theory, the peer-review process should work in such a way that publication opportunities are the same for all authors. Both the anonymity of the authors and the reviewers are guaranteed thanks to the double-blind principle. For many established scientists at top universities, "real" competition under these conditions would be a nuisance. After all, why did one work hard for a lifetime only to be subject to the same conditions as any newcomer? The critical debate on the peer-reviewed process discussed in the journal *Nature* in 2007, however, clearly showed that in practice the anonymity of the process for established scientists is rare. They know each other and know in advance which papers by colleagues or by scientists associated with them will be submitted. In expert networks maintained in research seminars, new papers are presented to each other, which successfully undermines the anonymity of the peer-review process.

  This fact can clearly be seen when looking at the origin of scientists who publish in top journals. For example, a study of the top five journals in economics (Frey et al. 2009, p. 153) shows that of the 275 articles published in 2007, 43 % originated from scientists working at only a few top American universities (Harvard, Yale, Princeton, MIT, Chicago, Berkeley, Stanford). The professors of these universities are basically set as authors and the rest must then go through an arduous competition for the few remaining publication slots. What George Orwell noted in his book "Animal Farm" can be paraphrased: All authors are equal but some are more equal than others.

---

[5] Just look at today's photos of highly praised young talents in sciences. In this case, images often say more than 1,000 words.

- *Revenge of frustrated experts*

  Ultimately, the entire publication process is a tedious and humiliating experience for many researchers. Constantly, submitted papers are rejected, and often for reasons that are not comprehensible. One has to be pleased if the reviewers have the grace to make recommendations for a revision of the article. In this case, in order to finally get it published, one needs to (or in fact "must") change the article according to the wishes of the reviewers. This is hardly a pleasant task as it is not uncommon that a revision is done "contre coeur." Therefore it is no wonder that many reviewers are at the same time frustrated authors, who can now pay back to innocent third authors the humiliation they had gone through themselves (Frey et al. 2009, p. 153): *They should not have it easier than us, and they should not think that getting a publication is so easy.* is the tenor. For this reason, articles are often rejected out of personal grudges, and the supposedly objective competition for publication becomes a subjective statement. This is particularly the case when it comes to approaches that are hated by the reviewers (in reality it is often the professor behind the publication who is hated) and they will not forgo the chance to make the life of this author a little bit more miserable.

The perverse incentives created by the peer-review process ensure that the steadily increasing number of published articles in scientific journals often does not lead to new or original insights and, therefore, many new ideas do not show up in established journals. They can rather be found in books and working papers, where there is no pseudo-quality control which hinders innovative ideas. Although the peer-review process prevents the publication of obvious platitudes and nonsense on the one hand, on the other hand it promotes the publication of formally and verbally dressed-up nonsense. The increasing irrelevance of content is the result of artificially staged competition for publication in professional journals. The next section deals with the use of publications and citations as indicators for the assessment of individual scientists and scientific institutions, and explains why we have more and more irrelevant publications.

# The Competition for Top-Rankings by Maximising Publications and Citations

Despite the great difficulties involved in publishing articles in professional journals, the number of publications is constantly growing because more and more journals exist simultaneously. These publications are important for the rankings of individual scientists as well as institutions and universities. Furthermore, if young scientists apply for a professorship, the list of publications is usually the most important criterion in the decision process of who will get the post. No wonder that scientists do everything to publish as much as possible despite the painstaking peer-review process. The question as to what to publish, where, and with whom has become essential to the modern scientist. Publication problems cause sleepless nights and the acceptance of an article in a top journal is the greatest thing that can happen in the life of a modern scientist. This is the case, although most of these publications are not of the slightest importance for anybody outside of the academic system. In most articles the opposite of what has been "proved" could also be "proved" and it would not change the course of the world at all.

How does the number of publications actually get into the evaluation and ranking process of scientists and their institutions? At first glance, this seems quite simple: one simply counts all the articles published by a scientist in scientific journals (or counts number of pages) and then gets to the relevant number of the scientist's publication output. However, there is a problem. As we have already seen, the journals differ dramatically in terms of their scientific reputation, and an article in an A journal is worth much more than an article in a B or C journal. So we must somehow take into account the varying quality of the journals in order to achieve a "fairly" assessed publication output. To this end, an entirely new science has developed, called scientometrics or bibliometrics, which deals with nothing else than measuring and comparing the publication output of scientists. This science has by now obtained its own professors and its own journals, and consequently the measurements are also becoming more complex and less transparent, which then in turn justifies even more bibliometric research.

The most important tool of bibliometric research is citation analysis, which has the purpose of determining the quantity of citations of the specific journal article to be analyzed. Based on this, the effect of scientific articles can be ascertained. The rationale behind this is simple: whoever is much quoted is read often, and what is often read must be of high quality. Hence, the quantity of citations can be used as a "quality indicator" of an article. This quality indicator can then be used to weigh up the articles published in various magazines. Thus, we obtain an "objective" number for a scientist's publication output which then can be easily compared and used for rankings. This is also done on a large scale and university administrators seem to put more energy and effort into these comparisons than into actual research.

The International Joint Committee on Quantitative Assessment of Research, consisting of mathematicians and statisticians, talks in a report dated 2008 (Adler et al. 2008, p. 3) about a Culture of Numbers and sums up the assessment of the situation as follows:

> The drive towards more transparency and accountability in the academic world has created a 'culture of numbers' in which institutions and individuals believe that fair decisions can be reached by algorithmic evaluation of some statistical data; unable to measure quality (the ultimate goal), decision-makers replace quality by numbers that they can measure. (...) But this faith in the accuracy, independence, and efficacy of metrics is misplaced.

This is a warning coming from experts, which we should take seriously. Also, the German Research Foundation (DFG 2002) warned a few years ago about believing too much in quantitative measures (translated by the author):

Quantitative indicators are comfortable, they seem objective and are (...) surrounded by an aura of hardly disputable authority. Nevertheless, the naive trust in numbers is a fatal misbelief which each faculty (...) should counteract.

However, the similarities between various publication rankings are low because different quality measurements lead to very different results (see e.g., Frey and Rost 2010; Maasen and Weingart 2008). However, "clever" researchers have found a solution even to that problem (see Franke and Schreier 2008). If rankings do not lead to clear results, we should simply calculate a weighted average from the different rankings. In other words, we construct a meta-ranking out of all existing rankings and again we have a clear result. And if in future several meta-rankings should exist, then one can also construct a meta-meta-ranking! Academic excellence at its best!

A measure which has become particularly popular among number-fetishists is the so-called "Impact Factor". This factor is widely used nowadays in order to calculate the "quality" of journals. The Impact Factor of a particular journal is a quotient where the numerator is the number of citations of articles published in that particular journal during previous years (mostly over the last two years) in a series of selected journals in a given year. The denominator comprises of the total number of articles published in that journal within the same period of time. For example, if a journal has an Impact Factor of 1.5 in 2010, this tells us that papers published in this journal in 2008 and 2009 were cited 1.5 times on average in the selected journals in 2010.

The Impact Factors used in science today are calculated annually by the American company Thomson Scientific; these then get published in the Journal Citation Reports. Thomson Scientific has a de facto monopoly for the calculation of impact factors, although the exact calculation is not revealed, which has been questioned repeatedly (see, e.g. Rossner et al. 2007). *The sciences have allowed Thomson Scientific to dominate them.* (Winiwarter and Luhmann 2009, p. 1). This is even more absurd if, on the one hand, the blessing of competition keeps being praised, but on the other hand, a monopoly for Thomson Scientific is allowed, which enables Thomson Scientific to sell its secretly fabricated Impact Factors to academic institutions at a high price, although in many sciences less than 50 % of today's existing scientific journals are included in the calculation.

A concrete example will show how numbers are fabricated mindlessly. The following proposal is from a 2005 research paper published by the Thurgau Institute of Economics at the University of Konstanz. The author, Miriam Hein (who studied economics) naively propagates a method for measuring quality without being aware of the perverse incentives that this would create. In the introduction we read (Hein 2005, p. 3):

An intended increase in research performance can probably be induced only by the use of incentive-compatible management tools. Research units and individual researchers who undertake high quality research must [an imperative!] be rewarded, and those who are less successful, should be sanctioned. It is therefore important to identify good and bad research. Well-designed ranking tools can serve this purpose.

The above-quoted section talks about "high quality research" within the same article and a few pages later a proposal for the measurement and calculation of the quality of research follows. The average "quality research" (DQ) of an institution shall be determined according to the following formula:

$$DQ = \frac{FX}{FX_S} = \frac{\sum_i \sum_k \frac{p_{ki} w_k}{n_{ki}}}{\sum_i \sum_k \frac{p_{ki}}{n_{ki}}}$$

Pki stands for the number of pages in publication k of scientist i, n denotes the number of authors of the publication k, and $w_k$ is a quality factor for the article k, which is typically the impact factor of the journal, in which the article was published. Therefore, the numerator shows the quality-weighted research output (FX) and the denominator simply consists of the number of published pages ($FX_S$). The content of an article, on the other hand, plays no role! The important thing is how long the article is and where it got published. Nevertheless, the just described "quality measure" is seriously praised as progress in quality measurement. The scientist is treated like a screw salesman: The more screws he has sold, the better he is. This attitude is already obvious from the term "research productivity", which according to Hein (2005, p. 24) *is an absolutely central unit of measure in research management.* Thus, pages published in scientific journals become ends in themselves.

The competition for top rankings established by the requirement for as many publications and citations as possible and the already perverse incentives due to the peer-review process have induced a great deal of perverse behavior among scientists. In particular, the following trends can be observed:

- *Salami tactics*
  Knowing that the ultimate goal is to maximize research output, researchers are trying to make as much out of very little and apply so-called "salami tactics". New ideas or records are cut as thin as salami slices in order to maximize number of publications (Weingart 2005). Minor ideas are presented in complex models or approaches in order to fill up an entire article. As a consequence, further publications can be written by varying these models and approaches. No wonder that in average the content of these papers gets increasingly irrelevant, meaningless, and redundant. Hence, it is becoming increasingly difficult to find new and really interesting ideas in the mass of irrelevant publications.
  The most extreme form of a Salami tactic is to publish the same result twice or even more often than that. Such duplication of one's own research output is of course not allowed, but in reality proves to be an entirely effective way to increase one's research productivity. As we have seen above, the peer-review process often fails to discover such double publications. Therefore, an anonymous survey on 3,000 American scientists from the year 2002 shows, at least 4.7 % of the participating scientists admitted to have published the same result several times (Six 2008).

- *Increase of the number of authors per article*
It can be observed that the number of authors publishing articles in scientific journals has largely increased over the recent decades. For example, in the Deutsche Ärzteblatt the average number of authors per article has risen from 1 author per article in 1957 to 3.5 in 2008 (see Baethge 2008). This is, on the one hand, due to the fact that experiments in particular have become increasingly complex and that experiments are no longer carried out by a single scientist, but rather by a team. An evaluation of international journals showed that today's average number of authors per article in modern medicine is 4.4, which is the highest number; this is followed by physics with 4.1 authors per article. In psychology, the average is 2.6 authors per article, while in philosophy, a field still free of experiments, the average number of authors of an article is 1.1 (Wuchty et al. 2007).

However, the increase in team research is not the only reason for the constant increase of authors per article. On the other hand, there is the incentive to publish as much as possible and to be cited as often as possible. So, especially those who have some power in the academic hierarchy (professors or project leaders) try to use their power by forcing all team members to include them as authors in all publications of their research team. And the larger the team, the more publications with this kind of "honorary authorship" are possible. Conversely, it may also be attractive to young scientists to include a well-known professor as a co-author because—thanks to the dubious nature of anonymity within the peer-review process—this improves the chances of publication (see above).

Instead of "honorary authorship" it would be also appropriate to speak of "forced co-authorship", as Timo Rager wrote in a letter to editor of the Neue Zürcher Zeitung at the end of 2008. There we read: *[Forced co-authorship] ... exists even at prestigious institutions at the ETH and at Max-Planck institutes. If you protest against it, you are risking your scientific career.* So in addition to the real authors of scientific articles there are more and more phantom authors, who did not actually contribute to an article, but want to increase the number of their publications. In medicine, this trend appears to be particularly prevalent, which also explains why the average number of authors per article in modern medicine is so high. Based on the articles published in 2002, every tenth name in the author list of the "British Medical Journal" and one in five in the "Annals of Internal Medicine", were phantom authors (see Baethge 2008). Furthermore, 60 % of all articles published in the "Annals of Internal Medicine" cited at least one phantom author. No wonder are there clinical directors with over 50 publications per year (see Six 2008), which, if they had really contributed to all these publications, would be beyond the capacity of a normal human being.

With the number of co-authors, however, not only the publication list of participating authors per article is growing, but also the number of direct and indirect "self-citations" (Fröhlich 2006), which triggers a snowball effect. The more authors an article has, the more all participating authors will be quoting this article again, especially if they are again involved as co-authors in another article: "I publish an article with five co-authors and we have six times as many friends who quote us" (Fröhlich 2006).

- *Ever-increasing specialization*

  To meet this enormous need for publication, new journals for ever more finely divided sub-areas of a research discipline are launched constantly. Thus, the total number of worldwide existing scientific journals is estimated between 100,000 to 130,000 (Mocikat 2009), and each year there are more. By getting increasingly specialized and narrow-minded, chances for publication are improved (Frey et al. 2009). It is advisable to be specialized in a very exotic but important-sounding topic which is understood only by very few insiders, and establish a scientific journal for this topic. Consequently, the few specialists within this field can promote their chances of publication by writing positive reviews in the peer-review process, so that they will all get published.

  Let us just take the topic of "wine" as an example: There is the "Journal of Wine Economics", the "International Journal of Wine Business Research", "Journal of Wine Research", the "International Journal of Wine Marketing," and so on. All of these are scientific journals that deal with wine on a "highly scientific" level, covering topics such as wine economics, wine marketing, or sales. Probably we will soon also have specialized journals for red-wine and white-wine economics and we also await the "Journal of Wine Psychology".

- *Forgery and fraud*

  Last but not least, the whole competition for as many publications and citations as possible leads to fraud and forgery. *The higher the pressure to increase productivity, the more likely it is to resort to doubtful means.* (Fröhlich 2006). The assumption that universities are committed to the search for truth (Wehrli 2009) becomes more and more a fiction. Modern universities are exclusively committed to excellence and the search for truth does not help very much in this respect. No wonder that quite a few cases of fraud have become publicly known more recently.

  A good example is the former German physicist Jan-Hendrik Schoen, born 1970, who was celebrated as the German Excellence prodigy until his case of fraud was discovered. For some time it was believed that he had discovered the first organic laser and the first light-emitting transistor, and accordingly he was highly praised and received a number of scientific awards. At the peak of his career, as a 31-year-old rising star at Bell Laboratories in the United States, he published an article in a scientific journal on average every eight days, of which 17 were published in highly respected journals such as "Nature" or "Science". No one seemed to notice that this is simply impossible if you do proper research. Instead the German scientific community was proud that they were able to come up with such a top performer. It took some time until co-researchers doubted his results and soon the data turned out to be forged in large parts. A lot of the results were simply simulated on the computer. The interesting thing is, as Reich (2009) writes in her book "Plastic Fantastic", that these forgeries would probably never have even been discovered if Schoen had not exaggerated so much with his publications. Otherwise, he would probably be a respected professor at a top university by now and part of an excellence cluster.

Cases of fraud such as the example of Jan Hendrik Schoen mainly affect the natural sciences, where the results of experiments are corrected or simply get invented. Social sciences often have gone already one step further. There, research is often of such a high degree of irrelevance that it does not matter anymore whether a result is faked or not. It does not matter one way or the other.

The overall effect of all these perverse incentives is that scientists produce more and more nonsense, which adds nothing to real scientific progress. In turn, because the articles also become increasingly out of touch with reality, they are read less and less. Moreover, the increase in citations is not a sign of increased dispersion of scientific knowledge because, presumably, most articles get quoted unread. This has been shown by research that documents how mistakes from the cited papers are also included in the articles which cite them. (Simkin and Roychowdhury 2005). Therefore, more and more articles are published but they are read less and less. The whole process represents a vicious circle that leads to a rapid increase in the publication of nonsense. In the past, researchers who had nothing to say at least did not publish. However, today, artificially staged competitions force even uninspired and mediocre scientists to publish all the time. Non-performance has been replaced by the performance of nonsense. This is worse because it makes it increasingly difficult to find the truly interesting research in the mass of insignificant publications.

# Side Effects of the Production of Nonsense in Science: 'Crowding-Out' Effects and New Bureaucracy

The artificially staged competitions in science for publications and citations, but also for third-party projects (financing), have caused the emergence of more and more nonsense in the form of publications and projects. This is associated with a variety of side effects, some of which have serious consequences. The intrinsic motivation of those scientists involved in research is increasingly replaced by a system of "stick and carrot". Indeed, this is not the only crowding-out effect that we can observe. In addition, a new bureaucracy has evolved which ensures that more and more people employed in the research system spend more and more time on things that have nothing to do with true research. Both effects cause a gradual deterioration within many scientific disciplines, but they are advertised under labels such as "more excellence" and "more efficiency".

*Crowding-Out Effects*

Some of the crowding out effects triggered by competitions for publications and projects were already previously addressed in this contribution. Here we will show how this crowding-out effects harm universities and the scientific world.

- *Crowding-out of intrinsic motivation by stick and carrot*
  Carrots and sticks replace the taste for science (Merton 1973) which is indispensable for scientific progress. A scientist who does not truly love his work will never be a great scientist. Yet exactly those scientists who are intrinsically motivated are the ones whose motivation is usually crowded out the most. They are often rather unconventional people who do not perform well in standardized competitions, and they do not feel like constantly being forced to work just to attain high scores. Therefore, a lot of potentially highly valuable research is crowded out along with intrinsic motivation as well.

- *Crowding-out of unconventional people and approaches by the mainstream*
  Both original themes and unconventional people have little in the way of chances in a system based on artificially staged competitions. The peer-review process causes potential authors and project applicants in both the competition for publication and the competition for third-party funding (their projects are also judged by peers) to converge upon mainstream topics and approaches, as novel ideas and approaches get rarely published or financed. However, scientific geniuses were hardly ever mainstream before their theories or methods were accepted. They are often quite unconventional in their way of working and, therefore, do not perform well in assessments which are based upon the number of publications in professional journals, citations, or projects acquired. Neither Albert Einstein nor Friedrich Nietzsche would be able to pursue a scientific career under the current system.

- *Crowding-out of quality by quantity*
  In the current system, scientific knowledge is replaced by measurable outputs. Not the content of an article or a project counts, but the number of published and cited articles or the number and the amount of money of the acquired projects. Since the measurable output is considered to be the indicator of quality, the true quality is more and more crowded out. The need to publish constantly leaves no time to worry too long about the progress of knowledge, although this should be the real purpose of scientific activity.

- *Crowding-out of content by form*
  Closely related to the crowding-out of quality by quantity is the crowding-out of content by form. As content gets more trivial and inconsequential, one tries to shine with form: With complicated formulas or models, with sophisticated empirical research designs, with extensive computer simulations, and with gigantic machinery for laboratories. The actual content of research drifts into the background and the spotlight is turned on formal artistry. For example, it does not matter anymore if comparing different data sets really brings benefit to the progress in knowledge. Important is the sophistication of the method which was used for the comparison of the data sets.

- *Crowding-out of research by bureaucracy*
  This crowding-out effect makes a significant contribution to the new bureaucracy described in the following section. The people employed in research such as professors, heads of institutes, research assistants, or graduate students actually spend an ever-larger portion of their time coping with research

bureaucracy. This obviously includes the time it takes to write (often unsuccessful) research proposals, and later on interim and final reports: This is time a researcher must spend as a price for actually participating in the project competition. In this way, the actual research is paradoxically repressed by its advancement because the administrative requirements no longer permit research. Furthermore, each journal article submitted for publication requires an enormous effort (strategic citing, unnecessary formalization, etc.), which has nothing to do with its content. Bureaucracy, and not research, ultimately consumes most of the time that is spent on writing scientific publications in journals and on carrying out projects that do not contribute anything to scientific knowledge, but have the goal of improving the measurable output.

- *Crowding-out of individuals by centers, networks, and clusters*
  Competitions for projects also cause individual researchers to disappear more and more behind competence centers, networks, and clusters. Research institutions prefer to pump research money into large research networks which are supposed to provide excellence. Scientists see themselves under pressure to reinvent preferably large cooperative and long-range projects with as many research partners (network!) as possible, bringing third-party funds to their institution. Large anonymous institutions such as the EU give money to other large anonymous institutions (e.g. an excellence cluster) where the individual researcher disappears, becoming a small wheel in a big research machine.

- *Crowding-out of "useless" basic research by application-oriented, "useful" research*
  The competition for third-party funded projects is especially driven in this way because it is believed to initiate more and more "useful" research; this will rapidly lead to marketable innovations and further on to more economic growth. In this way, both humanities and basic research is gradually crowded out because in these disciplines immediate usability can hardly be shown or postulated. For example, "useful" brain research displaces "useless" epistemology. However, anyone who is familiar with the history of scientific progress knows that often discoveries which were considered "useless" at their inception led to some of the most successful commercial applications. The at first sight "useless" field of philosophical logic has proven to be absolutely central to the development of hardware and software for computers.

The crowding-out effects described above vary from one scientific discipline to another, but nowadays they can found in almost every discipline. They have become obvious to such an extent that they cannot be ignored. However, politicians and managers in charge of science do not actually care about this because they want quick success that can be proven by measurable output. In turn, young scientists are socialized by the established scientific system in a way that the perverse effects caused by this development already appear to be normal to them.

# The Emergence of a New Research Bureaucracy

One of the crowding-out effects that was just described concerns the crowding-out of research by bureaucracy. From the outside, it looks just as if research activities grow at a fast pace. There are more and more people employed at universities and research institutions,[6] the number of scientific publications increases steadily, and more and more money is spent on research. However, the crowding-out effect gives rise to people who seem to do scientific work, but mostly are not engaged in research at all. Most scientists know about this phenomenon. What scientists at universities and other research institutions are mostly doing are things such as writing applications for funding of research projects, looking for possible partners for a network and coordination of tasks, writing interim and final reports for existing projects, evaluating project proposals and articles written by other researchers, revising and resubmitting a rejected article, converting a previously published article into a research proposal so that it can be funded retrospectively, and so on.

It is clear that there is hardly time to do research under such conditions. Project proposals of more than 100 pages are not uncommon today, and the application process at some institutions has become like a maze which only a few specialists can guide you through. An expert in this field, the sociologist Münch (2009, p. 8) writes:

> Staged competitions devour extensive stuff and resources for coordination, for application processes, for evaluation and implementation which eat into actual research work, so that exactly the very best researchers are falling into a newly created control machine and run the risk of drowning in its depths.

The actual research today rests largely on the shoulders of assistants and graduate students whose low hourly compensations still allow them to improve scientific knowledge. In contrast, opportunity costs of doing research are often too high for professors and research leaders, because they can contribute more to the measurable output of their institution by focusing on the organization and management of project acquisitions and publications. In turn, because the postgraduates are in fact often also forced to name their professors or institute directors as co-authors of their publications, the list of publications of professors and research leaders still grows despite their lack of continued research.

However, the above-described increase in the proportion of time that is lost due to the bureaucracy associated with the artificial competitions is only the first step of the new bureaucracy. The second step becomes evident by the ever-increasing number of people working in governmental committees who are in charge of the

---

[6] In Switzerland, the total number of employees at universities in Switzerland shows an increase of 24,402 in 1995 to 32,751 in 2008, which is about one-third. Of the 32,751 employees in 2008 were 2,900 professors, 2,851 were lecturers, 15,868 were assistants and research assistants, and 11,132 people were outside of research and teaching in the administration or engineering work (SBF 2007).

organization and the course of these artificially staged competitions. This is essential to both the traditional research institutions such as universities or research institutes as well as to the committees dealing with the organization and financing of research (European Research Council, Federal Ministry for Education and Research, etc.). Artificial competitions have enormously complicated research funding. Universities and their respective institutes do not directly receive money for research anymore. Instead, they have to write proposals for government-initiated research programs, which have to get evaluated and administered. This is a complex and time-consuming process in which each process is associated with complicated procedures and endless forms to be filled out. What is proudly called research-competition becomes, at a closer look, a labor-intensive and inefficient re-allocation of funds from some public institutions (Ministry of Research or the appropriate Federal Agency) to other public institutions (universities, research institutes).

The second step of the increase in bureaucracy is also due to the fact that universities, institutes, and even professors need to be evaluated and ranked. Numbers are needed to decide which institutions or professors are really excellent, and where it is worthwhile to promote excellence clusters or competence networks and what institutions can be awarded the status of a "lighthouse in research". There are already several public agencies (e.g. Centre d'Etudes de la science et de la Technology in Switzerland) and university institutions (e.g. Centre for Science and Technology Studies at the University of Leiden in the Netherlands), which deal exclusively with the measurement of research inputs and outputs on the basis of bibliometric and scientometric research. There the metrics are fabricated which are necessary for the artificial competitions and which form the basis for the rankings and, in turn, stimulate the publication and project competitions.

Research funding has reached its far highest level of bureaucracy by the EU research programs,[7] which appear to be especially sophisticated Keynesian employment programs. None of the "Research Staff" working for the EU actually does research because inventing increasingly complex application processes and new funding instruments already creates a sufficiently large workload for them. Therefore, a large portion of the research is just used to maintain this bureaucracy. Already in 1997, the European Court of Auditors criticized the EU in relation to the 4th Research Program as an "enormous bureaucracy and a useless waste of money". According to experts, only about 60 % of the 13 billion euros, which were provided to the 4th Research Program, were actually received by research institutions. Not much has been changed in the following programs. The responsible coordinator of the Budgetary Control Committee of the European Parliament, Inge Gräßle (CDU), after the end of the 6th Research Program (€ 16.7 billion in 4 years), came in 2007 to the conclusion that "the effort to simplify funding allocation within the EU research framework program has not yet been sufficient." That is an understatement. The 6th Program has invented a whole new, previously unknown form of networking bureaucracy, which has led to much more, and not less, bureaucracy.

---

[7]  See also Binswanger (2003).

The increase in bureaucracy outside of the actual research institutions also fosters an increase in bureaucracy within the research institutions. The large number of EU-research officers has managed to complicate the application process tremendously. In Germany alone hundreds of advisor posts have been created just to help scientists to make a successful project application. Even if you have completed the tedious work involved in making an application, the chance of success is low. Since the 6th Research Program which began in 2002, the success rate of applications lies between 15 and 20 %, while before the success rate of applications was at about one quarter. In other words, between 80 and 85 % of applications, involving about 12 researchers on average today, are not successful. You can imagine what enormous amounts of time and money are here wasted just to get funding from an EU project.

Of course, the new research bureaucracy has its positive impact on the economy. It creates new jobs and contributes to full employment. Keynes would probably be amazed at what creative level his ideas of a national employment policy have been developed within science. Back in the 1930s, the time of the Great Depression, he mentioned that, in such situations, even totally unproductive and useless activities would stimulate the economy and would therefore eliminate unemployment. The example he gave referred to a governmental construction project in which workers were employed digging ditches and then filling them up again. Even if useless, such a program paid by government funds will cause an increase in the demand for construction activities and thus stimulate the economy. Today's nonsense production in science is much more sophisticated than the nonsense of digging ditches and filling them up again as the nonsense is disguised to the general public.

# References

Adler, R., Ewing, J., & Taylor, P. (2008). *Citation statistics. A report from the joint committee on quantitative assessment of research (IMU, ICIAM, IMS).* Available at: http://www. mathunion.org/fileadmin/IMU/Report/CitationStatistics.pdf.

Atkinson, M. (2001). "Peer review" culture. *Science and Engineering Ethics, 7*(2), 193–204. doi:10.1007/s11948-001-0040-8.

Baethge, C. (2008). Gemeinsam veröffentlichen oder untergehen. *Deutsches Ärzteblatt, 105,* 380–383.

Berghoff, S., et al. (2009). CHE-Hochschulranking. Vorgehensweise und Indikatoren. In *Arbeitspapier Nr. 119.* Available at: http://www.che.de/downloads/CHE_AP119_Methode_ Hochschulranking_2009.pdf.

Binswanger, M. (2003). EU: Wie Forschungsmillionen in der Bürokratie verschwinden. *Die Weltwoche, 24,* 51–52.

DFG. (2002). *Perspektiven der Forschung und ihre Förderung. Aufgaben und Finanzierung 2002–2006,* Weinheim.

Franke, N., & Schreier, M. (2008). A meta-ranking of technology and innovation management/entrepreneurship journals. *Die Betriebswirtschaft, 68*, 185–216.

Frey, B. S. (2003). Publishing as prostitution? Choosing between one's own ideas and academic success. *Public Choice, 116*, 205–223.

Frey, B. S., Eichenberger, R., & Frey, R. L. (2009). Editorial ruminations: Publishing kyklos. *Kyklos, 62*(2), 151–160. doi:10.1111/j.1467-6435.2009.00428.x.

Frey, B. S., & Rost, K. (2010). Do rankings reflect research quality? *Journal of Applied Economics, 13*(1), 1–38. doi:10.1016/S1514-0326(10)60002-5.

Fröhlich, G. (2006). *Evaluation wissenschaftlicher Leistungen: 10 Fragen von Bruno Bauer an Gerhard Fröhlich*, Schweizerische Gesellschaft für Strahlenbiologie und Medizinische Physik: SGSMP Bulletin. Available at: http://www.sgsmp.ch/bullA62.pdf.

Fröhlich, G. (2007). Peer Review und Abweisungsraten: Prestigeschmuck wissenschaftlicher Journale. *Forschung und Lehre*, pp. 338–339.

Giusta, M. D., Tommaso, M. L., & Strøm, S. (2007). Who is watching? The market for prostitution services. *Journal of Population Economics, 22*(2), 501–516. doi:10.1007/s00148-007-0136-9.

Hein, M. (2005). Wie hat sich die universitäre volkswirtschaftliche Forschung in der Schweiz seit Beginn der 90er Jahre entwickelt? In *Research paper series*. Konstanz: Thurgauer Wirtschaftsinstitut.

Kohler, G. (2007). Über das Management der Universität. Anmerkung zu einer aktuellen Debatte. *Neue Zürcher Zeitung*. Available at: http://www.nzz.ch/aktuell/feuilleton/uebersicht/ueber-das-management-der-universitaet-1.538892.

Körner, C. (2007). Die Naturwissenschaft im Spannungsfeld zwischen individueller Kreativität und institutionellen Netzen. In W. Berka & W. Schmidinger (Eds.), *Vom Nutzen der Wissenschaften* (pp. 169–181). Wien: Böhlau.

Lawrence, P. A. (2003). The politics of publication. *Nature, 422*(6929), 259–261. doi:10.1038/422259a.

Maasen, S., & Weingart, P. (2008). Unternehmerische Universität und neue Wissenschaftskultur. In H. Matthies & D. Simon (Eds.), *Wissenschaft unter Beobachtung. Effekte und Defekte von Evaluationen. Leviathan Sonderheft ,24*, 141–160.

Merton, R. K. (1973). The normative structure of science. In R. K. Merton (Ed.), *The sociology of science: Theoretical and empirical investigations*. Chicago: University of Chicago Press.

Mittelstrass, J. (2007). Begegnungen mit Exzellenz.

Mocikat, R. (2009). Die Diktatur der Zitatenindizes: Folgen für die Wissenskultur. *Gaia, 2*(18), 100–103.

Münch, R. (2009). *Globale Eliten, lokale Autoritäten: Bildung und Wissenschaft unter dem Regime von PISA, McKinsey & Co*. Frankfurt, M.: Suhrkamp.

OECD (Organisation for Economic Co-operation and Development). (2008). OECD science, technology and industry outlook. Paris: OECD Publishing.

Osterloh, M., & Frey, B. S. (2008). Anreize im Wirtschaftssystem. CREMA Research Paper. In Universität Zürich.

Ouchi, W. G. (1980). Markets, bureaucracies and clans. *Administrative Science Quarterly, 25*, 129–141.

Partha, D., & David, P. A. (1994). Toward a new economics of science. *Research Policy, 23*(5), 487–521. doi:10.1016/0048-7333(94)01002-1.

Reich, E. S. (2009). *Plastic fantastic: How the biggest fraud in physics shook the scientific world* (1st ed.). New York: Palgrave Macmillan.

Rossner, M., Van Epps, H., & Hill, E. (2007). Show me the data. *The Journal of General Physiology, 131*(1), 3–4. doi:10.1085/jgp.200709940.

SBF (Staatssekretariat für Bildung und Forschung). (2007). *Bibliometrische Untersuchung zur Forschung in der Schweiz*, Bern, Schweiz.

Schatz, G. (2001). How can we improve European research?

Simkin, M. V., & Roychowdhury, V. P. (2005). Stochastic modeling of citation slips. *Scientometrics, 62*(3), 367–384. doi:10.1007/s11192-005-0028-2.

Six, A. (2008). Schreibkrampf unter Forschern. *Neue Zürcher Zeitung am Sonntag*, p. 67.

Starbuck, W. H. (2006). *The production of knowledge. The Challenge of Social Science Research.* Oxford: Oxford University Press.

Trow, M. (1997). Reflections on diversity in higher education. In M. Herbst, G. Latzel, & L. Lutz (Eds.), *Wandel im tertitären Bildungssektor: Zur Position der Schweiz im internationalen Vergleich* (pp. 15–36). Zürich, Schweiz: Verlage der Fachvereine.

Wehrli, C. (2009). Das hohe Gut wissenschaftlicher Redlichkeit. *NZZ.*

Weingart, P. (2005). Impact of bibliometrics upon the science system: Inadvertent consequences? *Scientometrics, 62*(1), 117–131. doi:10.1007/s11192-005-0007-7.

Winiwarter, V., & Luhmann, N. (2009). Die Vermessung der Wissenschaft. *Gaia, 1*(18), 1.

Wuchty, S., Jones, B. F., & Uzzi, B. (2007). The increasing dominance of teams in production of knowledge. *Science, 316*(5827), 1036–1039. doi:10.1126/science.1136099.

# Science Caught Flat-Footed: How Academia Struggles with Open Science Communication

**Alexander Gerber**

> *Change happens by listening and then starting a dialogue with the people who are doing something you don't believe is right.*
> —Jane Goodall, ethologist and devoted science communicator.

**Abstract** As high as the potential of Web 2.0 might be, the European academia, compared to that of the US, mostly reacts hesitantly at best to these new opportunities. Interestingly enough this scepticism applies even more to science communication than to scientific practice itself. The author shows that the supposed technological challenge is actually a cultural one. Thus possible solutions do not primarily lie in the tools or in the strategies used to apply them, but in the adaptation of the systemic frameworks of knowledge-creation and dissemination as we have practised them for decades, if not centuries. Permeating an 'Open Science Communication' (OSC) under closed paradigms can only succeed if foremost the embedding frameworks are adapted. This will include new forms of impact measurement, recognition, and qualification, and not only obvious solutions from the archaic toolbox of enlightenment and dissemination. The author also illustrates the causes, effects, and solutions for this cultural change with empirical data.

The swan song of what was meant to be an era of "Public Understanding of Science and Humanities" (PUSH) rings rather dissonantly today, given the wailing chorus of disorientation, if not existential fear, intoned by science communicators across Europe. Almost 30 years after the game-changing Bodmer report (Royal Society 1985), another paradigmatic shift is taking place, probably even more radical than any of the transitions during the previous four eras (Trench and Bucchi 2010; Gerber 2012). This fifth stage of science communication is being predominantly driven by interactive online media. Let us examine this from the same perspectives which the very definition of "science communication" as an

A. Gerber (✉)
German Research Center for Science and Innovation Communication, Berlin, Germany
e-mail: a.gerber@innokomm.eu

S. Bartling and S. Friesike (eds.), *Opening Science*,
DOI: 10.1007/978-3-319-00026-8_4, © The Author(s) 2014

umbrella-term also comprises of: (1) the communication about science, and (2) the communication by scientists and their institutionalised PR with different publics.

## Communication about Science

Journalists are witnessing a widespread disintegration of mass media outlets and their underlying business models. In terms of circulation and advertising revenue, this demise may not be as abrupt as in the U.S. (see Fig. 1), but is surely just as devastating for popular science publishers in Europe, and consequently their staff and freelancers in the long run (Gerber 2011, 2012). Brumfiel (2009) was among the first scholars to make the scientific community aware of the extent of the science journalism crisis, quoting blatant analyses by experienced editors, such as Robert Lee Hotz from The Wall Street Journal: "Independent science coverage is not just endangered, it's dying" (p. 275). Afflicted by low salaries and even lower royalties from a decreasing number of potential outlets, science journalism is additionally (or maybe consequently) suffering from a continuous decrease in credibility.

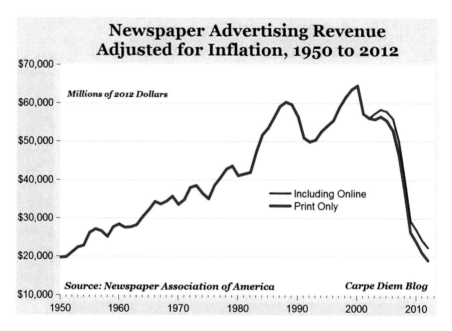

**Fig. 1** The business models of traditional print journalism in the U.S. have eroded remarkably fast: the industry has lost as much market share in five years as they had gained in the 50 years before. The disintegration of mass media outlets in terms of circulation and advertising revenue may not be as abrupt in Europe as it is in the U.S. Nonetheless, popular science publishers in Europe are also heavily under pressure

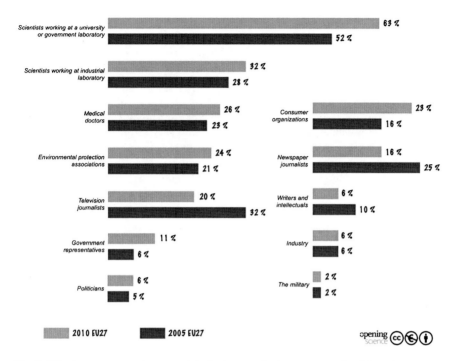

**Fig. 2** Who is most appropriate to explain the impact of science upon society? Less than one out of five Europeans nowadays name journalists, and the numbers are constantly decreasing (*light grey* 2010, *dark grey* 2005). In fact, a majority expects the scientists themselves to deliver their messages directly. Interactive online media offer new opportunities to do exactly that

Questioned about who is most appropriate to explain the impact of science upon society, only 16–20 % of Europeans nowadays name journalists—a further decrease from 25 to 32 % five years before (see Fig. 2). In fact, a majority expects the scientists themselves to deliver their messages directly: 63 %, increasing from 52 % five years earlier (European Commission 2010). Unfortunately, it has not yet been investigated properly as to what extent this credibility also (or particularly) extends over the science blogosphere and other online platforms, or whether interactive online media have even been catalysts, and not just enabling technologies, in this development.

Every discourse or effort to reinvent journalism regarding media economics (e.g. crowdfunding), investigation methods (e.g. data-driven journalism in the deep web), formats (e.g. slide casts), and distribution (e.g. content curation) almost inevitably seems to circle around interactive online media. Obviously the web is not only seen as the main cause of the crisis, but also as the main opportunity for innovations to solve it.

On the other hand, one could also argue that due to an increasing number of popular science formats on television, science journalism now reaches a much wider audience as compared to print publications which have always merely catered to a small fraction of society. Especially on TV, however, we as communication scholars should be wary of the distorted image of science reflected by conventional mass media. Coverage and content are mostly limited to either the explanation of phenomena in everyday life ("Why can't I whip cream with a washing machine?") or supposed success stories ("Scientists have finally found a cure for Cooties"). Thereby journalism neither succeeds in depicting the 'big science picture' of policy, ethics, and economics holistically, nor the real complexity of a knowledge-creation process authentically, which is everything but linear, being a process in which knowledge is permanently being contradicted or falsified, and is therefore never final.

However, the notion of what the essence of science really is could perfectly well be vulgarised through web technologies, in the sense of making the different steps within this process of knowledge-creation transparent, for instance by means of a continuous blog or other messaging or sharing platforms. Yet there are still only very few examples for such formats (see below), and they are particularly sparse in journalism.

The tendency to reduce science to supposed success stories is certainly also a result of its mediatisation, i.e. science and science policies reacting and adapting to the mass media logic by which it is increasingly being shaped and framed (Krotz 2007; Fuller 2010; Weingart 2001). This brings us to the second dimension of science communication.

## Communication by Scientists and the Institutionalised PR

Self-critical scholars as well as practitioners of science communication wonder how far we have effectively come since 1985, when the Royal Society envisioned a public which would understand "more of the scope and the limitations, the findings and the methods of science". Even then the "most urgent message" went to the scientists themselves: "Learn to communicate with the public, [...] and consider it your duty" (The Royal Society 1985, p. 24).

Almost 30 years later the resources for institutionalised science PR and marketing have multiplied remarkably. Compared to the early 1990s when professional communicators were rare exceptions, there is hardly a single university or institute left today without a communication department. Larger institutions employ up to 70 full-time communicators in the meantime. Yet less than one out of ten citizens in Europe actually show any interest whatsoever in science centres, public lectures, or science fairs (European Commission 2010, see Fig. 3)—albeit with a blanket coverage across the continent. Such obvious contrasts between the supply and demand of certain formats make science an easy prey for critics arguing that its communication is inherently elitist. At least the often misinterpreted decrease in naïve trust in science—66 % in 2010 compared to 78 % in 2005 (European Commission 2010)—is an encouraging sign of an increasingly critical public (Bauer 2009).

*Science and technology can sort out any problem*

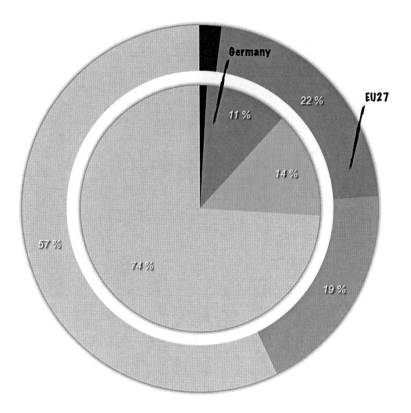

- ● Don't know
- ● Total "agree"
- ● Neither agree nor disagree
- ● Total "disagree"

**Fig. 3** Presumably as a direct result of mediatisation in the era of PUSH, the so-called "myth of science", the naïve trust in science being able to solve any problem, has decreased significantly. In some countries like Germany (*inner pie*) this trust is even lower than the European average. This development is often misinterpreted as a problem. It should instead be seen as an encouraging sign of an increasingly critical public

PR professionals have been 'PUSH-trained', so to speak, to focus on the dissemination of research results, ideally in the form of a well-told success story, as described above, and thereby significantly contribute to the distorted media image of scientific reality. Unfortunately just now that science, at least on an institutional level, seems to have come to terms with the mechanisms of mass media; PR and marketing are being shattered by a seismic shift towards a horizontalisation of communication better known as social media. Particularly the new media-savvy student generations have an entirely different understanding of how the relevant information should 'find them'. Even most communication scholars are still amazed of the pace of this transition. In countries like Germany, for instance, the Internet overtook television two years ago in terms of activated and structured demand for information, i.e. the medium of choice to look for quality information—an increase from 13 % in 2000 to 59 % in 2011 (IfD Allensbach 2011).

Unanimously most studies show, however, that science has as of yet largely avoided adapting both its communication efforts and its own media usage to the above mentioned changes in the information behaviour of laypeople (Procter et al. 2010; Bader et al. 2012; Allgaier 2013). In a web technology use and needs analysis Gerber (2012, 2013) showed that the use of even the most common online tools is still a niche phenomenon in the scientific community. Furthermore, the few well-known tools were also the ones to be the most categorically rejected, e.g. Twitter by 80.5 % of the respondents.

Yet the diffusion of Web 2.0 tools in academia is only partly a question of technology acceptance. For instance, online communication is still not taken into account in most cases of evaluation or allocation of research funding. Most experts in a Delphi study on science communication (Gerber 2011, 2012) therefore demand a critical discourse about possible incentives for scientists. If online outreach, however, became a relevant criterion for academic careers, we would also have to find more empirically sound ways to measure, compare, or even standardise and audit the impact of such an outreach. Approaches like 'Altmetrics' are promising but still in a conceptual phase. At least for another few years we will therefore have to deal with a widening gap between the masses of scientists communicating "ordinarily", on the one hand, and the very few cutting edge researchers and (mostly large and renowned) institutions experimenting extensively with the new opportunities, on the other. Thus the threat of increasing the already existing imbalances between scientific disciplines is just as evident as the opportunities for increasing transparency, flattening hierarchies, or even digitally democratizing the system itself, as sometimes hyperventilated by Open Science evangelists.

We must not forget that technologies only set the framework, whereas the real challenges and solutions for an 'Open Science Communication' are deeply rooted in scientific culture and the system of knowledge creation itself (Gerber 2012). Much will, therefore, depend upon the willingness of policy makers to actively steer the system in a certain direction. Yet they also have to reconsider whether they thereby risk fostering (even unintentionally) the above mentioned distortion of scientific practice. The ultimate challenge lies in balancing incentives and regulations, on the one hand, with the inevitable effect of a further mediatisation of science, on the other, since both remain two sides of the same coin.

Public relations and science marketing professionals will keep struggling with the increasing 'loss of control' as long as they hang on to their traditional paradigm of dissemination. An increasing number of social media policies in academia shows that the institutions have realised the challenges that they are facing in terms of governance. By accepting 'deinstitutionalisation' and involving individual scientists as authentic and highly credible ambassadors (see above), PR can make the most essential step away from the old paradigm to the new understanding of Open Science Communication (OSC).

The common ground for both above mentioned trends—the 'deprofessionalisation' of science journalism and the 'deinstitutionalisation' of science communication at large—is the remarkable amount of laypersons finding their voices online and the self-conception of civil society organisations demanding to be involved in the science communication process. As much as this inevitably shatters the economic base of science journalism and as much as it may force the science establishment to reinvent its communication practice, we should be grateful for the degree of communication from 'scientific citizens'. Thereby the challenge lies less in permitting (or even embracing) bottom–up movements as such, but rather more in resisting the use of public dialogue as a means to an end. While valorising 'citizen science' as an overdue 'co-production' of authoritative social knowledge, Fuller warns us not to treat broadcasts of consensus conferences, citizen juries, etc. simply as *better or worse amplifiers for the previously repressed forms of 'local knowledge' represented by the citizens who are now allowed to share the spotlight with the scientists and policy makers.* (2010, p. 292)

The questionable success of most of these public engagement campaigns has increasingly been challenged recently. Grassroots initiatives like 'Wissenschaftsdebatte' or 'Forschungswende' in Germany criticise openly the fact that pseudo-engagement has merely served as a fig leaf excuse for the legitimisation of research agendas which are still being built top–down. Instead it will be necessary to supplement the dragged-in rituals of 'end of pipe' dissemination with a fresh paradigm of 'start of pipe' deliberation.

Undoubtedly such initiatives cater to the transparency and true public engagement pursued by the ideal of Open Science. Thus within the 'big picture' we should embrace the opportunities of the OSC era, and in particular the interactive online technologies driving it.

## Outlook

Driven by interactive online media, OSC has the potential to exceed the outdated view of communication as a 'packaging industry'. In the next few years we can expect a second wave of professionalisation in science PR and marketing, e.g. through specialised social media training. The performance of communication professionals (and probably also the performance of scientists) will increasingly be measured by whether they succeed in truly engaging a much wider spectrum of society or not. New cultures of communication may foster a scientific citizenship but will also raise new questions regarding imbalances and distortion within the scientific system, and thus the challenge to measure communication impact properly, and even normalise and standardise these new measurements.

# References

Allgaier, J. (2013). Journalism and social media as means of observing the contexts of science. *BioScience, 63*(4), 284–287.

Bader, A., Fritz, G., & Gloning, T. (2012). *Digitale Wissenschaftskommunikation 2010–2011 Eine Online-Befragung*, Giessen: Giessener Elektronische Bibliothek. Available at: http://geb.uni-giessen.de/geb/volltexte/2012/8539/index.html.

Bauer, M. W. (2009). The evolution of public understanding of science–discourse and comparative evidence. *Science Technology & Society, 14*(2), 221–240. doi:10.1177/097172180901400202.

Brumfiel, G. (2009). Science journalism: Supplanting the old media? *Nature, 458*(7236), 274–277. doi:10.1038/458274a.

European Commission, DG Research/DG Communication. (2010). *Special Eurobarometer.* Available at: http://ec.europa.eu/public_opinion/archives/ebs/ebs_340_en.pdf.

Fuller, S. (2010). The mediatisation of science. *BioSocieties, 5*(2), 288–290. doi:10.1057/biosoc.2010.11.

Gerber, A. (2011). *Trendstudie Wissenschaftskommunikation - Vorhang auf für Phase 5. Chancen, Risiken und Forderungen für die nächste Entwicklungsstufe der Wissenschaftskommunikation*, Berlin: Innokomm Forschungszentrum. Available at: http://stifterverband.de/wk-trends.

Gerber, A. (2012). Online trends from the first German trend study on science communication. In Tokar (Ed.), *Science and the Internet* (pp. 13–18). Düsseldorf: Düsseldorf University Press. Available at: http://bit.ly/SMS_COSCI12.

Gerber, A. (2013). Open Science without scientists? Findings from the social media in science study. Available at: http://bit.ly/SMS_EISRI.

IfD Allensbach. (2011). Markt- und Werbeträger-Analyse (AWA).

Krotz, F. (2007). *Mediatisierung: Fallstudien zum Wandel von Kommunikation* 1. Aufl., Wiesbaden: VS, Verlag für Sozialwissenschaften.

Procter, R., Williams, R., & Stewart, J. (2010). *If you build it, will they come? How researchers perceive and use Web 2.0*, Research Information Network. Available at: http://www.rin.ac.uk/our-work/communicating-and-disseminating-research/use-and-relevance-web20-researchers.

The Royal Society. (1985). *The public understanding of science*, Available at: http://royalsociety.org/policy/publications/1985/public-understanding-science.

Trench, B., & Bucchi, M. (2010). Science communication, an emerging discipline. *Journal of Science Communication JCOM, 9*(3). Available at: http://jcom.sissa.it/archive/09/03.

Weingart, P. (2001). *Die Stunde der Wahrheit? Zum Verhältnis der Wissenschaft zu Politik, Wirtschaft und Medien in der Wissensgesellschaft* 1. Aufl., Weilerswist: Velbrück Wissenschaft.

# Open Science and the Three Cultures: Expanding Open Science to all Domains of Knowledge Creation

**Michelle Sidler**

*How knowledge circulates has always been vital to the life of the mind, which all of us share, just as it is vital, ultimately, to the well-being of humanity.*

—John Willinsky

**Abstract** The Open Science movement has been most successful in transforming disciplines traditionally associated with science. Social science and humanities disciplines, especially those in the United States, are less well represented. To include all domains of knowledge, the Open Science movement must bridge these 'three cultures' through projects that highlight multiple lines of inquiry, research methods, and publishing practices. The movement should also consider changing its moniker to Open Knowledge in order to include academic disciplines that do not self-identify as science.

In 1959, C. P. Snow's lecture, 'The Two Cultures,' argued that the sciences and the humanities were divided and at odds: *"Literary intellectuals at one pole—at the other scientists, and as the most representative, the physical scientists. Between the two a gulf of mutual comprehension—sometimes (particularly among the young) hostility and dislike, but most of all lack of understanding"* (p. 4). These divisions are felt perhaps most poignantly in American universities. Several cultural, economic, and historical events have led to increased divisions between not only the sciences and the humanities, but also the social sciences. Within each of these 'three cultures' (a term coined in Kagan's 2009 book of the same name), sub-disciplinary divides persist as well, creating pockets, or 'silos' of knowledge communities with their own methods, languages, professional organizations, identities, and so on.

These divisions have roots in the rise of American universities at the turn of the twentieth century. At that time, the liberal arts tradition of a shared curriculum was replaced in many schools by German educational philosophies that emphasized *Lernfreiheit*, freedom in learning. *Lernfreiheit* models encouraged students to

M. Sidler (✉)
Auburn University, Alabama, USA
e-mail: sidlema@auburn.edu

S. Bartling and S. Friesike (eds.), *Opening Science*,
DOI: 10.1007/978-3-319-00026-8_5, © The Author(s) 2014

choose their own courses and majors and prompted faculty to pursue specialized research; these changes eventually led to a model of higher education that replaced generalist courses and professors with individualist disciplinary departments (Hart 1874). Several national legislative acts were also passed during and after this philosophical change, and these moves privileged the sciences, writ large, over the humanities and fine arts while more or less neglecting the social sciences. First, the Morrill Act of 1862 established institutions of higher learning in service to the rising economic needs in industry and agriculture. Accordingly, these universities emphasized science-related disciplines over those in the social sciences and humanities.[1] Next, the mid-twentieth century saw the establishment of government agencies that fund science research, and the amount they make available to scientists far outweighs that of funding for the humanities and fine arts.[2] Add these historical factors to the rather abysmal job prospects for most humanities and social science majors in the present day, and one can easily understand how disciplinary divisions persist in American universities. Indeed, some scholars like Kagan argue that the privileging of the sciences *"created status differentials that eroded collegiality and provoked defensive strategies by the two less advantaged cultures"* (2009, p. ix).

Proponents of Open Science must understand these cultural divides as we move forward into a new era of knowledge, discovery, and collaboration. Nielsen (2012) and others[3] have noted that the immediate challenge for the Open Science movement is its ability to change the culture of science itself, which continues to operate within a print-based, proprietary, and closed framework for scientific discovery and communication. But a larger challenge looms on the horizon: if the Open Science movement hopes to advance change among all areas of knowledge and discovery, it must overtly articulate a larger mission, one that acknowledges the potential impact of networked technologies on all fields of knowledge. Perhaps this mission is tacitly assumed, but it cannot be so, especially when the movement has adopted the moniker, Open Science. At best, humanities and social science scholars, especially those in the U.S., will assume that this movement does not apply to them because 'science' is a term generally reserved for disciplines that employ the scientific method. Such a designation does not include most areas of the

---

[1]  The Morrill Act of 1862 apportioned 30,000 acres (120 km2) to each state. The land was sold or used for "the endowment, support, and maintenance of at least one college where the leading object shall be, without excluding other scientific and classical studies, and including military tactics, to teach such branches of learning as are related to agriculture and the mechanic arts ... in order to promote the liberal and practical education of the industrial classes in the several pursuits and professions in life" (The Morrill Act 1862).

[2]  The National Institutes of Health (NIH) and the National Science Foundation (NSF) provide approximately $38 billion in research funding annually (NIH: http://officeofbudget.od.nih.gov/br.html; NSF 2012). This number far outweighs the amount afforded by the major humanities and arts organizations, the National Endowment for the Humanities (NEH) and the National Endowment for the Arts (NEA), which combined have an annual budget of approximately $308 million (NEH: http://www.neh.gov/divisions/odh; NEA 2012).

[3]  See, for example, Lin (2012) and Willinsky (2006).

humanities and social sciences. At worst, non-science scholars will perceive Open Science as a threat, another way in which scientific disciplines dictate methods for knowledge production and maneuver for more resources.

This challenge is not insurmountable, but it will involve intensive collaboration and understanding among scientists, social scientists, and humanists. Most immediately, we should examine the term 'Open Science.' Scholars of language, rhetoric, and writing (like myself) are keenly aware of the power of words and their associations, and the word 'science' carries associations of division and inequality for some humanities and social science scholars.

Either the movement will have to create and foster a broader definition of 'science' or it will have to replace the term altogether. To use the moniker effectively, the Open Science movement will have to acknowledge and address disciplinary divisions and monetary reward systems that led to this acrimony. A first step might be a broader exploration of the potential impact that networked technologies will have on different knowledge areas. Knowledge discovery and communication practices vary among different disciplines, but no thorough taxonomy of these differences currently exists within the Open Science community. Figure 1 offers just a few examples of the differences between current publishing practices in the sciences and the humanities (although the social sciences are not included here, a similar comparison could be made between the sciences and social sciences). The figure makes clear that the scientific communication is already utilizing digital channels of communication much more deliberately and completely than the humanities. Moreover, digital technologies and Open Access principles (like those employed in Open Science initiatives) have so far achieved minimal impact on publications in the humanities. Such comparisons will be necessary to inventory the status of publishing and research in various disciplines, and then to devise ways new technologies might enhance research and communication across all fields of knowledge.

Another strategy that would alleviate the potential conflict with the moniker 'Open Science' is to substitute it with the phrase 'Open Knowledge.' This broader, more inclusive alternative is already employed by at least one organization, the Open Knowledge Foundation (OKF)[4]; their vision statement includes comprehensive, inspirational passages that foreground a desire to be as inclusive as possible: *"We promote the creation, dissemination and use of open knowledge in all its forms, from genes to geodata and from sonnets to statistics. Our projects, groups and tools work with this principle in different and varying ways to increase user access and ensure transparency."* OKF includes investigative examples from the social sciences and humanities ('sonnets and statistics'), emphasizing that their mission includes all forms of knowledge. Compare this to the description of the Science Online Conference, a major organizing body for Open Science advocates in the U.S.: *"ScienceOnline[5] is a non-profit organization … that facilitates*

---

[4]  OKF: http://okfn.org/about/vision/

[5]  ScienceOnline: http://scienceonline.com/about/

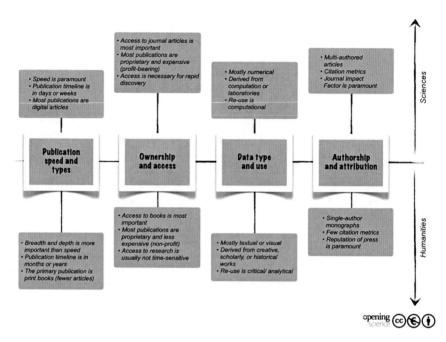

**Fig. 1** Publishing practices of the sciences and the humanities

*conversations, community, and collaborations at the intersection of Science and the Web.*" Few humanities and social science scholars in the U.S. would read this description and assume that their attendance at the conference would be appropriate, or that the issues discussed at the conference have much impact on their own disciplines.

Perhaps the most pragmatic strategy for bridging the 'three cultures' is to develop projects that adapt the digital tools of Open Science for research projects in the humanities and social sciences. OKF is a leader in this regard as well: they are pursuing initiatives such as the Shakespeare Project, a website that aims to provide multiple annotated editions of Shakespeare's plays. The Shakespeare Project leverages open source annotation tools, crowdsourcing, and literary works in the public domain to create a free, open, interactive, and ongoing space of knowledge production and access. These same principles are at the heart of perhaps the most extensive and exciting U.S. program that uses methods similar to Open Science in the humanities, the Office of Digital Humanities (ODH). ODH is a set-aside program within the National Endowment for the Humanities (NEH), and its express purpose is to enhance humanities research through technology. More specifically, ODH has been aggressively pursuing ways to promote digital methods of preserving, archiving, and accessing scholarly materials. One of its initiatives is a series of institutes around the country that train humanities researchers in the methods and tools of digital analysis, data curation, and text coding. Like OKF, ODH recognizes that humanities scholars have a different set of publishing priorities and technological expertise than that of scientists, so it leverages the most immediately applicable and effective tools to promote digital research in a community that has traditionally understood knowledge production as a print-based, textual enterprise.

While a similar claim can be made about a traditionalist culture in the sciences—and indeed, it has been made most emphatically by Nielsen (2012)—the degree to which the humanities and social sciences are engaged with technology is exponentially smaller. Moreover, the humanities and social sciences have a qualitatively different perspective—a different culture, to use Kagan's (2009) term—that requires investigation, interpretation, and engagement by Open Science advocates in order to expand this project more fully into other domains of knowledge.

# References

Hart, J. M. (1874). *German Universities: a narrative of personal experience, together with recent statistical information, practical suggestions, and a comparison of the German, English and American systems of higher education.* New York: Putnam & Sons.

Kagan, J. (2009). *The three cultures: natural sciences, social sciences, and the humanities in the 21st century.* New York: Cambridge University Press.

Lin, T. (2012, January 16). Cracking open the scientific process. NY Times, p.D1.

Morrill Act of July 2, 1862, Public Law 37–108, 37th Cong., 2nd Sess. (1862). Enrolled Acts and Resolutions of Congress, 1789–1996; Record Group 11; General Records of the United States Government; National Archives.

National Endowment for the Arts, (2012). Appropriations request for fiscal year 2013. Available at: http://www.arts.gov/about/Budget/NEA-FY13-Appropriations-Request.pdf.

National Endowment for the Humanities, (2012). *Fiscal year* 2013 *budget request,* Available at: http://www.neh.gov/about/legal/reports.

National Science Foundation, (2012). *FY 213 Budget Request to Congress,* Available at: http://www.nsf.gov/about/budget/fy2013/index.jsp.

Nielsen, M.A. (2012). Reinventing discovery: the new era of networked science, Princeton, NJ, Princeton University Press.

Snow, C.P. (1961). *The two cultures and the scientific revolution* 7th ed., New York: Cambridge University Press. Available at: http://sciencepolicy.colorado.edu/students/envs_5110/snow_1959.pdf.

Willinsky, J. (2005). *The access principle: the case for Open Access to research and scholarship.* Cambridge, MA: MIT Press.

# Part II
# Tools

# (Micro)Blogging Science? Notes on Potentials and Constraints of New Forms of Scholarly Communication

Cornelius Puschmann

**Abstract** Academic publishing, as a practice and as a business, is undergoing the most significant changes in its 350-year history. Electronic journals and books, both Open Access and behind digital pay walls, are increasingly replacing printed publications. In addition to formal channels of scholarly communication, a wide array of semi-formal and informal channels such as email, mailing lists, blogs, microblogs, and social networking sites (SNS) are widely used by scientists to discuss their research (Borgman 2007, p. 47; Nentwich and König 2012, p. 50). Scholarly blogs and services such as Twitter and Facebook are increasingly attracting attention as new channels of science communication (see Bonetta 2007; Kjellberg 2010; Herwig et al. 2009). Radically different conceptualizations of scholarly (micro)blogging exist, with some users regarding them as a forum to educate the public, while others see them as a possible replacement for traditional publishing. This chapter will provide examples of blogs and microblogs as tools for scientific communication for different stakeholders, as well as discuss their implications for digital scholarship.

## Framing the Issue: New Forms of Scholarly Communication and Science 2.0

There is a broad consensus that modern science is undergoing profound structural changes afforded by the rise of digital technology, and that this change is occuring on multiple levels of the scientific work process at once (Nielsen 2012; Nentwich and König 2012). The abundance of massive storage capacities, high volumes of processing power, and ubiquitous network access enables new forms of research which are contingent on large quantities of digital data and its efficient

C. Puschmann (✉)
Humboldt University, Berlin, Germany
e-mail: puschmann@ibi.hu-berlin.de

S. Bartling and S. Friesike (eds.), *Opening Science*,
DOI: 10.1007/978-3-319-00026-8_6, © The Author(s) 2014

computational analysis (Weinberger 2011). This development is underscored by the rise of *data science*, that is, science that is driven by the analysis of large quantities of data from a wide range of sources such as sensors, scanners, MRI, telescopes, but also human-generated data from social media and digital libraries, and interrogated through statistical procedures, machine learning algorithms, and other computational instruments, allowing researchers to discover previously unrecognized patterns. Such approaches are innovative in the sense that they surpass the capabilities of traditional research in making observations of changes in very complex systems as they unfold, and in that they potentially allow predictions regarding the future behavior of such systems (Golder and Macy 2012). Whereas research has in the past been based upon comparably scarce evidence, the promise of data science is that it will be both scalable and reproducible on a previously unimaginable level, providing novel insights into a wide array of areas, from climatology to social science (Lazer et al. 2009) (Fig. 1).

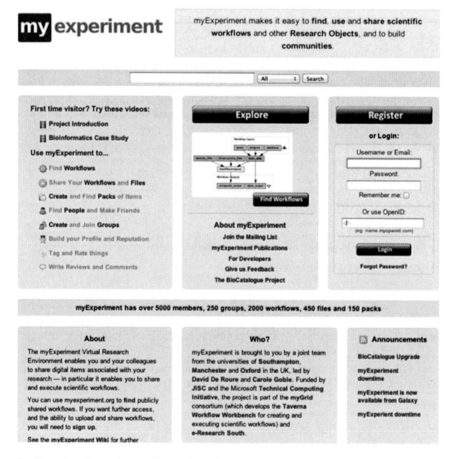

**Fig. 1** myExperiment is one of a number of new virtual research environments (VREs)

Beyond innovation of research methods, other aspects of how science is undertaken are also changing visibly, both as a result of technological shifts and because of economic and cultural changes in how research is financed and organized (cf. several contributions in this volume). From teaching and funding to publishing and peer review, it seems that a variety of aspects of how scientists work are changing, and that communication is at the forefront of this change, a change brought about primarily by the proliferation of technologies which are themselves the result of publicly funded scientific research. These technologies not only make it easier, cheaper, and quicker for scientists to exchange information with peers around the globe, they also have the potential to blur the line between internal communication among researchers and communication with the wider public. New formats must be adopted for scholarly use to fit the needs of academics while established genres evolve as a result of new technologies for the production and dissemination of scholarly publications (Cope and Kalantzis 2009).

Scientists have, of course, always been avid communicators. From Darwin's notebooks to the Large Hadron Collider, getting complex scientific issues across both to colleagues and laypersons has been at the top of the agenda for researchers for as long as modern science has existed. Successful communication is integral to scholarship because it allows scientific knowledge to proliferate, enable practical applications, and become entrenched societal knowledge, but also because frequently the outcomes of scientific research have far-reaching societal implications and are highly controversial (e.g., climate research, nuclear energy, genetics). Scientists must be able to explain what they do to a broader public to garner political support and funding for endeavors whose outcomes are unclear at best and dangerous at worst, a difficulty which is magnified by the complexity of scientific issues. They do so in an increasingly challenging environment, engaging with a public that has access to a wide range of sources of (by scientific standards) often dubious quality, many of them online (Puschmann and Mahrt 2012; König 2011). This public is increasingly critical and unimpressed by scientific authority and simple promises of scientific progress as an enabler of economic growth and societal welfare, and must be both won over and brought on board, rather than talked down to. Civil society expects to be engaged in a dialog with science, rather than being lectured. The affordances of social media (blogs, wikis, social networking sites) should accordingly be regarded as supporting a general long-term shift towards a more egalitarian relationship between experts and the lay public, rather than driving it (Fig. 2).

Intra-scientific discourse is changing as well, as a result of the move from paper to digital, which seems almost completed in much of the hard sciences. The majority of formal publishing in the STM disciplines takes place in academic journals and conference proceedings, with pre-prints, post-prints, reports, technical manuals, posters, and other formats also playing an important role (Borgman 2007). Increasingly, traditional academic genres (journal articles, conference papers, scholarly monographs) are published online, rather than in print, and disseminated through a variety of channels (email, blogs, online book reviews,

**Fig. 2** CERN's Twitter page

social media). Preprint archives such as *arXiv*[1] and *Social Science Research Network* (SSRN)[2] have proliferated in a variety of disciplines and continue to grow in popularity. Beyond Open Access, there is an increased push for adding features that make use of the affordances of digital publishing, such as interactive charts and figures, and towards providing raw data along with papers to encourage follow-up research, for example on sites such as *Figshare*.[3]

## Science Blogging as a New Form of Engaging with Science

While still an emergent phenomenon, new and genuinely digital forms of scholarly communication play an increasingly significant role in discussions about the future of academic discourse, especially as the existing system of knowledge dissemination is increasingly characterized as threatened or even dysfunctional (cf. Cope and Kalantzis 2009; Stein and Puschmann 2010). The phenomenon of science blogging has attracted significant attention and discussion in papers (e.g., Batts et al. 2008; Tola 2008; Shema et al. 2012) and at conferences (e.g., ScienceOnline '09, Science Blogging 2008: London). Sites such as *Nature Network, ScienceBlogs.com,* and

---

[1] http://www.arXiv.org

[2] http://www.ssrn.com/

[3] http://www.figshare.com/

*Hypotheses.org* act as hosting platforms of such specialized academic content, allowing researchers to present and discuss their work before a global audience, some with commercial publishers backing them, others funded publicly. Increasingly, universities and research institutes offer blog hubs which either aggregate externally-hosted content contributed by students and faculty members or allow direct publishing through the institutional website. Many academic researchers also rely on commercial hosting platforms such as *Wordpress.com* and *Blogger.com* to exchange information with peers and to document their projects.

A non-scholarly genre that has been adopted for scholarly communication, blogs are just one tool in a wider array of new formats. New platforms for publishing such as *Open Journal Systems* (OJS) and *Annotum* seek to make the processing and presentation of scholarly texts better adjusted to their digital environment. Monographs ·are also redefined in new approaches from initiatives such as *Press-Forward* or *OpenEdition*, which seek to modify both the dissemination of academic publications and the economics behind its distribution (costly production techniques, long delays between authoring and publication). Beyond making the results of scholarly research available online, efforts are being made to make scholarly formats themselves more innovative and better adjusted to the Internet (cf. Jankowski et al. 2012). The need to facilitate new means of knowledge production, presentation, and dissemination is widely felt, not only inside science itself, but also among policymakers. This need is fuelled both by the exponential growth of scholarly publishing (Jinha 2010) and the costs associated with the current model of subscription-based access. Different models have been proposed among the different varieties of Open Access (i.e. the 'gold road' model of immediate Open Access and the 'green road' model of delayed Open Access after an embargo period). Alternate funding schemes include author fees and institutional consortia, as well as direct public funding, for example via libraries (Houghton 2010).

Beyond the use outlined above—researchers using blogs to communicate their work, primarily to peers, a wide variety of other approaches to science (or, more broadly, scholarly) blogging exist, depending on communicators, target audience, and function. For example, it is widely assumed that because they are public, science blogs should be used to present the results of scientific research to a wider audience. Often blogging is seen as a new component of science journalism which is consequently something not just done by scientists, but also by journalists, or by enthusiasts with knowledge in a given area of science (Bonetta 2007). Frequently when the term *science blogging* (or *scholarly blogging*) is used, it is only implicitly clear which kind of blogging is meant, the variety that complements scholarly communication in journal articles and scholarly monographs, or the one that complements science journalism. It seems likely that different variants will continue to exist as a result of the freedom to innovate and create new genres online. In the following I will briefly discuss two different science blogs as examples of these different approaches in an attempt to underscore how blogging complements the needs of scientists and science communicators (journalists, activists, hobbyists) alike. While there is some overlap, it is important to be aware of the different needs of these actors.

**Table 1** Examples of actors, audiences, and functions of science blogs

| Actor | Target audience | Function | Analogy |
|---|---|---|---|
| Lab leader in genetics | Funders, general public | provide rationale f. research inform public & funders | Report |
| PhD student in physics | Peers, senior researchers | promote self practice writing | Lab notebook |
| Science journalist | General public | explain science broadly educate readers | Magazine piece |

**Table 2** Example motives of science bloggers

| Motive A: Visibility | Motive B: Networking | Motive C: Information |
|---|---|---|
| Increase own impact | Connect with peers | Be up to date |
| Be found by peers and other stakeholders | Stay in touch with colleagues | Be part of a conversation |
| Present self/own work | Be(come) part of a community | Anticipate trends |

When approaching science blogs and an emergent communicative practice, it is helpful to first outline the roles they play for different stakeholders in the ecosystem of scholarly communication. Tables 1 and 2 give an overview of the various roles played by different actors, and of some of the motives of scientists who blog for different reasons, respectively.

## Case 1: Rosie Redfield (RRResearch)

*RRResearch* is the blog of Rosemarie ('Rosie') Redfield, a microbiologist at the University of British Columbia, Vancouver, and head of the Redfield Lab at UBC's Department of Zoology. The blog was initially published on the commercial service *Blogspot*, but has since then moved to the independent blog network *Field of Science*[4] which uses the *Google Blogger* platform[5] as its technical backbone but is maintained so as to feature high quality scientific content contributed by experts from different fields.

Since August 2006, Redfield has posted over 900 entries on the blog, discussing various issues of her research. Her initial post gives a good idea about the direction of the blog:

---

[4] http://www.fieldofscience.com/

[5] http://www.blogger.com/

> *This is my first post to this new blog.*
>
> *The purpose of keeping the blog is to give me a semi-public place to describe the ongoing process of doing and thinking about my lab's research. I hope I'll use it to describe/explain (mainly to myself) the scientific issues I'm thinking about:*
>
> - *what experiments we've done*
> - *what the results were if they worked (or possible explanations for why they didn't work)*
> - *what I think the results mean for the questions we're trying to answer*
> - *what experiments I think we might do or should do when time and resources permit.*
>
> *The purpose of this post, however, is mainly to see what happens when I click on 'Publish Post'*

*(from: http://rrresearch.fieldofscience.com/2006_08_01_archive.html)*

While many posts are devoted to documenting and describing her research—often, as emphasized in the post above, seemingly with herself in mind as reader, quite a few touch related issues relevant to a less specialized audience. For example, several early posts cover Bayesian statistics and discuss its use in genetics research. Many posts are related to meta-issues in scientific work, i.e. grant proposals, journal submissions, and other aspects that are part of work processes at a genetics laboratory.

While Redfield's blog was known to an expert audience before, she attained major success as a result the post *"Arsenic-associated bacteria (NASA's claims)"* (Redfield 2010) that strongly critiqued the paper *"A Bacterium That Can Grow by Using Arsenic Instead of Phosphorus"* (Wolfe-Simon et al. 2010) which had been previously published in the journal *Science*. In the blog post, Redfield initially reports the findings of the paper and then proceeds with a detailed criticism of the methodology used by the authors of the study. As in other entries, she mixes a somewhat informal style with the vocabulary of a scientific paper. She also includes numerous figures, illustrations, and references, making the post comparable to a review in a scientific journal (Fig. 3).

The post received over 250 comments and a polished version was later published by *Science*, though the original article was not retracted. Redfield's success in using her blog to voice her criticism, rather than using the traditional channels, was seen by many as a turning point in the dynamics of science communication—a journal widely recognized for its rigour saw itself forced to react to criticism posted in a blog.

*RRResearch* is the blog of a scientist, who accordingly uses it as part of a wider communicative agenda. While most writing done by academics is geared towards peers and written to withstand their scrutiny and criticism, writing a blog "for oneself" amounts to a space where freer, less regimented expression is possible. Redfield is, of course, aware that her blog is widely read, but its status as something

**Fig. 3** The first post published on RRResearch in August 2006

other than a formally recognized publication is an asset, because it allows her to address issues that wouldn't generally fit into a formal publications. Yet *RRResearch* is also not a typical science blog in the sense that most journalists or science educators would interpret the term—understanding much of what is published in it presupposes in-depth knowledge of biochemistry and Redfield makes no attempt to dumb down her writing to make it more palatable to a lay audience.

## Case 2: Bora Zivkovic (A Blog Around the Clock)

Bora Zivkovic is a well-known blogger and science educator with a background in veterinary medicine and biology. He teaches introductory biology at North Caroline Wesleyan College, organizes *ScienceOnline* conference series, and has been a visiting scholar at New York University's Arthur L. Carter Journalism Institute.

Zivkovic started his site *A Blog Around the Clock* (ABATC) in 2006, after moving from *Blogger.com* to *ScienceBlogs*. In 2011, the blog was moved again, this time to *Scientific American*, where Zivkovic became the first Blog Editor. After he took up blogging in 2002, Zivkovic gradually gained wide recognition as a science blogger, not least because of the impressive volume of his activity. In the time before moving from *Blogger* to *ScienceBlogs* alone, he produced a total of 2420 posts about a variety of topics. While frequently these are short texts pointing to a news item, video, or other piece of information, many are detailed essays about (broadly) science and politics, science and the general public, etc. His style is not only less formal than that of Rosie Redfield, but he also uses considerably less scientific terminology. The considerable volume of content that flows through *ABATC* make it a virtual popular science magazine, covering a breadth of issues and formats (including blog carnivals and other outreach mechanisms that aim to strengthen connections with other blogs). Zivkovic both relays information from other sources, commenting on it and explaining it to readers, and provides longer commentaries, for example on issues of science policy. He assumes that his readers are interested in science, but does not generally presume in-depth knowledge of scientific topics. This approach is in line with Zivkovic's own background: while he is a trained scientist and writes from a first-hand perspective, his agenda is not that of someone paid for full-time research.

While *RRResearch* presents both the results of research (rarely) and frames scientific issues for a scientific audience, *ABATC* translates scientific topics for a more general, non-specialist audience. The issues are much broader there than they are in *RRResearch*, where they align much more strongly with the blogger's own research interests. The latter blog is a window into the mind and daily work of the researcher, not a friendly conversation with a lay audience. This is not to say that *RRResearch* doesn't engage—its success illustrates how well it achieves this goal—but whom it targets as its readership and what function it wants to realize remains at least partially unclear. Redfield uses her blog to frame issues for herself and her peers, while Zivkovic blogs for a readership with their needs squarely in mind. Much of the research that he relays is not his own, while much of what is discussed in *RRResearch* is Redfield's own work, or closely related to it. Whereas Redfield regards her blog as an instrument for communicating what she is currently working on or issues she is more generally interested in, Zivkovic provides a service and measures its success, at least in part, by its popularity and the amount of feedback he receives, a form of impact that may well be less relevant to a blogger like Redfield, who might be primarily concerned with her blog's reception among her students and peers (Fig. 4).

## The Uses of Microblogs for Science: Two Scenarios

Compared to blogging, which has a history that reaches back to the beginning of the Web itself, microblogs are still a relatively new form of communication. Microblogs share with "normal" blogs the sequential organization of information in dated entries, but they are usually constrained in length to facilitate scanning a large number of posts rapidly. Another point of distinction is that microblogs are typically centralized services rather than decentralized software packages that can be run from one's own webserver. *Twitter* is by far the most popular service, though competitors exist, both related specifically to science and for general use.[6]

---

[6] An example for a specialized microblogging for scientists is ScienceFeed, which is part of the social networking functionality offered by ResearchGate, while App.net is an advertising-free microblogging service that promises to put the interest's of its (paying) members first.

**Fig. 4** A Blog Around the Clock, Bora Zivkovic's blog at the scientific American Blog network

As with blogs, the potential uses of microblogs for scholarly communication are highly varied, ranging from virtual journal clubs (Reich 2011) and debates about current, science-related events, to self-help for graduate students (for example, under the #phdchat hashtag). Microblogs are also a way for scientists to stay up to date about what their colleagues are working on, while at the same time providing a window into current scientific research for science journalists and facilitating interaction between scientists and the general public (Puschmann and Mahrt 2012). The lack of a dividing line between scientists and non-scientists, as well as the great variety of topics that even scientists tweet about mean that *Twitter* is not comparable to the orderly world of science publishing, where every piece of information is assumed to be relevant. Instead, a typical user's timeline is likely to be populated both by scholarly content and personal remarks, more or less side by side. As the size of the network and the thematic broadness of *Twitter* is what makes it interesting to most users, it seems unlikely that this "problem" will ever be remedied at its core, but the ability to filter information from *Twitter* and similar services is likely to resolve the issue.[7] Tweets and other social media information can congregate around a journal article or piece of data—an approach that may also be beneficial for the development of dedicated science services. Such services could eventually become a reality as the strengths of services like *Twitter* are at once also a weakness: while timely, tweets are not accessible in the long term, and increased brevity also means less nuanced information in each tweet.

---

[7] As one example of a new approach to publishing powered by Twitter aggregation, see http://digitalhumanitiesnow.org/

Wide proliferation and ease of use may eventually be offset by problems regarding access to and long-term preservation of data. As with *FriendFeed*,[8] which was enthusiastically embraced by a small community of scientists, it is completely unclear how *Twitter* will evolve and the concerns of academics are likely to matter very little in respect to this. It is conceivable that policymakers will eventually put into place an infrastructure that will support the kind of communication taking place on *Twitter*, at least between scientists, rather than leaving vital issues to private companies that do not have scientific issues at the center of their attention. While it is impossible to tell how many scientists are already using *Twitter* and similar services and in what ways, it is safe to say that the significance of microblogging is growing, while its role for science communication continues to evolve (cf. Puschmann and Mahrt 2012). In the following, two common scenarios for the use of microblogs will be described in more detail: tweeting at scientific conferences and using *Twitter* to cite papers in Open Access journals and repositories.

## Case 1: Twitter at Conferences

Conferences are all about communication. When used in the context of scientific conferences, *Twitter* acts as a backchannel, in other words, it complements what happens at the conference itself, allowing attendees, and quite frequently also people who are unable to attend, to comment, ask questions, and participate in the discussion taking place. It is important to point out that this complements the face to face activity, rather than replacing it. It is a major advantage that a talk can take place uninterrupted while a lively discussion takes place about it on *Twitter*. A drawback of this approach is that the presenter cannot participate in the debate while it is underway and while being the the subject of discussion, sometimes also criticism. The use of a *Twitter* wall, i.e. a projection of hashtagged tweets usually shown next to or behind the presenter, can aggravate this problem. In November 2009, social media researcher Danah Boyd held a talk at the media industry event *WebExpo New York* that was accompanied by a *Twitter* wall showing tweets posted under the conference hashtag. As Boyd delivered her presentation, which was beset by technical difficulties, she was the subject of intense polemical remarks from spectators via *Twitter*; all the while, she herself could not see the projection of the offensive tweets as she spoke. Though this kind of incident is rare, it underlines the double-sidedness of a technology that is open and easy to use, but therefore also easy to abuse under certain circumstances. *Twitter* walls, apart from being a distraction, seem to add fairly little communicatively to the overall conference, although their precise placement (e.g. in the lobby, rather the main conference hall) seems a key issue to be aware of (Fig. 5).

---

[8]  http://friendfeed.com/

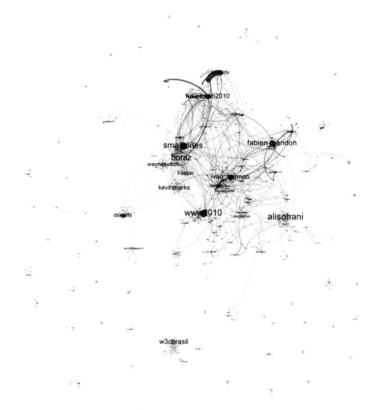

**Fig. 5** Network visualization of retweets among users at the World Wide Web 2010 Conference (#www2010), held in April 2010 in Raleigh, North Carolina

Examining the usage of *Twitter* during conferences, it is notable how specific the usage of scientists is compared to users of different backgrounds, and that at the same time microblogging is always more informal communication than traditional publishing, not just because of its brevity. Rather than chatting idly, researchers share information via *Twitter*—they point to papers and posters, to datasets online, and to websites related to their research (Weller and Puschmann 2011). Passing on (retweeting) this information is extremely popular, more so than just exchanging pleasantries or gossip. At the same time, academics also link to the same resources that other users do, such as online picture services such as *Instagram* or *Twitpic* or video platforms like *YouTube* and *Vimeo* (Thelwall et al. 2012), and they link to a variety of popular science content, i.e. science articles from newspapers (Weller et al. 2011). The continuum between personal and professional is frequently blurred on microblogging platforms. Conferences act as a sort of content filter—because the event that a conference hashtag is associated with is all about a professional activity, what is tweeted under the hashtag is usually related fairly closely to the topic of the event, though meta-topics such as the conference program or pointers to the venue of conference venue are also popular.

## Case 2: Twitter for Citations

Beyond conferences, *Twitter* also plays an increasingly important role for day-to-day communication among scientists. Academics are often interested in a variety of topics outside of their specific field of research and accordingly tweet about many things which are the not subject of their work or comment in ways that differ from traditional scholarly communication. This highlights an issue of informal digital communication online: it is extremely hard to determine what constitutes a scientifically "valuable" contribution and what does not. While some tweets are related to scholarly issues and others are obviously personal in nature, many occupy a meso-level between what is traditionally considered scholarly content and what usually is not. Counting every tweet mentioning a scholarly source as scientifically valuable is obviously too simplistic, as is discarding every personal remark as irrelevant.

This is a particularly salient issue because an increasing number of studies examine the relevance of social media for scientometrics, in other words, the role that social media can play in measuring and predicting the impact of scientific research (e.g., Weller and Puschmann 2011; Eysenbach 2011). By conservative estimates, popular sites such as *arXiv* received around 5,000 links per month[9] and this is bound to increase in the future. If the popular reception of scholarly literature among scientists and non-scientists alike via *Twitter* can be considered a form of impact (and many agree that it can), this means that citations on *Twitter* and via other channels may be introduced as a valid impact measure into the scientometric toolkit in the future [cf. the suggestions of Priem et al. (2011) in this direction].

## Who Uses Blogs and Microblogs for Scholarly Communication, and Why?

In the environment of change outlined above, it is only logical to ask why new forms of communication online—blogs, *Twitter*, social networks—haven't proliferated to a greater extent. If the examples of innovative usage of blogs and *Twitter* to communicate among scientists and more broadly about science give a reason to be optimistic, actual usage of such tools among scientists—defined here as the broad base of academics employed for research and teaching at universities and research institutes—should caution enthusiasts. International studies on the acceptance rate of social media among scientists vary considerably in their results, but many suggest widespread skepticism (cf. Procter et al. 2010; Bader et al. 2012).[10] While pointing to examples where new formats have succeeded is useful, it is also worth noting that

---

[9] Author's own estimate based on ongoing tracking of all tweets linking to the arXiv website.

[10] But see Priem et al. (2011), who suggests that usage of Twitter is steadily growing.

scientists are conservative when it comes to embracing new technologies, both for internal communication and in relation to new means of engaging with the general public. This may be changing, but it seems important to consider both the much-cited potential of social media for science communication and the reality of its yet-nascent acceptance among faculty members—especially those in senior positions. For policymakers it is imperative to have an accurate picture of the situation and the immediate future, beyond lofty promises. It is exceedingly likely that in those areas where change is occurring because it is being driven, at least in part, by researchers themselves, the changes will be more lasting than where new technologies are not well-integrated into established practices. Further factors able to spur innovation are payback in the form of funding, increased reputation, and other critical competitive aspects of institutional science. Yet it remains unproven whether social media tools are essential to improving scholarly communication or whether their usefulness is restricted to the margin of science and scholarship, rather than extending to the center.

Two key components that could facilitate the success of social media tools (blogging, microblogging, but also wikis and social networking sites for scientists) are the spread of alternative means of measuring scientific impact beyond traditional bibliometric indicators (a) and the increasing adaptation of social media formats for science and integration into "proper" scientific discourse (b). The former is at the focus of innovations in scientometrics and initial suggestions are likely to be made in the coming years to funders and research organizations about how to measure impact more holistically, though it remains to be seen whether established (and widely criticized) measures such as *Thompson* Scientific's Impact Factor (IF) can be displaced. In order to achieve the latter, the institutional enablers of science communication—publishers, libraries, science organizations and scholarly societies—will have to invent not only new technologies, but also re-brand familiar labels that scientists rely on. The French site *Hypotheses.org* and the lab platform *OpenWetWare.org* are examples of this approach: while the former is a technically a blog platform based on the popular Wordpress software and the latter is a wiki based on *Wikimedia's MediaWiki*, both clearly present themselves as pieces of scientific infrastructure, built for an academic audience. Success in these approaches lies not in engaging with the "newness" of social media to win skeptics over, but in promising that social media tools can be adapted to achieve similar aims as were previously realized through other channels, only quicker, cheaper and with broader effect.

The current consensus among scientists appears to be that blogs and *Twitter* are somewhat interesting to promote one's own research (to journalists and perhaps a few colleagues), and more broadly, one's field (to potential students, the general public), but that the payoff is not always worth the time and effort (Bader et al. 2012). If science was solely concerned with getting scholarly content across to as many people as possible, blogs would have displaced the established system of academic publishing by now, but it is no coincidence that the journal article has not been abandoned in favor of the blog post. In addition to overall conservatism, the lack of peer review in social media channels also hampers its adoption as a

**Table 3** Advantages and disadvantages of blogging and microblogging

| Blogs | | Twitter | |
|---|---|---|---|
| + | – | + | – |
| Rapidly disseminate content | Lack of formal recognition | Communicate with colleagues | Time-consuming |
| Cheap | Lack of prestige in the scientific community | Promote your research | Benefits unclear |
| Easy to use | No clear topical focus | Disseminate information | Increased self-exposure |
| Open to individuals | Time-consuming | Build personal influence | Not sufficiently informative |
| Promotional tool | Long-term availability unclear | Stay up to date about your field | Perceived as trivial |

replacement for traditional publications. Scholarly content, regardless of the discipline, must be valorized by the judgement of others, and frequently only after the criticism of peers has been taken into account and the original manuscript has been adjusted is a piece of writing deemed a genuine scholarly publication. Time is the scarcest resource in research and investing it in an activity of peripheral importance is widely regarded as wasteful. Taking the extreme goal-orientedness of scholarly communication into account is essential in understanding the perceived advantages and disadvantages of social media in the minds of many scientists (Table 3).

# Conclusion

A comparably small number of people across the globe actively works on complex scientific issues, communicating through channels and genres established over the course of decades, or in some cases centuries, which have been carefully designed to suit the needs of the respective communities. How can those on the outside reasonably argue for the need to profoundly change such a system without professing their own status as outsiders? The underlying claim of those challenging science to be more open is that it is closed to begin with, a perception not universally shared by scientists. Those who espouse the view that social media should be used to discuss scientific research tend to fall into one of either two camps: adaptionists or revolutionaries. Adaptionists believe that social media tools need to suit researchers needs in doing what they are already doing. Hard adaptationists believe that new formats should replace established ones because they are more efficient, cheaper, faster, and better than the established formats of institutionalized academia (e.g. that blog posts should replace journal articles). Soft adaptionists believe that new forms should augment existing ones, often filling unaddressed needs. A soft adaptionist would use *Twitter* to promote his research, but not publish a paper in his blog rather than *Nature*. In practice, most adaptionists probably act as soft adaptionists, but some would prefer to follow the hard, uncompromising route if they could. Adaptionists have in common the basic belief in the legitimacy and relevance of the existing system of institutional science, but see it as being in need of reform. They believe that certain aspects of the system need change, but are convinced of its overall soundness. Revolutionaries, by contrast, call more than just specific aspects of the system (e.g. publishing) into question, being, in fact, opposed to the system as such, which they perceive as elitist and deeply flawed. While to the adaptationists science is fundamentally open, it is fundamentally closed to the revolutionaries, who are rarely themselves part of the entrenched academic system, but tend to be either junior faculty members or amateurs. Whereas the adaptationists have been co-opted to varying degrees to uphold the established order, the revolutionaries imagine a future in which the the entrenched system is overturned. Though the latter seems much less likely than the former, both groups actively advance the significance of social media for science, in spite of widespread inertia on the part of much of the academic establishment.

It has yet to be seen how exactly blogs and microblogs will fit into the existing ecosystem of scholarly publishing. Their role could be complementary, providing an outlet for purposes which traditional publishing does not address—from reflections about teaching to the promotion of a researcher's work. Miscellaneous writing that does not fit into recognized publications however is strongly contingent on the time that a researcher has at their disposal. Blogging on a regular basis is time-consuming, therefore it is likely that full-time academics will actively blog only if they find it benefits their career. In the end, blogs and microblogs supplement, rather than replace, traditional formats, and act as tools for the promotion of one's research, rather than tokens of prestige and academic excellence. Changing blogs in order to make them functionally equivalent to recognized formal publications would mean changing them to a degree that could nullify their benefits (for example, by introducing peer review). Instead, they have a place in the larger ecosystem of science communication 2.0 which includes protocols (*OpenWetWare*) and workflows (*myExperiment*) as examples of entirely new scientific genres which are functionally different from blog posts.

# References

Bader, A., Fritz, G., & Gloning, T. (2012). *Digitale Wissenschaftskommunikation* 2010–2011 *Eine Online-Befragung*, Giessen: Giessener Elektronische Bibliothek. Available at: http://geb.uni-giessen.de/geb/volltexte/2012/8539/index.html [Accessed April 2, 2013].

Batts, S.A., Anthis, N.J., & Smith, T.C. (2008). Advancing science through conversations: Bridging the gap between blogs and the academy. *PLoS Biology, 6*(9), p.e240.

Bonetta, L. (2007). Scientists enter the blogosphere. *Cell, 129*(3), 443–445.

Borgman, C. L. (2007). *Scholarship in the digital age: information, infrastructure, and the Internet.* Cambridge, Mass: MIT Press.

Cope, W.W., & Kalantzis, M. (2009). Signs of epistemic disruption: Transformations in the knowledge system of the academic journal. First Monday, 14(46).

Eysenbach, G. (2011). Can tweets predict citations? metrics of social impact based on twitter and correlation with traditional metrics of scientific impact. *Journal of Medical Internet Research, 13*(4), e123.

Golder, S., & Macy, M. (2012). Social Science with Social Media. *ASA Footnotes*, 40(1). Available at: http://www.asanet.org/footnotes/jan12/socialmedia_0112.html.

Herwig, J. et al., (2009). *Microblogging und die Wissenschaft. Das Beispiel Twitter*, Available at: http://epub.oeaw.ac.at/ita/ita-projektberichte/d2-2a52-4.pdf.

Houghton, J.W. (2010). Alternative publishing models: exploring costs and benefits. In C. Puschmann & D. Stein, (Eds.), *Towards Open Access Scholarship. Selected Papers from the Berlin 6 Open Access Conference* (pp. 27–40). Düsseldorf: Düsseldorf University Press.

Jankowski, N.W. et al. (2012). Enhancing scholarly publications: developing hybrid monographs in the humanities and social sciences. *SSRN Electronic Journal.*

Jinha, A. E. (2010). Article 50 million: an estimate of the number of scholarly articles in existence. *Learned Publishing, 23*(3), 258–263.

Kjellberg, S. (2010). I am a blogging researcher: motivations for blogging in a scholarly context. First Monday, 15(8).

König, R. (2011). Wikipedia—participatory knowledge production or elite knowledge representation? Discussion pages as an arena for the social construction of reality. In *Contribution to the workshop Participatory knowledge production 2.0: Critical views and experiences* (pp.1–6). Virtual Knowledge Studio. Maastricht: Virtual Knowledge Studio.

Lazer, D., et al. (2009). Computational social science. *Science, 323*(5915), 721–723.

Nentwich, M., & König, R. (2012). *Cyberscience 2.0: research in the age of digital social networks*, Frankfurt; New York: Campus Verlag.

Nielsen, M. A. (2012). *Reinventing discovery: the new era of networked science.* Princeton, N.J.: Princeton University Press.

Priem, J., Piwowar, H., & Hemminger, B. (2011). Altmetrics in the wild: An exploratory study of impact metrics based on social media. Presented at Metrics 2011: *Symposium on Informetric and Scientometric Research.* New Orleans, USA, Oct 12, 2011.

Priem, J., Taraborelli, D., Groth, P., & Neylon, C. (2011). Almetrics: a manifesto. Available at: http://altmetrics.org/manifesto/.

Procter, R., et al. (2010). Adoption and use of Web 2.0 in scholarly communications. *Philosophical Transactions of the Royal Society A: Mathematical, Physical and Engineering Sciences, 368*(1926), 4039–4056.

Puschmann, C., & Mahrt, M. (2012). Scholarly blogging: A new form of publishing or science journalism 2.0? In A. Tokar et al. (Eds.), *Science and the Internet* (pp.171–181). Düsseldorf: University Press.

Redfield, R. (2010). Arsenic-associated bacteria (NASA's claims). RRResearch. Available at: http://rrresearch.fieldofscience.com/2010/12/arsenic-associated-bacteria-nasas.html.

Reich, E. S. (2011). Researchers tweet technical talk. *Nature, 474*(7352), 431–431.

Shema, H., Bar-Ilan, J., & Thelwall, M. (2012) research blogs and the discussion of scholarly information C. A. Ouzounis, (Ed.), *PLoS ONE, 7*(5), e35869.

Stein, D., & Puschmann, C. (2010). Timely or Timeless? The scholar's dilemma. thoughts on Open Access and the social contract of publishing. In D. Puschmann & D. Stein (Eds.), *Towards Open Access Scholarship. Selected Papers from the Berlin 6 Open Access Conference* (pp.5–10). Düsseldorf: Düsseldorf University Press.

Thelwall, M. et al. (2012) Chapter 9 Assessing the impact of online academic videos. In G. Widén & K. Holmberg (Eds.), *Social Information Research* (pp.195–213). Library and Information Science. Bingley: Emerald Group Publishing.

Tola, E. (2008). To blog or not to blog, not a real choice there. *JCOM Journal of Science Communication*, 2(2).

Weinberger, D. (2011). *Too big to know: rethinking knowledge now that the facts aren't the facts, experts are everywhere, and the smartest person in the room is the room.* New York: Basic Books.

Weller, K., & Puschmann, C. (2011). Twitter for scientific communication: How can citations/ references be identified and measured? In *Proceedings of the ACM WebSci'11* (pp. 1–4). Koblenz: ACM Publishers.

Weller, K., Dröge, E., & Puschmann, C. (2011). Citation analysis in Twitter. approaches for defining and measuring information flows within tweets during scientific conferences. In M. Rowe et al. (Eds.), *Proceedings of Making Sense of Microposts (#MSM2011). CEUR Workshop Proceedings.* (pp.1–12), Heraklion, Greece.

Wolfe-Simon, F., et al. (2010). A bacterium that can grow by using arsenic instead of phosphorus. *Science, 332*(6034), 1163–1166.

# Academia Goes Facebook? The Potential of Social Network Sites in the Scholarly Realm

Michael Nentwich and René König

> *This network is the seat of scientific opinion which is not held by any single human brain, but which is split into thousands of different fragments... each of whom endorses the other's opinion at second hand, by relying on the consensual chains which link him to all the others through a sequence of overlapping neighborhoods.*
> —Michael Polanyi (1962) in the Republic of Science

**Abstract** Social network sites (SNS) have not only become a fundamental part of the Web, but also increasingly offer novel communicative and networking possibilities for academia. Following a short presentation of the typical functions of (science-specific) SNS, we firstly present the state of knowledge regarding academic usage practices, both in general purpose SNS and in science-specific SNS. Secondly, we assess potential impacts by addressing identified key issues such as privacy, the role of pseudonymity, and the specific form of informal communication in question. In particular, we focus on the issue of network effects and the challenge of multiple channels, which presents itself as a major hurdle for an effective implementation of SNS in academia. Despite these difficulties, we come to the conclusion that SNS are, in principle, functional for scholarly communication and that they have serious potential within academia.

M. Nentwich (✉)
Institute of Technology Assessment, Austrian Academy of Sciences,
Strohgasse 45/5 1030 Vienna, Austria
e-mail: mnent@oeaw.ac.at

R. König
Institute of Technology Assessment and Systems Analysis, Karlsruhe Institute of Technology, PF 3640 76021 Karlsruhe, Germany
e-mail: rene.koenig@kit.edu

S. Bartling and S. Friesike (eds.), *Opening Science*,
DOI: 10.1007/978-3-319-00026-8_7, © The Author(s) 2014

# Introduction

Starting approximately around the year 2000, a growing number of social network sites (SNS) began populating the Internet, offering novel communicative possibilities; above all they link-up its members and map their offline networks. As this seemed to offer an attractive potential for academic communication as well, from the mid-2000s onwards, with a certain peak in 2007/2008, science-specific SNS also entered the market, both disciplinary-focused ones (like *AtmosPeer* or *Edumeres*) and more general examples with increasingly large numbers of members (like *ResearchGate, Mendeley, Academia.edu*). Most SNS provide a central web-based platform which cannot itself be modified by users. Some services give more options for this, for example *Ning*, which allows for the design of SNS for specific needs within the framework of the software. *Vivo*, a US-based science-specific SNS, offers even more flexibility as its software is open source and can be hosted on local servers.

Due to their manifold functions and complexity, various definitions exist of what a SNS constitutes (e.g. Mack et al. 2007; Richter and Koch 2007; Schmidt 2009; Boyd and Ellison 2007; Beer 2008; Fuchs 2009). As SNS have multiple functions, it is difficult to impose a selective definition of these; hence, it depends on the specific definition as to whether a platform will be here counted as a SNS. Following Schmidt (2009), we base our definition for this chapter on the possibility of setting up a sophisticated personal 'profile' with information about oneself, such as interests and activities, within a digital space that can usually only be reached after registration. Starting from this profile, users initiate and entertain social relationships with others, making them explicit through interlinking; the members interact and navigate on the platform, which is basically formed by these networks of 'contacts'. Focusing on the central function of profiles enables us to distinguish SNS from other services: Networking alone is also a characteristic of other platforms that are typically not seen as SNS such as the voice-over-IP service *Skype* or the microblogging service *Twitter*. As for the latter, the profiles are minimalist and the timeline of messages, not the profile, is at the center of the platform (see chapter C(Micro)Blogging Science? Notes on Potentials and Constraints of New Forms of Scholarly Communication). Similarly, online reference management platforms are organized around publications (see chapter Reference Management). We observe, however, that also in these other services increasingly SNS-like functions are added, so that the distinction is dynamic and not clear-cut.

Even among the SNS in the narrow sense, there are many differences, in particular when it comes to the available communication tools or how users can configure their profiles. Two core functions are always present: *identity management* and *contact management* (cf. Richter and Koch 2007). The profiles map—more or less in the public domain—the contacts of a person and enable access to further members on various paths, i.e. networking.

As the technical functionality and target groups vary, we may distinguish different types of SNS: There are variations according to the *intended usage forms*. In some SNS, private purposes prevail, in others professional fields of application dominate; furthermore, in others private and professional use overlap. *Requirements for access* also vary: some are open, that is, they only require a simple registration which, in principle, can be done by all Internet users (cf. Richter and Koch 2008). This is the case with many popular SNS. Other platforms offer limited free access, but charge user fees for the full service. However, most platforms are free of charge in order to attract a sufficient audience and paying advertisers (see section "Assessing the Potential Future and Impacts of SNS in Academia" for a discussion of the problems related to such business models). Finally, there are specialized networks that are open only for certain communities, such as a company or research group. The *available communication forms* vary according to different needs. For example, to nudge someone online is used in a private context, whereas many professional networks offer additional functions such as bibliographic searching (see section "Typical Functions of SNS").

In this chapter we discuss SNS only from the viewpoint of use in academia, based on, but extending the analysis in our book Cyberscience 2.0 (Nentwich and König 2012, pp. 19–50). Following a short overview on types of SNS, their typical functions, academic potential, and observable user practices, we focus on a few key issues that are essential for answering our title question, namely whether academia will indeed "go Facebook", that is, whether future communication among scholars will take place predominantly on these platforms, or even on one single dominant platform. These issues include privacy, the role of pseudonymity, and the specific form of informal communication in question. In particular, we focus on the challenge of multiple channels, which presents itself as a major hurdle for an effective implementation of SNS in academia.

# An Overview of Functions, Potential, and Usage Practices

## *Typical Functions of SNS*

Various functions and forms of communication are typical for SNS, though not all of them are necessarily available in each individual SNS. Science-specific SNS in particular try to develop technologies which meet the requirements of their particular audience.

1. *Profiles*: User profiles are digital representations of users and as such the central nodes of SNS. Various kinds of information can be made available to other members in a pre-structured way, from contact information to tracking of user activities. In some SNS it is also possible to have specific profiles for organizations. Thus profiles are like enhanced calling cards of individuals, organizations, and groups. Some SNS experiment with special scores to automatically

rate user activity on the basis of their activity in the SNS, thereby creating a potential metric for reputation (e.g. RG Score in *ResearchGate*, see Fig. 1).

2. **Communication**: The integration of multiple communication channels within one platform is a distinctive feature of SNS, as compared to various other web-based communication tools. Various tools are available in order to communicate with other members: messaging, chatting, discussion forums/groups, microblogging, nudging, videoconferencing, etc.

3. **Networking**: As networking is one of the basic functions of SNS, all sites offer various tools to promote it: contacts/friends, automated or manual propositions for further contacts, search functions (partly also automated), invitations, bookmarking of profiles, automatically generated requests to welcome new members or propose something or someone to them, and network presentation in various forms.

4. **Directing attention**: The great variety of opportunities to communicate and network in SNS suggests further tools to establish the relevance of content and to direct the attention of its members towards particular items: current issues on start page, external notifications (via e-mail), and the "Like this" button/ "Share this" function. These data may be used in the future as indicators for relevance, discussed under the label of social search (e.g. Biermann 2010).

5. **Groups**: All users can found thematic groups. By usually offering the following functions, groups enable the detection of and networking with members with similar interests and they provide a digital environment for discussion and collaboration: discussion forum, file upload, collaborative writing environments, tools to administer participants in events, selective access to groups, passive membership. Sometimes group-like options are labeled differently, e.g. "topics"/"projects" in ResearchGate.

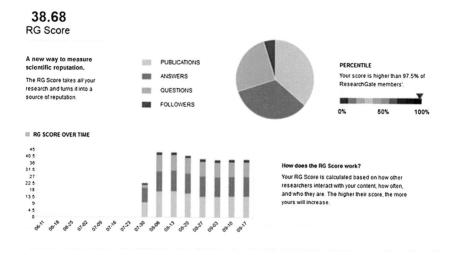

**Fig. 1** Excerpt of an RG score (screenshot)

6. *Calendar*: Some SNS offer their users calendars in order to coordinate dates, plan, and market events of all kinds.

7. *Literature-related functions*: Given the central position of publications in academia, science-specific SNS also offer a number of literature-related functions: searching for academic literature by giving access to other, external, mainly Open-Access databases, as well as internally in the publication lists and database entries of members; similar abstract search; compiling bibliographies; Open Access archive; various attention direction services like notifications, based on topicality, semantic relationships, "Have read" buttons, commenting or rating, "Share this" function, access statistics, and visualization of networks of co-authors.

8. *Further services*: In addition to these functions, further specialized and target-group-specific services are offered: job exchange services, blogging, embedding of services of external providers via apps (thus creating interfaces between the SNS and other services), and advertisement.

Given this broad variety of functions, services, and tools provided by SNS, one is tempted to consider SNS an umbrella for all kinds of features that Cyberscience 2.0—or Science 2.0—offer to the current and next generations of academics. From a technical point of view, this is a viable assessment. However, this is only a vision which still needs to be realized in practice, given some of the challenges addressed below.

## Potentials of SNS for Science and Research

Our systematic analysis of the potential for academic SNS use starts with the four core areas of scientific activity (Nentwich 2003, p. 24) and reveals that SNS provide functions for all these areas, namely knowledge production, processing and distribution, as well as institutional settings. The various functions of directing attention may be helpful in the process of acquiring information, particularly with regard to literature. Shared data archives potentially help working groups to administer their files. As the multiple possibilities for communication are the core of each SNS, they are, at least from a technical perspective, functional for academic communication as well. Through the various channels, knowledge can be presented and offered for academic discourse. The group functions may support collaboration. However, SNS are not currently an adequate place for publication, even though in principle documents may be published within the network, while access to documents is hampered, as it is usually necessary to register (which also hinders indexing the items in external search-engines). In addition, there is no formalized peer-review process in any of the observed SNS, thus the knowledge distributed via this channel will not be reputable, and less relevant to many. Hence, publication within SNS seem inappropriate at the moment. However, this could potentially change if thorough peer-review mechanisms are established. In contrast, SNS may be a valuable additional channel for pointing to texts that have been published elsewhere. They provide a number of functions in that respect: profiles, means of internal communication, tools to direct attention, group functions, and literature-related services. SNS may also be used as e-learning platforms and at the organizational level they are potentially useful as a digital infrastructure. For example, SNS serve as a dynamic list of "digital calling cards" and may help to set up networks of scientists with similar interests as a pool of potential cooperation and communication partners. The popular general-purpose SNS such as *Facebook* appear especially suitable for public relations, academic organizations such as research institutes, universities, scholarly associations, and networks, as well as for individual researchers.

In line with the multiple services SNS offer, different user practices are conceivable. SNS could serve multilaterally as a discussion forum or as a platform for exchanging information, similar to other web forums and in particular e-mail listservers. Furthermore, they may be used as bilateral communication channels, asynchronously via webmail or synchronously as chatting platforms. SNS may serve as platforms for (micro-)blogging to exchange science-related or day-to-day information, and for e-learning, and one can easily imagine more options for their scholarly application. Thus we note that SNS seem to be functional for a number of essential academic activities.

## *Academic Usage Practices in SNS*

As of yet, there are only very few, and mostly limited studies of how academics actually use SNS in practice. Therefore, the following account is based both on these few studies and the authors' own experiences and participatory observations over the last few years.

## The Diffusion of SNS in Academia and the Intensity of Usage

The number of members, mostly published by the SNS themselves, and their growth rates is a first indication for the diffusion of SNS in the academic world. *ResearchGate*, for example, had 150.000 members in August 2008, 700.000 in December 2010, announced a million by May 2011, and reached two million in September 2012. We observed similar growth in other SNS, but the figures may not hold in practice, given their origin. The member count, in any case, does not necessarily correlate with actual use, because there certainly are some (partly) inactive accounts. Therefore, more differentiated usage studies would be needed. Existing studies provide only first insights into the diffusion of SNS among scientists and students (Koch and Moskaliuk 2009; Kleimann et al. 2008; Procter et al. 2010; Bader et al. 2012): They generally show a rather low active usage, although the diffusion appears partly higher among young academics. The outcomes of such studies also vary depending on the exact target group and design of the surveys. We may expect that the proportion of SNS users among scientists will increase as the younger generations move up in academia.

We observed the following types of activity levels and usage intensities and propose to differentiate usage in future studies accordingly:

1. *Me-too presence*: Rudimentary profile; only occasional contacts and never, or only sporadically, become active—probably the most frequent case.
2. *Digital calling card*: More detailed profile like a type of additional personal homepage; practically no further activity—probably the second most frequent case at the moment.
3. *Passive networking*: Searching the network in the beginning and thereafter in irregular intervals for other (previously known) members, reacting to automated suggestions to contact other users, sporadic communication with other members.
4. *Active networking and communication*: Being regularly online, using further services, such as publication search, and participating in group forums, actively searching for potential networking partners beyond those they already know.
5. *Cyberentrepreneurship* (Nentwich 2003, 175ff.): Not only active participants in the network, but also serving as moderators or animators of group forums, administering groups, are in charge of institutional profiles, giving feedback to the site developers—obviously the rarest form of participation of researchers in SNS.

These are certainly ideal types and in practice appear mixed. We observed repeatedly the above usage types, but cannot offer results regarding their precise empirical distribution. There may also be activities which are not observable from an outside perspective, e.g. private messaging. In any case we need to consider that the activity levels and usage types vary considerably. Consequently, member counts do not lead to insights into the vitality of a SNS. This is confirmed by the study of Procter et al. (2010) on the scientific use of Web 2.0: only 13 % of the participants fall into the category "frequent users", 45 % are "occasional users", and 39 % do not actively use Web 2.0. A large qualitative study with 160 interviews and focus group discussions with US researchers (Harley et al. 2010) notes that SNS are not widely used in academia, with some exceptions.

Despite impressive and growing member counts, we may nevertheless draw the conclusion that SNS are not yet part of the academic mainstream. Given the theoretical potential (see above) we hypothesize that the trend will presumably continue in the future. On the question as to whether scientific SNS may reach the tipping point, see the section "The Hard Way to the Critical Mass".

## Academic Usage Practices in Science-Specific SNS

Many academics have become members of multi-purpose SNS, such as *Facebook*, *LinkedIn*, and *Xing*, not least because they are widespread and accepted. Usage practices are heterogeneous because these SNS are not particularly focused on academic users; among them we found communication with colleagues, e-teaching, public relations of research institutes, and self-marketing, as well as job exchange. While we have analyzed those practices elsewhere in more depth (Nentwich and König 2012, 38ff.)—our main conclusion being that general SNS play a minor role in the practice of research communication as of yet—we focus in this chapter on science-specific SNS.

We found the following main practices:

*Communication and cooperation*: One specific strength of science-specific SNS could be their potential to support communication and cooperation among researchers. We did not observe, however, many efficient and successful working groups in these SNS as of yet (they may, however, exist, but are hidden from outsiders). A few self-experiments in our own area have been only modestly successful. They mainly failed because of a lack of potential cooperation partners inside the chosen SNS as we were not able to motivate all relevant colleagues to actively participate in that particular SNS. In contrast to the attraction of large general SNS, the rather young and small science-specific networks suffer from a lack of sufficient numbers of active users (see the section "The Hard Way to the Critical Mass"). In addition, we observed the following further obstacles: technical limitations, lacking experience of users, skepticism regarding file security, the need to firstly develop a common culture of online collaboration, and, finally and notably, the problem of multiple channels (see the section "Multiple Channels, Information Overload and Filtering").

*Public relations and self-marketing*: Because of their limited target group (mainly peers), these SNS are of limited use for public relations, as you can hardly reach larger groups outside of the science communities in question. In contrast, it is potentially easier to target workers in particular fields by means of the sophisticated mechanisms for networking that most SNS provide. Similarly to general SNS, self-marketing is also possible in science-specific SNS when focused on one's peer group, for example, by drawing attention to one's own publications. Based on our observations, this is currently probably the most widely used activity. There is already a very high coverage of publications in certain fields in SNS like *Mendeley* (Li et al. 2011; Bar-Ilan 2012).

*E-teaching*: We did not observe that science-specific SNS are frequently used in teaching. There are specific functions to support it, for instance in *research.iversity*, but there is not much known yet about their actual usage. Obviously, these professional networks do not seem particularly attractive to students, in contrast to *Facebook* and other general SNS, because they fit less well with their day-to-day needs and more with the workaday life of a scientist. Hence, students are hardly reachable via this channel, except in experimental settings. However, certain effective student-orientated platforms exist, for example *Carnets2 Descartes* at Paris Descartes University. In any case, SNS may turn out being a good platform for exchange among teaching scientists when they prepare their courses.

*Job exchange:* These services have the advantage of having a preselected target group in science-specific SNS as opposed to general ones. In September 2012, for example, we found more than 1.000 job offers on *ResearchGate*, mainly from biomedical enterprises, and some 130 on *Academia.edu*. The extent to which these job exchanges are actually used is unknown to us.

# Assessing the Potential Future and Impacts of SNS in Academia

Will ever more and, perhaps at some point, most academics use SNS as they use e-mail today? What consequences may this have? In order to answer these questions, we will focus on the following puzzles: How important are network effects and will science-specific SNS reach the tipping point (section "The Hard Way to the Critical Mass")? What role will the very big players play in that game (section "The Hyper-Critical Mass: Too Big to Fail?")? Is the necessity to observe multiple channels in parallel possibly dysfunctional for science communication and will the trend towards multi-functionality and one-stop-services generate the necessary network effects (section "Multiple Channels, Information Overload and Filtering")? And finally (section "Social Issues"): What potential do SNS have for informal communication among academics, and with what effects? What roles do identity, pseudonymity, and anonymity play in scientific SNS? Which privacy-related conflicts occur?

## *The Hard Way to the Critical Mass*

Unlike many other Internet technologies, SNS necessarily require a certain critical mass of active users to be functional. This leaves them in a dilemma: They are only attractive with users, but users only come when they are attractive. SNS providers use different strategies to overcome this issue. Of course, they try to develop an infrastructure which is at least *potentially* useful once their target group has populated the platform. This might attract a number of early adopters who will eventually lure further users until a critical mass has been reached. While this strategy has worked for many Internet start-ups, it is not easily applicable for SNS. The problem here is that new members will only understand the early adopters' attraction once they have built up their own networks within the platform. Therefore, the effective usage of SNS requires a critical mass of users both on a global and also on an individual level. Even a highly populated platform can be dysfunctional for a single user if it does not represent people from his individual network or potentially relevant users for future interactions. Building individual networks takes time and effort, while the possible benefits of such an investment are not immediately clear to new users. This might be one of the reasons for the hesitant scholarly usage of SNS.

Another strategy to reach a critical mass can be to minimize the "mass" by addressing a smaller and thus easier reachable target group. *Facebook* can be seen as a successful example here, as it first aimed only at the Ivy League universities before it was opened up for larger audiences. *Carnets2 Descartes* is a popular example from the academic realm, focusing on students at the Descartes University in Paris. Although we are not aware of plans to reach beyond this circle, this example shows how a platform can become relevant for a limited audience. Another possible limitation for the academic realm is of course the focus on specific disciplines or even smaller thematic or organizational entities, as it is done by a number of academic SNS. However, smaller target groups can hardly be seen as a general way to success. For example, once the market leader of SNS in Germany, *StudiVZ* is now struggling with vast numbers of users migrating to *Facebook*. One reason for this is probably that it failed to address an international audience—in contrast to its main competitor.

Finally, a critical mass of scholars using SNS might be achieved by creating extrinsic incentives. Indirectly, this could be done with altmetrics which extend academic impact assessment beyond the established scientometrics by tracing SNS activities. If relevant institutions acknowledge scholarly engagement on these platforms via such measurements, it would certainly increase the participation of academics in SNS. Directly, incentives could be created by faculties and universities themselves: To a large extent, it is in their hands as to which software should be used for the various researching and teaching activities.

Evidently, such incentives need to be designed carefully and can easily result in unwanted consequences. For instance, altmetrics might get manipulated by "buying" friends, comments, recommendations, etc. There are already numerous companies offering such services for commercial users, which could in principle be used for academic users as well. Also, scholars or students could revolt against being pushed into SNS by their organizations. In particular, *Facebook* with its privacy issues seems problematic here. Indeed, there were reports on students rejecting approaches on *Facebook* from their university libraries due to privacy concerns (Connell 2008; Mendez et al. 2009). This points us to another issue: While SNS are undoubtedly dysfunctional without a critical mass, the mass itself can become problematic when it reaches a certain size.

## The Hyper-Critical Mass: Too Big to Fail?

Often *Facebook* is compared to nations or even whole continents in order to illustrate its massive size. Indeed, the platform does not only outnumber most countries' populations, but also has an enormous economic power and impact on various realms of modern societies. Therefore, one could argue that *Facebook* has not just reached the critical mass to survive, but a hyper-critical mass, overpowering its competitors. While the concentration of users in principle serves the functionality of a SNS and thereby also its users, the power which is accumulated in this way has to be critically observed. On a general level, this has been already a subject of intensive public as well as academic debates which we cannot discuss here in detail. The main concern seems to be privacy-related: *Facebook* gathers vast amount of data about personal lives and gives its users only very opaque options to control what can be seen by others, including external companies which may have access to this data. This is also a major obstacle for the academic usage of *Facebook*. On the one hand, the technical hurdle for the academic usage of *Facebook* is very low for users who already apply the platform for their private lives on a daily basis. On the other hand, this may be exactly what holds them back if they do not wish to blend their professional and their private lives in this way. At the same time, some researchers are reluctant to disseminate work in progress as they feel it is imperfect or because they fear competitiveness (Harley et al. 2010, p. 13). Although this is a general issue of academic social media usage, it is particularly pressing when a company's business model depends on the exploitation of user data as in the case of *Facebook* or *Google*.

Moreover, once a SNS has reached a hyper-critical mass, it creates new dependencies, as it works like a black hole: The bigger it gets, the more people are drawn to it, the more content is produced, and so on. Therefore, it becomes increasingly difficult to separate from it. A lot of time has been invested in learning to operate the platform, building networks, discussing issues, editing profiles, creating publication lists, tagging items, etc. Most of this data and effort cannot easily be extracted and imported into another platform, so the hurdle to leave it becomes higher and higher, especially if it is still frequently used by other relevant communication partners. Then it may be (perceived as a) significant part of an individual's or organization's social capital, leading to low mobility of users from social network sites with a hyper-critical mass, creating a self-stabilizing force in turn. This partially explains the "seductive power" (Oosthuyzen 2012) of such sites, making users stay even if they do not agree with its policies or are unsatisfied with its services. At the same time, it is very difficult for alternative SNS providers to compete with this accumulated power which also attracts third-party services like apps.

So, although the functionality of a SNS is increased when it concentrates a vast number of users, such a monopoly-like market situation comes at a price. In the academic context, this is particularly troubling when the SNS is outside the influence of the academic realm. Commercial providers like *Facebook* do not only have a questionable privacy policy, they also hardly let users participate in the platform design—especially when it comes to such specific needs as scientific ones. Science-specific SNS are more likely to take this into account but they are still mostly in the hand of companies who ultimately decide about the platform's design, policy, and existence. The worst case scenario is, of course, that a service is shut down because it is not profitable or does not fit anymore to a company's strategy. This is not just a hypothetical scenario: For instance, users of the blogging and networking platform *Posterous* could only helplessly witness as the company was acquired by its competitor *Twitter*, apparently just to let it die slowly and benefit from its staff's competence. In principle, this dependency also applies to non-commercial developers, although they are less driven by the needs of paying clients. They also might change their business model, as it was done in the case of *Couchsurfing* or *StudiVZ*, both SNS which started as non-profits but were later commercialized. Therefore, academic institutions should choose a platform carefully if they plan for a sustainable organized engagement. This may be challenging as a platform with a hyper-critical mass can be tempting, especially because of the difficulties in reaching a critical mass on competing platforms.

## Multiple Channels, Information Overload and Filtering

The current status of SNS in the scholarly realm is confusing: As pointed out above, there is no clear market leader with a sufficient critical mass of active scientists yet. Therefore, interested scholars are confronted with multiple potential platforms that they can choose from. Establishing and maintaining various SNS profiles is a time-consuming task, so most academics will rather select only one or a few than be active on various platforms at the same time. This means that the potential scholarly SNS users are spread over numerous services, instead of concentrating on one or two. At the same time, the present "cyberscientists 2.0" who actually use various platforms simultaneously have to face the challenges of these multiple channels: Maintaining their presences already becomes a time-consuming task under these circumstances. Partly, interoperability across different platforms via APIs solves this problem. For example, a number of social media tools allow the sending of one status update to several platforms. Yet such options are still very limited and not supported by all SNS. Due to the competition between the providers, it is unlikely that this will change fundamentally soon. Apart from maintaining multiple profiles, cyberscientists 2.0 also need to observe diverse channels. Even within one platform this can be a confusing task: Communication takes place in many virtual locations, e.g. via messaging, chatting, group conversations, or commenting. So far, SNS hardly provide options to effectively organize this stream of information, especially when it comes to archiving and retrieving older bits of communication. At the same time, the ongoing news stream via multiple channels can easily overwhelm SNS users, resulting in an information overload. Although the fear of such an information overload was already expressed decades ago (Toffler 1970), some Internet critiques regard this as a pressing issue of the fragmented and hyperlinked structure of the WWW, possibly swamping our neuronal capacities and hindering deeper and coherent thoughts (Carr 2010; Schirrmacher 2009; Spitzer 2012). Moreover, we need to remember that SNS only add up to the already existing communication channels—from other social media platforms to e-mail, telephone, and many more.

Partly, users will cope with the challenge of information overload by developing specific strategies. For example, they may limit their practices to intentional active usage, which is less likely to lead to endless distraction through non-targeted passive usage. One could also argue in favor of SNS that one of the main ideas of these services is an effective information selection by people who we trust. However, as soon as one's digital social network reaches a certain size, it becomes extremely time-consuming if not impossible to follow it. Then additional filter mechanisms are needed. In sophisticated platforms these are organized in the background through algorithms hidden from the user. While this creates additional opacity, the selection of information through peers within SNS *per se* leads to an individual bias depending on one's networks. The common argument in favor of this novel way of personalized gatekeeping is that it is more likely to deliver content which is relevant to the user. Critiques, however, fear it will lead us into a distorted "filter bubble" (Pariser 2011), lacking diversity and serendipity. In the first place, this is a concern for the public sphere. Yet we may also wonder what impact these new filter mechanisms will have upon the academic realm. Will this work against the general tendency of blurring (disciplinary) boundaries in the context of fluid digital networks? Might this re-define scholarly relevance and visibility to a certain extent? Will new metrics such as *ResearchGate*'s RG Score (see Fig. 1 above) one day become serious competition for established scientometrics? On the one hand, the current low penetration of SNS into the academic sector does not make these questions appear very urgent. On the other hand, these questions are highly relevant to those scholars who already use the emerging platforms. They change the way scientists interact and exchange information. Since this differs according to the individual digital networks and the phenomenon has not yet fulfilled its whole potential, one can hardly draw broader conclusions on the exact impact of these developments at this point.

## Social Issues

*Informal Academic Communication 2.0.* By offering multiple electronic paths to reach and chat with members of the research community, SNS increase the possibility and likelihood of informal communication. Fully-fledged Cyberscience 2.0—or Science 2.0—would certainly look different to today's interim state-of-affairs. It may be characterized by massive, ubiquitous, possibly transdisciplinary micro-communication among academics, and with interested lay observers (Nentwich and König 2012, p. 200f.). This is already happening in certain niches with very active academic cyberentrepreneurs, but it is anything but the norm as of yet. It will be interesting to see what impact this may have on the structure of the science system as it becomes more common. We may also ask whether SNS may contribute to formalize the informal by making social networks of researchers—the so-called "invisible colleges" (Crane 1972)—more transparent. Depending on factors like privacy settings and the chosen communication channels, SNS partly reveal who is connected to whom and how closely.

*The Ambiguous Roles of Identity, Pseudonymity and Anonymity.* With regard to private use of SNS, pseudonymity instead of having a profile with one's real identity is frequently practiced, though discouraged. Thus it is possible to differentiate between different roles. Anonymous accounts are usually not possible. By contrast, in professional SNS which often also serve as public calling card directories, pseudonymity would be counter-productive because the users need to get in touch with "real" people. Similarly, pseudonymity is mostly dysfunctional in academia. Science communication rests on the premise that you communicate, whatever the medium, with actual persons in order to be able to cooperate or co-author. In other words, merits need to be attributable: researchers definitely expect that behind a profile in a SNS is another researcher who has actually written the papers listed in the publications attached to the profile. Some SNS try to guarantee this by verifying the identity on registration (e.g. *BestThinking*). In most cases, researchers also desire to be recognized in order to better establish themselves and increase their reputation. However, there are two cases where temporal or functional anonymity is in the interest of academia: In many fields, the peer-review process is usually double-blind. We may conceive that also the various rating systems within SNS, most of which are not anonymous as of yet, may be implemented in a way that allows anonymous rating. The other case is when it comes to testing new ideas in a creative forum space or during collective brainstorming. Here it may fuel creativity when the relation between callow thoughts and the originator would not be registered permanently in a written archive. For many cases, it seems desirable to create several personal "micro-publics" which may overlap, but "allow for distinct foci" (Barbour and Marshall 2012), e.g. in order to address different fields and audiences, such as peers and students.

*Is Privacy an Issue in SNS?* Mixing private and professional roles is an obvious problem in general SNS (like *Facebook*) which almost inevitably blend both identities. This is less so in science-specific SNS where the related privacy conflicts are attenuated: We observed that most researchers reveal only their professional identity here. This is usually supported by the set of information one is supposed to enter when setting up one's profile: the forms ask for biographical information relevant to academia and less for private facts such as relationship status. Note, however, that even *ResearchGate* asks for pet books and hobbies, but only receives answers from a few according to our observations. In any case, people using SNS leave their digital marks and traces, and so do researchers. There is currently an intense discussion about privacy concerns in the general SNS. At least some of researchers' reluctance to join SNS may be explained by fear of losing control over their privacy. In science-specific SNS, the data needed to enable efficient networking based on automatically generated suggestions is to a very large extent professional in nature, such as curriculum vitae, publications, research interests, office contact information, etc. Nonetheless, if researchers are very active on various Web 2.0 platforms, they create significant digital traces that can be analyzed by data-mining tools. Identity theft (OECD 2008) is another salient issue. Profiles may be hacked with the intention of damaging somebody's reputation, or false identity may be assumed in order to gain some benefits. Barbour and Marshall argue that under these circumstances it is better to actively shape one's online persona than leaving this to others:

> Although many academics do contribute to their online persona creation, there are just as many who do not engage with new media in any meaningful way. However, this does not mean that they are not present online. The risk of not taking control of one's own online academic persona is that others will create one for you. This is what we are terming the 'uncontainable self' (Barbour and Marshall 2012).

## Conclusions

A close look at the technical functions of SNS shows that they are potentially useful for a number of scholarly activities. In fact, they offer so many services that they theoretically may serve as an encompassing platform, quasi a "one-stop-service 2.0" of use for all major tasks within academia—from knowledge production and distribution to communication and, even beyond the borders of academia's ivory tower, for public relations and other connections between science and its environment. A large-scale implementation of SNS would imply a number of major changes compared to the way scientists interact today. To begin with, it would diversify the possibilities for interaction, creating a number of fragmented pieces of information. Every single SNS does that due to the multiple channels that it provides. The currently unclear market situation in the field of science-specific SNS enforces this effect, since it creates even more channels. One could argue that this might also lead to social diversification of academia, as it comes with new possibilities for networking and increased transparency, including novel perspectives for informal communication. It may become visible with whom researchers interact with, what they read, discuss, and consider important. What is more, other researchers from various fields and positions, even students and lay people, might participate in these interactions. This tendency of lowering status-based communication hurdles might be regarded as democratization of science. Some would even argue that this would increase the quality of scientific work, as it may be checked by more peers in an ongoing process that is much faster than the regular circles of peer-reviewing.

However, we believe that these assumptions are far-fetched given the current state of affairs. The diffusion of SNS in academia is still fairly low and even lower when we focus on active scholars who make full use of the potential of these platforms. As pointed out above, this is crucial for SNS because their whole purpose is to create connections between active users. This limits the general potential of SNS, no matter whether one sees it as desirable or problematic. Even with today's rather low participation, it is obvious that the vast amount of frag-mented information distributed via multiple channels can quickly become dysfunctional and lead to information overloads. This will rather work against democratizing effects as scientists (or automated filter mechanisms) will have to limit their attention even more—most likely to already well-established scholars and channels. The transition to (Cyber-)Science 2.0 is to a large extent driven by younger academics who may partly benefit in this context as they often know "how to play the game" of Web 2.0 better than their more senior colleagues. For example, it is not unlikely that a young researcher will be rated higher by a novel SNS-based metric like the RG Score. However, this advantage will probably diminish if such numbers gain importance for evaluations. However, as long as altmetrics still play a minor role, it is anyway questionable how much such a benefit is really worth. In fact, it may even lower the status of a researcher because others might regard the active usage of SNS as a waste of time.

Despite all of these difficulties, especially with regard to reaching the tipping point of enough scientists actively using SNS, these services appear to be on the rise. Since a critical mass of users can turn into a hyper-critical mass—which in itself is problematic—we should make use of the opportunities of this current transition period. Academics can (and should) shape future developments instead of leaving it to commercial providers who follow their own interests. Coming back to the title of this contribution: Academia might indeed "go Facebook" if it does actively interfere by providing and further developing independent platforms. There are already attempts to do exactly that, most-notably *vivo*, which gives academic institutions a lot of freedom because it is based upon open source software which can be run on local servers. However, it has apparently not reached a critical mass yet and it will take more effort within academia to push such independent projects to the point that they can compete with the temptations of the global Internet players. Of course, commercial platforms may still simply create the better platforms with more engaged scholars and it is debatable as to whether it is desirable to interfere with this. This is very much a political question which can be answered differently, depending on one's point of view. Some will believe in the free market, others will favor an active involvement of scientific institutions and policy-makers, maybe even including regulation.

In the meantime, it seems likely that the unclear market situation in the field of scientific social networks is not going to be clearly solved very soon. Therefore, the best way to increase the functionality of these services is interface harmonization (e.g. via APIs), allowing the various services to connect to each other. There are also academic initiatives in this direction; for example, *ScholarLib* connects scientific thematic portals with SNS (Thamm et al. 2012). Again, such attempts are limited by the will of the providers to create such openness via suitable APIs. Obviously, we are witnessing a very dynamic development with both a promising potential for the future of science and research—and for reflection.

# References

Bader, A., Fritz, G., & Gloning, T. (2012). *Digitale Wissenschaftskommunikation 2010–2011 Eine Online-Befragung*. Giessen: Giessener Elektronische Bibliothek. Available at http://geb.uni-giessen.de/geb/volltexte/2012/8539/index.html.

Barbour, K., & Marshall, D. (2012). The academic online: Constructing persona through the World Wide Web First Monday. *First Monday, 17*(9). Available at: http://firstmonday.org/htbin/cgiwrap/bin/ojs/index.php/fm/article/view/3969/3292.

Beer, D. D. (2008). Social network(ing) sites…revisiting the story so far: A response to danah boyd & Nicole Ellison. *Journal of Computer-Mediated Communication, 13*(2), 516–529. doi:10.1111/j.1083-6101.2008.00408.x.

Biermann, K. (2010). Facebook, bing und Skype vernetzen sich. *ZEIT Online*. Available at http://www.zeit.de/digital/internet/2010-10/facebook-bing-skype.

Boyd, D. M., & Ellison, N. B. (2007). Social network sites: definition, history, and scholarship. *Journal of Computer-Mediated Communication, 13*(1), 210–230. doi:10.1111/j.1083-6101.2007.00393.x.

Carr, N. G. (2010). *The shallows: what the Internet is doing to our brains*. New York: W.W. Norton.

Connell, R. S. (2008). Academic libraries, Facebook and MySpace, and student outreach: A survey of student opinion. *Portal: Libraries and the Academy, 9*(1), 25–36. doi:10.1353/pla.0.0036.

Crane, D. (1972). *Invisible colleges; diffusion of knowledge in scientific communities*. Chicago: University of Chicago Press.

Fuchs, C. (2009). *Social networking sites and the surveillance society. A critical case study of the usage of studiVZ, Facebook, and MySpace by students in salzburg in the context of electronic surveillance*. Salzburg/Wien: ICT&S Center (University of Salzburg), Forschungsgruppe Unified Theory of Information. Available at http://twinic.com/duploads/0000/0509/ICT_Use_-_MySpace_Facebook_2008.pdf.

Harley, D., et al. (2010). *Assessing the future landscape of scholarly communication: An exploration of faculty values and needs in seven disciplines*. Berkeley, CA: Center for Studies in Higher Education.

Bar-Ilan, J. (2012). JASIST@mendeley. In *ACM Web Science Conference 2012 Workshop*. Evanston, USA. Available at http://altmetrics.org/altmetrics12/bar-ilan/.

Kleimann, B., Özkilic, B. & Göcks, M. (2008). Studieren im Web 2.0. Studienbezogene Web- und E-Learning-Dienste. Hannover: HIS Hochschul-Informations-System GmbH. Available at https://hisbus.his.de/hisbus/docs/hisbus21.pdf.

Koch, D., & Moskaliuk, J. (2009). Onlinestudie: Wissenschaftliches Arbeiten im Web 2.0. E-learning and education. *Eleed*, 5. Available at http://eleed.campussource.de/archive/5/1842.

Li, X., Thelwall, M., & Giustini, D. (2011). Validating online reference managers for scholarly impact measurement. *Scientometrics, 91*(2), 461–471. doi:10.1007/s11192-011-0580-x.

Mack, D., et al. (2007). Reaching students with Facebook: Data and best practices. *Electronic Journal of Academic and Special Librarianship, 8*(2). Available at http://southernlibrarianship.icaap.org/content/v08n02/mack_d01.html.

Mendez, J. P., et al. (2009). To friend or not to friend: Academic interaction on Facebook. *International Journal of Instructional Technology and Distance Learning, 6*(9), 33–47.

Nentwich, M. (2003). *Cyberscience: Research in the age of the Internet*. Vienna: Austrian Academy of Sciences Press.

Nentwich, M., & König, R. (2012). *Cyberscience 2.0: Research in the age of digital social networks*. Frankfurt, New York: Campus Verlag.

OECD, 2008. *Scoping Paper on Online Identity Theft*, Seoul: Organisation for Economic Co-operation and Development. Available at: http://www.oecd.org/dataoecd/35/24/40644196.pdf.

Oosthuyzen, M. (2012). The seductive power of Facebook. *Unlike us blog.* Available at http://networkcultures.org/wpmu/unlikeus/2012/05/24/the-seductive-power-of-facebook.

Pariser, E. (2011). *The filter bubble what the Internet is hiding from you.* New York, USA: Penguin.

Procter, R., Williams, R., & Stewart, J. (2010). *If you build it, will they come? How researchers perceive and use Web 2.0.* Research Information Network. Available at http://www.rin.ac.uk/our-work/communicating-and-disseminating-research/use-and-relevance-web20-researchers.

Richter, A., & Koch, M. (2008). Funktionen von Social-Networking-Diensten. In M. Bichler et al. (Eds.), *Multikonferenz Wirtschaftsinformatik 2008* (pp. 1239–1250). Berlin: GITO-Verlag. Available at http://ibis.in.tum.de/mkwi08/18_Kooperationssysteme/04_Richter.pdf.

Richter, A., & Koch, M. (2007). *Social software—status quo und Zukunft.* München: Fakultät für Informatik, Universität der Bundeswehr München. Available at http://www.unibw.de/wow5_3/forschung/social_software.

Schirrmacher, F. (2009). *Payback warum wir im Informationszeitalter gezwungen sind, zu tun, was wir nicht tun wollen, und wie wir die Kontrolle über unser Denken zurückgewinnen.* München: Blessing.

Schmidt, J. (2009). *Das neue Netz: Merkmale, Praktiken und Folgen des Web 2.0.* Konstanz: UVK Verlagsgesellschaft.

Spitzer, M. (2012). *Digitale Demenz: wie wir uns und unsere Kinder um den Verstand bringen.* München: Droemer.

Thamm, M., Wandhöfer, T., & Mutschke, P. (2012). ScholarLib—Ein Framework zur Kopplung von Sozialen Netzwerken mit wissenschaftlichen Fachportalen. In M. Ockenfeld, I. Peters, & K. Weller (Eds.), *Social Media and Web Science das Web als Lebensraum; 64. Jahrestagung der DGI, Düsseldorf, 22. bis 23. März 2012; Proceedings* (pp. 205–212). 2. DGI-Konferenz, 64. Jahrestagung der DGI. Frankfurt a. M.: DGI.

Toffler, A. (1970). *Future shock.* New York: Random House.

# Reference Management

**Martin Fenner, Kaja Scheliga and Sönke Bartling**

> *If I have seen further it is by standing on the shoulders of Giants.*
>
> — Isaac Newton

**Abstract** Citations of relevant works are an integral part of all scholarly papers. Collecting, reading, and integrating these references into a manuscript is a time-consuming process, and reference managers have facilitated this process for more than 25 years. In the past 5 years, we have seen the arrival of a large number of new tools with greatly expanded functionality. Most of the newer reference managers focus on the collaborative aspects of collecting references and writing manuscripts. A number of these newer tools are web-based in order to facilitate this collaboration, and some of them are also available for mobile devices. Many reference managers now have integrated PDF viewers (sometimes with annotation tools) for scholarly papers. Reference managers increasingly have to handle other forms of scholarly content, from presentation slides to blog posts and web links. Open source software and open standards play a growing role in reference management. This chapter gives an overview of important trends in reference management and describes the most popular tools.

M. Fenner (✉)
Public Library of Science, San Francisco, CA, USA
e-mail: mfenner@plos.org

K. Scheliga
Alexander von Humboldt Institute for Internet and Society, Berlin, Germany

S. Bartling
German Cancer Research Center, Heidelberg, Germany
e-mail: soenkebartling@gmx.de

S. Bartling
Institute for Clinical Radiology and Nuclear Medicine, Mannheim University Medical Center, Heidelberg University, Mannheim, Germany

S. Bartling and S. Friesike (eds.), *Opening Science*,
DOI: 10.1007/978-3-319-00026-8_8, © The Author(s) 2014

# Introduction

Reference management is perceived to be tedious and time consuming by many researchers, especially when it is done manually. In the past, references used to be written on index cards and stored in boxes. Now, reference management software allows for the digitalization of a personal collection of relevant scholarly publications. The earliest programs to manage the basic task of storing references and adding them to manuscripts have been around for over 25 years (including Endnote and BibTeX/LaTeX-based programs which are still popular today), but each individual entry had to be typed by hand. In the last 15 years we have seen a number of significant developments that have made reference management much easier for the researcher:

1. Retrieval of reference information from online bibliographic databases
2. DOIs and other persistent identifiers for bibliographic information
3. Automated management of PDF files
4. Open Access for easier access to full-text content
5. Web-based reference management for easier collaboration and use across multiple devices

In this chapter we describe what reference managers are and provide an overview of some reference management products. We do not make recommendations as to which reference manager may be the best as this is a personal choice and depends on the workflow of the individual researcher.

# What is a Reference Manager?

A reference manager supports researchers in performing three basic research steps: searching, storing, and writing (Fenner 2010a). It helps researchers find relevant literature, allows them to store papers and their bibliographic metadata in a personal database for later retrieval, and allows researchers to insert citations and references in a chosen citation style when writing a text. To support those steps, a reference manager should have the following functionalities as identified by Gilmour and Cobus-Kuo (2011):

1. Import citations from bibliographic databases and websites
2. Gather metadata from PDF files
3. Allow organization of citations within the reference manager database
4. Allow annotation of citations
5. Allow sharing of the reference manager database or portions thereof with colleagues
6. Allow data interchange with other reference manager products through standard metadata formats (e.g. RIS, BibTeX)
7. Produce formatted citations in a variety of styles
8. Work with word processing software to facilitate in-text citation

A reference manager is a software package that allows scientific authors to collect, organize, and use bibliographic references or citations. The terms citation manager or bibliographic management software are used interchangeably. The software package usually consists of a database that stores references and citations. Once a citation is inserted into the database, it can be reused to create bibliographies which are typically found at the end of a scientific text.

Almost all reference managers allow direct importing from bibliographic databases through direct access from the reference manager and/or bookmarklets that import content from the web browser. Alternatively, references can be imported from other reference managers or from files in the BibTeX standard format with the help of import tools.

The reference database can then be searched, indexed, and labeled. Most reference managers offer tools for organizing the references into folders and subfolders. Some reference managers allow the inclusion of full-text papers in PDF format. References can be shared via the Internet and organized into workgroups so that all members can use the same reference database.

Reference managers offer tools for exporting citations and references into word processing programs by selecting relevant items from the database. The citation style can be selected from a corresponding database which contains styles that aim to cover the requirements of a large number of scholarly publishers. Some reference managers allow for styles to be edited and saved.

There is a wide variety of reference management software, and the strengths and weaknesses of reference management software are perceived differently depending on the workflows of individual scientists. The deciding factor for a particular reference manager is often its popularity within a particular community, as collaboratively writing a manuscript is facilitated if all authors use the same reference manager (see chapter How This Book was Created Using Collaborative Authoring and Cloud Tools). Reference managers have been commercially available for a long time, but free solutions offer comparable functionalities and are increasingly gaining importance.

Some reference managers allow sharing, collaborative editing, and synchronization of reference databases across a private workgroup and/or publicly via the Internet. Public sharing of references is the focus of online-only social bookmarking tools such as CiteULike and Bibsonomy, but is also available with other reference managers. This functionality makes it possible to share Open Access papers online (see chapter Open Access: A State of the Art) and to generate usage statistics as a novel means of measuring scientific impact (see chapter Altmetrics and Other Novel Measures for Scientific Impact).

## Getting References into the Reference Manager

All reference managers provide the functionality to manually enter bibliographic data. However, it is more convenient if the references are automatically extracted from an online bibliographic database such as Web of Science, Scopus, PubMed, or Google Scholar. Most reference managers can also import references directly from a webpage, usually using information embedded via CoinS. All reference managers can import/export references in the BibTeX and/or RIS format; this is a convenient way to share reference lists with colleagues.

## Bibliographic Databases

Some of the largest bibliographic databases (Web of Science, Scopus, and others) are only available via a subscription. In the last 10 years we have seen the emergence of an increasing number of openly available bibliographic databases. This trend started with PubMed in the late 1990s, includes Google Scholar, and, more recently, Microsoft Academic Search and the CrossRef Metadata Search, and now also includes bibliographic databases built by reference managers themselves (e.g. Mendeley or CiteULike). The availability of these databases increases the options for researchers to automatically import citation information, either via direct integration into the reference manager, or via a bookmarklet that captures the bibliographic content on the web page.

## COinS: Hassle-Free Import of Bibliographic Data

ContextObjects in Spans (COinS) is a method that includes relevant bibliographic metadata of a scientific publication into the HTML code of a web page. If appropriate plugins are installed in a standard web browser, the bibliographic information of a reference can be easily retrieved by a reference manager, thus omitting tedious copy and paste processes. For example, if a reference is found in PubMed, a little symbol appears in the browser address line if the Zotero plugin is installed. At the click of a button, all important bibliographic information will be transferred into the Zotero database. Many scientific databases, scientific social networks, and journals support COinS (Fig. 1).

## Digital Object Identifiers and Other Unique Identifiers

Most journal articles can now be uniquely identified by a digital object identifier (DOI). DOIs for journal articles are issued by CrossRef, a non-profit organization that has most scholarly publishers as its members. DOIs can also be used for other content, e.g. conference proceedings or book chapters. DataCite is another non-profit organization that can issue DOIs, focusing on DOIs for datasets. There are also other unique identifiers for scholarly content, e.g. the PubMed ID, PubMed Central ID, or the ArXiV ID. These identifiers make it much easier to handle bibliographic information: reference managers can extract the DOI from imported PDFs, obtain more citation information using the DOI, store the DOI internally to help find duplicate records, etc. Authors only need to worry about the DOI (or other unique identifier), all the other information they need (authors, title, journal, link to the full-text) can be obtained from it.

## Standardized Bibliographic Data Formats: BibTeX and RIS

BibTeX and RIS are the two most established file formats for storing bibliographic data, and one or both of these formats are supported by all reference managers. Exporting data in a standardized format is important because it allows users to backup their reference lists independently of the reference management software, to switch from one reference manager to another, or to use multiple reference managers in parallel.

- **BibTeX** has existed since the mid 1980s and was designed to be used in combination with the typesetting system LaTeX. The format is now widely supported by reference managers that work with Microsoft Word and other authoring tools, and by online bibliographic databases such as Google Scholar.
- **Research Information Systems** (RIS) is a standardized tag format originally invented by Research Information Systems (now part of Thomson Reuters). The format is widely supported and has been adapted over time, e.g. to include a field for digital object identifiers (DOIs).
- **Endnote XML and Citeproc JSON** are newer formats which are not yet as widely supported. BibTeX and RIS are plain text formats. XML and, more recently, JSON have evolved into the standard data exchange formats of the Web, and are easier to process automatically. They may therefore over time become the predominant formats for exchanging bibliographic information.

## Citation Styles and Citation Style Language

Citations can be formatted in many different ways: what information to include (authors, title, journal, year, issue, pages), how to order and format this information, and how to reference these citations in the main text (e.g. by number or author/year). These so-called citation styles are important for printed documents, but are not really relevant for digital content (where citations are exchanged in BibTeX and other data formats). Unfortunately, most manuscript submission systems do not accept references in digital format, and authors are forced to format their references in the style requested by the publisher and include them as plain text at the end of the manuscript (and, in turn, publishers then spend time and money to get these references back into a bibliographic data format).

What publishers are really interested in are unique identifiers, such as the DOI, for all references. This allows them to double-check the reference information against

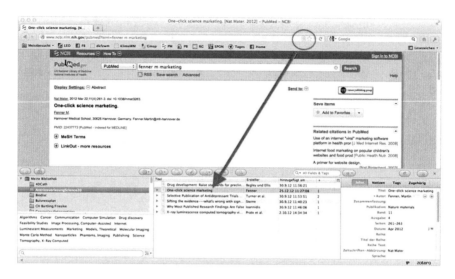

**Fig. 1** Showing COinS in action. At the click of a button, a reference is included into the reference manager software (Zotero) from information that is contained in the COinS information in the displayed web page: No need to manually copy references

bibliographic databases (using tools such as eXtyles), and to format the citations into their preferred style. Citation information in free-text format can contain errors, and these errors are propagated if citations are entered manually (see Specht 2010).

Citation styles are needed not only to correctly identify all references (for which bibliographic formats and digital identifiers are better suited), but also to help the researcher while reading the text. Citations are an important part of all scholarly documents, and citation styles should facilitate that process. Even though a number of common styles exist (e.g. APA, MLA, Chicago, Vancouver), there is no standard style for citations in scholarly documents, and with the differences in citation practices between disciplines, it is not likely to ever happen. Some disciplines use simple reference lists at the end of the document, whereas other disciplines use footnotes at the bottom of pages and/or make heavy use of annotations.

Until it becomes standard practice to submit references in a bibliographic file format together with manuscripts (some publishers do this already), authors must resultingly deal with a large number of citation styles. This also often means changing the citation style when a paper has to be resubmitted to another journal. This is a time consuming endeavor, thus automating the process of adjusting to the various citation styles is an important feature of all reference managers.

Most reference managers support a large number of citation styles: EndNote[1] supports over 5,000 bibliographic styles, and Mendeley, Zotero, and Papers all support 2,750 citation styles. Some reference managers include a style editor, in

---

[1] EndNote Output Styles: http://endnote.com/downloads/styles

**Examples of citation styles**
**DOI**
http://dx.doi.org/10.1126/science.1197258
**shortDOI**
http://doi.org/dc3dhn
**APA**
Wolfe-Simon, F., Blum, J. S., Kulp, T. R., Gordon, G. W., Hoeft, S. E., Pett-Ridge, J., &
   Oremland, R. S. (2011). A Bacterium That Can Grow by Using Arsenic Instead of
   Phosphorus. Science, 332(6034), 1163-1166. doi:10.1126/science.1197258
**Vancouver**
Wolfe-Simon F, Blum JS, Kulp TR, Gordon GW, Hoeft SE, Pett-Ridge J, et al. A Bacterium That
   Can Grow by Using Arsenic Instead of Phosphorus. Science [Internet]. American Association
   for the Advancement of Science; 2011 Jun 2;332(6034):11636. Available from: http://
   dx.doi.org/10.1126/science.1197258
**Nature**
Wolfe-Simon, F. et al. A Bacterium That Can Grow by Using Arsenic Instead of Phosphorus.
   Science 332, 1163-1166 (2011)
**BibTeX**
@article{_Webb_Weber_Davies_et_al__2011, title = {A Bacterium That Can Grow by Using
   Arsenic Instead of Phosphorus}, volume = {332}, url = {http://dx.doi.org/10.1126/
   science.1197258}, DOI = {10.1126/science.1197258}, number = {6034}, journal = {Sci-
   ence}, publisher = {American Association for the Advancement of Science}, author =
   {Wolfe-Simon, F. and Blum, J. S. and Kulp, T. R. and Gordon, G. W. and Hoeft, S. E. and
   Pett-Ridge, J. and Stolz, J. F. and Webb, S. M. and Weber, P. K. and Davies, P. C. W. and
   et al.}, year = {2011}, month = {Jun}, pages = {1163-1166}}
**RIS**
TY—JOUR
T2—Science
AU—Wolfe-Simon, F.
AU—Blum, J. S.
AU—Kulp, T. R.
AU—Gordon, G. W.
AU—Hoeft, S. E.
AU—Pett-Ridge, J.
AU—Stolz, J. F.
AU—Webb, S. M.
AU—Weber, P. K.
AU—Davies, P. C. W.
AU—Anbar, A. D.
AU—Oremland, R. S.
SN—0036-8075
TI—A Bacterium That Can Grow by Using Arsenic Instead of Phosphorus
SP—1163
EP—1166
VL—332
PB—American Association for the Advancement of Science

(continued)

(continued)

---

DO—10.1126/science.1197258
PY—2011
UR—http://dx.doi.org/10.1126/science.1197258
ER—

**Citeproc JSON**

{ "volume":"332","issue":"6034","DOI":"10.1126/science.1197258","URL":"http://dx.doi.org/10.1126/science.1197258","title": "A Bacterium That Can Grow by Using Arsenic Instead of Phosphorus","container-title":"Science","publisher":"American Association for the Advancement of Science","issued":{ "date-parts":[[2011,6,2]]},"author":[{ "family":"Wolfe-Simon","given":"F." },{ "family":"Blum","given":"J. S." },{ "family":"Kulp","given":"T. R." },{ "family":"Gordon","given":"G. W." },{ "family":"Hoeft","given":"S. E." },{ "family":"Pett-Ridge","given":"J." },{ "family":"Stolz","given":"J. F." },{ "family":"Webb","given":"S. M." },{ "family":"Weber","given":"P. K." },{ "family":"Davies","given":"P. C. W." },{ "family":"Anbar","given":"A. D." },{ "family":"Oremland","given":"R. S." }],"editor":[],"page":"1163-1166","type":"article-journal" }

---

case a particular style is not yet supported. Citation styles used to be in proprietary format and owned by the publisher of the reference manager, but the Citation Style Language[2] (CSL) has evolved as an open XML-based language to describe the formatting of citations and bibliographies. Originally written for Zotero, CSL is now also used by Mendeley, Papers, and many other tools and services. In 2012, a web-based editor[3] to create and edit CSL styles was launched, facilitating the creation of additional styles.

## Managing Full-Text Content

Reference management has traditionally been about managing information about scholarly content (authors, title, journal, and other metadata). With the switch to digital publication and the availability of content in PDF, as well as other formats, reference management increasingly dealt with managing this digital content: linking references to the full-text document on the computer, performing full-text search, making annotations in the PDF, managing the PDF files on the hard drive, etc. Papers was the first reference manager to focus on this aspect, but most reference managers now have functionality to manage PDF files.

Most scholarly journal articles are currently distributed via subscription journals. This makes it important to store a copy on the local hard drive for easier access, but it can also create problems when these PDF files are shared with collaborators (which most publishers do not allow, even within the same institution). Reference management software therefore has to make decisions as to what

---

[2] Citation Style Language: http://citationstyles.org/

[3] Find and edit citation styles: http://editor.citationstyles.org/about/.

is technically possible and convenient for researchers vs. what is possible under copyright law (see chapter Intellectual Property and Computational Science).

Content published as Open Access does not have these limitations. This not only makes it much easier to share relevant full-text articles with collaborators, but it also means that we often do not need to store a copy of the full-text on the local hard drive, as the content is readily available.

## Reference Management Tools

From the large number of available reference managers, we have chosen seven popular products that are described in more detail below. We have included a table that gives an overview of their basic features. A feature list is not the only criterion in picking a reference manager though; ease of use, stability, price, and available support in case of questions are equally important factors.

### *EndNote*

EndNote is a commercial reference management software package produced by Thomson Reuters. Endnote is one of the most popular reference managers and has been around for more than 20 years. It allows collecting references from online resources and PDFs. References from bibliographic databases can be imported into EndNote libraries. Full-text can be imported too. EndNote provides plugins for Microsoft Word and OpenOffice. References can be exported to BibTeX. While EndNote does not include any collaborative features, EndNote Web provides the functionality for collaboration with other users. Users can give group members read/write access to their references and import references from other people's libraries. Endnote also integrates with other bibliographic tools produced by Thomson Reuters, including Web of Science and ResearcherID.

### *Mendeley*

Mendeley is a reference manager developed by a London based startup, but has been bought by Elsevier earlier this year. Its strength lies in its networking and collaborative features, and also in providing facilities for easily managing PDF files. It offers both a desktop and a web version with synchronized bibliographic information, allowing access from several computers and collaboration with other users. PDF files can be imported into Mendeley desktop and metadata such as authors, title, and journal are automatically extracted. It is possible to do a full-text search, highlight text in PDFs, and add sticky notes.

The web version recommends papers to users based on their profiles and the content in their libraries. Users can create both private and public groups and share papers and annotations. Mendeley is free to use, but costs a monthly fee if the number of documents in Mendeley web or the number of private groups exceeds a limit.

## Zotero

Zotero is a popular open source reference manager, originally developed as a plugin for the Firefox browser. The newer Zotero Standalone offers the same functionality but runs as a separate program and works with Firefox, Chrome and Safari. Zotero also includes a hosted version in order to synchronize references across devices and share them in private or public groups.

Zotero allows users to collect and to organize a variety of web sources such as citations, full-texts, web pages, images and audio files directly in the browser. Citations from Zotero can be integrated into Microsoft Word and OpenOffice.

## RefWorks

RefWorks is a commercial web-based reference manager by ProQuest. The Write N Cite utility enables the integration of references into Microsoft Word where in-text citations and reference lists can be formatted into various styles. RefWorks makes it easy to collaborate with others as all references are stored in the web-based version. The Write N Cite utility can also work offline, but RefWorks is not the right tool for researchers with intermittent or poor Internet connectivity.

## Papers

Papers is a commercial reference management software, now part of Springer Science+Business media. Initially Papers was only available for Mac, but now there are also versions for iPad and PC. Its main strength is its excellent handling of PDF documents (including metadata extraction) and its polished user interface, whereas the collaborative features are less developed than in some of the other products. Papers uses the Citation Style Language and provides a word processor plugin.

## JabRef

JabRef is an open source bibliography reference manager popular with LaTeX users. It runs on Java and is thus compatible with Windows, Linux, and Mac. The native file format is BibTeX which is the standard LaTeX bibliography format. The strength of JabRef is that references can be formatted directly in LaTeX, thus

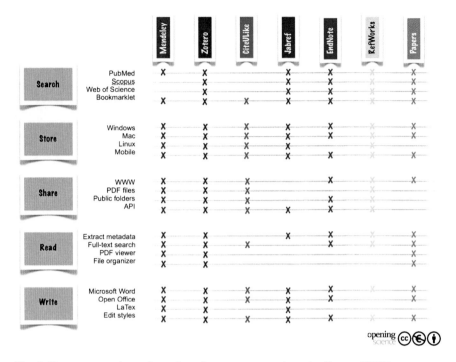

**Fig. 2** Feature comparison of popular reference managers (see also Fenner 2010b)

providing access and control over a wide range of citation styles. JabRef provides direct search and downloads from PubMed and IEEEXplore. There are plugins for word processing programs and also other Java based plugins, which expand the general functionality.

## CiteULike

CiteULike is a free online reference manager and social bookmarking tool. References are primarily entered via a bookmarklet that captures bibliographic content in web pages. New entries are public by default and are added to the common library, but entries can be also made private. Users can assign tags to entries which make it easier to organize and search through content. References can be exported in BibTeX and RIS formats. The social networking features are the strength of CiteULike. Users can create profiles, connect with other researchers, and create and join groups where they can collaborate on library content.

## Other Reference Management Products

Many other reference managers are available, including Citavi which is popular in some disciplines and also helps with knowledge management, and ReadCube which has a very nice user interface and a good PDF viewer. An extensive list and comparison of available reference management software can be found on Wikipedia (Fig. 2).[4]

## Outlook

Reference management has become easier, cheaper, and more social in the past few years, and this trend will continue. We will see the integration of unique author identifiers (ORCID, etc.) into bibliographic databases and reference management tools (see case in chapter Unique Identifiers for Researchers), and this will facilitate the discovery of relevant literature and the automatic updating of publication lists. We will increasingly see citations of datasets and other non-text content (see chapter Open Research Data: From Vision to Practice). Digital identifiers for content and support for the open Citation Style Language will also increase, as will the availability of open bibliographic information. Three areas still need improvement. Firstly, the automatic importing of the references of a particular publication, and the integration of reference managers into authoring tools. Secondly, the word processor plugins for reference managers still do not work together, and some of the newer online authoring tools (Google Docs, etc.) need to be better integrated with reference managers. Finally, instead of having references in plain text, which makes it difficult to get to the full-text and reformat it into a different citation style, publishers, institutions, and funders should start to ask for reference lists in standard bibliographic formats using digital identifiers.

## References

Fenner, M. (2010a). Reference management meets Web 2.0. *Cellular Therapy and Transplantation, 2*(6), 1–13.
Fenner, M. (2010b). Reference manager overview. *Gobbledygook*. Available at http://blogs.plos.org/mfenner/reference-manager-overview/.

---

[4] Comparison of reference management software: http://en.wikipedia.org/wiki/Comparison_of_reference_management_software

Gilmour, R. & Cobus-Kuo, L. (2011). Reference management software: A comparative analysis of four products. In *Issues in Science and Technology Librarianship*. Available at http://www.istl.org/11-summer/refereed2.html.

Specht, C. G. (2010). Opinion: Mutations of citations. Available at http://www.the-scientist.com/?articles.view/articleNo/29252/title/Opinion–Mutations-of-citations/.

# Open Access: A State of the Art

**Dagmar Sitek and Roland Bertelmann**

> *Open Access saves lives.*
> —Peter Murray-Rust

**Abstract** Free access to knowledge is a central module within the context of Science 2.0. Rapid development within the area of Open Access underlines this fact and is a pathfinder for Science 2.0, especially since the October 2003 enactment of the "Berlin Declaration on Open Access to Knowledge in the Sciences and Humanities". Berlin Declaration on Open Access to Knowledge in the Sciences and Humanities (http://oa.mpg.de/files/2010/04/berlin_declaration.pdf)

## Introduction

The past years have shown that Open Access is of high relevance for all scientific areas but it is important to see that the implementation is subject-tailored. In all journal based sciences two both well-established and complementary ways used are "OA gold" and "OA green". These two ways offer various advantages that enhance scientific communication's processes by allowing free access to information for everybody at any time.

Furthermore, it is necessary to break new ground in order to expand, optimize, and ensure free worldwide access to knowledge in the long run. All involved players need to re-define their role and position in the process. This challenge will lead to new, seminal solutions for the sciences.

D. Sitek (✉)
DKFZ German Cancer Research Center, Heidelberg, Germany
e-mail: d.sitek@dkfz-heidelberg.de

R. Bertelmann
GFZ German Research Centre for Geosciences, Potsdam, Germany
e-mail: roland.bertelmann@gfz-potsdam.de

S. Bartling and S. Friesike (eds.), *Opening Science*,
DOI: 10.1007/978-3-319-00026-8_9, © The Author(s) 2014

# Definition of Open Access

Open Access implies free access to scientific knowledge for everybody. In the "Berlin Declaration on Open Access to Knowledge in the Sciences and Humanities", the term scientific knowledge is defined as "original scientific research results, raw data and metadata, source materials, digital representations of pictorial and graphical materials and scholarly multimedia material."[1] Most scientific knowledge is gained in a publicly funded context; basically it is paid for by the taxpayer. In many fields, journals are the main channel of scholarly communication, therefore Open Access has especially developed in this sector. At the moment, most scientific journal articles are only accessible to scientists who are working in an institution with a library that has licensed the content. According to the "Berlin Declaration", not only a "free, irrevocable, worldwide, right of access" should be granted, but also a "license to copy, use, distribute, transmit and display the work publicly and to make and distribute derivative works, in any digital medium for any responsible purpose (...) as well as the right to make small numbers of printed copies for their personal use."[1]

Authors have several possibilities in publishing their research results. Open Access maximizes the visibility and outreach of the authors' publications and the results of public funding (Fig. 1).

# State of the Art

Open Access today is an accepted and applauded scientific publication strategy. In summer 2012, a number of statements impressively showed the state of the art as it was seen by national and international actors of science politics and science management.

The European Commission published its vision on how to improve access to scientific information. Two citations from this occasion's press release and the related communication represent this perspective:

> As a first step, the Commission will make Open Access to scientific publications a general principle of Horizon 2020, the EU's Research & Innovation funding program for 2014–2020. As of 2014, all articles produced with funding from Horizon 2020 will have to be accessible: articles will either immediately be made accessible online by the publisher ('Gold' Open Access)—up-front publication costs can be eligible for reimbursement by the European Commission; or researchers will make their articles available through an Open Access repository no later than six months (12 months for articles in the fields of social sciences and humanities) after publication ('Green' Open Access).[2]

---

[1]  http://oa.mpg.de/files/2010/04/berlin_declaration.pdf

[2]  Press Releases RAPID: http://europa.eu/rapid/press-release_IP-12-790_en.htm

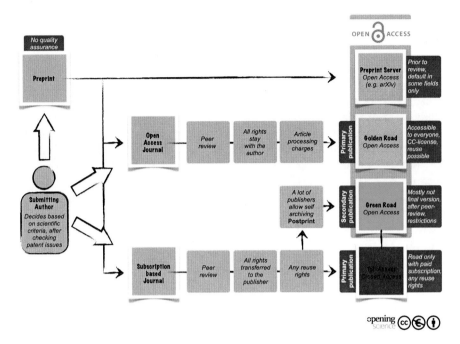

**Fig. 1** The Open Access process, an overview

The European Commission emphasises Open Access as a key tool to bring together people and ideas in a way that catalyses science and innovation. To ensure economic growth and to address the societal challenges of the 21st century, it is essential to optimize the circulation and transfer of scientific knowledge among key stakeholders in European research—universities, funding bodies, libraries, innovative enterprises, governments and policy-makers, non-governmental organizations (NGOs) and society at large.[3]

Hence, we can expect that results from the European research program Horizon 2020 should be fully Open Access. Already in the current program, published results from the fields of energy, environment, health, information and communication technologies, and research infrastructures are expected to be Open Access, according to an Open Access Pilot for these subjects.

... *beneficiaries* shall deposit an electronic copy of the published version or the final manuscript accepted for publication of a scientific publication relating to *foreground* published before or after the final report in an institutional or subject-based repository at the moment of publication. *Beneficiaries* are required to make their best efforts to ensure that this electronic copy becomes freely and electronically available to anyone through this repository:

---

[3] European Commission: http://ec.europa.eu/research/science-society/document_library/pdf_06/era-communication-towards-better-access-to-scientific-information_en.pdf

- immediately if the scientific publication is published "Open Access", i.e. if an electronic version is also available free of charge via the publisher, or
- within [X] months of publication …[4]

In June 2012, the Royal Society published a report named "Science as an open enterprise" which aimed for research data to be an integral part of every researcher's scientific record, stressing the close connection of open publication and open accessible research data (see chapter Open Research Data: From Vision to Practice: Open Research Data). "Open inquiry is at the heart of scientific enterprise … We are now on the brink of an achievable aim: for all science literature to be online, for all of the data to be online and for the two to be interoperable" (Boulton 2012).

In several countries, initiatives are afoot to build a legal foundation to help broadening the road to a world of openly accessible scientific results. Just to name a few:

- In Great Britain, the minister for universities and science, David Willetts, strongly supports a shift to free access to academic research. The British government actually plans to Open Access to all publicly funded research by 2014 (cf. Willetts 2012).
- In the United States, an initiative called Federal Research Public Access Act (FRPAA) is on the way, requiring "free online public access".[5]
- In Germany, the Alliance of German Science Organizations is a strong supporter of an initiative for a change in German Copyright law which is supposed to secure a basic right for authors to publish their findings in accordance to the idea of providing scientists free access to information.[6]

Since the Budapest Open Access Initiative (BOAI 2002)[7] was inaugurated, a number of declarations of different bodies have paved the way. Indeed, the list of signatories of the "Berlin Declaration on Open Access to Knowledge in the Sciences and Humanities"[8] read like a gazetteer of scientific institutions and organizations worldwide.

Due to a series of follow-up conferences, the number of supporters of the Berlin Declaration is still growing. Moreover, some US universities took the opportunity to join in when the conference took place Washington DC in December 2011.[9]

Already at an early stage, funding bodies like the National Institutes of Health (NIH)[10] stepped in and created rules for the openness of their funded research.

[4] Annex 1: http://ec.europa.eu/research/press/2008/pdf/annex_1_new_clauses.pdf
[5] Berkman: http://cyber.law.harvard.edu/hoap/Notes_on_the_Federal_Research_Public_Access_Act
[6] Priority Initiative "Digital Information": http://www.allianzinitiative.de/en/core_activities/legal_frameworks
[7] Budapest Open Access Initiative: http://www.soros.org/openaccess/read
[8] http://oa.mpg.de/files/2010/04/berlin_declaration.pdf
[9] B9 Open Access Conference: http://www.berlin9.org/
[10] NIH Public Access Policy: http://publicaccess.nih.gov/policy.htm

National funders like DFG in Germany, SURF in the Netherlands, JISC in GB, and others not only asked for open results of their funded projects, but also featured change by funding calls for projects to do research on Open Access and to develop appropriate infrastructure.

One of the boosters for this rapid development of support for Open Access was, of course, the "journal crisis". Since the early 1990s, we have seen a dramatic change in the scientific publication landscape, especially for journals which had basically not changed since they were established. One other aspect was a long series of mergers of publication houses, leaving us with four big players controlling about 60–70 % of journal titles worldwide. Here, stock exchange perspectives and risk money from private equity funds are playing an important and shaping role. Another change factor lies in the possibilities of the Internet. Already in the early days of the Internet, ArXiv was established.[11] ArXiv already displayed the benefits of Open Access within a small, and for a long time closely cooperating community, Particle Physics. Publishers used their monopoly and increased journal prices over the years at very high rates; at least 10 % per year was the standard for years. Although these rates have lowered a little in the last few years (five to six percent per year), since the late nineties, most libraries have had problems keeping up with the subscriptions to journals which they should hold for the benefit of researchers. As a result, they have cancelled journal subscriptions. Even today, big and famous libraries cancel journal subscriptions, like the Faculty Advisory Council suggested for Harvard in 2012.[12] In former days, moderate prices guaranteed that, at least in the Western world, the possibility somehow of providing access to scientific output. In these times of a continuing "journal crisis", fewer and fewer scientists get access to journals, especially in science, technology, and medicine, and therewith to scientific knowledge, because not all institutions can afford the ever rising subscription fees. This day to day experience of many scientists enormously helped to build the vision of science based on openly accessible publications.

In economic theory, Nobel laureate Elinor Ostrom extended her concept of "the commons" to also include "understanding knowledge as a commons" (Hess and Ostrom 2011). Open Access activist Peter Suber showed how Open Access fits perfectly in such a theoretical background: "Creating an Intellectual Commons through Open Access" (Suber 2011).

Interviews with scientists showed that a change in attitude has already taken place. More and more scientists admit that they quickly change to another content related, but accessible article if they experience access problems. Also, Open Access seems to be a modern prolongation of a central traditional scientific habit for many scientists: make your work accessible to colleagues. This was done in former times with the help of offprints. Open Access to an article may be seen as a modern solution for such scientific needs.

---

[11] Arxiv: http://arxiv.org/

[12] Faculty Advisory Council Memorandum on Journal Pricing: http://isites.harvard.edu/icb/icb.do?keyword=k77982&tabgroupid=icb.tabgroup143448

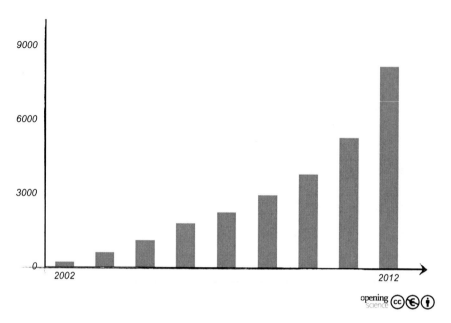

**Fig. 2** Number of Open Access journals by year (*Source* DOAJ)

Some numbers show how broad the idea of Open Access is, how many already are using Open Access, and how quickly it is still growing. 'Base',[13] a service built by the University Library Bielefeld, is harvesting the world of repositories (Green Open Access) and indexing their contents. It now contains over 35 million items, which compares to a total of about 1 million collected items in 2005.[14] The Directory of Open Access Journals (DOAJ)[15] gives an overview of Open Access Journals (Gold Open Access). In 2002, they counted 33 journals. Currently, the steadily increasing number has reached more than 8,000 Open Access journals (Fig. 2).

"Green" and "Gold" are the two well established and complimentary used roads to Open Access. Open Access depends upon these basic concepts, but, of course, a number of mixed concepts have also been established (for detailed information see Suber 2012b).

## A Closer Look at Green and Gold Open Access

Traditional journal subscription denies access to all those whose institution cannot afford to pay yearly subscription fees. In contrast, Gold Open Access describes a business model for journal publishing which gives free access to all potential readers and sees other models to cover expenses for a publication. Although there

---

[13]  BASE: http://www.base-search.net/?fullbrowser=1

[14]  BASE Statistics: http://www.base-search.net/about/en/about_statistics.php?menu=2

[15]  Directory of Open Access Journals: http://www.doaj.org/

is a broad range of models, a majority of notable Open Access journals rely on publication fees, also known as article processing charges (ACP), which are often also incorrectly referred to as author fees. These sums are usually paid by the author's institution. Especially in science, technology, and medicine, this follows the practice of paying for color images, too many pages, or other factors, which has been familiar since pre-Internet times in subscription-based journals. On the other hand, society journals in particular have opened access to their journal articles without charging authors. Others, like PNAS, give access after an embargo of half a year.

In the early times of Open Access an often heard argument against golden journals was the question of quality. Open Access journals differ only in terms of the publisher's business model from subscription-based journals; they pass through the same peer review processes as the traditional journals and there are no differences regarding the quality of the published articles. Newly founded journals need some time to build a positive resonance in their research community. Today, Open Access journals are, of course, embedded within the high ranking journals in their fields. More and more get listed, e.g. in the Journal Citation Report of *Thomson-Reuters* (more than ten percent of all ranked titles).[16] Laakso et al. (2011) give a comprehensive overview of the development using a distinction between "The pioneering years (1993–1999), the innovation years (2000–2004), and the consolidation years (2005–2009)". For the future a more numerous migration from existing and valued subscription journals to the Gold model is desirable.

However, Open Access is not only possible for articles in journals with these respective business models. The Green Road of Open Access stresses the possibility of authors to deposit their articles, which are primarily published on publisher's sites, additionally on another server. Usually an institutional or a subject-based repository is used for this purpose. "A complete version of the work and all supplemental materials, including a copy of the permission as stated above, in an appropriate standard electronic format is deposited (and thus published) in at least one online repository using suitable technical standards" (Berlin Declaration).[17] An institutional repository is organized by an institution and contains the publications of its scientists. Opposed to the affiliation to an institution as a criterion for content, a subject-based repository comprises publications which belong to some specific fields of science. A famous example of a subject-based repository is ArXiv[18] which already laid the grass roots for Open Access in the nineties. PubMedCentral[19] is another example within the field of biomedical and life sciences research.

---

[16] Thomson Reuters Intellectual Property and Science: http://science.thomsonreuters.com/cgi-bin/linksj/opensearch.cgi?

[17] http://oa.mpg.de/files/2010/04/berlin_declaration.pdf

[18] http://arxiv.org/

[19] NCBI: http://www.ncbi.nlm.nih.gov/pmc/

In principle, between 70 and 80 % of scientific journals allow such a method of self-archiving. Generally there are some restrictions which have to be complied by the authors. In the majority of cases, depositing a version of the original article is not allowed, but rather a preprint or a version of the final draft. Depending on the journal, this can either be done immediately, or an embargo period between the publication of the original article and the self-archiving has to be considered. This period is usually between six (for STM journals) and twelve months (for social sciences and humanities journals). All journals which allow self-archiving are listed in the SHERPA/Romeo database which also lists the specific restrictions.[20]

Meanwhile, many scientific institutions run an institutional repository to deposit green Open Access articles. Usually the library is responsible for this task. The deposit of their articles in such a repository has numerous advantages for the scientists.

One large benefit is made up of the support the repository operator offers its users. The scientists in question may ask for advice in all questions concerning the workflow of posting their publications. This includes, for example, when and in which form there are allowed to deposit a journal article. Digital preservation of the stored material is ensured as soon as explicit identification like persistent identifiers is provided. Furthermore, they make sure that all publications are tagged with precise and standardized metadata. Only in this way is cross-linking with other sources or other repositories possible, and, in turn, future features like semantic web functions will be possible. Correctly prepared data also enhances search engine exposure. In future, the linking between publications and the data which belongs to them, for example supplementary material or research data, will be relatively easy to establish on this level.

The content of an institutional repository is not limited to journal articles. By posting all of their publications, like reports, talks, conference proceedings, teaching materials, and so forth, into the repository, the scientists can present their work openly as a whole within the context of their research group and institution. If this Open Access repository is combined with an institutional research information system (CRIS), numerous benefits can emerge. Authors can re-use this content by linking to their openly accessible publications from social networks for scientists, their own homepage, etc. Through this linking, it is possible to connect the advantages of an institutional repository with the scientist's personal needs. It can also be used as a helpful tool for the management of publications.

Scientists should demand such a database from their institutions if such a service is not yet offered. Not only the scientists in question, but also the whole institution benefit from a well-run institutional repository. A presentation of the research output of an institution in this way can constitute an important element for science marketing. For example, a Google search on articles shows the institutional homepage with the repository output, instead of a publisher's homepage.

---

[20] SHERPA/RoMEO: http://www.sherpa.ac.uk/romeo/

It hence serves as a showcase of the research output of an institution (cf. Armbruster and Romary 2010). Therefore, it should also be in their interest to build such systems.

Institutional repositories mostly deal with final drafts. Subject-oriented repositories are based on specific traditions in certain scientific fields. Surely the most famous is ArXiv,[21] founded in the early nineties for researchers in Theoretical Physics. Today it is a preprint archive for a broad range of scientific subjects. A recent Nature article states: "Population biologists turn to pre-publication server to gain wider readership and rapid review of results" (Callaway 2012).

PubMedCentral,[22] on the other hand, is a subject repository which, amongst others, hosts NIH-sponsored manuscripts, while Research Papers in Economics (RePEc)[23] has successfully built a service based on the long tradition of publishing reports in economics. In future, both repository types should get better linked. If an article is deposited in one type, linkage to the other should become a standard.

## Green or Gold: Which is the Better Way?

The recommendations of the British Working Group on Expanding Access to Published Research Findings, the Finch Report[24] preferred Gold to Green. This triggered a discussion on what the best way to Open Access is (see, for example, Harnad 2012 or Suber 2012a). Obviously, seen from a scientist's point of view, both ways have the right to exist. Looking at the green road means publishing an article wherever one thinks it is the best for one's career. At the same time, one makes use of the opportunity to give access to all relevant readers. Funders' mandates will not be a problem, the green road is compliant. If self-archiving is supported by a well made institutional infrastructure, this way works quickly and easily. Additional costs are generated from infrastructural needs. In too many institutions there is still poor help for researchers; too often they are still left alone to self-archive. Hence, institutions should not only state policies, but actively support their scientists and strengthen infrastructural backing.

Meanwhile, the golden road is part of an axiomatic change of the publication landscape. It is a primary publication, which gives immediate access to an article in the context of its journal, including linkage to all additional services of a publisher. *"… journals receive their revenues up front, so they can provide immediate access free of charge to the peer-reviewed, semantically enriched published article, with minimal restrictions on use and reuse. For authors, gold means that decisions on how and where to publish involve balancing cost and quality of service. That is how most markets operate, and ensures that competition*

---

[21] http://arxiv.org/

[22] http://www.ncbi.nlm.nih.gov/pmc/

[23] RePEc: http://repec.org/

[24] Research Information Network: http://www.researchinfonet.org/publish/finch/

*on quality and price works effectively. It is also preferable to the current, non-transparent market for scholarly journals."*, as the secretary to the Finch committee puts it (Jubb 2012).

Naturally of course, again, the respective traditions of research fields matter. Björk et al. write *"There is a clear pattern to the internal distribution between green and gold in the different disciplines studied. In all the life sciences, gold is the dominating OA access channel. The picture is reversed in the other disciplines where green dominated. The lowest overall OA share is in chemistry with 13 % and the highest in earth sciences with 33 %."* (Björk et al. 2010).

## New Models

Of course, publishing has its costs and whatever way is followed, someone has to cover these. In the case of green repositories, infrastructure needs to be supported by institutions. Article processing charges for gold publishing are paid by funders or institutions. Most funders have already reacted and financing at least a part of open publishing fees has become a standard. Unfortunately, many institutions currently lack an appropriate workflow for this new challenge. Traditional journal subscription is generally paid for by libraries. In institutions it often is not clear to scientists, by whom and how these Open Access charges can be managed. Initiatives like the "Compact for Open-Access Publishing Equity"[25] are paving the way to such workflows in order to make them a matter of course. The Study of Open Access Publishing (SOAP)[26] gave evidence of this challenge: "Almost 40 % [scientists] said that a lack of funding for publication fees was a deterrent …". (Vogel 2011) Institutional libraries must face this challenge and take on a new role. This new role is not too far from their traditional role: paying for access to information as a service for scientists. Björn Brembs even sees the future in a "library-based scholarly communication system for semantically linked literature and data" instead of the traditional processes dominated by publishers (Brembs 2012). Sponsoring Consortium for Open Access Publishing in Particle Physics (SCOAP3) "is currently testing the transition of a whole community",[27] integrating scientific institutions, their libraries, and publishers.

Some publishers feature a hybrid model. They still back the traditional subscription model, but also offer an opportunity to buy out an individual article for Open Access. Seen from a scientist's point of view this may be interesting, but usually the price level is high and only a few authors utilize this option. Seen from an institutional point of view, this is a problematic business model, as article fees

---

[25] Compact for Open-Access Publishing Equity: http://www.oacompact.org/compact/

[26] SOAP: http://project-soap.eu/

[27] SCOAP3: http://scoap3.org/

and subscription fees are normally not yet combined. Therefore, institutions pay twice to a publisher (Björk 2012). Obviously such a hybrid is not a transition path to Gold.

Since traditional publishers have adopted the Open Access business model (e.g. Springer in 2010), we have definitely reached a situation in which Open Access has grown-up.

All stakeholders of the scholarly communication have to check carefully and adjust their roles in future, as new stakeholders will arise. They have been closely connected with each other for a long time. Open Access brought new functions and tasks for each stakeholder within the classical distribution; not all have already faced up to that challenge. For example, a lot of publishers are still locked up in thinking in print terms. In parallel, a common fear is that ACPs will go up and up when traditional publishers adopt the gold model and will become unaffordable. Charges differ within a broad range of some hundred Euros up to over 3,000 Euros (Leptin 2012).

We now see a mixture of the roles mentioned. As an example, libraries can, in certain cases like grey literature, switch to a publisher's role. On the other hand, "Nature" experimented with preprint publication, opening in 2007 "Nature precedings",[28] closing down the platform again in 2012. Due to Open Access, new publishing houses were set up. Some have quickly become respectable and successful, others may be under suspicion to be predatory.[29] Besides, new players are in the game and it is not yet decided as to where their role will lie. Publication management systems and scientific social networks are merging, often relying on Open Access full-texts.

But not only the players have to re-define their role within the scientific publications process; the format of scientific knowledge is also changing: *"It no longer consists of only static papers that document a research insight. In the future, online research literature will, in an ideal world at least, be a seamless amalgam of papers linked to relevant data, stand-alone data and software, 'grey literature' (policy or application reports outside scientific journals) and tools for visualization, analysis, sharing, annotation and providing credit. … And 'publishers' will increasingly include organizations or individuals who are not established journal publishers, but who host and provide access and other added value to this online edifice. Some may be research funders, such as the National Institutes of Health in its hosting of various databases; some may be research institutions, such as the European Bioinformatics Institute. Others may be private companies, including suppliers of tools such as the reference manager Mendeley and Digital Science, sister company to Nature Publishing Group"* (Nature 2012a).

---

[28] Nature Precedings: http://precedings.nature.com/

[29] see Code of Conduct of the Open Access Scholarly Publishers Association—OASPA: http://oaspa.org/membership/code-of-conduct/

## Books and Grey Literature

For a long time, scientific journals were in the center of Open Access discussions. Since e-books in scholarly publication are also emerging very quickly, we will soon see more developments in this field. Of course, business models are not one to one transferable from journals to monographs. Nevertheless, it already is clear that there is also a model for commercial publishers. Often an electronic version of a book is published Open Access and the publisher gets revenues by selling the printed version. In some fields, monographs mostly consist of a compilation of articles. In these cases, their handling could be comparable to journals. Maybe Springer's move in August 2012 to introduce Open Access Books will be copied by other publishers. In the sciences it is familiar and a long standing tradition that an institution supports publishing a book by paying high contributions to publishers. It is just a matter of establishing a new culture to change the underlying standardized contracts in two points. Firstly, to retain rights for authors and institutions, secondly, to introduce some kind of Open Access, perhaps including an embargo.[30]

So called "grey literature" has always played a role in scholarly communication and was mostly defined by its poor findability and dissemination. Usually, grey literature was published by scientific institutions in print with a low circulation rate. But if the content is trusted, reviewed, and is published Open Access by a reputable institution in its own electronic publishing infrastructure, grey literature is up for playing a new and sustainable role in a future publication landscape. Some even see this as a nucleus for a rearrangement of roles (see Huffine 2010). Hereby, libraries could be one of the key players. Important for an Open Access future of grey literature is a thoroughly-built infrastructure which guarantees quality, persistence, and citability. New and emerging ways of scholarly communication can be included in such a structure.

The important role of research data for an Open Science is discussed elsewhere in this book (see Pampel and Dallmeier-Tiessen in this volume). Scholarly text publication and data publication cannot be separated in the future. On the side of Open Access for texts, a close connection to related data needs to become part of scholarly common sense. Text and data should be seen as an integral unit which represents the record of science of a researcher. As Brembs puts it: "Why isn't there a 'World Library of Science' which contains all the scientific literature and primary data?" (Brembs 2011). Talking about data mining will always have both parts in mind: text and related research data.

---

[30] OApen: http://project.oapen.org/index.php/literature-overview

# Impact of Open Access on Publishing

In addition to establishing new business models, Open Access has featured and accelerated elementary changes in scientific publishing. The general impact of Open Access upon the development of scholarly publishing is tremendous.

Peer review is one issue. Already ten years ago, for example, Copernicus Publications, the largest Open Access publisher in geosciences, combined Open Access publishing with a concept of open interactive peer review (Pöschl 2004).

The rise of PLOS One,[31] an Open Access mega journal promising quick peer review and publication and accepting articles from all fields, has changed the scene. PLOS, which is now the largest scientific journal worldwide with around 14.000 articles per year, has been followed by a chain of new established journals from other publishers copying the model. Just to name a few new Open Access journals, and having a look at the publishers in the background, this following list shows how important mega journals have become: Springer Plus, BMJ open, Cell reports, Nature communications, Nature Scientific Reports, and Sage Open.

Giving away all rights to the publisher when signing an author's contract has been one of the strongest points of criticism for years. Discussions on how authors can retain copyright brought Creative Commons licenses into the focus. Today, Creative Commons licenses like CC-BY or CC-BY-SA have become a de facto standard in Open Access publishing (see as an example Wiley's recent move to CC-by).[32] "Re-use" is the catchword for the perspective which has been opened by introducing such licenses.

# Benefits

Open Access publications proved to have citation advantages (Gargouri et al. 2010) resulting from open accessibility of scholarly results formerly only available in closed access. It guarantees faster communication and discussion of scientific results. Therefore, it perfectly assists in fulfilling the most basic scholarly need: communication. Open Access also promotes transparency and insight for the public into scientific outcomes (Voronin et al. 2011). The outreach of scientific work is stimulated.

Tools for a new and comprehensive findability and intensive data mining to openly accessible texts will certainly be available. This will make interdisciplinary work easier and productive. Reuse, due to open licenses, the "possibility to translate, combine, analyze, adapt, and preserve the scientific material" is easier and will lead to new outcomes (Carroll 2011).

---

[31] PLOS: www.plosone.org

[32] Wiley Moves Towards Broader Open Access Licence: http://eu.wiley.com/WileyCDA/PressRelease/pressReleaseId-104537.html

The statement "In the online era, researchers' own 'mandate' will no longer just be 'publish-or-perish' but 'self-archive to flourish'" (Gargouri et al. 2010) can be extended to "researchers' own 'mandate' will no longer just be 'publish-or-perish' but give Open Access to flourish".

# References

Armbruster, C., & Romary, L. (2010). Comparing repository types—challenges and barriers for subject-based repositories, research repositories, national repository systems and institutional repositories in serving scholarly communication. *International Journal of Digital Library Systems, 1*(4), 61–73.

Björk, B.-C. (2012). The hybrid model for Open Access publication of scholarly articles: A failed experiment? *Journal of the American Society for Information Science and Technology, 63*(8), 1496–1504. doi:10.1002/asi.22709.

Björk, B.-C. et al. (2010). Open Access to the scientific journal literature: Situation 2009. In E. Scalas (Ed.) *PLoS ONE, 5*(6), e11273. doi:10.1371/journal.pone.0011273.

Boulton, G. (2012). *Science as an open enterprise*, UK: The Royal Society. Available at: http://royalsociety.org/policy/projects/science-public-enterprise/report/.

Brembs, B. (2011). A proposal for the library of the future. *björn.brembs.blog*. Available at: http://bjoern.brembs.net.

Brembs, B. (2012). Libraries are better than corporate publishers because… *björn.brembs.blog*. Available at: http://bjoern.brembs.net.

Callaway, E. (2012). Geneticists eye the potential of arXiv. *Nature, 488*(7409), 19–19. doi:10.1038/488019a.

Carroll, M. W. (2011). Why full Open Access matters. *PLoS Biology, 9*(11), e1001210. doi:10.1371/journal.pbio.1001210.

Eckman, C. D., Weil, B. T. (2010). Institutional Open Access funds: Now is the time. *PLoS Biology, 8*(5), e1000375.

Evans, J. A., & Reimer, J. (2009). Open Access and global participation in science. *Science, 323*(5917), 1025–19.

Gargouri, Y. et al. (2010). Self-selected or mandated, Open Access increases citation impact for higher quality research. In R. P. Futrelle (Ed.), *PLoS ONE, 5*(10), e13636. doi:10.1371/journal.pone.0013636.

Grant, B. (2012). Whither science publishing? *The Scientist*. Available at: http://www.the-scientist.com.

Harnad, S. (2012). Open Access: A green light for archiving. *Nature, 487*(7407), 302–302. doi:10.1038/487302b.

Hawkes, N. (2012). Funding agencies are standing in way of Open Access to research results, publishers say. *BMJ, 344*(1 jun 11), pp. e4062–e4062.

Hess, C., & Ostrom, E. (2011). *Understanding knowledge as a commons: from theory to practice*. Cambridge: MIT Press.

Huffine, R. (2010). Value of grey literature to scholarly research in the digital age. Available at: http://cdn.elsevier.com/assets/pdf_file/0014/110543/2010RichardHuffine.pdf.

Jubb, M. (2012). Open Access: Let's go for gold. *Nature, 487*(7407), 302–302. doi:10.1038/487302a.

Laakso, M. et al. (2011). The development of Open Access journal publishing from 1993 to 2009. In M. Hermes-Lima (Ed.) *PLoS ONE, 6*(6), e20961. doi:10.1371/journal.pone.0020961.

Leptin, M. (2012). Open Access–pass the buck. *Science, 335*(6074), 1279–1279. doi:10.1126/science.1220395.

Nature. (2010). Open sesame. *Nature, 464*(7290), 813–813.

Nature. (2012a). Access all areas. *Nature, 481*(7382), 409–409. doi:10.1038/481409a.

Nature. (2012b). Openness costs. *Nature, 486*(7404), 439–439.

Noorden van, R. (2012). Journal offers flat fee for 'all you can publish.' *Nature 486*(166).

Pöschl, U. (2004). Interactive journal concept for improved scientific publishing and quality assurance. *Learned Publishing, 17*(2), 105–113. doi:10.1087/095315104322958481.

Science. (2012). The Cost of Open Access. *Science, 336*(6086), 1231–1231.

Shotton, D. (2009). Semantic publishing: the coming revolution in scientific journal publishing. *Learned Publishing, 22*(2), 85–94.

Suber, P. (2011). Creating an intellectual commons through Open Access. In C. Hess, E. Ostrom (Eds.), *Understanding knowledge as a commons. From theory to practice* (pp. 171–208). USA: MIT Press.

Suber, P. (2012a). Ensuring Open Access for publicly funded research. *British Medical Journal,* 345, e5184

Suber, P. (Ed.). (2012b). *What is Open Access? In Open Access* (pp. 1–27). USA: MIT Press.

Vogel, G. (2011). Open Access gains support; fees and journal quality deter submissions. *Science, 331*(6015), 273–273. doi:10.1126/science.331.6015.273-a.

Voronin, Y., Myrzahmetov, A., Bernstein, A. (2011). Access to scientific publications: The scientist's perspective. In K. T. Jeang (Ed.) *PLoS ONE, 6*(11), e27868. Doi:10.1371/journal.pone.0027868.

Whitfield, J. (2011). Open Access comes of age. *Nature, 474*(7352), 428–428.

Willetts, D. (2012). Open, free access to academic research? This will be a seismic shift. *The guardian.* Available at: http://www.guardian.co.uk/commentisfree/2012/may/01/open-free-access-academic-research?CMP=twt_gu. For interested readers, further information and interesting discourses are provided here:

# Novel Scholarly Journal Concepts

**Peter Binfield**

*It is not the strongest of the species that survives, nor the most intelligent, but the one most responsive to change.*
—Charles Darwin

**Abstract** Recent years have seen a great deal of experimentation around the basic concept of the journal. This chapter overviews some of the more novel or interesting developments in this space, developments which include new business models, new editorial models, and new ways in which the traditional functions of the journal can be disaggregated into separate services.

## Introduction

For a long period following the invention of the Academic Journal in the 17th Century, the journal evolved very little, and certainly did not change substantially from the original format. It was perhaps with the formalization of the Peer Review process (as we have come to know it) that the concept of the journal made its greatest leap. Other than that development, very little changed in over 300 years...

However, since the advent of the Internet, the 'traditional' concept of the Academic Journal has been under pressure. Although subscription titles moved online quite early in the Internet era, it has only been with the more recent, and still accelerating, move towards Open Access (an innovation which was made possible thanks to the enabling technology of the Internet) that there has been a considerable amount of experimentation around what a journal is, or could be.

Because of the size of this industry and the scale of experimentation which is underway, the examples listed in this chapter are not intended to represent a comprehensive list, but simply to highlight some of the representative experiments that are happening today.

P. Binfield (✉)
PeerJ, CA, USA
e-mail: pete@peerj.com

S. Bartling and S. Friesike (eds.), *Opening Science*,
DOI: 10.1007/978-3-319-00026-8_10, © The Author(s) 2014

## Novelty in the Business Model

Clearly the predominant business model in journal publishing has always been the subscription model, however there have been several recent developments which aim to provide alternatives to this established model. The most obvious alternative in today's marketplace is the Open Access 'author pays' Article Publication Charge (APC) model which has been successfully used by the likes of BioMed Central, PLOS, Hindawi, and Frontiers, to name a few. This model will be well understood by most readers, so we shall not dwell on it here. Instead it is interesting to consider some of the other Open Access business models which are in the marketplace today:

**Free to Publish:** e-Life[1] is a highly selective, Open Access journal which is entirely financed by research funders (Max Planck Society, the, Welcome Trust and the HHMI). Because of this funding, the journal does not charge authors a publication fee (hence it is free to publish, as well as free to read). E-Life is perhaps the most recent, and visible, example of a 'free-free' journal but clearly many other journals are funded by entities such as Institutions, or Societies to the extent that their costs can also be entirely covered.

**Individual Membership Models:** PeerJ[2] (see Fig. 1) is an Open Access journal which offers authors a Lifetime Membership, in return for which authors can publish freely for life. Membership fees start at $99 (allowing authors to publish once per year) and rise to $299 (which allows authors to freely publish as many articles as they wish). All co-authors need to be paying members with the correct Membership level. Membership fees can be paid either before editorial Acceptance; or authors can submit for free and become a Member only at the time of Editorial Acceptance (for a slight price increase). This model is very new, and clearly orthogonal to a traditional APC fee (as it shifts payment from a "fee per publication" to a "fee per author")—therefore it is being watched with some interest, to see how the model might affect the approach of the publisher towards its 'customers' (who are now Members).

**APC Fees Centrally Negotiated:** SCOAP3 (the Sponsoring Consortium for Open Access Publishing in Particle Physics) has been a multi year project by a consortium of high energy physics laboratories aiming to flip their entire field from a subscription basis to Open Access. SCOAP3 has raised committed funding from major libraries and research centers worldwide such that it has been able to take that commitment and approach the publishers of the main subscription titles in their field, requesting that they tender for the Open Access business of the community. The arrangement comes along with a promise that committed institutions will no longer subscribe to journals, but will instead fund the Open Access fees of the researchers in the field.

---

[1] eLIFE: http://www.elifesciences.org/the-journal/

[2] Disclosure: The author of this chapter is a Co-Founder of PeerJ.

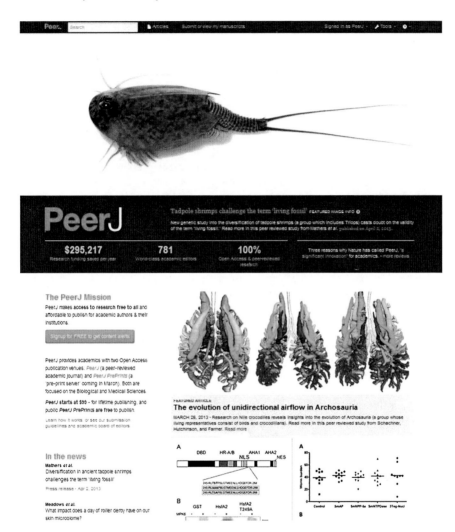

**Fig. 1** The PeerJ homepage

## Novelty in the Editorial Model

For a very long period there was no formal peer review process in the sciences and as recently as the 1970s, many journals did not formally peer review everything they published. However, since that time, the process of peer review has become firmly intertwined with the concept of the scholarly journal. The peer review which has evolved in this way has largely tried to do two things at the same time: (1) to comment on the validity of the science, and suggest ways in which it could be improved; and (2) to comment on the interest level (or 'impact') of that science, in an attempt to provide a sorting, or filtering mechanism on the mass of submitted content. However, with the advent of the Internet; the development of online only 'author pays' business models; and the development of improved methods of search and discovery, this second aspect of peer review has become increasingly less important.

It was in this environment that PLOS ONE (from the Public Library of Science) was conceived [3] a journal which would peer review all content, but only ask the reviewers to comment on the scientific and methodological soundness, not on the level of interest (or 'impact', or 'degree of advance') of the article. PLOS ONE has proven to be wildly successful—it launched in December 2006, and in 2012 alone it published 23,464 articles[4] (approximately 2.5 % of all the content indexed by PubMed in that year, and making it the largest journal in the world by several multiples) and continues to grow year on year. This success did not go unnoticed - PLOS ONE coined a new category of journal, the "Open Access Megajournal" and, with it, gave rise to a number of similar journals (employing similar editorial criteria).

The archetypal features of a MegaJournal seem to be: (1) editorial criteria which judges articles only on scientific soundness; (2) a very broad subject scope (for example the whole of Genetics or the whole of Social Sciences); (3) an Open Access model employing a payment model (typically APC) which is set up for each article to pay its own costs; (4) a large editorial board of academic editors (as opposed to a staff of professional editors).

Although some megajournals are not completely transparent about their editorial criteria (perhaps for fear of harming their brand), a non-exhaustive list of these 'MegaJournals' would currently include (in no particular order) BMJ Open,[5] SAGE Open,[6] PeerJ, Springer Plus, Scientific Reports (from Nature),[7] Q Science Connect,[8] Elementa,[9] Optics Express,[10] G3 (from the Genetics Society of America),[11] Biology Open (from the Company of Biologists),[12] IEEE Access,[13] AIP Advances, The Scientific World Journal, Cureus, F1000 Research and FEBS

---

[3] Disclosure—the author of this chapter previously ran PLOS ONE

[4] PLOS ONE Search: http://www.plosone.org/search/advanced?pageSize=12&sort=&query-Field=publication_date&startDateAsString=2012-01-01&endDateAsString=2012-12-31&unformattedQuery=publication_date%3A[2012-01-01T00%3A00%3A00Z+TO+2012-12-31T23%3A59%3A59Z]+&journalOpt=some&filterJournals=PLoSONE&subjectCatOpt=all&filterArticleTypeOpt=all.

[5] BMJ open:http://bmjopen.bmj.com/.

[6] SAGE Open: http://sgo.sagepub.com/.

[7] Scientific Reports: http://www.nature.com/srep/index.html.

[8] Q Science Connect: http://www.qscience.com/loi/connect.

[9] Elementa: http://elementascience.org/connect.

[10] Optics Express: http://www.opticsinfobase.org/oe/home.cfm.

[11] G3: http://www.g3journal.org/.

[12] Biology Open: http://bio.biologists.org/.

[13] IEEE Access: http://www.ieee.org/publications_standards/publications/ieee_access.html.

Open Bio.[14] In addition, it has been argued that the BMC Series,[15] the "Frontiers in…" Series,[16] and the ISRN Series from Hindawi[17] (all of which apply similar editorial criteria, but attempt to retain subject-specific identity to each journal in their Series) should also be considered megajournals, although they typically seem to downplay that association.

## Novelty in the Peer Review Model

Although the megajournals have successfully implemented a single change to the peer review process (not judging based on impact), there are other innovators who have journals (or 'journal-like') products which are trying other variations with their peer review. Some illustrative examples are:

Hindawi's ISRN Series algorithmically identifies suitable peer reviewers (mainly from its pool of Editorial Board members), and then operates an anonymous peer review process which culminates in a 'vote' between the peer reviewers. If all peer reviewers are in agreement to either accept or reject the article then it is accepted or rejected. However, if there is any disagreement as to the decision, then the reviews are shown to all the peer reviewers and they are invited to change their opinion. After this second round, the decision goes with the majority opinion (even if not unanimous). Once accepted, the authors are given the option of voluntarily revising their manuscript based on the feedback. This process is described, for example, at Hindawi's Website.[18]

By contrast, F1000 Research receives submissions and places them publicly online before peer review. Reviews are then solicited (typically from the Editorial Board) and reviewers must sign their reports. The reports can be 'approved', 'approved with reservations', or 'not approved' (Fig. 2). Provided an article accrues at least one 'approved' and two 'approved with reservations' (or simply two 'approved' reports) then it is considered to be 'published' and subsequently it is indexed in PubMed Central, and Scopus. Authors are not obliged to revise their manuscripts in light of feedback. Because content is posted online even before peer review has started, F1000 Research is thus composed of content in varying states of peer review, and as such can be thought of as a cross between a journal and a preprint server.

---

[14] FEBS Open Bio: http://www.journals.elsevier.com/febs-open-bio/.

[15] BMC Series: http://www.biomedcentral.com/authors/bmcseries.

[16] Frontiers: http://www.frontiersin.org/about/evaluationsystem

[17] Hindawi Journals: http://www.hindawi.com/isrn/.

[18] Hindawi ISRN Obstetrics and Gynecology Editorial Workflow: http://www.hindawi.com/isrn/obgyn/workflow/.

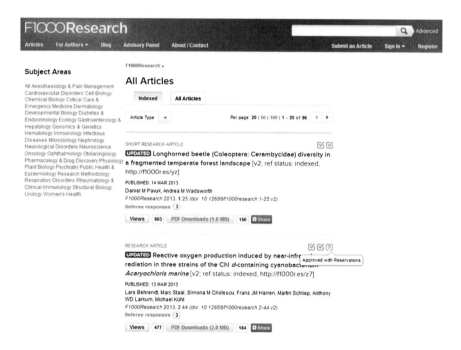

**Fig. 2** The article listing for F1000 Research, highlighting the way that evaluations are presented

The PLoS Currents series[19] of 6 titles can also be thought of as a cross between a journal and a preprint server. There is no publication fee and any content posted to a PLOS Current is submitted using an authoring tool which automatically generates XML. The content is evaluated by an editorial board, and these boards typically look to make very rapid decisions as to whether or not to publish the content (they are not typically recommending revisions or performing a full peer review). Because of this process, articles can go online within a day or two of submission, and are then indexed by PubMed Central. Although an interesting concept, to date PLOS Currents have not received a large number of submissions.

And then, of course there are the true '*PrePrint Servers*'. Two defining features of the preprint server are that (i) the content is typically un-peer reviewed, and (ii) they are usually free (gratis) to submit to. Because a preprint server is rarely thought of as a 'journal' (and this chapter is devoted to innovations around the journal concept) we shall not spend much time on them, other than to provide an illustrative list which includes the arXiv (in Physics and Mathematics), PeerJ PrePrints (in the Bio and Medical sciences), Nature Precedings[20] (now defunct), FigShare (a product which is 'preprint-like', and covering all of academia); the

---

[19] PLOS Currents: http://currents.plos.org/.

[20] Nature Precedings: http://precedings.nature.com/.

Social Sciences Research Network (SSRN), and Research Papers in Economics (RePEc).


## The Disaggregation of the Journal Model

Historically, a journal has performed several functions such as 'archiving', 'registration', 'dissemination', and 'certification' (there are others, but these four have historically defined the journal). However it is increasingly evident that these functions do not need to all take place within a single journal 'container'—instead each function can be broken off and handled by separate entities.

Several interesting companies are arising to take advantage of this way of thinking. Although each service can be thought of as an attempt to 'disaggregate' the journal, they are also being used by existing journals to enhance and extend their features and functionality. As with preprint servers, none of these products are really thought of as a journal, but it is certainly useful to be aware of them when considering the future development of the journal model:

Rubriq is a company which attempts to provide "3rd party peer review"—authors submit to Rubriq who then solicit (and pay) appropriate peer reviewers to provide structures reports back to the author. Another example of this kind of thinking is with the Peerage of Science (Fig. 3). By using services like this, authors can either improve their articles before then submitting to a journal; or they can attempt to provide their solicited peer reviews to the journal of their choice in the hope that this will shorten their review process.[21]

'Alt-Metrics',[22] or 'Article Level Metrics' (ALM) are tools which aim to provide 3rd party 'crowdsourced' evaluation of published articles (or other scholarly content). If we envision a future state of the publishing industry where most content is Open Access, and a large proportion of it has been published by a megajournal, then it is clear that there are considerable opportunities for services which can direct readers to the most relevant, impactful, or valuable content for their specific needs. Pioneered by the likes of PLOS[23] (who made their ALM program entirely open source), the field is being pushed forward by newly started companies. The major players in this space are Impact Story (previously Total Impact), Altmetric and Plum Analytics and all of them attempt to collate a variety of alt-metrics from many different sources, and present them back again at the level of the article (Fig. 4).

One particularly interesting provider of 'alt metrics' is F1000Prime[24] (from the "Faculty of 1,000"). Previously known simply as 'Faculty of 1000', F1000Prime

---

[21] Disclosure—the author of this chapter is on the (unpaid) Advisory Panel of Rubriq

[22] Altmetrics Manifesto: http://altmetrics.org/manifesto/.

[23] PLOS Article-Level Metrics: http://article-level-metrics.plos.org/.

[24] F1000Prime: http://f1000.com/prime.

**Fig. 3** The peerage of science homepage

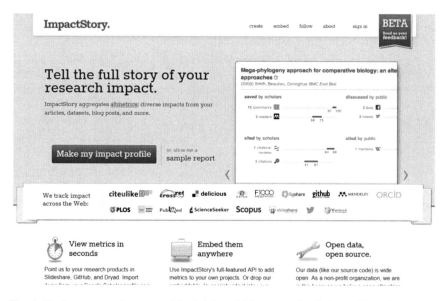

**Fig. 4** The impact story homepage, highlighting which sources they index and how they present metrics for a single article

makes use of a very large board of expert academics who are asked to evaluate and rate published articles regardless of the publisher. In this way, they form an independent review board which attempts to direct readers towards the articles of most significance. Although F1000Prime only evaluates perhaps 2 % of the literature (and hence is not comprehensive), it is clear that an approach like this fits well with a concept of disaggregating the role of 'content evaluation' (or 'content filtering') from the journal process.

## Conclusion

As can be seen from this chapter, there is a great deal of experimentation happening in the journal space today. It remains to be seen which experiments will succeed and which will fail, but it is certainly the case that the last decade has seen more experimentation around the concept of the journal than its entire 350 year history prior to this point. We live in interesting times.

# The Public Knowledge Project: Open Source Tools for Open Access to Scholarly Communication

James MacGregor, Kevin Stranack and John Willinsky

**Abstract** This chapter describes how the Public Knowledge Project, a collective of academics, librarians, and technical genies, has been, since 1998, building open source software (free) publishing platforms that create an alternative path to commercial and subscription-based routes to scholarly communication. It sets out how its various website platforms, including Open Journal Systems, Open Conference Systems, and, recently, Open Monograph Press, provide a guided path through the editorial workflow of submission, review, editing, publishing and indexing. Thousands of faculty members around the world are now using the software to publish independent journals on a peer-reviewed and Open Access basis, greatly increasing the public and global contribution of research and scholarship.

## Introduction

The digital transformation of scholarly communication has given rise to a wealth of new publishing strategies, models, ands tool over the last two decades. Many of these developments revolve around this new technology's seeming promise to increase the extent and reach of knowledge dissemination on a more equitable and global scale (cf. Benkler 2006). At first reluctantly, but now with increasing levels of interest, scholarly publishing is turning to the Internet as the preferred method of dissemination. This poses a set of core challenges: How can scholars, regardless of geographic location or institutional resources, participate in, learn from, and contribute to the global exchange of knowledge? How can those involved in

J. MacGregor (✉) · K. Stranack
Simon Fraser University Library, Burnaby, Canada
e-mail: jmacgreg@gmail.com

J. Willinsky
Stanford University, Stanford, USA

S. Bartling and S. Friesike (eds.), *Opening Science*,
DOI: 10.1007/978-3-319-00026-8_11, © The Author(s) 2014

publishing scholarly work maintain high standards of quality for this work, while further advancing the long-standing research goals of openness and increased access to knowledge?

The responses to such challenges are prolific and growing, proving to be source of exciting research and development for scholarly communication. The whole arena is complicated by the mix of, on the one hand, large corporate publishing entities, seeking to preserve some of the highest profit margins in publishing, and, on the other, small independent scholar-publishers who see their work as a service to their colleagues and a commitment to the pursuit of learning, while in the middle are scholarly associations that have grown dependent over the years on publishing revenues for their survival (cf. Willinsky 2009).

Within this larger picture, the Public Knowledge Project (PKP) represents a modest instance of research and experimentation in a new generation of publishing tools that would lower the barriers among scholars and scientists interested in playing a more active role in publishing and in seeing this work reaching a much wider audience. What success the project has achieved over the years in developing software that is used by journals in many different parts of the world can be attributed to the collective wisdom, as well as trial and error, of the team involved in this project. This wisdom has found its expression in, for example, the early adoption of open source and community development models; the active development of the international PKP community; and the feedback of users in guiding software and workflow design decisions that reflected principles of simplicity, interoperability, accessibility, and openness, without sacrificing capability.

## History of the Project

The Public Knowledge Project was started at the University of British Columbia (UBC) in Vancouver, Canada in 1998 with a small number of student developers working under the direction of John Willinsky, a faculty member in the Faculty of Education. The project began on two levels. It was involved in researching various models for creating a more coordinated approach to scholarly publishing that would increase its public value (cf. Willinsky 1999). It also sought to develop something practical and useful, in the form of online software, for the journal community, which was only beginning, at the turn of the twenty-first century, to think about moving its publishing operations and its journals to a web-based environment. The project's goal from the outset was to find ways of increasing public and global access to research and scholarship. As such, it was an early participant in the Open Access movement that sought to develop ways of creating peer-reviewed journals that did not charge readers for access to their content (cf. Suber 2012).

In 2005, Willinsky led PKP into a partnership with Lynn Copeland and Brian Owen at the Simon Fraser University (SFU) Library. It was becoming clear that the research library was emerging as a key player in efforts to reform scholarly communication around technology. And SFU Library quickly demonstrated how productively this sort of partnership could work, by providing management and systems support. In 2007, Willinsky left UBC to take up a position at Stanford University in the Graduate School of Education, creating a strong institutional link for the project between Stanford and the SFU Library, with a greater emphasis at Stanford on the related research questions in scholarly communications, while matters of technology development and innovation are centered around the SFU Library.

As for PKP's software, an early result of the project was the creation and 2001 release of Open Journal Systems (OJS) 1.0, a free, open source journal publication management system, which provided an online platform for accepting submissions, performing double blind peer review, editing, publishing, and dissemination. OJS provided the necessary technological infrastructure for many journals making the transition from print to online, as well as being the foundation for emerging "born-digital" journals. Today, PKP has not only created OJS, but also Open Conference Systems (OCS, for managing conferences), Open Monograph Press (OMP, for managing book publication), and Open Harvester Systems (OHS, for metadata harvesting).

The Project currently employs over a dozen developers, librarians and library staff at Simon Fraser University, Stanford University, and elsewhere in the world. Most are active academically as students and/or as scholars. There is no physical PKP "office": while most PKP associates live in Vancouver, others live in New Brunswick, Palo Alto, Brazil, and elsewhere. As with other open source software initiatives, community collaboration is at the forefront of the PKP development model, and the PKP user community continues to grow and influence application development.

To take one community example, the PKP Support Forum has over 4,500 members and more than 33,000 posts, and generates upwards of ten new posts a day; many of these posts contain vital bug reports and feature requests.[1]

Translation support across all PKP applications is growing: OJS alone now includes 27 community-contributed translations. And the global install base of PKP applications expands from month to month, with over 3,500 active journals currently using OJS. Half of these titles are edited and published in developing countries. Close to 90 percent of the titles publish Open Access editions, with very few charging article processing fees. Their secret is operating on very low-overhead and obtaining some measure of institutional support (cf. Edgar and Willinsky 2010).

In both its research and development initiatives, PKP continues to be funded, as it was originally, by a range of different government and foundation grants.[2] In 2012, however, PKP introduced two new funding models to ensure its sustainability, which involved growing responsibilities around the expanded number of

---

[1]  PKP: http://pkp.sfu.ca/support/forum

[2]  PKP Funding Partners: http://pkp.sfu.ca/funding_partners

journals and conferences dependent on its software. The two models involved, first of all, strengthening PKP's hosting services for journals and conferences using its free software, and, secondly, the creation of an institutional sponsorship program for research libraries, many of which were now providing PKP software to their institutions.

On the hosting side, what was once a fledgling, ad-hoc initiative at Simon Fraser University Library to mount journals was established as a distinct venture, dubbed PKP Publishing Services (PKP|PS).[3]

The growth and professionalization of PKP|PS has required a deeper level of commitment to infrastructure: hardware, network uptime, and software management across hundreds of installed instances of OJS, OCS and OMP. PKP|PS currently hosts over 200 journals and conferences (with a small number of OMP instances on the way), and now acts as a significant funding resource for PKP, not to mention a critical vector for feedback from invested, informed, and day-to-day users of the software.

Perhaps more significant for giving PKP a stronger institutional base, however, is its sponsorship program, which has now over 30 participating institutions.[4]

Interested research libraries can sponsor the project directly on an annual basis, or can become more involved as development partners. Development partners are just that: they have access to the core PKP development team and are deeply involved in long-term technical and administrative planning. This represents a new model for PKP, which has traditionally been a very small and tight-knit group of developers. Opening the team to a larger community is not without its challenges in coordinating the work among different teams and locations. It is important to stress here, however, that this isn't simply a solution to PKP's financial problem. The sponsorship program provides a venue for PKP to interact with the larger scholarly community in a way that previously did not exist. It is an open invitation to participate as a patron and a peer in this project, and the investment of participation is equally if not more important to the fundamental goals of the project as any financial contribution.

## The PKP Systems

In introducing the operating principles at work in PKP's software, we are focusing on the themes of simplicity and interoperability that underlie are approach to supporting the managers, editors, authors, reviewers, copyeditors, layout designers, and proofreaders, among others involved in the workflow that defines scholarly publishing. Our goal has always been to build systems that are not simply free to use, but are easier to use to do the quality work that those in scholarly

---

[3] PKP Publishing Services: http://pkpservices.sfu.ca

[4] PKP Sponsorships: http://pkp.sfu.ca/sponsorships

publishing has always involved. We have sought to build systems that not only support the workflow that results in a sharing of research but that are instructive and informative around the standards that have historically developed around these practices, so that others who have not been previously part of the scholarly publishing community could begin to participate and contribute, as they were walked through the process by the software design. We have, in this process, pursued a number of holy grails, among them, the design of intuitive systems and the production of automated systems. We continue down this path, not without our Monty Python moments, having realized that scholarly publishing is not an inherently intuitive process nor one that can be readily automated. We have reduced the clerical tasks and greatly increased the portability of the editorial office, and a good deal more than that, of course, as we outline in what follows.

## (a) Simplicity in Technical Administration

All PKP application system requirements are both *low* and *broad*: all that is needed to run OJS, OCS or OMP is a web server running PHP and a common database system (MySQL or PostgreSQL). PKP also actively supports older versions of PHP, MySQL and PostgreSQL, out of consideration for users who may not have access to newer technology. Users who download and install PKP applications are often definitively non-technical, and so special care has been taken to ensure that the installation and maintenance processes and documentation is easy to understand and uncomplicated. The installation process is straightforward and can be accomplished in a matter of minutes. Application maintenance, including backing up files and general upkeep, is also simple and well documented. After installing OJS, OCS or OMP, the site administrator can create one or more journal, conference or press instance on the site. Each instance takes only a second to create; after they have been created, separate journal managers can be enrolled in each instance, and these journal managers subsequently take over day-to-day administration tasks.

## (b) Simplicity in Management

After the journal, conference or press has been created, the manager completes a guided setup process where all core components related to publishing workflow, author and submission management, guidelines (author, reviewer, editing, etc.), publishing, indexing, and the look and feel of the site are configured. (In OJS, the setup is a five-step process; in OCS, it is a six-step process; in OMP the process is a bit more extensive, with separate setup steps for press, website, publication, distribution and user management; there is an initial wizard available for quick press configuration, however.)

This stepwise workflow has been created and adhered to with different goals in mind. For the new manager, these workflows provide a guided tour through many of the options they must consider before they publish: OJS includes prompts for ISSN information and a publication schedule, for example, while OMP provides comprehensive series and category configuration options. For the experienced manager, these setup options are easily and centrally accessible for periodic review.

This isn't a case of "simple is as simple does," however. A great deal of behind-the-scenes automation and task/service management is included in OCS, OJS and OMP, and all three applications offer far more capability than may be assumed from their relatively straightforward configuration processes. Most of these services involve promoting accessibility and visibility of the journal's published content on the web. For example, Google Scholar requires article information to be available to its web crawlers in very specific ways; OJS does this automatically, with no further configuration needed.[5]

### (c) Simplicity of Submission

Each application's submission process has been refined to be as simple as possible for new and experienced authors alike. Each application uses a multi-step submission process (no more than five steps in any application). Each step serves a specific purpose, from informing the author of any copyright or other requirements; to providing submission indexing metadata; to requesting submission and/ or supplementary files; to confirming the submission. Authors are aware at all times of which step they are on, and what is needed of them. This process ensures that all information relevant to the submission is gathered at the very beginning, saving editors valuable time during later stages.

### (d) Simplicity of Review

While implementations differ as required by the publishing format, all three applications approach review and editing workflows in a philosophically similar way. Peer review is the key quality control for scholarly communication, as well as a source of improvement for this work. The review process, in particular for reviewers, must be kept as simple and quick as possible, as reviewers often have the least incentive to use the system and may balk at any impediment between themselves and the review proper. Typically, in the review process, the reviewer needs to agree to complete the review; download the submission files; and upload review comments and/or review files to the system. Reviewers may log in directly to the system to complete the review process, or editors may act on their behalf. To assist editors in selecting reviewers, the system tracks a reviewers previous record on areas of interest, time taken, number of reviews, and editor rating.

### (e) Simplicity of Editing and Production

All three systems handle editing differently. OCS includes a relatively minor editing step only if full paper submissions are being accepted by the conference, whereas OJS and OMP both have full-scale editing workflows which can include input from copyeditors, proofreaders, layout editors, and others. In the case of OMP, editing and production workflows are handled separately: copyediting of

---

[5] See Google Scholar: http://scholar.google.ca/intl/en/scholar/inclusion.html

final draft files are handled in an editing stage, and the creation of production-ready files (eBooks, PDFs, and so on) and the completion of all catalog information for that particular manuscript are managed in a final production stage.

# The PKP Program

## (a) Enhancing Interoperability

The PKP development team actively pursues software interoperability with different applications, frameworks and platforms where appropriate. Interoperability is ideally facilitated via open, widely used and time-tested APIs, standards and protocols. A number of interoperability standards common to the library and scholarly publishing worlds have enjoyed a long history of support within PKP, and support for new standards is added regularly (and in many cases in the form of contributed plugins from the larger community).

Various information interchange mechanisms enjoy broad support across the PKP applications. All three applications support the Open Archives Initiative Protocol for Metadata Harvesting (OAI-PMH), which provides machine access to published article (or book, or presentation) metadata for the use of indexing systems. Another source of interoperability comes from following XML standards, particularly journal publishing standards such as the National Library of Medicine (NLM) Journal Publishing Tag Set, have proven crucial to PKP's efforts to provide open, structured access to published scholarly content. XML is particularly well-suited to sharing data and metadata online between applications, as it is human- and machine-readable.

Other discrete interoperability projects are currently underway. PKP is partnering with the Dataverse Network initiative at Harvard to develop a set of plugins that will provide deposit and display functionality between OJS and Dataverse repositories.[6] At the same time, the project is also working with the Public Library of Science (PLoS) to provide Altmetrics[7] for PKP applications, and with ORCID to provide author disambiguation services.[8] These services are usually implemented as plugins, and allow different levels of access to data and metadata for different online services and platforms, typically with very little needed in terms of additional setup. Most importantly however, the service standards and protocols are open, understood, and widely accepted throughout the scholarly and academic library communities, ensuring a broad level of support and interoperability for PKP applications.

---

[6] Dataverse Network. http://thedata.org

[7] PLOS Article-Level Metrics: http://article-level-metrics.plos.org/alm-info/

[8] Altmetrics: http://www.altmetric.com/; Orcid: http://about.orcid.org/

(b) **Enhancing Accessibility**

PKP promotes access to scholarly content in a number of ways. Interoperability via open standards and services, discussed above, is of key importance to accessibility: providing multiple access methods to content will of course increase exposure. In this fashion, journals may have their content harvested by OAI-capable metadata harvesters, can provide article DOI information to CrossRef, can deposit into PubMed's MEDLINE indexing service.[9] All PKP applications are search-engine-friendly, and include special HTML "meta" tags that are used by Google Scholar to identify and present content properly. In addition, the application's HTML is written to specific standards, and special care is taken to ensure general accessibility across a wide variety of browsers and operating system.

(c) **Enhancing Openness**

*Open Source Software*
PKP software applications have always been released as open source software, under the General Public License.[10]

The software is free in two ways: It is free to download and use; and the source code is freely available to download, view, and modify. There are a number of reasons why PKP publishes these applications as open source software.

Firstly, our mandate to improve the access to and quality of scholarly research has been helped immensely by providing the software free of charge: Researchers from all over the world can download and use our software; in a very real sense, journals from Indonesia and Sri Lanka can operate on the same field (or quality of platform) as journals from the United States and Germany.

Secondly, our software has benefitted immeasurably from source code contributions from many, many members of the scholarly community. Almost all translations of the software have been contributed as code; bugs have been identified and in many cases fixed by community members; and new features (many in plugin format) have been contributed as well. Simply put, we would not have been able to attain the quality and breadth of our software without following an open source software community model.

Thirdly, while Open Access to scholarly research and open source software models are not necessarily explicitly interlinked, they do share some of the same philosophical underpinnings: Open Access to material; community collaboration; etc. Following an open Source licensing model makes as much sense as promoting an Open Access approach to scholarly research and to Open Science, more generally (cf. Willinsky 2005).

*Open Community*
PKP is a community project in many ways. The Project provides direct developer access to anyone, via the PKP support forums and wiki. Anyone can

---

[9]  CrossRef: http://www.crossref.org/

[10]  Specifically, the GPL V2. See GNU Operating System.

register on the forum and interact directly with the PKP development team for technical support or development inquiries. The support forum also exists as an active venue for questions and conversations from editors, with questions ranging from accessibility, indexing and DOIs to how typical review and editorial work-flows typically work.

This community engagement is international. PKP seeks to cooperate with different community partners around the world (including translators, developers, and supportive institutions in Europe, Africa, Latin America, China, and else-where). PKP has worked with INASP and other organizations in delivering scholarly publishing workshops in many parts of the world. It was worked with INASP to build portals such as African Journals Online and Asia Journals Online, which have created an online presence in Google Scholar and elsewhere for hundreds of title.[11] In addition, many independent user and training groups have popped up throughout the world, operating without direct PKP support—for example, one partner in Spain has developed an entire OJS training program and support forum, while another, with IBICT in Brasilia has been offering workshops across the country for years.[12] That these community initiatives are blossoming internationally, and largely without direct support from PKP, is a welcome marker of success, and an indication of the broad acceptance of PKP software as a scholarly publishing standard internationally.

*Open Access*

A key goal of PKP is to promote Open Access to scholarly research. As such it is part of growing Open Access movement. Open Access was initially, at the turn of the century, a radical challenge to the old print model, but it is now increasingly embraced not just by small independent scholar-publishers, where it got its start, but by the largest of scholarly publishing corporations, just as it is being supported by government legislation requiring Open Access for funded research, with every sign that Open Access may well become the norm for publishing research (cf. Laakso and Björk 2012; Björk and Peatau 2012). With the development of mega-journals, such as *PLoS One* publishing tens of thousands of Open Access articles a year, and increasing use of "article processing fees" to guarantee that Open Access can be a source of revenue, the momentum and incentive is transforming the industry (cf. Frank 2012). While PKP continues to largely serve smaller Open Access journals operated by scholar-publishers, efforts are underway to adapt its approach to make the mega-journal model among the options that it offers to the academic community.

*Open Education*

One of the challenges for sustaining, enhancing, and increasing Open Access is lack of professional publishing experience among many in the growing commu-nity. A new initiative of PKP is the development of tuition-free, open, online training courses in the use of PKP software and online publishing and management

---

[11]  African Journals Online: http://www.ajol.info/; Asia Journals Online: http://www.asiajol.info/

[12]  OJS.es: http://www.ojs.es/; IBICT: http://www.ibict.br/

skills.[13] Working in conjunction with partners such as the International Network for the Availability of Scientific Publications (INASP) and the Publishing Studies Department at Kwame Nkrumah University Of Science and Technology (KNUST) in Ghana, this new education program will help build local capacity for online publishing and sustainable Open Access.[14]

### (d) Enhancing Knowledge

The fundamental purpose of the Public Knowledge Project is to enhance the quality of scholarly communication and global knowledge sharing. By providing free and open source tools for professional monograph, journal, and conference management, PKP has enabled scholars from around the world to launch their own online publications with little or no money, and to build scholarly communities around their areas of interest, and to share the results of their research with all (cf. Willinsky and Mendis 2007).

Discussions of the developing world and Open Access often revolve around making research from the leading publications from the developed world more widely available. Programs such as HINARI, AGORA, and OARE have made significant gains in this area.[15] While this is no doubt important, it is equally important for researchers in the developed world (and elsewhere) to hear the voices from the South. In the past, a leading publisher may have rejected the knowledge generated by a Ghanaian researcher because the significance of her work was not understood or valued. She could instead publish it in a local print-based research publication, but it would have a very limited readership, with physical copies not making it far beyond her country's borders. With the increasing availability of the Internet in Africa, although still a challenge, and the existence of free and open source tools for professional publishing, she has new options. Locally produced online journals, with a global community of editors, authors, and reviewers are increasingly available as a forum for her work, and where a suitable local option doesn't exist, she can now choose to collaborate with colleagues to start her own online journal.

## Conclusion

The Public Knowledge Project has worked hard with a good number of organizations and institutions, editors and publishers, over the course of the last decade-and- a-half to increase the options and alternatives available to the global community of scholars and researchers. In the face of this new publishing medium that has transformed so many aspects of communication, and with even more

---

[13] PKP School: http://pkpschool.org

[14] INASP: http://www.inasp.info/; KNUST: http://www.knust.edu.gh/pages/

[15] Research4Life: http://www.research4life.org/

changes clearly in the offing, it is too early to know or even predict what models and methods are going to prevail as the digital era of scholarly communication continues to unfold. Our project has always been to demonstrate ways in which these new directions and opportunities might uphold long-standing historical principles of openness, community, cooperation, experimentation, and questioning that continue to underwrite the work of research and learning. The continuing success of this work relies not only on the open nature of the project, but on the passion and interests of this larger community in their desire to contribute ideas and knowledge, as well as the always appreciated instances of well-formed code.

# References

Benkler, Y. (2006). *The wealth of networks: How social production transforms markets and freedom*, New Haven, USA: Yale University Press. Available at: http://cyber.law.harvard.edu/wealth_of_networks/.

Björk, B.-C., & Paetau, P. (2012). Open Access to the scientific journal literature—status and challenges for the information systems community. *Bulletin of the American Society for Information Science and Technology, 38*(5), 39–44. doi:10.1002/bult.2012.1720380512.

Edgar, B.D., & Willinsky, J. (2010). A survey of scholarly journals using Open Journal System. *Scholarly and Research Communication*, 1(2). Available at: http://src-online.ca/index.php/src/article/view/24/41.

Frank, (2012). Megajournals. *Trading Knowledge*. Available at: http://occamstypewriter.org/trading-knowledge/2012/07/09/megajournals/.

Laakso, M., & Björk, B.-C. (2012). Anatomy of Open Access publishing: a study of longitudinal development and internal structure. *BMC Medicine, 10*(1), 124. doi:10.1186/1741-7015-10-124.

Suber, P. (Ed.), (2012). What is Open Access? *In Open Access*. Massachusetts (pp.1–27). USA: MIT Press.

Willinsky, J. (1999). *Technologies of knowing: a proposal for the human sciences*. Boston, Mass.: Beacon Press.

Willinsky, J. (2005). The unacknowledged convergence of open source, Open Access, and Open Science. *First Monday*, 10(8). Available at: http://firstmonday.org/htbin/cgiwrap/bin/ojs/index.php/fm/article/view/1265/1185.

Willinsky, J. (2009). The stratified economics of Open Access. *Economic Analysis and Policy, 39*(1), 53–70.

Willinsky, J., & Mendis, R. (2007). Open Access on a zero budget: a case study of Postcolonial Text. *Information Research*, 12(3). Available at: http://www.aughty.org/pdf/postcolonial_text.pdf.

# Part III
# Vision

# Altmetrics and Other Novel Measures for Scientific Impact

**Martin Fenner**

*Good science, original work, always went beyond the body of received opinion, always represented a dissent from orthodoxy. However, then, could the orthodox fairly assess it ?*
—Richard Rhodes mod. from Michael Polanyi in "Making of the Atomic Bomb"

**Abstract** Impact assessment is one of the major drivers in scholarly communication, in particular since the number of available faculty positions and grants has far exceeded the number of applications. Peer review still plays a critical role in evaluating science, but citation-based bibliometric indicators are becoming increasingly important. This chapter looks at a novel set of indicators that can complement both citation analysis and peer review. Altmetrics use indicators gathered in the real-time Social Web to provide immediate feedback about scholarly works. We describe the most important altmetrics and provide a critical assessment of their value and limitations.

## Introduction

Impact assessment of researchers and their research is central to scholarly communication. In the last 25 years, we have seen a shift from individual qualitative assessment by peers to systematic quantitative assessment using citation analysis of journal articles. Arguably the impact of research can not be quantified, and citation analysis falls short of a comprehensive analysis, but the journal as a filter for relevant scholarly content and the Journal Impact Factor as a tool to quantify the relevance of journals are at the core of how research is communicated and evaluated today.

The central role of the journal (to distribute, filter, and help evaluate scholarly content) has dramatically changed with the shift from print to electronic publishing, and is no longer appropriate for the assessment of impact. We can look at

M. Fenner (✉)
Public Library of Science, San Francisco, CA, USA
e-mail: mfenner@plos.org

S. Bartling and S. Friesike (eds.), *Opening Science*,
DOI: 10.1007/978-3-319-00026-8_12, © The Author(s) 2014

citations of individual articles, and at other measures of impact using usage stats and the Social Web. Moreover, impact assessment does not have to be confined to journal articles; research outputs such as data publication can also be assessed.

Altmetrics is a young discipline that looks at new metrics based on the Social Web for analyzing scholarship. Altmetrics are complementary to the citation-based filters which we have relied upon for the past 50 years and try to overcome some of their shortcomings: citations are slow to accumulate, and often miss new forms of scholarly content such as datasets, software, and research blogs (Priem et al. 2012a).

Altmetrics are challenging this established system, and are therefore seen by many as either an opportunity or a threat to the current system of scholarly communication. This potential makes altmetrics both fascinating and challenging, as many discussions about altmetrics are often intermixed with other ideas about how to change scholarly communication.

## Terminology

**Scientometrics** is the science of measuring and analysing science.

**Bibliometrics** is a major subdiscipline of scientometrics which measures the impact of scientific publications. Citation analysis is the most popular application of bibliometrics.

**Usage-based metrics** use usage data (pageviews, document downloads, etc.) to assess scholarly impact. The concept was popularized by the COUNTER (Counting Online Usage of NeTworked Electronic Resources) and MESUR (MEtrics from Scholarly Usage of Resources) projects.

**Altmetrics** is the creation and study of new metrics based on the Social Web for analyzing and informing scholarship (Altmetrics Manifesto[1]). Altmetrics is a sub-discipline of scientometrics. Altmetrics typically looks at individual research outputs, including journal articles or datasets.

**Article-level metrics** are a comprehensive and multidimensional suite of trans-parent and established metrics at the article level.[2] They collect and provide metrics for individual articles, rather than aggregating them per journal. Article-level metrics include citations, usage data, and altmetrics. Article-level metrics are typically associated with the publisher Public Library of Science (PLOS), who

---

[1]  Altmetrics: http://altmetrics.org/about

[2]  PLOS Article-Level Metrics: http://article-level-metrics.plos.org/alm-info/

introduced them for all of their articles in 2009. Altmetrics and article-level metrics are sometimes used interchangeably, but there are important differences:

- Article-level metrics also include citations and usage data
- Altmetrics can also be applied to other research outputs, such as research data

**Metrics for other research works**—presentations, datasets, software, etc.—typically include usage statistics and altmetrics, but also citations.

**Author-level metrics** aggregate the metrics of all research by a specific author. Metrics can also be aggregated by institution, discipline, etc.

**Post-publication peer review** is the process whereby scientific studies are absorbed into the body of knowledge (Smith 2011). This definition is much broader and does not just include activities that are traditionally described as peer review. In contrast to metrics, the focus is on the discussion of a paper in comments, blog posts, and citations. A broader term with similar meaning is post-publication activity.

## History

In 2008 Dario Taraborelli published a paper on soft peer review, advocating social bookmarking tools for post-publication peer review (Taraborelli 2008). Neylon and Wu described the PLOS Article-Level Metrics service launched in 2009 in an article published the same year (Neylon and Wu 2009). Priem and Hemminger published an article in July 2010 that describes scientometrics 2.0 and called for new metrics based on Web 2.0 tools (Priem and Hemminger 2010). Groth and Gurney studied chemistry science blogging about scholarly papers and presented their findings at the Web Science Conference 2010 (Groth and Gurney 2010). The Altmetrics manifesto was published in October 2010 by Jason Priem, Dario Taraborelli, Paul Groth and Cameron Neylon (Priem et al. 2010).

ReaderMeter is a web service that tracks the number of Mendeley readers of all papers of a particular author. ReaderMeter was launched in late 2010 and is the first working altmetrics service. The first altmetrics workshop was was altmetrics11, held at the ACM Web Science Conference 2011 Workshop[3] in June 2011. Hackathons are an important part of altmetrics history: a working prototype for Total Impact (now ImpactStory) was put together at the Beyond Impact conference in May 2011, and the idea of the ScienceCard project started at the Science Online London conference in September 2011. Three of the 11 finalists of the Mendeley/PLOS Binary Battle programming contest in September 2011 were altmetrics applications. In 2012, we saw the launch of several altmetrics services, more publishers implementing altmetrics for their journal articles, and an increasing number of presentations and workshops dedicated to altmetrics.

---

[3] ACM Web Science 2011: http://www.websci11.org/

## Scholarly Research

Two workshops dedicated to altmetrics research and associated with the ACM Web Science conference were held: June 2011 in Koblenz, Germany and June 2012 in Evanston, IL.

PLOS ONE launched the Altmetrics collection in October 2012, with initially 7 research articles published since June 2009.[4]

Much early altmetrics research has examined reference managers, particularly Mendeley and CiteULike. Li et al. (2011) found 92 % of Nature and Science articles in their sample had been bookmarked by one or more Mendeley users, and 60 % by one or more CiteULike users. Bar-Ilan (2012) showed 97 % coverage of recent JASIST articles in Mendeley. Priem et al. (2012) reported that the coverage of articles published in the PLOS journals was 80 % in Mendeley and 31 % in CiteULike. Sampling 1,397 F1000 Genomics and Genetics papers, Li and Thelwall (2012) found that 1,389 of those had Mendeley bookmarks.

Studies have consistently found moderate correlation between reference manager bookmarks and Web of Science (WoS) citations. Li et al. (2011) showed $r = 0.55$ of Mendeley and $r = 0.34$ of CiteULike readers with WoS citations respectively. Weller and Peters (2012) report similar correlation values for a different article set between Mendeley, CiteULike, BibSonomy, and Scopus. Bar-Ilan (2012) found a correlation of $r = 0.46$ between Mendeley readership counts and WoS citations for articles in JASIST. User-citation correlations for sampled Nature and Science publications were 0.56 (Li et al. 2011); Priem et al. (2012b) report a correlation of 0.5 between WoS citations and Mendeley users articles published by the Open-Access publisher PLOS.

Twitter has also attracted significant interest from altmetrics researchers. Priem and Costello (2010) and Priem and Costello (2011) report that scholars use Twitter as a professional medium for discussing articles, while Eysenbach (2011) found that highly-tweeted articles were 11 times more likely become highly-cited later. Analyzing the use of Twitter during scientific conferences, Weller and Puschmann (2011) and Letierce et al. (2010) report that there was discipline-specific tweeting behavior regarding topic and number of tweets, as well as references to different document types including journal articles, blogs, and slides. Other sources have examined additional data sources besides reference managers and Twitter, investigating examined citation from Wikipedia articles (Nielsen 2007) and blogs (Groth and Gurney 2010; Shema et al. 2012) as sources of alternative impact data.

---

[4] PLOS Collections: http://www.ploscollections.org/altmetrics

# Use Cases

Altmetrics can complement traditional bibliometrics in a number of scenarios:

- Metrics as a discovery tool
- Data-driven stories about the post-publication reception of research
- Business intelligence for a journal, university or funder
- Evaluation of the impact of research and researchers

## *Metrics as a Discovery Tool*

Information overflow has become a major problem, and it has become clear that relying on the journal as a filter is no longer an appropriate strategy. Altmetrics have the potential to help in the discovery process, especially if combined with more traditional keyword-based search strategies, and with the social network information of the person seeking information. The advantage over citation based metrics is that we don't have to wait years before we can see meaningful numbers. The free Altmetric PLOS Impact Explorer[5] is an example for a discovery tool based on altmetrics and highlights recently published PLOS papers with a lot of social media activity. Altmetric.com also provides a commercial service for content from other publishers.

## *Data-Driven Stories About The Post-Publication Reception of Research*

Altmetrics can help researchers demonstrate the impact of their research, in particular if the research outputs are not journal articles, but datasets, software, etc., and if the impact is best demonstrated in metrics other than citations. ImpactStory[6] focuses on this use case. Often creators of web-native scholarly products like datasets, software, and blog posts are hard pressed to demonstrate the impact of their work, given a reward system built for a paper-based scholarly publishing world. In these cases, ImpactStory helps to provide data to establish the impacts of these products and allow forward-thinking researcher. ImpactStory also gathers altmetrics to demonstrate wider impacts of traditional products, tracking their impact through both traditional citations and novel altmetrics.

---

[5] Altmetric: http://www.altmetric.com/demos/plos.html

[6] ImpactStory: http://impactstory.org

## Business Intelligence for a Journal, University or Funder

The focus is not on the individual article, but rather on overall trends over time and/or across funding programs, disciplines, etc. This is an area that the typical researchers is usually less interested in, but is important for strategic decisions by departments, universities, funding organizations, publishers, and others. This area has been dominated by large commercial bibliographic databases such as Web of Science or Scopus, using citation data. Plum Analytics[7] is a new service that also provide altmetrics and is focusing on universities. The publisher PLOS[8] makes a comprehensive set of citations, usage data and altmetrics available for all articles they published.

## Altmetrics as an Evaluation Tool

Traditional scholarly metrics are often used as an evaluation tool, including inappropriate uses such as using the Journal Impact Factor to evaluate publications of individual researchers. Before altmetrics can be used for evaluation, the following questions need to be addressed:

• Can numbers reflect the impact of research, across disciplines and over time?
• Does the use of metrics for evaluation create undesired incentives?
• Do the currently available altmetrics really measure impact or something else?
• How can we standardize altmetrics?
• How easily can altmetrics be changed by self-promotion and gaming?

The first two questions relate to more general aspects of using scientometrics for evaluation, whereas the last three questions are more specific for altmetrics. All these issues can be solved, but it will probably take some time before altmetrics can be reasonably used for evaluation.

Author-level metrics can also include citations and usage stats. Citations are a more established metric for impact evaluation, and citations based on individual articles are much more meaningful than the metrics for the journal that a researcher has published in. The Hirsch-Index (or h index, Hirsch 2005) is a popular metric to quantify an individual's scientific research output. The h index is defined as the number of papers with citation number $\geq h$, e.g. an h index of 15 means a researcher has published at least 15 papers that have been cited at least 15 times.

---

[7] Plum Analytics: http://www.plumanalytics.com

[8] PLOS Article-Level Metrics: http://article-level-metrics.plos.org

## Example Metrics and Providers

A growing number of metrics are used by the altmetrics community, and the most important metrics and providers are listed below. Not all metrics measure scholarly impact, some of them are indicators of attention, and in rare cases self-promotion. Some metrics are good indicators of activity by scholars (e.g. citations or Mendeley bookmarks), whereas other metrics reflect the attention by the general public (e.g. Facebook or HTML views) (Table 1).

Metrics describe different activities: usage stats look at the initial activity of reading the abstract and downloading the paper, whereas citations are the result of much more work, they therefore account for less than 0.5 % of all HTML views. Altmetrics tries to capture the activities that happen between viewing a paper and citing it, from saving an article to informal online discussions.

## *Mendeley*

Mendeley is one of the most widely used altmetrics services—the number of articles with Mendeley bookmarks is similar to the number of articles that have ciations. Mendeley provides information about the number of readers and groups. In contrast to CiteULike no usernames for readers are provided, but Mendeley provides basic information regarding demographics such as country and academic position. Mendeley is a social bookmarking tool used by scholars and the metrics probably reflect an important scholarly activity—adding a downloaded article to a reference manager.

## *CiteULike*

CiteULike is another social bookmarking tool, not as widely used as Mendeley and without reference manager functionality. One advantage over Mendeley is that usernames and dates for all sharing events are publicly available, making it easier to explore the bookmarking activity over time.

**Table 1** Categorizing metrics into target audiences and depth of interaction (cf. ImpactStory 2012)

|             | Scholars                                   | Public                        |
|-------------|--------------------------------------------|-------------------------------|
| Discussed   | Science blogs, journal comments            | Blogs, Twitter, Facebook, etc.|
| Recommended | Citations by editorials, Faculty of 1,000  | Press release                 |
| Cited       | Citations, full-text mentions              | Wikipedia mentiones           |
| Saved       | CiteULike, Mendeley                        | Delicious, Facebook           |
| Viewed      | PDF downloads                              | HTML views                    |

## *Twitter*

Collecting tweets linking to scholarly papers is challenging, because they are only stored for short periods of time (typically around 7 days). There is a lot of Twitter activity around papers, and only a small fraction is from the authors and/or journal. With some journals up to 90 % of articles are tweeted, the number for new PLOS journal articles is currently at about 50 %. The Twitter activity typically peeks a few days after publication, and probably reflects attention rather than impact.

## *Facebook*

Facebook is almost as popular as Twitter with regards to scholarly content, and provides a wider variety of interactions (likes, shares and comments). Facebook activity is a good indicator for public interest in a scholarly article and correlates more with HTML views than PDF downloads.

## *Wikipedia*

Scholarly content is frequently linked from Wikipedia, covering about 6 % of all journal articles in the case of PLOS. The Wikipedia Cite-o-Meter[9] by Dario Taraborelli and Daniel Mietchen calculates the number of Wikipedia links per publisher. In the English Wikipedia the most frequently cited publisher is Elsevier with close to 35,000 links. In addition to Wikipedia pages, links to scholarly articles are also found on user and file pages.

## *Science Blogs*

Blog posts talking about papers and other scholarly content are difficult to track. Many science bloggers use a blog aggregator, Research Blogging, Nature Blogs and ScienceSeeker being the most popular ones. The number of scholarly articles discussed in blog posts is small (e.g. less than 5 % of all PLOS articles), but they provide great background information and can sometimes generate a lot of secondary activity around the original paper (both social media activity and downloads).

---

[9] Wikipedia Cite-o-Meter: http://toolserver.org/~dartar/cite-o-meter/

## Altmetrics Service Providers

Comprehensive altmetrics are currently only available from a small number of service providers. This will most likely change in the near future, as more organizations become interested both in analyzing altmetrics for their content (publishers, universities, funders) or for providing altmetrics as a service.

The Open Access publisher Public Library of Science (PLOS) was the first organization to routinely provide altmetrics on a large number of scholarly articles. The first version of their article-level metrics service was started in March 2009, and PLOS currently provides usage data, citations and social web activity from 13 different data sources. The article-level metrics data are provided via an open API[10] and as monthly public data dump.

Altmetric.com is a commercial start-up that started in July 2011. They maintain a cluster of servers that watch social media sites, newspapers and magazines for any mentions of scholarly articles. The data are available to individual users and as service for publishers.

ImpactStory is a non-profit service providing altmetrics since late 2011. They provide both altmetrics and traditional (citation) impact metrics for both traditional and web-native scholarly products, and are designed to help researchers better share and be rewarded for their complete impacts.

Plum Analytics is a start-up providing altmetrics data to universities and libraries. They also provide usage stats and citation data, and track research outputs beyond journal articles, e.g. presentations, source code and datasets.

At this time it is unclear how the altmetrics community will develop over the next few years. It is possible that one or a few dominant commercial players emerge similar to the market for citations, that a non-profit organization is collected these numbers for all stakeholders, or that we see the development of a more distributed system with data and service providers, similar to how usage data for articles are distributed.

## Challenges and Criticism

Many challenges remain before we can expect altmetrics to be more widely adopted. A big part of the challenge is the very nature of the Social Web, which is much more difficult to analyze than traditional scholarly citations.

1. the constantly changing nature of the Social Web, including the lack of commonly used persistent identifiers
2. self-promotion and gaming, inherit to all Social Web activities, and aggravated by the difficulty of understanding who is talking

---

[10] GitHub: https://github.com/articlemetrics/alm/wiki/API

3. Altmetrics is more interested in things that can be measured, rather than things that are meaningful for scholarly impact. We therefore measure attention or self-promotion instead of scholarly impact.

These challenges are less of a problem for discovery tools based on altmetrics, but are hard to solve for evaluation tools. Altmetrics is still a young discipline and the community is working hard on these and other questions, including standards, anti-gaming mechanisms, and ways to put metrics into context.

# References

Bar-Ilan, J. (2012). *JASIST@mendeley*, Available at: http://altmetrics.org/altmetrics12/bar-ilan/.
Eysenbach, G. (2011). Can Tweets predict citations? metrics of social impact based on Twitter and correlation with traditional metrics of scientific impact. *Journal of Medical Internet Research*, 13(4), p.e123. doi:10.2196/jmir.2012.
Groth, P., & Gurney, T. (2010). Studying scientific discourse on the web using bibliometrics: A chemistry blogging case study. In *Proceedings of the WebSci10: Extending the Frontiers of Society On-Line, April* 26–27th 2010. Raleigh, NC, USA. Available at: http://journal.webscience.org/308/.
Smith, R. (2011). What is post publication peer review? *BMJ Group Blogs*. Available at: http://blogs.bmj.com/bmj/2011/04/06/richard-smith-what-is-post-publication-peer-review/.
Hirsch, J.E. (2005). An index to quantify an individual's scientific research output. *Proceedings of the National Academy of Sciences*, 102(46), pp.16569–16572. doi:10.1073/pnas.0507655102.
ImpactStory, (2012). A new framework for altmetrics. *ImpactStory blog.* Available at: http://blog.impactstory.org/2012/09/14/31524247207/.
Letierce, J. et al. (2010). Using Twitter during an academic conference: The #iswc2009 Use-Case. In *Proceedings of the Fourth International AAAI Conference on Weblogs and Social Media.* Available at: http://www.aaai.org/ocs/index.php/ICWSM/ICWSM10/paper/view/1523.
Li, X., & Thelwall, M. (2012). F1000, Mendeley and traditional bibliometric indicators. Available at: http://sticonference.org/Proceedings/vol2/Li_F1000_541.pdf.
Li, X., Thelwall, M., & Giustini, D. (2011). Validating online reference managers for scholarly impact measurement. *Scientometrics, 91*(2), 461–471. doi:10.1007/s11192-011-0580-x.
Neylon, C., & Wu, S. (2009). Article-Level metrics and the evolution of scientific impact. *PLoS Biology*, 7(11), p.e1000242. doi:10.1371/journal.pbio.1000242.
Nielsen, F.A. (2007). Scientific citations in Wikipedia. *First Monday*, 12(8). Available at: http://firstmonday.org/article/view/1997/1872.
Priem, J. et al. (2010). altmetrics: a manifesto. *altmetrics.* Available at: http://altmetrics.org/manifesto/.
Priem, J., & Costello, K.L. (2010b). How and why scholars cite on Twitter. *Proceedings of the American Society for Information Science and Technology*, 47(1), pp.1–4. doi:10.1002/meet.14504701201.
Priem, J., Costello, K.L., & Dzuba, (2011). *Poster at Metrics* 2011: *Symposium on Informetric and Scientometric Research.*

Priem, J., & Hemminger, B.M. (2010). Scientometrics 2.0: Toward new metrics of scholarly impact on the social web. *First Monday*, 15(7). Available at: http://firstmonday.org/htbin/cgiwrap/bin/ojs/index.php/fm/article/view/2874/2570.

Priem, J., Groth, P., & Taraborelli, D. (2012a). The Altmetrics Collection Ouzounis C. A. (Ed.), *PLoS ONE*, 7(11), p.e48753. doi:10.1371/journal.pone.0048753.

Priem, J., Piwowar, H.A., & Hemminger, B.M. (2012b). Altmetrics in the wild: Using social media to explore scholarly impact. Available at: arXiv:1203.4745v1.

Shema, H., Bar-Ilan, J., & Thelwall, M. (2012). Research Blogs and the discussion of scholarly information Ouzounis C. A. (Ed.), *PLoS ONE*, 7(5), p.e35869. doi:10.1371/journal.pone.0035869.

Taraborelli, D. (2008). Soft peer review: social software and distributed scientific evaluation. In P. Hassanaly et al. (Eds.), *Proceedings of the 8th International Conference on the Design of Cooperative Systems, Carry-le-Rouet*. Aix-en-Provence, France: Institut d'Etudes Politiques d'Aix-en-Provence, pp.99–110.

Weller, K., & Peters, I. (2012). Citations in Web 2.0. Available at: http://nfgwin.uni-duesseldorf.de/sites/default/files/Weller.pdf.

Weller, K., & Puschmann, C. (2011). *Poster presented at the 3rd International Conference on Web Science (ACM WebSci'11)*, Available at: http://files.ynada.com/posters/websci11.pdf.

# Dynamic Publication Formats and Collaborative Authoring

Lambert Heller, Ronald The and Sönke Bartling

*"We are Wikipedians. This means that we should be: kind, thoughtful, passionate about getting it right, open, tolerant of different viewpoints, open to criticism, bold about changing our policies and also cautious about changing our policies. We are not vindictive, childish, and we don't stoop to the level of our worst critics, no matter how much we may find them to be annoying."*
—*Jimmmy Wales*—one of the founders of *Wikipedia.*

**Abstract** While Online Publishing has replaced most traditional printed journals in less than twenty years, today's Online Publication Formats are still closely bound to the medium of paper. Collaboration is mostly hidden from the readership, and 'final' versions of papers are stored in 'publisher PDF' files mimicking print. Meanwhile new media formats originating from the web itself bring us new modes of transparent collaboration, feedback, continued refinement, and reusability of (scholarly) works: Wikis, Blogs and Code Repositories, to name a few. This chapter characterizes the potentials of Dynamic Publication Formats and analyzes necessary prerequisites. Selected tools specific to the aims, stages, and functions of Scholarly Publishing are presented. Furthermore, this chapter points out early examples of usage and further development from the field. In doing so, Dynamic Publication Formats are described as (a) a 'parallel universe' based on the commodification of (scholarly) media, and (b) as a much needed complement, slowly recognized and incrementally integrated

L. Heller (✉)
German National Library of Science and Technology, Welfengarten 1B 30167 Hanover, Germany
e-mail: heller@ub.fu-berlin.de

R. The
University of Design, Schwäbisch Gmünd, Germany
e-mail: rt@infotectures.com

S. Bartling
German Cancer Research Center, Heidelberg, Germany
e-mail: soenkebartling@gmx.de

S. Bartling
Institute for Clinical Radiology and Nuclear Medicine, Mannheim University Medical Center, Heidelberg University, Mannheim, Germany

S. Bartling and S. Friesike (eds.), *Opening Science*,
DOI: 10.1007/978-3-319-00026-8_13, © The Author(s) 2014

into more efficient and dynamic workflows of production, improvement, and dissemination of scholarly knowledge in general.

## Introduction

The knowledge creation process is highly dynamic. However, most of current means of scholarly publications are static, that means, they cannot be revised over time. Novel findings or results cannot contribute to the publications once published, instead a new publication has to be released. Dynamic publication formats will change this. Dynamic publication formats are bodies of text/graphic/rich media that can be changed quickly and easily while at the same time being available to a wide audience.

In this chapter we will discuss dynamic scholarly publication formats with respect to their chances, advantages, and challenges. First, we begin with a revision of existing and past publishing concepts. We discuss how the growing body of scholarly knowledge was updated and evolved using static forms of publishing. This will be followed by a structured analysis of the characteristics of dynamic publication formats, followed by a presentation of currently implemented solutions that employ concepts of dynamic publications.

## Historic Dynamic Publishing Using Printed Journals and Books: Revising Editions or Publishing Novel Books and Articles

For centuries scholarly books were improved and updated with new content. This happened through releasing new editions. In subsequent editions, mistakes were corrected, recent results incorporated, and feedback from the readership used to improve the overall book. A sufficient demand for the reprinting of editions was a necessity. Before reprinting the publisher invited the author to revise the next edition ('revised editions'[1]). The changes were usually marked and introduced in the preface of the consecutive editions.

Many encyclopedias, handbooks, and schoolbooks became established brands, which have been revised over and over again, sometimes over the space of decades. In many examples the authors changed. In successive revisions parts were changed, paragraphs rewritten, and chapters removed or added. In particularly vivid fields a different 'genre' of book—the loose-paper-collections—were invented. Here, carefully revised pages were sent out to subscribers on a regular basis.

---

[1]  see *Wikipedia*: http://en.wikipedia.org/wiki/Edition_(book)#Revised_edition

Libraries provided not only access to the most recent version of books, but also kept earlier editions for interested readers. Earlier editions were of historical and epistemological interest. Recurrent book editions made it necessary to add the consecutive edition number when referencing revised books.

Revising books allowed authors to keep track with novel developments. A book usually presented a closed 'body of knowledge', a mere collection of indisputable knowledge, often with a review character. Textbooks or encyclopedias were specially structured books.

In contrast to books, scholarly articles were a snapshot of certain scientific knowledge. In most scholarly fields, research results were published only once. Scientific journal articles were not to be revised—if new findings occurred, new articles were published. Publishing became the currency of research and around the journal article methods to measure the performance of researchers were developed.

The scholarly journal article and its 'life cycle' are currently under debate and development. New mechanisms to publish scientific results are being widely discussed; most opportunities have been opened up by the new possibilities that were enabled by the Internet.

Some of the most prominent changes that have already found wide acceptance so far are being reviewed in the following:

## Preprint, Postprint and (Open) Peer Review

The fundamental interest of researchers is to publish their research results in a straightforward fashion. This is in conflict with the publishers' duties of filtering good research from faulty research, rejecting papers with methods that are insufficient to draw the stated conclusion, or denying research publication that are out of the scope of the journal's audience. The current gold standard supporting editorial decisions is the peer-review process as organized by the publishers. Since the peer-review process takes a significant amount of time and is one of the main causes of delaying publications, some research disciplines developed a culture of publishing so-called *preprints*. Preprints are preliminary, pre-peer-review versions of original research articles which are submitted to repositories such as arXiv (arxiv.org). It is acceptable to exchange preliminary versions with updates, for example updates with applied changes that occur during peer-review, but older versions are always available and cannot be removed. A publication identifier points to the most recent version of the article, but older versions can be assessed through a history function. Preprints are legally accepted by most journals. Some journals even combine the acceptance with preprints together with an open peer-review process in which all comments and changes can be tracked (Pöschl 2012). *Postprints* are versions of the article which are published after peer-review, usually by storing the article in repositories (see chapter Open Access: A State of the Art) or by sending them via email. They contain all the changes that have resulted from discourse with the peer-reviewers.

## Follow-Ups and Retractions

Publishing preprints, postprints, or even the peer-review process allows the tracking of the development of a final version of a scholarly article. Usually, after peer-review, a final version of an article exists which must not be further changed.

After publication of the article, it is of interest to see how the article is being received by the community. Its impact is measured by counting the amount of citations to it, references which result at article-level (see chapter Altmetrics and Other Measures for Scientific Impact). Databases such as the *Web of Science, Scopus, Google Scholar, ResearchGate*, and non-commercial services such as *Inspire* count these citations and provide more meta-analysis of articles. References to the article are visible and so follow-up articles can be identified. Current databases do not give information about the context of a citation. It remains unclear as to whether the article is referenced as a citation within the introduction, a reference to similar 'Materials and methods', or whether the cited article is being disputed in the discussion.

In cases of scientific misconduct, articles are retracted. Obviously, this happens more and more often (cf. Rice 2013). Similarly, universities retract dissertations and other scientific publications. Obviously, printed or downloaded articles cannot disappear in the same way that online version of articles can be deleted. Libraries and repositories keep the retracted books, articles, or dissertations in the archives and just change the catalogue status to 'retracted'. Publishers delete the online version and books are no longer sold.

## Current Aspects of the Publication System in Regard to the Dynamic Knowledge Creation Process

### *The Production Process is not Visible to the Reader*

With the advancement of the Internet, methods to cooperatively compile a text ('collaborative authoring tools') are finding wider application. It is now possible to trace each individual's contribution to a text. Technically, it would be possible to track all versions and comments that occur during the production process. Currently, final versions of scholarly publications do not contain traces of their production process. The final version of a publication is a kind of finalized consent from all its authors without any traces of the production process itself.

## *The Contribution of Individual Authors is not Visible*

Usually contributors to a scientific publication are stated in the list of authors. Large research organizations provide guidelines on the requirements to qualify as an author of an article. Only contributors should be listed as authors and there exist guidelines of good scientific practice so as to clarify what acceptable contributions are. Honorary authorships, e.g. authorships that are based on political considerations, are not considered appropriate.[2] The listing itself happens independently of the quantifiable amount of actual text contribution. However, often the placement and order of the authors give a hint on the amount and of the kind of contribution. Various cultures exist; in many disciplines (e.g. life sciences) the first and the last authors contributed most significantly to an article.

The distribution of third party funding is more and more based upon scientometric measurements which depend on authorship. Since the incentives are set that way, it is now very important to a researcher to have his contribution appropriately acknowledged. In this context, conventions on the good scientific practice guiding authorship qualifications have become much more important than in earlier times. This is especially true in the context of growing author lists and increasing manipulations. In practice, the distribution of authorship positions is a complex process, often involving a non-transparent system of social and professional dependencies.

## *Finalized Versions do not Allow Changes, Thus Making Corrections and Additions Nearly Impossible*

Despite the fact that the Internet allows for other procedures, the publication of a scholarly manuscript is organized around the release date of the publication. After the release of a scientific publication no corrections, additions, or changes are possible. Only in strong cases of scientific misconduct, falsicification or manipulation of findings will a retraction occur, usually with sweeping consequences for the authors in question. Minor mistakes cannot be corrected. Only a couple of journals provide online commenting functionality and these are not currently being used in a relevant matter. However, this might change quite soon, for example by merging in trackback functions as already used by weblogs. A scientific discourse around a publication cannot occur, and if so, channels such as comments or discussion forums are being used which are currently not credited. Only the discussion sections of new peer-reviewed publications are a chance for accredited scholarly criticism.

---

[2] *Wikipedia*: http://en.wikipedia.org/wiki/Academic_authorship#Honorary_authorship

## *Redundancy in Scientific Publications—Currently no Reuse and Remixing*

The scientific knowledge creation process is usually incremental. Once a certain amount of scientific knowledge is gathered, a novel publication is released. Depending on discipline, a full paper, thesis, or book is the most accepted form of publication. Each release is considered to be a self-contained body of text, understandable to fellow-scientists in the field. This makes redundancy in the introduction, material, and methods a necessity. With this come certain legal and ethical implications. The authors are currently in danger of not only being accused of self-plagiarism, but also of copying from fellow scientists. Even if sections are correctly referenced and citations are placed, many scientists reword phrases for fear of being accused of plagiarism and scientific misconduct. Current conventions prevent scientific authors from *reusing* well-worded introductions or other paragraphs, despite the fact that from a truly scientific point of view, this would be totally acceptable if enough new content and results besides the copied and reused parts is present (Fig. 1). Also, obvious *remixing* of phrases and content from

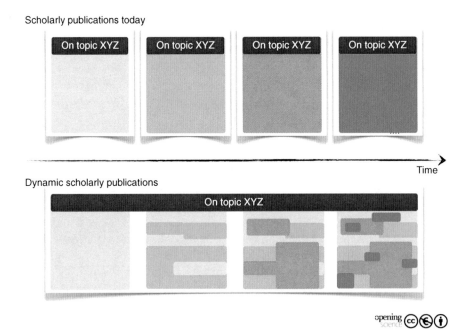

**Fig. 1** Today's scientific publications are static—meaning finalized versions exist that cannot be changed. Dynamic publication formats have become possible with the Internet. The publication can now evolve with the development of new knowledge. In dynamic publications many parts and texts can be 'reused' (as represented by the parts of the text that keep the color; new additions represent novel scientific knowledge)

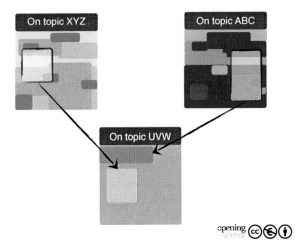

**Fig. 2** Remixing is the concept of using text and parts of earlier publications to build a novel publication; remixing is currently restricted through legal and scientific cultures, however, remixing may become much more acceptable in the future—remixing has to be distinguished from scientific plagiarism

several sources is currently not accepted (Fig. 2). This results in unnecessary rewording, a greater workload, and potentially sub-optimal phrasing. The same introduction, methodology description, and statements are rewritten over and over again, making it sometimes difficult to identify the truly new contribution to a scientific field (Mietchen et al. 2011). It is important to notice that in many disciplines and scientific cultures, mainly humanities, textual reproduction with precious words and in a literary manner is a considerable feat which is beyond the pure transportation of information. Here, the reusing and remixing of content has to be seen in a different context.

## *Legal Hurdles to Make Remixing and Reuse Difficult*

Most publishers retain the copyright of a publication, which strictly limits the reuse of text, pictures, and media. This banishment of remixing seems outdated in the age of the Internet. Novel copyright concepts such as Creative Commons (CC-BY) (see chapter Creative Commons Licences) will change this and will make reuse and remixing possible.

## Technical Hurdles in Reusing Content—"Publisher PDF" Files are Mimicking Print

Some scientific publications are being reproduced in a way that makes the reuse of articles and parts of articles technically difficult. Sometimes, the PDF version is the only available version of an article. More open formats, such as HTML, XML, LaTeX source code, or word documents are not always released and remain with the publisher. Even the author themself suffers from significant hurdles in accessing the final version of his or her personal publications (cf. Schneider 2011; Wikiversity[3]).

The current publication system is a consequence of a scholarly knowledge dissemination system which developed in times before the Internet when printing and disseminating printed issues of papers were the only means of distributing scientific results. The Internet made it possible to break with the limitations of printed publications and allowed the development of dynamic publication formats.

## Dynamic Publication Format—General Concept

Science as a whole is constantly developing. Novel insights, results, and data are permanently being found. The prevailing current publication system is dynamic, but its changes and iterations are too slow. The publication system developed long before the Internet. With the Internet came new possibilities for publishing, transporting results, and defining the nature of 'a publication'. Dynamic publications can adapt to the development of knowledge. Just as *Wikipedia* is developing towards completeness and truth, why not have scientific publications that develop in pace with the body of scientific knowledge?

## Dynamic Publication—Challenges

In the past a modality of publication was mainly shaped by the prevailing medium (paper) and its distribution (mailing). New scientific results had to cross a certain threshold to be publishable. This threshold was defined by the amount of effort that was necessary to produce this publication and to distribute it. A publication had to be somewhat consistent and comprehensible by itself. The forms of publications that were available in the past are abstracts, talks, papers, reviews, and books (Fig. 3).

Since the Internet, the available publication methods are no longer limited to this list. It became possible that virtually everybody can publish at very little or no

---

[3] Wikiversity: http://en.wikiversity.org/wiki/Wikiversity:Journal_of_the_future

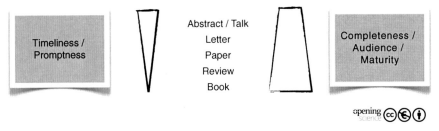

**Fig. 3** Classical publication formats before the Internet

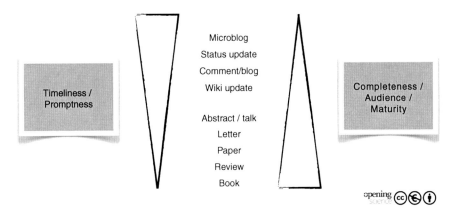

**Fig. 4** Today's publication formats

cost. The limiting factor of the medium of paper and its distribution vanished. Novel publication methods such as blogs, microblogs, comments, wiki updates, or other publication methods complement the prevailing publishing methods (Fig. 4) (Pochoda 2012).

## Aspects of Dynamic Publication Formats

### *Dynamic*

Dynamic publication formats are—as the name says—dynamic (Fig. 5), meaning that no static version exists. Dynamic publications evolve. The changes can be done on several formal levels, from letters and single words ('collaborative authoring tools', 'wikis'), to a few sentences ('status updates') and whole paragraphs ('blogs', 'comments'). Changes include deletions, changes, and additions. However, implementations vary in terms of how permanent a deletion may be.

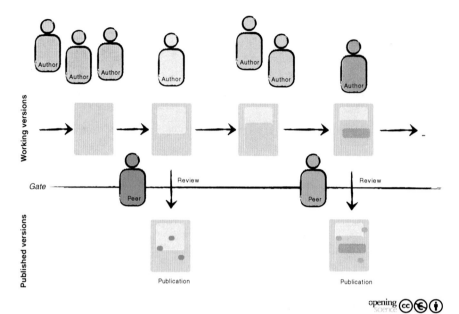

**Fig. 5** Dynamic publications: Working and public versions. The working versions are collaboratively edited by a small group of authors. The authors can decide when a version or a revision should become widely available. Depending on the platform, a formalized 'gate-keeping' mechanism (consent among authors) and/or 'peer-review' as organized by a quality-granting authority (journal) has to be passed. Working as well as published versions can be reused by other authors

## *Authorship*

In collaborative authoring tools it is quite technically easy to precisely trace who typed which text and who drew which figures. However, authorship in a scientific publication currently represents much more than just an actual textual contribution. It defines whose ideas and theories lead to it, in addition to the actual work that was necessary to gather the scientific results. This is not adequately represented by the actual contribution of the text. Authorship is a guarantor of quality and here the personal reputation of a researcher is at stake. Therefore, clear statements of the kind of contribution to a work provided by an author should be associated with a publication. For example, many scientific journals request a definition of the role each author played in the production process of the work. The contributions range from the basic idea, actual bench work to revision of the article.

## *Openness*

Technically the whole textual creation process including all typing and editing could be open. Furthermore, all commentary and discussion can be open. Certain consequences are related to such openness. Not all versions of a document and discussions are meant to be public. While openness can be seen as a tool for assuring quality and preventing scientific misconduct, at the same time it puts researchers under great pressure. Usually early versions of documents are full of spelling mistakes and errors and not meant to be seen by the public; furthermore, they usually lack approval from all coauthors.

A possible solution allows for some parts of the publication and editing process to take place with limited visibility in a *working version*. After all authors have approved a version or a revision, this version can become part of the *public version* (Fig. 5). The step from working version to public version would be based on some internal 'gatekeeping' criteria, such as the discussion and consent of all authors, making the process similar to that of the peer-review process. However, the peer-review is done by people other than the authors themselves and the peer-reviewing process can be organized by a quality-granting authority such as a journal.

## *Tranclusion, Pull-Requests, and Forking—Lifecycle and History*

The lifecycle of a dynamic publication is much harder to define than the life cycle of a static, traditional publication. Concepts such as *'transclusion'*,[4] *'pull-requests'*, and *'forking'*[5] allow for different kinds of *remixing* and *reuse* of earlier publications (Fig. 6). An important feature of dynamic publications is the availability of a history functionality so that older versions of the publication are still available and referencing to the older versions can occur. This might not only be of interest to historians of science, but may also be very valuable in assessing the merits of earlier scientific discoveries and documenting scientific disputes.

Many of these remixing and reuse concepts stem from collaborative software development and many of these are in turn far removed from the current perception of the life cycle of scientific publications. It remains to be seen whether they can be integrated into the scientific publishing culture so that the systems in question benefit from it, and usability, as well as readability, can be assured.

---

[4]  *Wikipedia*: http://en.wikipedia.org/wiki/Transclusion

[5]  A concept derived from software development, but also applicable to texts. *Wikipedia*: http://en.wikipedia.org/wiki/Fork_(software_development)

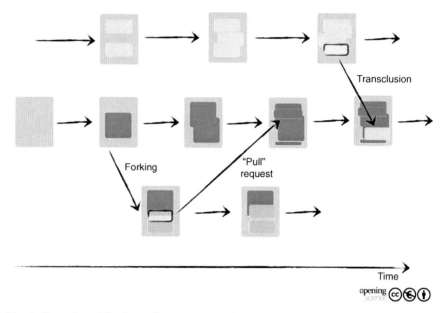

**Fig. 6** Dynamic publications allow many novel concepts such as 'forking' (dividing one publication into two branches of working versions), 'transclusion' (reuse of text or images from another publication, potentially with live updates) and 'pull requests' (a certain way of including updates from one forked working version into another: a 'one time transclusion')

## Publication Formats

Various publication formats exist. There are books, chapters, abstracts, tweets, reviews, full-papers, and so on. Some publication formats are more likely to benefit from the many remixing concepts of dynamic publications than others. In many science cultures, reviews are constantly being released on similar topics, sometimes on an annual basis. A dynamic publication concept would be ideally suited to providing reviews of current developments: instead of publishing completely novel reviews, reviews could constantly be updated.

## Content and Quality Control

The authors as the primary guarantors of quality remain untouched by the concepts of dynamic publications. However, while the pre-publication peer-review of static publications and the decision of editorial boards or publishers assured content in the past, this is more flexible in dynamic publications. An open commenting functionality can be seen as a form of post-publication review. The public pressure that is associated with potentially unmasking comments urges the authors to provide a high standard of output. If the commenting functionality is anonymous it should be clear to all readers that non-qualified comments may occur; at the same time, an anonymous commenting functionality may encourage true criticisms.

In actual implementations of dynamic publications, visibility of transclusions as well as pull-requests has to be assured—otherwise misunderstanding of the actual authorship may occur.

## *Cultural Background*

Dynamic publications are a completely novel tool in scholarly publishing. Scientists have to learn to use them and to understand their benefits and limitations. Furthermore, scientometrics have to learn how to assess contributions that occur in dynamic publications.

Some research fields are more suited to dynamic publication concepts, while others are less so. There are research cultures that might implement dynamic publications faster than others. Hard sciences/lab sciences are more suited for dynamic publications. Here, often novel, incremental findings just require small changes to a text, whereas in humanities comprehensive theories and interpretations might not be as suitable to be expressed in well-circumscribed changes of text.

## Current Implementation of Dynamic Publications

Traditional scholarly publication methods exist—and novel tools and platforms that technically allow the realization of dynamic publication concepts have originated from the web. Tools that implement aspects of dynamic publishing are presented here and their limitations explained.

## *Journal Articles and Books*

Journal articles and books represent the gold-standard of scientific publishing. In the world of books and journal articles there exists a point in time that clearly divides the production phase from the reception phase of a scientific publication. This point in time is when the publication is released and available to readers. With this comes the expectation that the results and discussion of released scientific results provided are 'complete' and 'final'. When the neutral and often anonymous peer-review process is finished, a publication is 'fit to print'[6]. In most

---

[6] Journalists of the New York Times in 19th century stated "All the news that's fit to print" (cf. Encyclopædia Britannica Online: http://www.britannica.com/EBchecked/topic/850457/All-the-News-Thats-Fit-to-Print).

**Table 1** Characteristics of current methods of dynamic content (selection)

| | Scholarly articles | Blogs/microblogs | Wikis or other collaborative authoring tools | Social coding/GitHub |
|---|---|---|---|---|
| **Application** | One-time and nonrecurring release of a novel scientific finding | Irregular contributions, with novel findings, ongoing research and comments on third party findings | Collaborative writing, structuring of knowledge, work-flow processes, or as a tool to collaboratively prepare publication with several authors | Closed projects with a clear defined aim, e.g. producing a running computer code |
| **'Reviewability': Quality assurance and evaluation through others** | Independent peer-review; retraction and comments only through publisher; comments; delayed assessment through citation data, in progressive journals usage statistics and altmetrics | Comments, usage data, social network metrics | A group of authors or a community releases and accepts novel content using a structured reviewing process, whereof the reviewing process is usually open; open comment functionality; usage data and social network metrics | Usage data by tracking code pull requests; third party reuse |
| **Continuity and integration with the scientific knowledge creation process** | Referencing; Development of the article only during creation and peer-review process; Usually hidden from the public | Serial publishing of novel contribution; links to other blog posts/articles; comments and trackbacks allow dynamic interaction | Continuous collaborative creation and changing of content; history function available | Continuous working as a team on a common project; results can be reused by other projects |
| **Authorship and accountability of contributions** | Authors provide information about their contribution; author position is negotiated | Usually the blogger is the only author | Exact labelling of the contribution, independent from size | Exact labelling of the contribution, independent from size |

(continued)

**Table 1** (continued)

| | Scholarly articles | Blogs/microblogs | Wikis or other collaborative authoring tools | Social coding/GitHub |
|---|---|---|---|---|
| **Collaborative content control** | The content is provided only by the authors; content and relevance controlled by the editorial board of the journal | Single author is responsible for content; commenting is allowed | Wide consent on the scope of the project; conflicts will be addressed and solved by majority decisions; everybody can contribute | 'Maintainer' decides about acceptance or rejection of changes; if conflicts exists, project can be divided into two sub projects ('forking') |
| **Technical reusability** | Potentially possible, but practically limited by PDF format; little use of markup languages and remixing mechanisms such as "forking" or "transclusion" | Usage of markup languages including HTML; but no implementation of remixing or forking mechanisms | Highly reusable; content is highly structured; flexible markup language; transclusion within the platform; easily traceable transclusion | Highly reusable; examples for usage of markup languages such as Markdown and Pandoc for text publications; forks easily and often done; traceable |
| **Legal reusability** | More and more use of more open copyright licenses; | Almost only use of open copyright licenses that allow reuse | Very high; *wikipedia*-like or creative commons licenses | Very high; free licenses that allow reuse |
| **Implementations** | Proprietary journal platforms or open journal platforms such as Open Journal System of public knowledge project (see chapter The Public Knowledge Project: Open Source Tools for Open Access to Scholarly Communication) | WordPress with wide spread use; other blogging solutions | MediaWiki with wide spread use; proprietary tools such as Google Docs | GitHub or free repository platform Git; Sourceforge or CVS |
| **History function** | Traces of creation process usually deleted; no history function | No traces of creation process; no history function | Complete traces of creation process and history of articles; seamless traces of discussion | Complete traces of creation process and history of articles; seamless traces of discussion |

(continued)

**Table 1** (continued)

| | Scholarly articles | Blogs/microblogs | Wikis or other collaborative authoring tools | Social coding/GitHub |
|---|---|---|---|---|
| **Openness, in general** | Closed, after publication after paywall/Open Access | Closed until publication than open | Form very beginning open to a wide community | Form very beginning open to a wide community |
| **Readability in style/ Redundancy: 1. In the best case** | Ability to frame a finished research result, in homogenous writing style by one (or a few) author(s) | Direct reporting of research results with readability of (good) science journalism. | Capacity for continuous refinement and correction of text; authors allowed to remix/translate from previously existing articles | Capacity for continuous refinement and correction of text |
| **Readability in style/ Redundancy: 2. Challenges and problems** | External pressures to 'publish or perish' and therefore diluted and dispersed results Compared e.g. to wiki/social coding writing style: unusual to "remix" previously existing text and/or make later corrections in style | Often "serialized" reporting of ongoing, not yet finished research. As such mostly addressing peers in same research topic area (e.g. by not making clear research aims, presumptions, methods used, etc. in each new blog post) | Hard to maintain consistent encyclopaedia-level content and readability with large author community. In addition, this often leads to wiki-bureaucracy, e.g. meta-level of templates, rules, acceptance of proposed changes, etc. | At present, few experiences with article-style collaborative knowledge production in code repositories; by now mostly used for production/ collection /integration of code and data |
| **Acceptance within scientific community** | Together with books in most disciplines the essential part of scientific publishing; officially credited | Somewhat accepted, but most often not credited | Widely used, but contribution not credited | Used, e.g. for production and maintenance of software code, in some cases data collections/documentation; Most often not credited |

scientific cultures, it is not expected that something should be published before the peer-review is concluded. The production process is usually only open to the work group and authors. This is being changed through the use of Preprint-Repositories [like arXive.org (since 1991)], or the opening of the peer-review process in some journals (cf. Pöschl 2012). After peer-review critical comments, extensions, hints, and reviews have to go to other publications.

## Blogs

Blogs are fundamentally different: Only the author decides on the medium, the structure of publication, and the point in time of the release. Usually blogs are produced by single persons and even in the case of blogging platforms the responsibility for the content of one blog usually rests with the author of that explicit blog. This results in certain expectations with respect to the content of the blog. In typical scientific blogs, scientists publish reviews and review-like aggregations of already published scientific publications. Blogs can often be seen as a method of science journalism. On the other hand, some scientists blog about their ongoing research, e.g. about the progress of a doctoral thesis (cf. Efimova 2009). In some cases a blog is a public form of the scientific knowledge creation process—the blog becomes a diary of the personal knowledge creation process, with novel ideas and results being constantly published. Even preliminary results and unproven hypotheses can be presented to a limited audience (limited in terms of real readers— most blogs are indeed completely open) which, on the other hand, provides useful feedback in the form of comments or other feedback. In this context, a blog post is usually based on earlier blog posts and it is not considered to be a 'full publication' with sufficient background information. A high level of very specialized knowledge is assumed (also see the discussion round including Mike Taylor; Taylor 2012). In conclusion, it could be said that blog postings are no replacement for, but rather a useful adjunct to old-fashioned, peer-reviewed journal or book publications. Blog postings seem to already be on their trajectory to become a valuable part of the publication mix. (Cf. to the development around the project ScienceSeeker.[7])

## Wikis

While blog postings represent conclusive texts of individual authors, wikis are much more different from traditional ways of publishing. Wikis were initially introduced to document practices for developing software,[8] however, they became commonly

---

[7] ScienceSeeker: http://scienceseeker.org/

[8] Ward Cunningham: http://de.wikipedia.org/wiki/Ward_Cunningham; Wiki Wiki Web: http://c2.com/cgi/wiki?WikiWikiWeb

known through the open and freely available online encyclopedia *Wikipedia* (wikipedia.org, since 2001). Wikis represent websites with content that can be collaboratively changed by potentially very large groups of users. Despite the fact that the usage of wikis grew far beyond the remit of software development and encyclopedias, *Wikipedia* significantly influenced the wide reception of wikis.

Wikis are hosted as open platforms in the public web. In most cases, a registration for the wiki is easily possible and new wiki topics can be proposed from anyone, while the triage of new articles or concurrent changes and their acceptation to the public version of wiki is done by the project founders or a special user group. Usually, these are authors who have become especially trustworthy through their engagement with, or past contributions to the wiki. Usually the founding group provides style and content guidelines. Strict adherence to these guidelines is especially relevant since the content of articles is more or less implicitly approved of by all authors of the wiki community. To resolve disputes is particularly challenging since only one version of the articles exists. If disputes are unsolvable usually all viewpoints are elucidated and the reason for the dispute is mentioned.

The fact that many people can contribute to articles possesses the advantage that virtually anybody can become a co-author. Errors and biased viewpoints can be corrected much quicker than in traditional ways of publishing. This is under the assumption that all contributors adhere to the consensus of the wiki—potentially at the expense of personal writing styles and viewpoints.

The individual author has to accept that statements might be edited or modified by the community. Similarly, he has to accept its principles of meritocracy and the potential consequences that might arise from such principles.

On the other side, contributions to a continuously evolving wiki-project present the possibility of contributing to a work with an ongoing relevance. Even far into the future, relevant contributions by an individual author can be traced in detail in the revision history of the wiki text. This might also be used to scientometrically quantify the quality or relevance of contributions to wikis—for example current approaches include algorithmic modeling of the revision history (Kramer et al. 2008).

In contrast to scientific blogging and some dedicated wiki-projects, *Wikipedia* itself was never considered to be a platform to exchange originary research results. *Wikipedia* keeps an encyclopedic character, however, despite this, there are multiple examples of scientists who actively contribute to *Wikipedia*. Ever more so, some academic organizations propose a lively contribution to *Wikipedia* (Farzan & Kraut 2012).

A cointegration of a scientific journal and *Wikipedia* was started with *Topic Pages* by PLoS Computational Biology (Wodak et al. 2012). Topic Pages are a version of a page to be posted to (the English version of) *Wikipedia*. In other words, *PLoS Computational Biology* publishes a version that is static, includes author attributions, and is indexed in PubMed, all with the reviews and reviewer identities of Topic Pages available to the readership. The aim of this project is that the *Wikipedia* pages subsequently become living documents which will be updated and enhanced by the *Wikipedia* community.

## Stack Exchange—Message Boards Where Threads are Initiated by Posting Open Questions

Question centered message boards ("stack exchange") like *MathOverflow* and *BioStar* (Parnell et al. 2011) consists of comment threads that are posted under a known ID. A thread is centered on a question, which is in contrast to blogs which provide more or less opinions, reviews, comments, overviews, or novel hypotheses. A reputation ('Karma') can be built by earning 'likes' or 'views' from other users within the community (initially introduced by *Slashdot* in the 1990s). The questioner and the community (Paul et al. 2012) assesses as to whether the answers are sufficient and whether the thread should be closed, maximizing the potential gain in Karma. The incentives set by this leads to many useful and comprehensible answers at the end of a good browseable question thread. Orienting threads around questions leads to a question-centered discussion and the discussions in turn stay on topic.

## SNS for Scientists

Social networking systems (SNS) have found widespread use in the Internet. Early examples are *Friendster*, *Sixdegrees.com*, *Myspace*, while *Facebook* made the concept widely available. In 2012 *Facebook* hit the first billion of users worldwide. After signing into a SNS, users can set up a profile page with a multitude of information about themselves. Besides adopting the information, posting so-called 'status updates' has become very popular, ranging from personal feelings to more or less useful information on one's current task or whereabouts, often together with some rich media such as pictures or movies.

Other users can follow the status update of particular members. Members that are 'followed' contribute to their own personal 'timeline'—a collection of all status updates of fellow members. Other users can be added to the list of friends. Friending another user results in a mutual exchange of status updates, media, pictures, and many more things.

Usually, all friendship and follower connections are visible to a wider audience. This fact, together with many other aspects of proprietary SNS, resulted in privacy concerns which the provider tried to counteract by establishing selective privacy settings. Other SNS such as *Twitter* incorporated a full and mandatory openness into their strategy. With the advancement of SNS users are becoming more and more aware of the chances and dangers of SNS's.

Most SNS's create a rich social experience with a mixture of status updates from friends, personalized news, and the possibility of interacting with the postings of others by 'liking' or commenting on them. If the user decides that certain postings might be of interest to their friends or followers, they can share it with them—often with the click of a mouse button.

Dedicated SNS's for scientists were established around 2008 (see chapter Academia Goes Facebook? The Potential of Social Network Sites in the Scholarly Realm). Scientists started to share status updates related to their scientific work, in many cases information about published articles, abstracts, and talks. They provide a platform for users to post their research articles in compliance with copyright laws, since a profile page is considered to be a personal homepage (Green road to Open Access [see chapter Open Access: A State of the Art]). More and more often, scientists have started to take the opportunity to incorporate media as well as some interesting, novel findings into their status updates. The providers use information and connections between users to support scientists, using suggestions about interesting topics, other publications, and fellow researchers that work in similar fields. *Mendeley.com*, *Academia.edu*, and *ResearchGate.net* have reached several millions of users.

Most users of SNS's for scientists maintain a profile in a non-scientific SNS. At the dawn of the SNS, it seemed like there was only need for one SNS that could serve all personal, professional, and scientific (and many more) networking needs. However, this impression was wrong. It seems to be more suitable for users to maintain several profiles in several SNS's, whereof the facets of the personal profile as well as the shared information depends on the purpose of the SNS (cf. Nentwich and König 2012). Users do not want to mix holiday pictures with their scientific publications.

In the past, SNS's were not considered to be a means of sharing original scientific results. However, this may undergo profound changes. For example, in 2011, *FigShare* (a commercial service) was introduced, serving as a free repository for the archiving and presentation of scientific results. *Researchgate as well as Mendeley* allow the publication of preprints; *Mendeley* allows the finding of dedicated reviewers for certain publications.

SNS's carry the potential of becoming a means of publishing scientific results in accordance with the ongoing decoupling of scientific communication channels from the journal system (e.g. Priem and Hemminger 2012).

The status updates in SNS's for scientists could be used to publish ideas, exciting findings, as well as links to other interesting sources. Commenting, as well as the 'like' functionality could act as a kind of peer-review. In SNS's for scientists, status updates, comments, and likes are not anonymously done— therefore their creator together with their profile are visible to other scientists who can then assess the 'credibility' and the background of the contributing scientists. The 'question' functionality of *ResearchGate* provides a platform with vivid scientific discussions that were not possible in such a manner, were the users to hide behind anonymous acronyms.

Furthermore, SNS's can analyze the activity of scientists and provide easily accessible, novel 'impact' metrics of scientists—based on their activity and reputation within a SNS or based on established metrics.

A SNS for scientists combined with a text editing and publishing platform might be the ideal platform to realize a dynamic publication system.

# References

Efimova, L. (2009). *Passion at work: Blogging practices of knowledge workers*. Enschede: Novay. Available at http://blog.mathemagenic.com/phd/dissertation/.

Farzan, R., & Kraut, R. (2012). *Eight months of APS Wikipedia initiative*. Available at http://de.slideshare.net/PsychScience/recruiting-and-engaging-psychologists-to-the-aps-wikipedia-initiative.

Kramer, M., Gregorowicz, A., & Iyer, B. (2008). Wiki trust metrics based on phrasal analysis. In *Proceedings of the 4th International Symposium on Wikis* (p. 1). ACM Press, doi:10.1145/1822258.1822291.

Mietchen, D., Hagedorn, G., & Förstner, K. U. (2011). Wikis in scholarly publishing. *Information Services and Use, 31*(1–2), 53–59. doi:http://dx.doi.org/10.3233/ISU-2011-0621.

Nentwich, M., & König, R. (2012). *Cyberscience 2.0: Research in the age of digital social networks*. Frankfurt, New York: Campus Verlag.

Parnell, L. D., et al. (2011). BioStar: An online question & answer resource for the bioinformatics community. *PLoS Computational Biology, 7*(10), e1002216. doi:10.1371/journal.pcbi.1002216. (P. E. Bourne, ed.).

Paul, S. A., Hong, L., & Chi, E. H. (2012). Who is authoritative? Understanding reputation mechanisms in Quora. In *Collective Intelligence Conference*. doi:arXiv:1204.3724.

Pochoda, P. (2012). The big one: The epistemic system break in scholarly monograph publishing. *New Media and Society*. doi:10.1177/1461444812465143.

Pöschl, U. (2012). Multi-stage open peer review: Scientific evaluation integrating the strengths of traditional peer review with the virtues of transparency and self-regulation. *Frontiers in Computational Neuroscience, 6*. doi:10.3389/fncom.2012.00033.

Priem, J., & Hemminger, B. M. (2012). Decoupling the scholarly journal. *Frontiers in Computational Neuroscience, 6*. doi:10.3389/fncom.2012.00019.

Rice, C. (2013). Science research: Three problems that point to a communications crisis. *Theguardian. Higher Education Network*. Available at http://www.guardian.co.uk/higher-education-network/blog/2013/feb/11/science-research-crisis-retraction-replicability.

Schneider, J. (2011). Beyond the PDF. *Ariadne, 66*(January). Available at http://www.ariadne.ac.uk/issue66/beyond-pdf-rpt.

Taylor, M. (2012). What is the difference between a paper and a blog post? *Sauropod Vertebra Picture of the Week*. Available at http://svpow.com/2012/10/14/what-is-the-difference-between-a-paper-and-a-blog-post/.

Wodak, S. J., et al. (2012). Topic pages: *PLoS computational biology* meets *Wikipedia*. *PLoS Computational Biology, 8*(3), e1002446. doi:10.1371/journal.pcbi.1002446.

# Open Research Data: From Vision to Practice

**Heinz Pampel and Sünje Dallmeier-Tiessen**

> *To make progress in science, we need to be open and share.*
> —Neelie Kroes (2012)

**Abstract** "To make progress in science, we need to be open and share." This quote from Neelie Kroes (2012), vice president of the European Commission describes the growing public demand for an Open Science. Part of Open Science is, next to Open Access to peer-reviewed publications, the Open Access to research data, the basis of scholarly knowledge. The opportunities and challenges of Data Sharing are discussed widely in the scholarly sector. The cultures of Data Sharing differ within the scholarly disciplines. Well advanced are for example disciplines like biomedicine and earth sciences. Today, more and more funding agencies require a proper Research Data Management and the possibility of data re-use. Many researchers often see the potential of Data Sharing, but they act cautiously. This situation shows a clear ambivalence between the demand for Data Sharing and the current practice of Data Sharing. Starting from a baseline study on current discussions, practices and developments the article describe the challenges of Open Research Data. The authors briefly discuss the barriers and drivers to Data Sharing. Furthermore, the article analyses strategies and approaches to promote and implement Data Sharing. This comprises an analysis of the current landscape of data repositories, enhanced publications and data papers. In this context the authors also shed light on incentive mechanisms, data citation practises and the interaction between data repositories and journals. In the conclusions the authors outline requirements of a future Data Sharing culture.

H. Pampel (✉)
GFZ German Research Centre for Geosciences, Potsdam, Germany
e-mail: pampel@gfzpotsdam.de

S. Dallmeier-Tiessen
Scientific Information Service, CERN, Geneva, Switzerland

S. Bartling and S. Friesike (eds.), *Opening Science*,
DOI: 10.1007/978-3-319-00026-8_14, © The Author(s) 2014

# The Vision of Open Research Data

Digitization has opened up new possibilities for scientists in their handling of information and knowledge. The potential of networked research was recorded in the "Berlin Declaration on Open Access to Knowledge in the Sciences and Humanities" (2003). This declaration was signed by leading scientific organizations and is regarded as the central reference for the demands of access and sharing of scientific results in the digital age. Previous definitions of Open Access were related to free access to peer-reviewed literature,[1] whereas the "Berlin Declaration" considers this in a wider sense. Not only articles, but also "raw data and metadata, source materials, digital representations of pictorial and graphical materials and scholarly multimedia material" should be openly accessible and usable.

This demand is also evident on the political level. An example is the statement made in a publication of the Organisation for Economic Co-operation and Development (OECD) 2007, entitled "Principles and Guidelines for Access to Research Data from Public Funding": "Sharing and Open Access to publicly funded research data not only helps to maximise the research potential of new digital technologies and networks, but provides greater returns from the public investment in research" (OECD 2007). The European Commission also strives for Open Access to research data. In the "Commission Recommendation on Access to and Preservation of Scientific Information" which was published in 2012, European member states are requested to ensure that "research data that result from publicly funded research become publicly accessible, usable and re-usable through digital e-infrastructures" (European Commission 2012a).

The discussion on the realisation of this aim is present in the scientific communities (Nature 2002, 2005, 2009a, b; Science 2011). The term Open Research Data can be applied on a cross-disciplinary layer. It covers the heterogeneity of the data with its diverse characteristics, forms and formats in the scientific disciplines. Further to this, the term Open Research Data is distinct to Open Data, which is mainly used in the context of Open Government initiatives and neglects the special requirements of science.

The two central arguments for Open Access to research data are a) the possibility to re-use data in a new connection and b) the verifiability it guarantees for ensuring good scientific practice. The OECD (2007) added a further argument: "Sharing and Open Access to publicly funded research data not only helps to maximise the research potential of new digital technologies and networks, but provides greater returns from the public investment in research."

The vision of the High Level Expert Group on Scientific Data for the year 2030 is that, scientists in their role as data user, "are able to find, access and process the

---

[1] Compare: Budapest Open Access Initiative, 2002: http://www.opensocietyfoundations.org/openaccess/read & Bethesda Statement on Open Access Publishing, 2003: http://www.earlham.edu/~peters/fos/bethesda.htm

data they need", and in their role as data producer "prefer to deposit their data with confidence in reliable repositories" (High Level Expert Group on Scientific Data 2010).

The demand for Open Research Data effects individual researchers and their data handling. In a report of The Royal Society (2012) entitled "Science as an open enterprise" which is worth reading, the recommendation is given that: "[s]cientists should communicate the data they collect and the models they create, to allow free and Open Access, and in ways that are intelligible, assessable and usable for other specialists in the same or linked fields wherever they are in the world. Where data justify it, scientists should make them available in an appropriate data repository. Where possible, communication with a wider public audience should be made a priority, and particularly so in areas where openness is in the public interest." This recommendation makes it clear that diverse basic conditions must be created before Data Sharing can become a standard in scientific practice. Access and usage conditions must be defined. Murray-Rust et al.[2] for example demands the free accessibility in the public domain in their "Panton Principles": "By open data in science we mean that it is freely available on the public Internet permitting any user to download, copy, analyse, re-process, pass them to software or use them for any other purpose without financial, legal, or technical barriers other than those inseparable from gaining access to the Internet itself." The majority of the disciplines are still far away from the implementation of these "[p]rinciples for open data in science", however. In addition, there are many cases in the life sciences and social science disciplines in which, because of data protection and personal rights, Data Sharing is not possible, or only possible under narrowly defined conditions.

## The Status of Data Sharing Today

In a consultation carried out in 2012, the European Commission determined that there were massive access barriers to research data. Of the 1,140 of those questioned, 87 % contradicted the statement that "there is no access problem to research data in Europe" (European Commission 2012b). In a revealing study made by Tenopir et al. (2011), 67 % of the more than 1,300 researchers pointed to a "lack of access to data generated by other researchers or institutions" that is a hindrance to advances in science. Scientists frequently see the potential offered by Open Research Data, but most are reticent with regard to the open accessibility of their own data. Tenopir et al. found, for example, that "only about a third (36 %) of the respondents agreed that others can access their data easily". This is not in accordance with the researchers attitudes, as three-quarters state that they "share their data with others". The study also sheds light on different disciplinary

---

[2]  Panton Principles: http://pantonprinciples.org/

practices: Whereas 90 % of scientists working in atmospheric science were willing to sharing their data, only 58 % of the questioned social sciences scientists were ready to do this. The authors conclude: "there is a willingness to share data, but it is difficult to achieve or is done only on request."

Further insights in disciplinary practices are presented by the studies Wicherts et al. (2006) in psychology and Savage and Vickers (2009) in medicine, for example. Wicherts et al. approached authors of 141 articles published in 2004 in journals of the American Psychological Association (APA) and requested access to data that was the basis of the articles. Within the next six months, they only received positive replies from one third of the authors, 73 % of the authors were not prepared to share their data. Savage & Vickers came to a similar result. They asked authors of ten articles that were published in the PLoS Medicine or PLoS Clinical Trials journals to allow them access to the underlying data of the articles. Despite the clear demands for Open Access to data in den editorial policies of each of the Open Access journals, only one author permitted access to the requested data. A further insight in the status of Data Sharing is presented by the analysis of Campbell et al. (2002) in genetics. In this study that involved about 1,800 life science scientists, they identified two central factors that hinder Data Sharing: "Lack of resources and issues of scientific priority play an important role in scientists' decisions to withhold data, materials, and information from other academic geneticists."

Alongside these very reserved attitudes, however, there are numerous examples which underline that open exchange of research data can successfully be realized. The "Bermuda Principles" that were adopted in human genetics in the framework of the Human Genome Project in 1996, for example. These principles require that "[a]ll human genomic sequence data generated by centers funded for large-scale human sequencing should be freely available and in the public domain to encourage research and development and to maximize the benefit to society" (Smith and Carrano 1996). Over time the pre-publication of data comes off as common practice, i.e. gene sequencies are made openly accessible prior to the description of them in a peer reviewed article.[3] Alongside Data Sharing in large scientific projects, in which data is made openly available in trustworthy research data repositories, there are also examples of spontaneous Data Sharing. Research on a disease-causing strain of the Escherichia coli (O104:H4) bacteria is such a case. This caused more than 4,000[4] people to fall ill in Germany in 2011. The publication of sequence data under a Creative Commons licence and the use of the widely popular GitHub[5] as an exchange platform enabled scientists all over the

---

[3] See also the Fort Lauderdale Principles (Wellcome Trust 2003) and the Toronto Statement (Birney et al. 2009).

[4] See: http://www.rki.de/DE/Content/Service/Presse/Pressemitteilungen/2011/11_2011.html (Retrieved 20 August 2012).

[5] GitHub is a hosting service for the collaborative development of software. See: https://github.com/ehec-outbreak-crowdsourced (Retrieved 20 August 2012).

world to make a contribution to a rapid investigation of the bacterium (Kupferschmidt 2011; Turner 2011; Check Hayden 2012).

A further example of successful Data Sharing is the operation of the World Data System (WDS) of the International Council of Science (ICSU) which - even before the coming into being of the Internet - resulted from the International Geophysical Year (1957–1958). This network of disciplinary data centers ensures "full, open, timely, non-discriminatory and unrestricted access to metadata, data, products and services".[6]

## Understanding the Barriers

So-called data policies have an increasing effect on scientists and how they handle research data.[7] Recommendations and mandatory requirements by funding agencies and scientific journals stand out here. They request the beneficiary of funds to ensure the preservation and accessibility of data created in the framework of a funded project or a publication. The National Institute of Health (NIH) was a pioneer in this respect. It anchored its "Data Sharing Policy" in 2003: Applicants for a grant upwards of 500,000 US dollar are requested to make statements on Data Sharing.[8] From 2011 on, the National Science Foundation (NSF) requires receivers of funds "to share with other researchers, at no more than incremental cost and within a reasonable time, the primary data, samples, physical collections and other supporting materials created or gathered in the course of work under NSF grants" (National Science Foundation 2011a). Measures for the implementation of this guideline must be specified in a "Data Management Plan" (National Science Foundation 2011b). This request is being increasingly taken up by scientific journals via editorial policies. Exemplary for these are the requirements of the Nature journals, in which "authors are required to make materials, data and associated protocols promptly available to readers without undue qualifications in material transfer agreements". It is suggested that the data be made accessible "via public repositories".[9]

It must be noted that implementation of the requirements formulated in the data policies will not run by itself (Pampel and Bertelmann 2011). To promote Data Sharing it is necessary to identify the barriers, which influence scientists with regard to the sharing of their own data. Surveys carried out by Kuipers and Van der Hoeven (2009) and Tenopir et al. (2011) allow the following barriers to be named:

---

[6] ICSU World Data System: http://icsu-wds.org/images/files/WDS_Certification_Summary_11_June_2012_pdf

[7] For details see: Pampel & Bertelmann (2011).

[8] National Institutes of Health: http://grants.nih.gov/grants/guide/notice-files/NOT-OD-03-032.html.

[9] Guide to Publication Policies of the Nature Journals: http://www.nature.com/authors/gta.pdf

"legal issues", "misuse of data" and "incompatible data types" (Kuipers and Van der Hoeven 2009), as well as "insufficient time" and "lack of funding" (Tenopir et al. 2011). These barriers make it clear that a dedicated framework is required for the publication of research data. The conception and implementation of such a framework is being increasingly discussed under the Research Data Management term.[10] The aim is to develop organisational and technical measures to ensure a trustworthy infrastructure for permanent integrity and re-use of data. The centre of attention hereby is the operation of information infrastructures, such as research data repositories, in which research data can be permanently stored. To make re-use of the stored data possible, the Research Data Management framework must ensure that the data are described via metadata. Documentation of the instruments and methods used to obtain the data is necessary for reliable re-use of the data, for example. Such an enhanced documentation of data is often a time-consuming task that is competing with many other activities on the researchers priority list. Further to this, in many disciplines there are no standards in which the data can be described.

Recently, it can be observed that libraries, data centers and other institutions are increasingly collaborate and begin to build up information infrastructures to support scientists in the handling of their data and so also to promote Data Sharing (Pampel et al. 2010; Osswald and Strathmann 2012; Reilly 2012).

Van der Graaf and Waaijers (2011) have formulated four central fields of action for the realization of a "collaborative data infrastructure" which enables the "use, re-use and exploit research data to the maximum benefit of science and society". Incentives must be given to stimulate Data Sharing (1); in addition, the education and training of scientists and service providers on and around the handling of data must be intensified (2). Further to these the authors point to the importance on the structuring and networking of research data infrastructures that serve for a permanent and reliable data storage (3) and point out the challenge of the long-term financing of these infrastructures (4).

## Overcoming the Barriers

A central barrier to of the pervasiveness of Data Sharing is the lack of incentives for the individual scientist to make his data openly accessible. In particular in projects, in which data management was not already discussed in the preparatory phase, the individual scientist has good reasons for not making his or her data openly accessible, as there are no incentive mechanisms for the sharing of research data in the competitive scientific system (Borgman 2010; Klump 2012).

---

[10] For details see: Büttner et al. (2011) and Pryor (2012).

The slogan "[c]redit where credit is overdue" (Nature Biotechnology 2009) clearly expresses that: Data Sharing will only be successful when it is worthwhile for a scientist to make his data openly accessible. Against this background, a growing number of publication strategies are appearing with a view to the implementation of Data Sharing on the basis of the established scientific reputation system. Three of these strategies are as follows[11]:

1. The publication of research data as an independent information object in a research data repository.
2. The publication of research data as a textual documentation in the form of a so-called data paper.
3. The publication of research data as enrichment of an article, a so-called "enriched publication".

Whereas the first named practice has long been established in the life sciences with the use of data repositories such as GenBank (Benson et al. 2012)[12] , the second named data paper strategy has been gaining more and more attention recently. Chavan and Penev (2011) define this publication type as follows: "a journal publication whose primary purpose is to describe data, rather than to report a research investigation. As such, it contains facts about data, not hypotheses and arguments in support of those hypotheses based on data, as found in a conventional research article." Experience with data papers has been made, among others, in the geosciences[13] and ecology.[14] The use of this model has recently been widened to include so-called data journals. The pioneer of this development is the Open Access journal Earth System Science Data (ESSD). It has published descriptions of geosciences data sets since 2008. The data sets themselves are published on a "reliable repository" (Pfeiffenberger and Carlson 2011). The data sets and descriptive publications described are permanently persistently addressed by means of a digital object identifier (DOI) which also facilitate data citation. Thanks to this procedure that was developed within the Publication and Citation of Scientific Primary Data (STD–DOI) project (Klump et al. 2006) and expanded by DataCite (Brase and Farquhar 2011), it is possible to link publications and the underlying data. This procedure also supports the visibility of the data. Some publishing houses, for example, have therefore already integrated freely accessible research data in their platforms (Reilly et al. 2011). A number of data journals

---

[11] The following categorization is based on Dallmeier-Tiessen (2011).

[12] For the GenBank history see: Cravedi (2008).

[13] The AGU Journals have published data papers for many years. See: http://www.agu.org/pubs/authors/policies/data_policy.shtml (Retrieved 20 August 2012).

[14] See the Data Papers of the Journals Ecological Archives of the Ecological Society of America (ESA): http://esapubs.org/archive/archive_D.htm (Retrieved 20 August 2012).

have been brought into being in the meantime.[15] It must be noted here that the establishment of data journals is only feasible when data, metadata and the corresponding text publication are freely accessible, as only then can a barrier free re-use of the data be possible.

The linking of articles and data is also addressed in the third named enriched publication strategy (Woutersen-Windhouwer et al. 2009). The aim is to build and sustain a technical environment to relate all relevant information objects around an article so that a knowledge space is created, in which the research data that are the basis of the article can be made freely accessible.[16]

The implementation of the three strategies requires trustworthy repositories on which the data can be made permanently accessible. A differentiation must be made here between institutional, disciplinary, multi-disciplinary and project-specific infrastructure (Pampel et al. 2012). Prominent examples of disciplinary research data repositories are GenBank in genetics and PANGAEA in geosciences and Dryad in biodiversity research.[17] A look at the access conditions of repositories highlights some differences: GenBank states that there are "no restrictions on the use or distribution of the GenBank data, PANGAEA licences the data under the "Creative Commons Licence Attribution" and Dryad makes the data accessible under the "Creative Commons License CC0" in the public domain.

A number of studies have been published that show the impact of Data Sharing on citation rates. Articles for which the underlying data is shared are more frequently cited than articles for which this is not the case. This is substantiated in studies from genetics (Piwowar et al. 2007; Botstein 2010), astronomy (Henneken and Accomazzi 2011; Dorch 2012) and paleoceanography Sears (2011). Such results need to be considered when discussing the lack of incentives for Data Sharing. The same holds true for data citation and data papers, which could contribute to the researchers publication profile and thus current research assessments and incentive systems.

---

[15] Examples: Atomic Data and Nuclear Data Tables (Elsevier); Biodiversity Data Journal (Pensoft Publishers); Dataset Papers in Biology (Hindawi Publishing Corporation); Dataset Papers in Chemistry (Hindawi Publishing Corporation); Dataset Papers in Ecology (Hindawi Publishing Corporation); Dataset Papers in Geosciences (Hindawi Publishing Corporation); Dataset Papers in Materials Science (Hindawi Publishing Corporation); Dataset Papers in Medicine (Hindawi Publishing Corporation); Dataset Papers in Nanotechnology (Hindawi Publishing Corporation); Dataset Papers in Neuroscience (Hindawi Publishing Corporation); Dataset Papers in Pharmacology (Hindawi Publishing Corporation); Dataset Papers in Physics (Hindawi Publishing Corporation); Earth System Science Data—ESSD (Copernicus Publications); Geoscience Data Journal (Wiley); GigaScience (BioMed Central); Nuclear Data Sheets (Elsevier); Open Archaeology Data (Ubiquity Press); Open Network Biology (BioMed Central). Please note that the majority of the journals are still developing and a narrow definition of the type of publication is difficult because of this early development stage.

[16] Potential offered by this strategy under use of Linked Open Data.

[17] An overview of existing data repositories is offered by re3data.org (http://re3data.org).

## Translating Vision into Practice

The developments in recent years have shown that numerous initiatives have emerged in Data Sharing. The hesitation among researchers in many disciplines is met by new strategies that work on barriers such as the lack of incentives. A professionalization of the Research Data Management, which supports scientists in the sharing of their data, is necessary to ensure the permanent accessibility, however. In this context, priority must be given to the structuring and networking of the research data repositories and their long-term financing.

A more detailed analysis for the identification and overcoming of barriers to Data Sharing has been created in the framework of the EU-project Opportunities for Data Exchange (ODE).[18] This project takes the various players involved in scholarly communication and data management (policy-makers, funders, researchers, research and education organisations, data centres and infrastructure service providers and publishers) into consideration, names variables that have an effect on the sharing and points out strategies for overcoming barriers to Open Access (Dallmeier-Tiessen et al. 2012). Many of the strategies that are outlined show that, to counter the diverse challenges, close cooperation is necessary between the players named above. As an example, the successful implementation of data policies of supporting organizations requires a Research Data Management and infrastructures that support scientists and create a regulatory framework. All of these measures will only lead to success, however, when scholarly societies and other disciplinary players who support the anchoring in the disciplinary communities take part. All players in the scientific process are therefore requested to make their contribution to Open Access of research data.

The publication strategies outlined show that there really is a possibility for the anchoring of Data Sharing in the scientific reputation system. Further innovation is desirable, though. The implementation of the increasing demand for Open Science from society[19] and academic policy (Kroes 2012), as is assumed, for example, by the federation of national academies ALLEA - ALL European Academies (2012), needs a culture of sharing. The establishment of this culture is a far reaching challenge. It appears that implementation of it can only then be successful when changes are made in the scientific reputation system. Scientific performances should in the future be valued with a "sharing factor" that not only judges the citation frequency in the scientific community, but also rates the implementation of sharing of information and knowledge for the good of society.

The demand for openness in science is loud and clear. All players in the scientific area should direct their practices to this demand. The publication strategies for research data have up to now been important approaches towards Open Science. The following citation from the "Berlin Declaration" (2003) makes it

---

[18] See: http://ode-project.eu

[19] See here, for example, the Vision of the Open Knowledge Foundation (OKF): http://okfn.org/about/vision/ (Retrieved 20 August 2012).

clear, that further steps are necessary for the realization of Open Science: "Our mission of disseminating knowledge is only half complete if the information is not made widely and readily available to society."

# References

All European Academies. (2012). Open Science for the 21st century, Rome, Italy. Available at: http://cordis.europa.eu/fp7/ict/e-infrastructure/docs/allea-declaration-1.pdf.

Benson, D.A., et al. (2012). GenBank. *Nucleic Acids Research, 40*(D1), D48–D53. doi:10.1093/nar/gkr1202.

Birney, H., et al. (2009). Prepublication data sharing. *Nature, 461*(7261), 168–170. doi:10.1038/461168a.

Borgman, C. L. (2010). Research data: Who will share what, with whom, when, and why? *SSRN Electronic Journal.* doi:10.2139/ssrn.1714427.

Botstein, D. (2010). It's the data! *Molecular Biology of the Cell, 21*(1), 4–6. doi:10.1091/mbc.E09-07-0575.

Brase, J. & Farquhar, A. (2011). Access to research data. *D-Lib Magazine, 17*(1/2). doi:10.1045/january2011-brase.

Büttner, S., Hobohm, H.-C., & Müller, L. (eds.) (2011). *Handbuch Forschungsdatenmanagement,* Bad Honnef: Bock + Herchen.

Campbell, E.G., et al. (2002). Data withholding in academic genetics: Evidence from a national survey. *JAMA: The Journal of the American Medical Association, 287*(4), 473–480.

Chavan, V., & Penev, L. (2011). The data paper: a mechanism to incentivize data publishing in biodiversity science. *BMC Bioinformatics, 12*(Suppl 15), S2. doi:10.1186/1471-2105-12-S15-S2.

Check Hayden, E. (2012). Open-data project aims to ease the way for genomic research. *Nature.* doi:10.1038/nature.2012.10507.

Cravedi, K. (2008). GenBank celebrates 25 years of service with two day conference. Leading scientists will discuss the DNA database at April 7-8 Meeting. National Institutes of Health. Available at: http://www.nih.gov/news/health/apr2008/nlm-03.htm.

Dallmeier-Tiessen, S., et al. (2012). Compilation of results on drivers and barriers and new opportunities. Available at: http://www.alliancepermanentaccess.org/wp-content/uploads/downloads/2012/08/ODE-CompilationResultsDriversBarriersNewOpportunities1.pdf.

Dorch, B. (2012). On the citation advantage of linking to data: Astrophysics. Available at: http://hprints.org/docs/00/71/47/34/PDF/Dorch_2012a.pdf.

European Commission. (2012a). Commission recommendation on access to and preservation of scientific information. C(2012) 4890 final, Available at: http://ec.europa.eu/research/science-society/document_library/pdf_06/recommendation-access-and-preservation-scientific-information_en.pdf.

European Commission. (2012b). Online survey on scientific information in the digital age, Luxembourg: Publications Office of the European Union. Available at: http://ec.europa.eu/research/science-society/document_library/pdf_06/survey-on-scientific-information-digital-age_en.pdf.

Henneken, E.A. & Accomazzi, A. (2011). Linking to data—effect on citation rates in astronomy. Digital Libraries; Instrumentation and Methods for Astrophysics. Available at: http://arxiv.org/abs/1111.3618v1.

High Level Expert Group on Scientific Data. (2010). Riding the wave. How Europe can gain from the rising tide of scientific data. Available at: http://cordis.europa.eu/fp7/ict/e-infrastructure/docs/hlg-sdi-report.pdf.

Klump, J. (2012). Offener Zugang zu Forschungsdaten. In U. Herb (ed), *Open Initiatives: Offenheit in der digitalen Welt und Wissenschaft*. Saarbrücken: Universaar, pp. 45–53. Available at: http://hdl.handle.net/10760/17213.

Klump, J., et al. (2006). Data publication in the Open Access initiative. *Data Science Journal, 5*, 79–83. doi:10.2481/dsj.5.79.

Kroes, N. (2012). Opening Science Through e-infrastructures. Available at: europa.eu/rapid/pressReleasesAction.do?reference=SPEECH/12/258.

Kuipers, T. & van der Hoeven, J. (2009). Insight into digital preservation of research output in Europe. Available at: http://www.parse-insight.eu/downloads/PARSE-Insight_D3-4_Survey Report_final_hq.pdf.

Kupferschmidt, K. (2011). Scientists rush to study genome of lethal *E. coli*. *Science, 332*(6035), 1249–1250. doi:10.1126/science.332.6035.1249.

National Science Foundation. (2011a). Award and administration guide. Chapter VI other post award requirements and considerations, Available at: http://www.nsf.gov/pubs/policydocs/pappguide/nsf11001/aag_6.jsp#VID4.

National Science Foundation. (2011b). Proposal and award policies and procedures guide. Grant proposal guide. Chapter II proposal preparation instructions. Available at: http://www.nsf.gov/pubs/policydocs/pappguide/nsf11001/gpg_2.jsp#dmp.

Nature. (2002). How to encourage the right behaviour. *Nature, 416*(6876), 1. doi:10.1038/416001b.

Nature. (2005). Let data speak to data. *Nature, 438*(7068), 531. doi:10.1038/438531a.

Nature. (2009a). Data for the masses. *Nature, 457*(7226), 129. doi:10.1038/457129a.

Nature. (2009b). Data's shameful neglect. *Nature, 461*(7261), 145. doi:10.1038/461145a.

Nature Biotechnology. (2009). Credit where credit is overdue. *Nature Biotechnology, 27*(7), 579. doi:10.1038/nbt0709-579.

Organisation for Economic Co-operation and Development (OECD). (2007). OECD principles and guidelines for access to research data from public funding. Retrieved from http://www.oecd.org /dataoecd /9/61/38500813.pdf.

Osswald, A., & Strathmann, S. (2012). The role of libraries in curation and preservation of research data in Germany: Findings of a survey. In *78th IFLA General Conference and Assembly*. Available at: http://conference.ifla.org/sites/default/files/files/papers/wlic2012/116-osswald-en.pdf.

Pampel, H., & Bertelmann, R. (2011). "Data policies" im Spannungsfeld zwischen Empfehlung und Verpflichtung. In S. Büttner (ed.), *Handbuch Forschungsdatenmanagement*. Bad Honnef: Bock + Herchen, pp. 49–61.

Pampel, H., Bertelmann, R., & Hobohm, H.-C. (2010). "Data librarianship" Rollen, Aufgaben, Kompetenzen. In U. Hohoff & C. Schmiedeknecht (eds.), *Ein neuer Blick auf Bibliotheken*. Hildesheim: Olms, pp. 159–176. Available at: http://econpapers.repec.org/paper/rswrswwps/rswwps144.htm.

Pampel, H., Goebelbecker, H.-J., & Vierkant, P. (2012). *re3data.org: Aufbau eines Verzeichnisses von ForschungsdatenRepositorien. Ein Werkstattbericht (Forthcoming)*. Jülich: Forschungszentrum Jülich.

Pfeiffenberger, H., & Carlson, D. (2011). "Earth system science data" (ESSD) a peer reviewed journal for publication of data. *D-Lib Magazine, 17*(1/2). doi:10.1045/january2011-pfeiffenberger.

Piwowar, H.A., Day, R.S., & Fridsma, D.B. (2007). Sharing detailed research data is associated with increased citation rate J. Ioannidis, ed. *PLoS ONE, 2*(3), 308. doi:10.1371/journal.pone.0000308.

Pryor, G. (2012). *Managing research data*. London: Facet Publishing.

Reilly, S., et al. (2011). *report on integration of 15 data and publications*, Available at: http://www.alliancepermanentaccess.org/wpcontent/uploads/downloads/2011/11/ODE-ReportOnIntegrationOfDataAndPublications-1_1.pdf.

Reilly, S. (2012). The role of libraries in supporting data exchange. In *78th IFLA General Conference and Assembly*. Available at: http://conference.ifla.org/sites/default/files/files/papers/wlic2012/116-reilly-en.pdf.

Savage, C.J. & Vickers, A.J. (2009). Empirical study of data sharing by authors publishing in PLoS Journals C. Mavergames, ed. *PLoS ONE*, *4*(9), e7078. doi:10.1371/journal.pone.0007078.

Science. (2011). Challenges and opportunities. *Science*, *331*(6018), 692–693. doi:10.1126/science.331.6018.692.

Sears, J.R., (2011). Data sharing effect on article citation rate in paleoceanography. IN53B1628. In *AGU Fall Meeting 2011*. Available at: http://static.coreapps.net/agu2011/html/IN53B-1628.html.

Smith, D., & Carrano, A. (1996). International large-scale sequencing meeting. *Human Genome News*, *6*(7). Available at: http://www.ornl.gov/sci/techresources/Human_Genome/publicat/hgn/v7n6/19intern.shtml.

Tenopir, C., et al. (2011). Data sharing by scientists: Practices and perceptions C. Neylon, ed. *PLoS ONE*, 6(6), p.e21101. doi:10.1371/journal.pone.0021101.

The Royal Society. (2012). Science as an open enterprise. The Royal Society Science Policy Centre report, Available at: http://royalsociety.org/uploadedFiles/Royal_Society_Content/policy/projects/sape/2012-06-20-SAOE.pdf..

Turner, M. (2011). The German *E. coli* outbreak: 40 lives and hours of crowdsourced sequence analysis later. *Nature News Blog*. Available at: http://blogs.nature.com/news/2011/06/the_german_e_coli_outbreak_40.html.

van der Graaf, M. & Waaijers, L. (2011). A Surfboard for riding the wave. Towards a four country action programme on research data, Wellcome Trust. Available at: http://www.knowledge-exchange.info/Admin/Public.

Wellcome Trust. (2003). Sharing data from largescale biological research projects. A system of tripartite responsibility. Available at: http://www.genome.gov/Pages/Research/WellcomeReport0303.pdf.

Wicherts, J. M., et al. (2006). The poor availability of psychological research data for reanalysis. *The American psychologist*, *61*(7), 726–728. doi:10.1037/0003-066X.61.7.726.

Woutersen-Windhouwer, S., et al. (2009). *Enhanced publications: Linking publications and research data in digital repositories*. Amsterdam: Amsterdam University Press. Available at: http://dare.uva.nl/aup/nl/record/316849.

# Intellectual Property and Computational Science

Victoria Stodden

**Abstract** This chapter outlines some of the principal ways United States Intellectual Property Law affects the sharing of digital scholarly objects, particularly for those who wish to practice reproducible computational science or Open Science. The sharing of the research manuscript, and the data and code that are associated with the manuscript, can be subject to copyright and software is also potentially subject to patenting. Both of these aspects of Intellectual Property must be confronted by researchers for each of the these digital scholarly objects: the research article; the data; and the code. Recommendations are made to maximize the downstream reuse utility of each of these objects. Finally, this chapter proposes new structures to manage Intellectual Property to accelerate scientific discovery.

## Introduction

A deep digitization of the scientific enterprise is taking place across the research landscape and generating new ways of understanding our surroundings. As a result, our stock of scientific knowledge is now accumulating in digital form. Our DNA is encoded as genome sequence data, scans of brain activity exist in functional magnetic resonance image databases, and records of our climate are stored in myriad time series datasets—to name but a few examples. Equally as importantly, our reasoning about these data is recorded in software, in the scripts and code that analyze and make sense of our digitally recorded world. Sharing the code and data that underlie scientific findings is a necessary step to permit the transfer of knowledge embodied in the results, so that they can be independently verified, re-used, re-purposed, understood, and applied in new areas to solve new problems.

V. Stodden (✉)
Columbia University, Manhattan, USA
e-mail: victoria@stodden.net

S. Bartling and S. Friesike (eds.), *Opening Science*,
DOI: 10.1007/978-3-319-00026-8_15, © The Author(s) 2014

The inability to access scientific data and code stands as a barrier to the verification of scientific findings, and as a barrier to the knowledge transfer needed to both facilitate scientific advancement and spurn innovation and entrepreneurship around scientific findings (Stodden 2011).

These computational advances have taken place in parallel with the development of the Internet as a pervasive digital communication mechanism, creating an unprecedented opportunity to broaden access to scientific understanding. In this chapter I describe Intellectual Property barriers to the open sharing of scientific knowledge, and motivate solutions that coincide with longstanding scientific norms. In "Research Dissemination: The Narrative", I frame scientific communication as a narrative with a twofold purpose: to communicate the importance of the results within the larger scientific context and to provide sufficient information such that the findings may be verified by others in the field. With the advent of digitization, replication typically means supplying the data, software, and scripts, including all parameter settings and other relevant metadata, that produced the results (King 1995; Donoho et al. 2009). Included in this discussion is the importance of access to the primary research narrative, the publication of the results. "Research Dissemination: Data and Raw Facts" and "Research Dissemination: Methods/Code/Tools" then discuss Intellectual Property barriers and solutions that enable data and code sharing respectively. Each of these three research outputs, the research article, the data, and the code, require different legal analyses in the scientific context.

## Research Dissemination: The Narrative

A typical empirical scientific workflow goes something like this: a research experiment is designed to answer a question; data are collected, filtered, and readied for analysis; models are fit, hypotheses tested, and results interpreted; findings are written up in a manuscript which is submitted for publication. Although highly simplified, this vignette illustrates the integral nature of narrative, data, and code in modern scientific research. What it does not show is the limited nature of the research paper in communicating the many details of a computational experiment and the need for data and code disclosure. This is the subject of the sections "Research Dissemination: Data and Raw Facts" and "Research Dissemination: Methods/Code/Tools." This section motivates the sharing of the research paper, and discusses the conflict that has arisen between the need for scientific diss00emination and modern intellectual property law in the United States.

A widely accepted scientific norm, labeled by Robert K. Merton, is *Communism* or *Communalism* (Merton 1973). With this Merton described an ideal in scientific research, that property rights extend only to the naming of scientific discoveries (Arrow's Impossibility Theorem for example, named for its originator Kenneth Arrow), and all other intellectual property rights are given up in exchange for recognition and esteem. This idea underpins the current system of publication and citation that forms the basis for academic rewards and promotions. Results are described in the research manuscript which is then published, typically in established academic journals, and authors derive credit through their publications and other contributions to the research community. They do not receive financial or other material rewards beyond recognition by peers of the value of their contributions. There are many reasons for the relinquishment of property rights over discoveries in science, but two stand out. It is of primary importance to the integrity of our body of scientific knowledge that what is recognized as scientific knowledge has as little error as possible. Access not just to new discoveries, but also to the methods and derivations of candidates for new knowledge, is imperative for verification of these results and for determining their potential admission as a scientific fact. The recognition that the scientific research process is error prone—error can creep in at any time and in any aspect of research, regardless of who is doing the work—is central to the scientific method. Wide availability increases the chances that errors are caught - "many eyes make all bugs shallow." The second reason Intellectual Property rights have been eschewed in scientific research is the historical understanding that scientific knowledge about our world, such as physical laws, mathematical theorems, or the nature of biological functions, is not subject to property rights but something belonging to all of humanity. The U.S. federal government granted more than $50 billion dollars for scientific research last year in part because of the vision that fundamental knowledge about our world isn't subject to ownership but is a public good to be shared across all members of society.[1] This vision is also reflected both in the widespread understanding of scientific facts as "discoveries" and not "inventions," denoting their preexisting nature. Further, current intellectual property law does not recognize a scientific discovery as rising to the level of individual ownership, unlike an invention or other contribution. Here, we focus on the interaction of intellectual property law and scientific research article dissemination.

Copyright law in the United States originates in the Constitution, when it states that "The Congress shall have Power ... To promote the Progress of Science and useful Arts, by securing for limited Times to Authors and Inventors the exclusive Right to their respective Writings and Discoveries".[2] Through a series of laws and interpretations since then, copyright has come to automatically assign a specific set of rights to original expressions of ideas. In the context of scientific research, this means that the written description of a finding is copyright to the author(s) whether or not they wish it to be, and similarly for code and data (discussed in the following two sections). Copyright secures exclusive rights vested in the author to both reproduce the work and prepare derivative works based upon the original. There are exceptions and limitations to this power, such as Fair Use, but none of these provides an intellectual property framework for scientific knowledge that is

---

[1] The Science Insider: http://news.sciencemag.org/scienceinsider/budget_2012/

[2] U.S. Const. art. I, §8, cl. 8.

concordant with current scientific practice and the scientific norms described above. In fact far from it.

Intellectual property law, and how this law is interpreted by academic and research institutions, means that scientific authors generally have copyright over their research manuscripts. Copyright can be transferred, and in a system established many decades ago journals that publish the research manuscripts typically request that copyright be assigned to the publisher for free as a condition of publication. With some notable exceptions, this is how academic publication continues today. Access to the published articles requires asking permission of the publisher who owns the copyright owner, and usually involves paying a fee. Typically scientific journal articles are available only to the privileged few affiliated with a university library that pays subscription fees, and articles are otherwise offered for a surcharge of about $30 each.

A transformation is underway that has the potential to make scientific knowledge openly and freely available, to everyone. The debate over access to scientific publications breaks roughly into two camps. On one side are those who believe tax-payers should have access to the fruits of the research they've funded, and on the other side are those who believe that journal publishing is a business like any other, and the free market should therefore be left unfettered.[3] The transformation started in 1991 when Paul Ginsparg, Professor of Physics at Cornell University, set up an open repository called arXiv.org (pronounced "archive") for physics articles awaiting journal publication. In the biosciences, a new publishing model was brought to life in 2000—Open Access publishing—through the establishment of the Public Library of Science, PLoS.[4] PLoS publishes scientific articles by charging the authors the costs upfront, typically about $1300 per article, and making the published papers available on the web for free.[5] The PLoS model has been extraordinarily successful, gaining in prestige and publishing more articles today than any other scientific journal.[6]

The U.S. government has joined in this movement toward openness in scientific literature. In 2009 the National Institutes for Health (NIH) began requiring all published articles arising from research it funds to be placed in the publicly accessible repository PubMed Central[7] within 12 months of publication. In January of 2011, President Obama signed the America COMPETES Reauthorization Act of 2010.[8] This bill included two key sections that step toward the broad implementation of Open Access mandates for scientific research. The Act both

---

[3] Association of American Publishers Press Release: http://www.publishers.org/press/56/

[4] See: http://blogs.plos.org/plos/2011/11/plos-open-access-collection-%E2%80%93-resources-to-educate-and-advocate/ for a collection of articles on Open Access.

[5] See http://www.plos.org/publish/pricing-policy/publication-fees/ for pricing information.

[6] See http://scholarlykitchen.sspnet.org/2011/06/28/plos-ones-2010-impact-factor/ for recent impact factor information.

[7] PubMed Central: http://www.ncbi.nlm.nih.gov/pmc/

[8] America COMPETES Reauthorization Act of 2010: http://www.gpo.gov/fdsys/pkg/BILLS-111hr5116enr/html/BILLS-111hr5116enr.htm

required the establishment of an Interagency Public Access Committee to coordinate dissemination of peer-reviewed scholarly publications from research supported by Federal science agencies, and it directed the Office of Science and Technology Policy in the Whitehouse to develop policies facilitating online access to unclassified Federal scientific collections. As a result, on November 3, 2011 the Whitehouse announced two public requests for information on, "Public Access to Peer-Reviewed Scholarly Publications Resulting From Federally Funded Research" and "Public Access to Digital Data Resulting From Federally Funded Scientific Research," As this chapter goes to press, the Office of Science and Technology Policy at the Whitehouse is gathering plans to enable Open Access to publications and to data from federal funding agencies.[9]

These events indicate increasing support for the public availability of scientific publications on both the part of regulators and the scientists who create the content.[10] The paradoxical publishing situation of sustained high charges for content generated (and subsidized) for the public good came about in part through the scientific norm of transparency. As mentioned earlier, establishing a scientific fact is difficult, error-prone work. The researcher must convince skeptics that he or she has done everything possible to root out error, and as such expose their methods to community scrutiny in order to flush out any possible mistakes. Scientific publication is not an exercise in *informing* others of new findings, it is an active dialog designed to identify errors and maximize the integrity of the knowledge. Scientific findings and their methodologies that are communicated as widely as possible have the best chance of minimizing error.

Scientific knowledge could be spread more widely, more mistakes caught, and the rate of scientific progress improved. Scientists should be able to share their published articles freely, rather than remitting ownership to publishers. Many journals have a second copyright agreement that permits the journals to publish the article, but leaves copyright in the hands of the authors.[11] We are in need of a streamlined and uniform way of managing copyright over scientific publications, and also copyright on data and code, as elaborated in the next section.

---

[9] See http://www.whitehouse.gov/blog/2013/02/22/expanding-public-access-results-federally-funded-research

[10] Unsurprisingly, the journal publishers are not so supportive. Just before the 2011 winter recess, House representatives Issa and Maloney introduced a bill that would do enormous harm to the availability of scientific knowledge and to scientific progress itself. Although no longer being considered by Congress (support was dropped the same day that publishing giant Reed-Elsevier claimed it no longer supported the bill), the "Research Works Act" would have prohibited federal agencies and the courts from using their regulatory powers to make scientific articles arising from federally funded research publicly available.

[11] See for example Science Magazine's alternative license at http://www.sciencemag.org/site/feature/contribinfo/prep/lic_info.pdf (last accessed January 29, 2013).

# Research Dissemination: Data and "Raw Facts"

Computational science today is facing a credibility crisis: without access to the data and computer code that underlies scientific discoveries, published findings are all but impossible to verify (Donoho et al. 2009). This chapter discusses how Intellectual Property Law applies to data in the context of communicating scientific research. Drawing on our vignette introduced in the beginning of "Research Dissemination: The Narrative," data is understood as integral in the communication of scientific findings. Data can refer to an input into scientific analysis, such as a publicly available dataset like those at Data.gov[12] or one gathered by researchers in the course of the research, or it can refer to the output of computational research. In short, it is typically inference, and array of numbers or descriptions, to which analysis interpretation is applied.

In 2004, Gentleman and Temple Lang (Gentleman and Temple Lang 2004). introduced the concept of the *compendium*: a novel way of disseminating research results that expands the notion of the scientific publication to include the data and software tools required to reproduce the findings. At core, the research compendium envisions computational results not in isolation, but as components in a description of a meaningful scientific discovery.

Reproducible computational science has attracted attention since Stanford Professor Jon Claerbout wrote some of the first really reproducible manuscripts in 1992.[13] Since then a number of researchers have adopted reproducible methods (Donoho and Buckheit 1995; Donoho et al. 2007; Stodden et al. 2012) or introduced them in their role as journal editors[14] (Trivers 2012). Mature responses to the ubiquity of error in research have evolved for both branches of the scientific method: the deductive branch relies on formal logic and mathematical proof while the empirical branch has standards of statistical hypothesis testing and standardized communication of reproducibility information in the methods section. Unifying the scholarly record to include digital objects such as code and data with the published article facilitates the new types of information flows necessary to establish verifiability and reproducibility in computational science.

As we saw in the previous section, copyright attaches to the original expression of ideas and not to the ideas themselves. In the case of data, U.S. copyright does not attach to raw facts.[15] In 1991 the U.S. held that raw facts are not copyrightable although the original "selection and arrangement" of these raw facts may be.[16] The Supreme Court has not ruled on Intellectual Property in data since and it

---

[12]  See https://explore.data.gov/

[13]  See http://sepwww.stanford.edu/doku.php?id=sep:research:reproducible

[14]  Journal of Experimental Linguistics: http://elanguage.net/journals/jel

[15]  Although copyright does attach to raw facts under European Intellectual Property Law. This is a key distinction between European and U.S. Intellectual Property systems in the context of scientific research.

[16]  Feist Publications v. Rural Telephone Service Co., 499 U.S. 360 (1991).

seems plausible that in modern scientific research the original selection and arrangement of facts may create a residual copyright in a particular dataset, if there was "original selection and arrangement" of these raw facts. Collecting, cleaning, and readying data for analysis is often a significant part of scientific research.

The *Reproducible Research Standard* (Stodden 2009a, b) recommends releasing data under a Creative Commons public domain certification (CC0) in part because of the possibility of such a residual copyright existing in the dataset.[17] Public domain certification means that as the dataset author you will not exercise any rights you may have in the dataset that drive from copyright (or any other ownership rights). A public domain certification also means that as the author you are relying on downstream users' ethics, rather than legal devices, to cite and attribute your work appropriately.

Datasets may, of course, have barriers to re-use and sharing that do not stem from Intellectual Property Law, such as confidentiality of records, privacy concerns, and proprietary interests from industry or other external collaborators that may assert ownership over the data. Good practice suggests planning for data release before beginning a research collaboration, whether it might be with industrial partners who may foresee different uses for the data than really reproducible research, or with scientists subject to a different Intellectual Property framework for data, such as those in Europe (Stodden 2010, 2011).

## Research Dissemination: Methods/Code/Tools

Computational results are often of a complexity that makes communicating the steps taken to arrive at a finding prohibitive in a typical scientific publication, giving a key reason for releasing the code that contains the steps and instructions that generated the published findings. Of the three digital scholarly objects discussed in this chapter, code has the most complex interactions with Intellectual Property Law as it is both subject to copyright and patent law.

Software is subject to copyright, as it is an original expression of an underlying idea. The algorithm or method that the code implements is not subject to copyright, but copyright adheres to the actual sequence of letters and numbers that is the code. Copyright prohibits others from reproducing or modifying the code—for scientific applications this would prohibit running the code on a different system (reproducing) or adapting the code to a new problem (re-using). These action are openly encouraged in scientific research and again, scientific norms are at odds with Intellectual Property Law. An open license that permits others to re-use scientific code is essential.

---

[17] Creative Commons was founded in 2001 by Larry Lessig, Hal Abelson, and Eric Eldred to give creators of digital artistic works the ability to set terms of use on their creation that differ that those arising from copyright. Creative Commons provides a set of licenses with terms of use for work that differ from, and are usually more permissive than, the default copyright.

The Creative Commons licenses discussed in the previous section were created for digital artistic works and they are not suitable for code. There are, however, a great number of open licenses written for software. Each of these licenses sets some specific terms of use for the software (none of them rescind the underlying copyright). Software can exist in two forms, source and compiled, and for modification transmission of the compiled form alone is not sufficient. In the context of scientific research, source code is often in the form of scripts, python or R for example, that execute in association with an installed package and are not compiled. Communication of the source code, whether intended to be compiled or not, is essential to understanding and re-using scientific code.

There are several open licenses for code that place few restrictions on use beyond attribution, creating the closest Intellectual Property framework to conventional scientific norms. The (Modified) Berkeley Software Distribution (BSD) license permits the downstream use, copying, and distribution of either unmodified or modified source code, as long as the license accompanies any distributed code and the previous authors' names are not used to promote any modified downstream software. The license is brief enough it can be included here:

Copyright (c) <YEAR>, <OWNER>

All rights reserved.

Redistribution and use in source and binary forms, with or without modification, are permitted provided that the following conditions are met:

- Redistributions of source code must retain the above copyright notice, this list of conditions and the following disclaimer.
- Redistributions in binary form must reproduce the above copyright notice, this list of conditions and the following disclaimer in the documentation and/or other materials provided with the distribution.
- Neither the name of the <ORGANIZATION> nor the names of its contributors may be used to endorse or promote products derived from this software without specific prior written permission.

This template is followed by a disclaimer releasing the author from liability for use of the code. The above copyright notice and list of conditions, including the disclaimer, must accompany derivative works. The Modified BSD license is very similar to the MIT license, with the exception that the MIT license does not include a clause forbidding endorsement. The Apache 2.0 license is also commonly used to specify terms of use on software. Like the Modified BSD and MIT licenses, the Apache license requires attribution. It differs from the previously discussed licenses in that it permits users the exercise of patent rights that would otherwise only extend to the original author, so that a patent license is granted for any patents needed for use of the code. The license further stipulates that the right to use the software without patent infringement will be lost if the downstream user of the code sues the licensor for patent infringement. Attribution under Apache 2.0 requires that any modified code carries a copy of the license, with notice of any modified files and all copyright, trademark, and patent notices that pertain to the work must be included. Attribution can also be done in the notice file.

The *Reproducible Research Standard* (Stodden 2009a, b) recommends using one of these three licenses, Modified BSD, MIT, or Apache, for scripts and software released as part of a scientific research compendium, or a similar open license whose only restriction on reuse is attribution.

Patents are a second form of intellectual property that can be a barrier to the open sharing of scientific codes. For example, as noted of the University of British Columbia's website,

> Members of faculty or staff, students and anyone connected with the University are encouraged to discuss and publish the results of research as soon and as fully as may be reasonable and possible. However, publication of the details of an invention may make it impossible to seek patent protection.[18]

Publication is, of course, the primary way research findings are made available, and authors who seek patents may be less likely to openly release their software, as software is a patentable entity (Stodden 2010, 2011). As university technology transfer offices often encourage startups based about patentable technology and software, the incentive to release code that permits others to replicate published findings is reduced. These two systems, technology transfer through patents and scientific integrity through openly available software, can co-exist. A dual-licensing system, for example, can be introduced that enables patent revenues for commercial downstream use, while permitting Open Access for research use such as verification of findings and re-use of code for research application (Stodden and Reich 2011).

It should be made clear that the code and scripts alone are not generally sufficient to ensure reproducible research, nor to understand the scientific findings in question. The accompanying narrative, documentation, and meta-data are an essential part of understanding the research findings and for their verification and replication.

# Conclusion

The current set of scientific norms evolved to maximize the integrity of our stock of scientific knowledge. Hence they espouse independent verification and transparency, and historically this has been part of the rationale for the publication of research findings. The complexity of modern computational science means that in order to make reproducibility possible new types of scholarly objects, data and code, must be communicated. In this chapter I have traced how Intellectual Property Law creates barriers to scholarly communication, through both the copyright and patent systems and suggested solutions and workarounds.

---

[18] University of British Columbia Policy on Patents and Licensing, March 1993, http://www.universitycounsel.ubc.ca/files/2010/08/policy88.pdf

For broad reuse, sharing, and archiving of code to be a possibility, it is important that open licenses be used that minimize encumbrances to access and reuse, such as attribution only licenses like the MIT license or the Modified BSD license. A collection of code with an attribution only licensing structure, or public domain certification, permits archiving, persistence of the code, and research on the code base itself. Similarly for collections of research articles. The current system of distributed permission-based ownership makes archiving, research extensions, and scholarly research on publications next to impossible. For these reasons, as well as the integrity of our body of scholarly knowledge, it is imperative to address the barriers created by current Intellectual Property Law in such a way that access, reuse, and future research are promoted and preserved.

# References

Donoho, D., & Buckheit, J. (1995). *WaveLab and reproducible research*. Stanford Department of Statistics Technical Report.

Donoho, D., Stodden, V., & Tsaig, Y. (2007). About sparseLab. Available at: http://www.stanford.edu/~vcs/papers/AboutSparseLab.pdf.

Donoho, D. L., et al. (2009). Reproducible research in computational harmonic analysis. *Computing in Science & Engineering, 11*(1), 8–18. doi:10.1109/MCSE.2009.15.

Gentleman, R., & Temple Lang, D. (2004). Statistical analyses and reproducible research. Available at: http://biostats.bepress.com/bioconductor/paper2/.

King, G. (1995). Replication, replication. *Political Science and Politics, 28*, 443–499.

Merton, R. K. (1973). The normative structure of science. In R. K. Merton (Ed.), *The sociology of science: Theoretical and empirical investigations*. Chicago: University of Chicago Press.

Stodden, V. (2009a). *Enabling reproducible research: Licensing for scientific innovation* (pp. 1–25). Law and Policy: International Journal of Communications.

Stodden, V. (2009b). The legal framework for reproducible research in the sciences: Licensing and copyright. *IEEE Computing in Science and Engineering, 11*(1), 35–40.

Stodden, V. (2010). The scientific method in practice: Reproducibility in the computational sciences. MIT Sloan Research Paper No. 4773-10. Available at http://papers.ssrn.com/sol3/papers.cfm?abstract_id=1550193.

Stodden, V., et al. (2011). Rules for Growth: Promoting Innovation and Growth Through Legal Reform. Yale Law and Economics Research Paper No. 426, Stanford Law and Economics Olin Working Paper No. 410, UC Berkeley Public Law Research Paper No. 1757982. Available at SSRN: http://ssrn.com/abstract=1757982 or http://dx.doi.org/10.2139/ssrn.1757982..

Stodden, V., & Reich, I. (2011). Software patents as a barrier to scientific transparency: An unexpected consequence of bayh-dole. *SSRN Working Paper*. Available at: http://papers.ssrn.com/sol3/papers.cfm?abstract_id=2149717.

Stodden, V., Hurlin, C., & Perignon, C. (2012). RunMyCode.Org: A novel dissemination and collaboration platform for executing published computational results. *SSRN Electronic Journal*. Available at: http://www.ssrn.com/abstract=2147710.

Trivers, R. (2012). Fraud, disclosure, and degrees of freedom in science. *Psychology Today*. Available at: http://www.psychologytoday.com/blog/the-folly-fools/201205/fraud-disclosure-and-degrees-freedom-in-science.

# Research Funding in Open Science

**Jörg Eisfeld-Reschke, Ulrich Herb and Karsten Wenzlaff**

> *"The ultimate act of Scholarship and Theater is the art of selling"*
>
> George Lois

**Abstract** The advent of the Open Science paradigm has led to new interdependencies between the funding of research and the practice of Open Science. On the one hand, traditional revenue models in Science Publishing are questioned by Open Science Methods and new revenue models in and around Open Science need to be established. This only works if researchers make large parts of their data and results available under Open Access principles. If research funding wants to have an impact within this new paradigm, it requires scientists and scientific projects to make more than just text publications available according to the Open Access principles. On the other hand, it is still to be discussed how Research Funding itself could be more open. Is it possible to generate a new understanding of financing science shaped by transparency, interaction, participation, and stakeholder governance—in other words reach the next level as Research Funding 2.0? This article focuses on both of the aspects: Firstly, how Research Funding is promoting Open Science. Secondly, how an innovative and open Research Funding might look like.

J. Eisfeld-Reschke · K. Wenzlaff
Institut für Kommunikation in sozialen Medien, Berlin, Germany
e-mail: eisfeld-reschke@ikosom.de

K. Wenzlaff
e-mail: wenzlaff@ikosom.de

U. Herb (✉)
Saarland University, Saarbrücken, Germany
e-mail: u.herb@sulb.uni-saarland.de

S. Bartling and S. Friesike (eds.), *Opening Science*,
DOI: 10.1007/978-3-319-00026-8_16, © The Author(s) 2014

# Research Funding Policies: Pushing forward Open Science

In the past decades, with new technology allowing interactive communication between content producers, content consumers, and intermediaries such as the publishing industry, there has been tremendous pressure on journalists, politicians, and entrepreneurs to become more accessible. The Web 2.0, a buzzword comprising of phenomena such as blogs and social networks, is shaping not just communication, but also decision-making in communities ranging from Parliamentarians to CEOs, and from TV staff to newspaper editors.

The scientific community has not felt the same amount of pressure. Nevertheless, a few scientists have taken the lead: Science blogs are increasingly popular and scientists tweet and interact with a larger audience. Universities have opened pages on Facebook and other social networks, or have created internal networks for communication. We have even witnessed the rise of social networks that exclusively address scientists (see Academia Goes Facebook? The Potential of Social Network Sites in the Scholarly Realm). A silent revolution is on its way with more and more students entering the ivory tower of academia with a set of communication expectations based on real-time communication across borders, cultures, and scientific clubs. The ivory tower opened up some windows which are now being showcased as Science 2.0.

Meanwhile, a second silent revolution has been taking place. In 2002, the Soros-founded Budapest Open Access Initiative[1] called for more publications along their principles. Ten years later, Open Access has spread to a plethora of scientific communities, publishers and journals (Björk et al. 2010; Laakso et al. 2011; Laakso & Björk 2012). The more common Open Access has become, the more people start to think about what other sorts of scientific information might be available openly. As is the case with Open Access, for many initiatives striving for Openness in the context of scientific information it is quite unclear what kind of Openness they are claiming or how they define Openness. Some Open Access advocates are satisfied if scientific publications are available online and free of charge (so called Gratis Open Access) while others want these publications to be made available according the principles of the Open Definition,[2] that applies the Open Source paradigm to any sort of knowledge or information, including the rights to access, reuse, and redistribute it.

Considering the Open Science concepts as an umbrella, there are several initiatives (see Herb 2012) that want to open up nearly every component or single item within research and scientific workflows, e.g.:

- *Open Review*, which includes both review of funding proposals and articles that are submitted for publication, the latter traditionally conducted as a peer review. Open Review does not so much aim for Openness according to the Open

---

[1]  Budapest Open Access Initiative: http://www.soros.org/openaccess

[2]  Open Definition: http://opendefinition.org/

Definition or the Open Source Principles, rather it is meant to make the review processes more transparent, impeding cliquishness between colleagues as submitting scientists and reviewers (Pöschl 2004).

- *Open Metrics* as a tool for establishing metrics for the scientific relevance of publications and data that are independent from proprietary databases like the *Web of Science* or the *SCOPUS* database which do not only charge fees, but also disallow unrestricted access to their raw data.
- *Open Access to scientific data* according to the Panton Principles.[3]
- *Open Access* to scientific publications.
- *Open Bibliography*, meaning Open Access to bibliographic data.

As we can see, some of these initiatives focus on free or Open Access to science related information (in the shape of scientific data, scientific publications, or bibliographic data), while others promote a more transparent handling of the assessment processes of scientific ideas and concepts (such as Open Review and Open Metrics).

Many prominent funding agencies have already adopted policies that embrace single elements of an Open Science. Among others, the National Institutes of Health NIH,[4] the Wellcome Trust,[5] the European Research Council,[6] and the upcoming European Commission Framework Horizon 2020[7] also require funded projects to make project-related research data and publications freely available.

The unfolding science of the future will be characterized not only by seamless and easy access, but also by interaction, networked and integrated research information workflows and production cycles, openness, and transparency. Science (at least in the Western hemisphere) was an open process in antiquity, having been debated in agoras in the centre of Greek cities. Even in the Roman Empire, the sharing of ideas across the Mediterranean Sea had a profound impact on civilisation—the French, Swedish, English, Italian and German languages attest to the common linguistic principles that developed in this era. Only with the ideological dominance of the Catholic doctrines following the collapse of the Roman Empire did science retreat to monasteries, and scholarly debate to universities and peer-reviewed science communities. The Enlightenment ensured that the educated citizenry became involved in science, but only the Internet has pushed the possibility for a complete citizen science, not unlike how the Greek science community would have seen the debate.

Even though the online media and the initiatives mentioned above brought *Openness* back to scientific communication, one might ask what research funding which is compliant with the paradigms of Openness and Science 2.0 might look

---

[3] Panton Principles: http://pantonprinciples.org/

[4] SHERPA/JULIET. NIH: http://www.sherpa.ac.uk/juliet/index.php?fPersistentID=9

[5] SHERPA/JULIET. Wellcome Trust: http://www.sherpa.ac.uk/juliet/index.php?fPersistentID=12

[6] SHERPA/JULIET. European Research Council: http://www.sherpa.ac.uk/juliet/index.php?fPersistentID=31

[7] European Commission: http://ec.europa.eu/research/horizon2020/index_en.cfm

like. As we have seen, many funding agencies require fundees to make their project-related research results (as data or text publication) more or less open, or at least freely available, but until now the processes of research funding are hardly ever considered to be relevant to Open Science scenarios and appear to be closed, hidden, and opaque (in contradiction to any idea of Openness).

## Research Funding at Present: Limitations and Closed Discourses

Usually, applications for research funding are reviewed and assessed in closed procedures similar to the review and assessment of articles submitted for publication in scientific journals. This also entails that the reviewers are unknown to the applicant, while, on the other hand, the applicant is known to the reviewers (so-called *single blind review*). Horrobin describes the process of evaluating a funding application as follows:

"A grant application is submitted. The administrators send it to reviewers (usually two) who are specialists in the field and therefore competitors of the applicant. A committee (usually between ten and 30 members) assesses the application and the reviewers' reports, perhaps with a commentary from the administration." (Horrobin 1996, p. 1293). Not only the sequence of events involved in the funding process, but also the results achieved through the funding as well as the publication of the results show similarities: in both contexts, the so-called *Matthew Effect* (Merton 1968) is evident. This effect describes the fact that authors with an already high citation quotient are more likely to keep receiving a high number of citations in the future, and that in the same vein, institutions already attracting vast amounts of funding can expect to pull in more funds than other institutions (see The Social Factor of Open Science, Fries: The Social Factor in Open Science). A current study of the Sunlight Foundation reveals this effect for example in the funding patterns of the National Science Foundation NSF: "Twenty percent of top research universities got 61.6 % of the NSF funding going to top research universities between 2008 and 2011." (Drutman 2012).

Even the handing-over of the final funding decision from the peers to so-called *Selection Committees*, whose verdicts are supposed to incorporate the judgments of the peers, has led to similar results (v. d. Besselaar 2012). Furthermore, peer decisions on research funding from the review process do not appear to be objective: Cole, Cole & Simon presented reviewers with a series of accepted as well as declined funding applications and examined the consistency of the (second) judgment. The result: No significant connection between the first and the second decision on the eligibility of a funding proposal could be established. The results indicate "that getting a research grant depends to a significant extent on chance. The degree of disagreement within the population of eligible reviewers is such that whether or not a proposal is funded depends in a large proportion of cases upon which reviewers happen to be selected for it" (Cole et al. 1981, p. 881). A study by Mayo et. al. produces similar conclusions, it "found that there is a considerable amount of chance associated with funding decisions under the traditional method of assigning the grant to two main reviewers" (Mayo et al. 2006, p. 842). Horrobin even diagnosed in 2001 "an alarming lack of correlation between reviewers' recommendations" (Horrobin 2001, p. 51).

Although the review process for publications as well as for funding proposals is similar, the consequences of distortions in the reviewing of funding applications are far more dramatic. Whereas even a mediocre article, after a series of failed submissions, can hope to be eventually accepted by some lesser journal, an application for research funding is stymied from the beginning by the paucity of funding organizations: "There might often be only two or three realistic sources of funding for a project, and the networks of reviewers for these sources are often interacting and interlocking. Failure to pass the peer-review process might well mean that a project is never funded." (Horrobin 2001, p. 51).

Horobin suggests that the review process for research funding is inherently conservative as evidenced by the preference for established methods, theories, and research models, and that reviewers are furthermore "broadly supportive of the existing organization of scientific enterprise". He summarizes: "it would not be surprising if the likelihood of support for truly innovative research was considerably less than that provided by chance." (2001, p. 51). Consequently, the funding bodies fund "research that is fundamentally pedestrian, fashionable, uniform, and second-league—the sort of research which will not stand the test of time but creates an illusion that we are spending money wisely. The system eliminates the best as well as the worst and fails to deliver what those providing the funds expect." (Horrobin 1996, p. 1293). The preference for mainstream research is thus an impediment to innovation: "The projects funded will not be risky, brilliant, and highly innovative since such applications would inevitably arouse broad opposition from the administrators, the reviewers, or some committee members." (Horrobin 1996, p. 1293). In addition, traditional research funding promotes uniformity: "Diversity—which is essential, since experts cannot know the source of the next major discovery—is not encouraged." (Horrobin 1996, p. 1294). In a meta-study on the effect of peer reviewing in the funding process, Demicheli and De Pietrantonj came to the sobering conclusion that: "No studies assessing the impact of peer review on the quality of funded research are presently available." (Demicheli and Di Pietrantonj 2007, p. 2).

Critics of classic research funding are therefore demanding among other alternatives the allocation of a part of the available funds by lot through an innovation lottery (Fröhlich 2003, p. 38) or through the assignment of funds in equal parts to all researchers: "funds [should be] distributed equally among researchers with academic (...) positions" (Horrobin 1996, p. 1294). Additionally, the application of the Open Review described above would ensure greater transparency of the review

process as well as prevent or counteract distortions; however, in actual fact, Open Review is hardly practiced in funding processes.[8]

In the following, the question as to what extent crowdfunding and other innovative funding procedures and channels may serve as an alternative to traditional research funding will be examined.

## Open Research Funding

Open Science and Open Research Funding share mutual spheres of interest. Both want to advance science through the involvement of citizens, and both want to make content available that was previously hidden behind paywalls of traditional science publishers, informal boundaries of scientific-peer-communities, or formal boundaries established by private or public funding-bodies. It can be compared as to how two areas of content creation with similar situation have addressed this demand for open content: journalism and arts. In both realms, the suppliers of content vastly outnumber the financiers of content.

There are many more journalists, writers, photographers out there willing to provide content than there are people willing to invest in large news corporations, which before the digital era were the only institutions capable of funding large-scale news publishing. Notwithstanding the bromide that the Internet has allowed everybody to publish, it has also allowed everyone to find a financier for publishing—through self-publishing on the eBook market through micropayments to crowdfunding sites like Spot.us[9] or Emphas.is[10] we have seen the gradual development of democratized news funding.

Similarly in the arts. While true skills in the arts still require perseverance, endurance, and none-the-least talent, the Internet has allowed artists to broaden their audience and reach out to fans, thus converting them into patrons for the arts. Therefore artists now enjoy avenues outside of the traditional mechanism in which content is being produced, sold, and licensed.

Let us examine some cases where this new freedom to find financiers for content has blended dynamically with Open-Access principles. In 2011, the Kickstarter[11] project "Open Goldberg variations"[12] reached US-$ 23.748 by recording the Bach Goldberg Variations for release into the public domain[13]:

---

[8] At least some scientists make their funding proposals available after the review is finished (on their motivation see White 2012).

[9] Spot.us: http://spot.us/

[10] Emphas.is: http://www.emphas.is

[11] Kickstarter: http://www.kickstarter.com/

[12] Open Goldberg Variations: http://www.opengoldbergvariations.org/

[13] Kickstarter: http://www.kickstarter.com/projects/293573191/open-goldberg-variations-setting-bach-free

> We are creating a new score and studio recording of J.S. Bach's Goldberg Variations, and we're placing them in the public domain for everyone to own and use without limitations on licensing. Bach wrote his seminal work over 270 years ago, yet public domain scores and recordings are hard or impossible to find. Until now! read the introduction at the Kickstarter project.

The focus of the project is to generate funds for a piece of music that can be found across the world in music stores, but not in the Public Domain with easy redistribution, sharing, and mash-up-possibilities.

A similar idea drove the German platform Sellyourrights.org.[14] Artists were encouraged to release their music into the public domain by having the music crowdfunded through the fans. Unfortunately, that experiment was stopped when the German GEMA—a collective rights union for artists—prohibited musicians (not just GEMA members) from share their work on the platform.[15]

Spot.us—an American platform to crowdfund journalism—was also motivated by public access to investigative journalism. All crowdfunded articles were released under a CC-by-license, thus allowing attribution and sharing.[16] Again, the motivation to create content outside of traditional publishing avenues is a key factor in the success of crowdfunding.

## *Open Research Funding: Some Considerations*

A consideration of the criticism voiced against the traditional models of research funding suggests that innovative procedures of research funding should exhibit certain characteristics. For example, the decision-making process leading to a verdict for or against a funding request should be transparent. Ideally, the decision would be taken not only by a small circle of (frequently) only two reviewers, but also involve the entire academic community of the subject in question. Moreover, the question arises as to whether in the age of electronic communication research funding still has to be based on bureaucratic models of delegating responsibility, or whether the direct participation and involvement of researchers as well as citizens might conceivably be practiced. Since research funding is not only subject to the inherent conservative tendencies mentioned above, but also thematically restricted by the available funding programs, it can also be asked as to whether there might not be more flexible vehicles that are better suited for the funding of niche projects unrelated to the buzzwords or academic discourses of the day.

---

[14] Sell your rights. The Blog: http://blog.sellyourrights.org/

[15] Unreturned Love: http://blog.sellyourrights.org/?p=252

[16] Poynter: http://www.poynter.org/latest-news/top-stories/89906/break-the-mold-brainstorming-how-newspapers-could-make-money/

## *Crowdfunding*

Obviously, crowdfunding meets several of the aforementioned criteria. Jim Giles, while commenting also on the public nature of crowdfunding, states in this context: "*Crowd-funding*—raising money for research directly from the public—looks set to become increasingly common." (Giles 2012, p. 252). In principle, crowdfunding can also be more closely intertwined with the model of *Citizen Science* than traditional research funding organizations—for those organizations only a select and narrowly defined circle of applicants, whether institutions or individuals, are eligible. While this pre-selection of fundees may be justified by quality assurance considerations, it also effectively excludes researchers on the basis of institutional (and thus non-academic) criteria—a practice that in an age of rising numbers of *Independent Researchers* conducting their research outside of the university framework may well be put into question. Giles also points out the connection between research and the civic society established through crowdfunding: "It might help to forge a direct connection between researchers and lay people, boosting public engagement with science." (2012, p. 252)

Publicly financed research nevertheless does not appear well-suited to crowdfunding in the classic sense: research as a process is lengthy, institutionally anchored, and team-based. It is also expensive. The results of the research process in many disciplines are not immediately 'tangible'—rather they are documented in articles, books, or conference presentations, and more rarely in patents and new products. Researchers are normally not judged or evaluated according to how well they can explain their research to the public (not to mention to their students), but according to how successfully they present themselves to their peers in the academic journals, conferences, and congresses of their respective fields.

However, the most important impediment is the research process itself. In ancient times, the ideal of gaining knowledge was the open dialogue in the Agora. Our notion of science since the advent of modernity has been marked by the image of the solitary researcher conducting research work in splendid isolation either in a laboratory or library. Although this myth has long since been destroyed by the reality of current research, it is still responsible for the fact that a substantial part of the publicly financed academic establishment feels no pressure to adequately explain or communicate their research and its results to the public. In particular, there is no perceived need to involve the public even in the early stages of the research project, for example in order to discuss the research motivations and methods of a project.

An alternative model of research is described by Open Science. Open Science aims to publish research results in such a manner that they can be received and newly interpreted by the public, ideally in an Open Access journal or on the Internet. However, Open Science also means that research data are made public and publicly accessible. Yet this concept of Open Access is incompatible with current financing models which profit from limited access to research. The concept is, however, compatible with the basic notion underlying crowdfunding—that of the democratization of patronage of the arts, which bears many similarities to the public patronage of the sciences. A quick glance at the mutually dependent relationship existing between the 'free' arts and company sponsors, wealthy individuals, and the funding agencies of the public sector reveals that the supposedly 'free' sciences are tied up in an equally symbiotic relationship with political and economic interests.

The democratization of research financing does not necessarily lead to a reduction in dependency but rather increases reciprocity. Nevertheless, in analog fashion to the creative industries, crowdfunding can also be used as an alternative, supplementary, or substitute financing instrument in research funding. Just as crowdfunding does for film, music, literature, or theatre projects, crowdfunding in research has one primary purpose: To establish an emotional connection between the public and an object.

If seen in this way, the ideal of the 'rational scientist' seems to contrast with 'emotional science'. Yet the enormous response elicited in our communications networks by a small NASA robot operating thousands of miles away on another planet testifies to the emotional potential inherent in science. The example of CancerResearchUK[17] demonstrates that this potential can also be harnessed for crowdfunding. As part of the CancerResearchUK initiative, attempts were made to increase donations to scientific projects by means of crowdfunding. The special draw of the campaign was the chance for supporters to reveal their personal connection to cancer—be it the death from cancer of a friend or relative, the recovery, the effect of medicines, medical advances, or research.

What then should a crowdfunding platform for science look like, if it is supposed to be successful? One thing is clear. It will not look like Kickstarter, Indiegogo,[18] or their German equivalents Startnext,[19] Inkubato,[20] Pling,[21] or Visionbakery.[22] The Kickstarter interface we have become accustomed to in the creative industries which can increasingly be considered as 'learned' or 'acquired' would make little sense in a scientific research context. Kickstarter is successful because four key information elements are made so easily graspable and transparent: Who started the crowdfunding project? How much money is needed overall? How much still has to be accumulated? What do I get for my contribution?

Presumably, crowdfunding for science and research will have to rely on entirely different types of information. A film, for example, is inextricably bound up with the name of a director, or producer, or actors; a team of a different stripe will not be able to replicate this effect. In science, however, the replicability of methods,

---

[17] Cancer Research UK: http://supportus.cancerresearchuk.org/donate/

[18] Indiegogo: http://www.indiegogo.com/

[19] Startnext: http://www.startnext.de/

[20] Inkubato: http://www.inkubato.com/de/

[21] Pling: http://www.pling.de/

[22] Visionbakery: http://www.visionbakery.com/

arguments, and results is key—therefore research and researcher must be independent of each other. The knowledge gap a crowdfunding project is supposed to close is much more salient than the individual researcher. Thus, the big challenge faced by a crowdfunding platform for research is to visualize this gap.

The target amount is of much lesser concern in research crowdfunding than in crowdfunding in the creative industries. In the CancerResearchUK project, this information was visualized—the score of funds received up to the current point was visually indicated on the site—but for most donors the decisive factor in joining was not whether the total amount needed was £ 5,000 or £ 50,00,000, but the concrete result that a contribution of £ 5 or £ 50 from crowdfunding would bring about.

Last, but not not least, the rewards: For many research projects, much thought and creativity will have to be devoted to the rewards, if a reward-based system of crowdfunding is to be favored over a donation-based system like Betterplace[23]. Reward-based crowdfunding on sites like Kickstarter make it essential to provide some material or immaterial rewards to incentivize a contribution; donation-based crowdfunding relies solely on the charitable appeal of a project.

Finding material rewards that are closely connected to the research process for science projects is not an easy proposition—after all, the results of such a project are much more complex than in most crowdfunding projects. Of much greater relevance than the question of what the scientist can give back to the community is hence the problem of what the community can give to the researcher. For this reason, the reward actually lies in the access to science and the research process that participation in the funding initiative allows.

A crowdfunding platform should therefore conceptualize and visualize the following three elements as effectively as possible: (a) visualization of knowledge gaps, (b) results achieved by funds, (c) participation options for supporters.

Although crowdfunding is still the exception among the financing instruments used for research projects, it has nonetheless advanced beyond the merely experimental stage. Among other projects, scientists were able to raise $ 64,000 through the crowdfunding platform Open Source Science Project[24] OSSP for a study on the water quality of the Mississippi River (Giles 2012, p. 252). The way a scientific crowdfunding platform works so far is largely identical to the way platforms devoted to other content categories operate: "Researchers start by describing and pricing a project, which they submit to the site for approval. If accepted, the pitch is placed online and donors have a few weeks or months to read the proposal and make a donation. Some sites operate on a non-profit basis and channel all proceeds to researchers; others are commercial concerns and take a cut of the money raised." (Giles 2012, p. 253).

---

[23] Betterplace: http://www.betterplace.org/de/

[24] The Open Source Science Project: http://www.theopensourcescienceproject.com/

## *Social Payments in Science*

Related to crowdfunding, but not entirely the same, are new tools known as social payments. Typically, these are micropayments given for content that already exists on the net. They share with crowdfunding the notion of many small payments generating large income through accumulation. Flattr[25] and Kachingle[26] are two tools commonly associated with social payments. They are a little different from each other, but share the idea that a content creator embeds a small button on its webpage, and a content financer in pushing that button ships a small payment to the content creator.

When the New York Times put their blogs behind a flexible paywall in 2010, Kachingle rose to the occasion and allowed the readers to "kachingle" the New York Times blogs, in other words transferring a little bit of money to the writers behind the blogs every time they visited the site. The New York Times was not amused and sued Kachingle for using their trademarks—which in the eyes of most commentators was a reaction to new forms of financing typical of a news monolith.

Flattr, another social payment provider, has deep connections with the Creative Commons ecosphere. The website Creative Commons employs a Flattr-button to earn micropayments[27] and many bloggers are putting their content both under a CC license and a Flattr-button. However, there is also one mishap present: Creative Commons are typically shared under a Non-Commercial Clause, which would prohibit the use of Flattr on any blog licensing content into the public domain.[28]

How can social payments be applied to science? Already Scienceblogs are using the social payment system—not necessarily for monetary gains but also for sharing content, engaging in conversation with readers, and measuring relevance[29]:

> "It is easy to find out how many people access a certain Internet site—but those numbers can be deceiving. Knowing that X number of people have clicked on my article on Y is no doubt a good start. But I have no real insight on how many had a genuine interest in precisely this article and have read my article and appreciated it and how many only found my site after a Google search and left after 5 s. There may be tools allowing me to find answers to these questions, but they will most likely require a lot of work and analysis. But if I have a Flattr-button under each of my articles, I can assume that only people who really appreciated reading them will click on it—after all, this click costs them real money." *says Florian Freistetter, author of a blog on Astronomy.*

---

[25] Flattr: http://flattr.com/

[26] Kachingle: http://www.kachingle.com/

[27] FlattrBlog: http://blog.flattr.net/2011/08/great-things-creative-commons/

[28] Techdirt: http://www.techdirt.com/articles/20120828/00585920175/should-creative-commons-drop-its-noncommercial-noderivatives-license-options.shtml

[29] Science Blogs: http://scienceblogs.de/astrodicticum-simplex/2010/06/05/warum-ich-flattr-gut-finde/, translated by the authors.

The real potential of social payments lies in combination with Open Access journals, archives, and publications. Imagine, for instance, databases of publicly available data which allow the users of content to flattr or kachingle the site whenever they visit it? This would allow the making of money from scientific content beyond the traditional licensing systems of universities and libraries. Imagine if a university has a Flattr account filled with 100,000 Euros per year. Every time a university member accesses a scientific journal, the 100,000 Euro is divided among the clicks. This could generate a demand-based but fully transparent way of funding science.

Social payments could also be integrated into direct funding: For instance, through scientists receiving a certain amount of public money or money from funding institutions which cannot be used for their own projects but must be donated to other projects in their discipline. Funds as yet unassigned would remain in a payment pool until the end of the year and then be divided up equally among all projects.

There seems to be some evidence[30] showing that distributions of social payments follow roughly the sharing and distribution behavior of content. In other words, content which is often liked, shared, and tweeted is more likely to receive funds through Flattr.

Social payments are thus likely to generate an uneven distribution of science funding—controversial, popular articles and data might generate more income than scientific publications in smaller fields.

Groundbreaking research might profit from such a distribution mechanism, especially if a new idea applies to a variety of disciplines. The established citation networks of scholars and the Matthew Effect mentioned above might even be stabilized.

Social payments in combination with measuring social media impact could provide an innovative means of measuring relevance in science. Such indices would not replace traditional impact scores, such as appearances in journals, invitations to congresses, and third-party funding, but would allow assessment of the influence of scientific publications within the public sphere.

## Virtual Currencies in Science

All of the tools described above relate in one way or another to real cash-flows in the overall economy. However, these mechanisms might also work with virtual currencies which may be linked to existing currencies, but not in a 1-to-1-relationship.

In Flattr, it is customary to be able to use the earned income within the system to Flattr new content, without having to withdraw cash. The Flattr ecosystem

---

[30] Medien-Ökonomie-Blog: http://stefan-mey.com/2010/05/02/deutsches-flattr-ranking/

generates its own value of worth. Similarly, on crowdfunding sites such as Sellaband[31] or Sonicangel,[32] fans can use some of the rewards they receive to fund new artists. The money stays inside the ecosystem of the platform. Virtual currencies are used often in games, whereby gamers can turn real money into virtual money such as Linden Dollars on Second Life or Farmdollars on Farmville; the virtual money buys goods and services inside the game, both from other players and the game provider, and the earned income can be withdrawn at any time. It might be conceivable that a scientific community creates its own virtual currency. The currency could be used to trade and evaluate access to data, publications, or other scientific resources. Let us imagine for instance that a scientist receives a certain amount of 'Aristotle-Dollars' for every publication in the public domain. Based on the amount of 'Aristotle-Dollars' which they earn, they receive earlier access to public data.

# Some Critical Reflections

## *Quality Assurance and Sustainability*

One advantage of the peer review system is seen in the provision of quality assurance, although the procedure, as stated before, has been criticized. Some of the crowdfunding platforms hosting scientific project ideas also use peer review (for further details, see Giles 2012); for instance, SciFlies[33] and OSSP only publish project ideas after an expert review. Moreover, only members of scientific institutions are allowed to present project ideas via OSSP. In one possible scenario, researchers could identify themselves in crowdfunding environments by means of an author identifier such as the Open Researcher and Contributor ID ORCID[34] and document their expert status in this way (see Unique Identifiers for Researchers, Fenner: Unique Identity for a Researcher). Project proposals from the #SciFund Challenge,[35] on the other hand, were not subject to proper peer review but were scrutinized only in passing. Since the crowdfunding model, however, demands that each submission reveals the research idea and the project realization, a mechanism of internal self-selection can be posited: It can be assumed that scientists will only go public in crowdfunding environments with projects that are carefully conceived.

The same applies to plagiarism and idea or data theft—these types of academic misbehavior would almost certainly be revealed through the public nature of the procedure. The same arguments have also been offered in support of Open Review.

---

[31] Sellaband: https://www.sellaband.de/

[32] Sonicangel: http://www.sonicangel.com/

[33] SciFlies: http://sciflies.org/

[34] ORCID: http://about.orcid.org/

[35] #SciFund Challenge: http://scifundchallenge.org/

Ulrich Pöschl, editor of the journal Atmospheric Chemistry and Physics[36] (ACP), stresses the fact that the transparency of the submissions process in ACP increases the quality of submissions because authors are discouraged from proposing articles of mediocre or questionable quality (Pöschl 2004, p. 107): In the interest of self-protection and self-preservation, scientists can be expected to refrain from exposing and potentially embarrassing themselves in their community with premature or ill-conceived publications. Furthermore, crowdfunding relies upon self-regulation through the expertise of donors who in most cases are able to judge the merits of a proposal themselves, so that weak proposals, if they are made public at all, will have very poor prospects. Some crowdfunding platforms also use forums as additional mechanisms of quality assurance; in FundaGeeks[37] "Geek Lounge", for instance, potential donors can exchange their thoughts on the weaknesses or strong points of a project idea. Thanks to an expert discussion in the Kickstarter forum, a questionable project could be stopped without financial loss for the donors (Giles 2012, p. 253).

In spite of the positive outlook outlined above, scientific crowdfunding has yet to prove the advantages claimed for it. To conclude with Jim Giles: "For crowdfunding to make a real difference, advocates will have to prove that the process—which sometimes sidesteps conventional peer review — channels money to good projects, not just marketable ones." (Giles 2012, p. 252). Also somewhat questionable is the long-term perspective of the projects: Unlike classic research funders, crowdfunding donors can hardly require fundees to only develop sustainable service infrastructures, for example. Conversely, crowdfunding, social payments, and virtual currencies may create new funding avenues facilitating the funding of specific individual researchers rather than abstract projects with fluctuating staff. Small projects with a funding volume below the funding threshold of classic funders could also be financed with these instruments.

## *Plagiarism*

As already mentioned, the public character of proposals for crowdfunding is more likely to expose plagiarism in projects than closed review procedures. For the same reason, researchers submitting their project ideas for crowdfunding demonstrate their claim to a scientific idea or method in a manner that can hardly be ignored, thus discouraging the plagiarizing of 'their' project. To put things into perspective, it must be mentioned that plagiarism or idea theft has also been reported for closed review procedures (Fröhlich 2003, p. 54).

---

[36] Atmospheric Chemistry and Physics: http://www.atmospheric-chemistry-and-physics.net/

[37] FundaGeek: http://www.fundageek.com/

## *Pop Science, Self-Marketing, and Verifiability*

On account of its proximity to citizens and its public character, crowdfunding also bears the inherent danger of unduly popularizing research, especially if any individual may donate to a project. Even though internal platforms for crowdfunding in which only researchers can donate to a project proposal may develop faster, it is conceivable—as with the peer review in traditional funding—that mainstream research is favored. Some also suspect that crowdfunding, but also social payments, could establish a disproportionate preference of applied research over basic research (Giles 2012, p. 253). The same could also be suspected for popular science or science that lends itself easily to media portrayal.

Crowdfunding, social payments, and virtual currencies place new demands on researchers' self-marketing (Ledford 2012), but these demands need not be a bad thing, since a clear, succinct, and understandable presentation of a project proposal can only enhance and augment the verifiability and testability of scientific concepts by eliminating the dense prose and difficult wording found in many funding applications (language that is often mandated by funders' requirements), thus promoting the intersubjective verifiability of scientific concepts called for by science theory and philosophy of science.

A more solid grounding in the scientific community might be achieved if crowdfunding, social payments and virtual currencies were not applied in entirely open contexts, but rather only within scientific communities (if necessary under the umbrella of discipline-specific associations or learned societies). In such a scenario, however, the aspect of involvement of civic society would be lost.

## *What About Openness?*

Although crowdfunding, social payments, and virtual currencies appear as more transparent than traditional avenues of research financing, the question of the 'openness' or accessibility of the research results nevertheless arises. Whereas traditional financing institutions may require fundees to make project results publicly available, it is as yet unclear how projects funded through the innovative procedures detailed above might be mandated to make their project results accessible for the public. Of equal importance may be the question of who owns the rights to a project's results. In the interest of transparency, it might be desirable to make the names of donors who contributed to a project public, so as to identify and prevent potential conflicts of interest. Conversely, the risk of *sponsorship bias* must not be neglected. The term *sponsorship bias* refers to the production of results—consciously or unconsciously—that are consistent with the presumed expectations or desires of the financiers. To minimize the risks posed by *conflicts of interest* as well as sponsorship bias, it may be advisable to keep the identity of the financiers hidden from the fundees until the project's end.

# Appendix: A List of Crowdfunding Platforms for Scientific Projects

- *#SciFund Challenge* hostet by RocketHub, http://scifundchallenge.org/
- *Open* Source *Science Project OSSP*, http://www.theopensourcescienceproject.com/
- *SciFlies*, http://sciflies.org/
- *PetriDish*, http://www.petridish.org/
- *iAMscientist*, http://www.iamscientist.com/
- *Sciencestarter* (by now the only German crowdfunding service for scientific projects), www.sciencestarter.de

# References

Björk, B.-C. et al. (2010). Open Access to the scientific journal literature: situation 2009 E. Scalas, ed. *PLoS ONE, 5*(6), e11273. doi:10.1371/journal.pone.0011273.

Cole, S., Cole, J. R., & Simon, G. A. (1981). Chance and consensus in peer review. *Science, 214* (4523), 881–886. doi:10.1126/science.7302566.

Demicheli, V., & Di Pietrantonj, C. (2007). Peer review for improving the quality of grant applications. In The Cochrane Collaboration & V. Demicheli, (eds.). *Cochrane database of systematic reviews*. Chichester: Wiley. Available at: http://doi.wiley.com/10.1002/14651858. MR000003.pub2.

Drutman, L. (2012). How the NSF allocates billions of federal dollars to top universities. *Sunlight foundation blog*. Available at: http://sunlightfoundation.com/blog/2012/09/13/nsf-funding/.

Fröhlich, G. (2003). Anonyme Kritik: Peer review auf dem Prüfstand der Wissenschaftsforschung. *Medizin—Bibliothek—Information, 3*(2), 33–39.

Giles, J. (2012). Finding philanthropy: Like it? Pay for it. *Nature, 481*(7381), 252–253. doi:10.1038/481252a.

Herb, U. (2012). Offenheit und wissenschaftliche Werke: Open Access, open review, open metrics, Open Science & open knowledge. In U. Herb (Ed.), *Open Initiatives: Offenheit in der digitalen Welt und Wissenschaft* (pp. 11–44). Saarbrücken: Universaar.

Horrobin, D. F. (1996). Peer review of grant applications: A harbinger for mediocrity in clinical research? *The Lancet, 348*(9037), 1293–1295. doi:10.1016/S0140-6736(96)08029-4.

Horrobin, D. F. (2001). Something rotten at the core of science? *Trends in Pharmacological Sciences, 22*(2), 51–52. doi:10.1016/S0165-6147(00)01618-7.

Laakso, M. et al., (2011). The development of Open Access journal publishing from 1993 to 2009 M. Hermes-Lima, ed. *PLoS ONE, 6*(6), e20961. doi:10.1371/journal.pone.0020961.

Laakso, M., & Björk, B.-C. (2012). Anatomy of Open Access publishing: A study of longitudinal development and internal structure. *BMC Medicine, 10*(1), 124. doi:10.1186/1741-7015-10-124.

Ledford, H. (2012). Alternative funding: Sponsor my science. *Nature, 481*(7381), 254–255. doi:10.1038/481254a.

Mayo, N., et al. (2006). Peering at peer review revealed high degree of chance associated with funding of grant applications. *Journal of Clinical Epidemiology, 59*(8), 842–848. doi:10.1016/j.jclinepi.2005.12.007.

Merton, R. K. (1968). The Matthew effect in science: The reward and communication systems of science are considered. *Science, 159*(3810), 56–63. doi:10.1126/science.159.3810.56.

Pöschl, U. (2004). Interactive journal concept for improved scientific publishing and quality assurance. *Learned Publishing, 17*(2), 105–113. doi:10.1087/095315104322958481.

van den Besselaar, P. (2012). Selection committee membership: Service or self-service. *Journal of Informetrics, 6*(4), 580–585. doi:10.1016/j.joi.2012.05.003.

White, E. (2012). On making my grant proposals Open Access. *Jabberwocky Ecology*. Available at: http://jabberwocky.weecology.org/2012/08/08/on-making-my-grant-proposals-open-access/.

# Open Innovation and Crowdsourcing in the Sciences

**Thomas Schildhauer and Hilger Voss**

**Abstract** The advent of open innovation has intensified communication and interaction between scientists and corporations. Crowdsourcing added to this trend. Nowadays research questions can be raised and answered from virtually anywhere on the globe. This chapter provides an overview of the advancements in open innovation and the phenomenon of crowdsourcing as its main tool for accelerating the solution-finding process for a given (not only scientific) problem by incorporating external knowledge, and specifically by including scientists and researchers in the formerly closed but now open systems of innovation processes. We present perspectives on two routes to open innovation and crowdsourcing: either asking for help to find a solution to a scientific question or contributing not only scientific knowledge but also other ideas towards the solution-finding process. Besides explaining forms and platforms for crowdsourcing in the sciences we also point out inherent risks and provide a future outlook for this aspect of (scientific) collaboration.

## What is Open Innovation and What is Crowdsourcing?

Nowadays, companies use online co-creation or crowdsourcing widely as a strategic tool in their innovation processes (Lichtenthaler and Lichtenthaler 2009; Howe 2008). This open innovation process and opening up of the creation process can be transferred to the field of science and research, which is called Open science.

Here we see Open Science on a par with open innovation: both incorporate external knowledge in a research process. One way of doing this is "crowdsourcing". Companies use open innovation when they cannot afford a research and

T. Schildhauer (✉) · H. Voss
Institute of Electronic Business e.V., Affiliate Institute of Berlin University of the Arts, Berlin, Germany
e-mail: schildhauer@ieb.net

S. Bartling and S. Friesike (eds.), *Opening Science*,
DOI: 10.1007/978-3-319-00026-8_17, © The Author(s) 2014

development department of their own but still need external or technical knowledge, or when they want to establish an interdisciplinary route to problem-solving processes. This can be an interesting working milieu for scientists as their involvement in these open innovation processes may lead to third-party funding.

Firms usually initiate open innovation processes by setting up challenges of their own or using dedicated platforms; participation is often rewarded by incentives. The kinds of problems that crop up in the context of open innovation can be very diverse: Challenges can include anything from a general collection of ideas to finding specific solutions for highly complex tasks. IBM's "Innovation Jam" (www.collaborationjam.com) or Dell's "IdeaStorm" (www.ideastorm.com) (Baldwin 2010) quote companies that involve employees of all departments and partners in open innovation as an example. They also interact with external experts, customers and even researchers from universities and other scientific institutions, who do not necessarily belong to the research and development department, in order to pool and evaluate ideas. This concept was introduced by Chesbrough (2003).

Firms tend to favor tried-and-tested solutions and technologies when working on innovations: Lakhani (2006) defined this behavior as local search bias. To his way of thinking, co-creation can be seen as a tool for overcoming the local search bias by making valuable knowledge from outside the organization accessible (Lakhani et al. 2007). Hippel names various studies that have shown some favorable impacts that user innovation has on the innovation process (Hippel 2005).

The advantages of open innovation are not only of interest to companies and firms: it is also becoming increasingly popular with the scientific community in terms of collaboration, co-creation and the acceleration of the solution-finding process (Murray and O'Mahony 2007). In the fields of software development (Gassmann 2006; Hippel and Krogh 2003) and drug discovery (Dougherty and Dunne 2011) in particular, scientists have discovered the advantages of open collaboration for their own work: Open Science—which, for the sake of simplicity, we can define as the inclusion of external experts into a research process.

Most open innovation initiatives do not necessarily address the average Internet user. Often scientists and other specialists from different disciplines are needed: Lakhani et al. (2007) find that the individuals who solve a problem often derive from different fields of interest and thus achieve high quality outcomes.

Open innovation accordingly refers to the inclusion of external experts into a solution-finding process. This process was hitherto thought to be best conducted solely by (internal) experts (Chesbrough 2003). Opening up the solution-finding process is the initial step of using participatory designs to include external knowledge as well as outsourcing the innovation process (Ehn and Kyng 1987; Schuler and Namioka 1993). Good ideas can always come from all areas. Special solutions, however, require specialized knowledge and, of course, not every member of the crowd possesses such knowledge ("mass mediocrity", Tapscott and Williams 2006, p. 16). The intense research on open innovation confirmed this conjecture (Enkel et al. 2009; Laursen and Salter 2006).

Before the term "open innovation" came into existence it was already common for companies to integrate new knowledge gained from research institutes and development departments into their innovation processes (Cooper 1990; Cooper and Kleinschmidt 1994; Kline and Rosenberg 1986).

Crowdsourcing refers to the outsourcing of tasks to a crowd that consists of a decentralized, dispersed group of individuals in a knowledge field or area of interest beyond the confines of the given problem, who then work on this task (Friesike et al. 2013). Crowdsourcing is used by businesses, non-profit organizations, government agencies, scientists, artists and individuals: A well-known example is Wikipedia, where people all over the world contribute to the online encyclopedia project. However, there are numerous other ways to use crowdsourcing: On the one hand, the crowd can be activated to vote on certain topics, products or questions ("crowd voting"), or they can also create their own content ("crowd creation"). This input can consist of answering more or less simple questions (such as Yahoo Answers), creating designs or solving highly complex issues, like the design of proteins (which we will revert to further down).

Figure 1 provides an overview of the different aims and tasks of open innovation and crowdsourcing. The position of the varying fields in the diagram mirrors a certain (not necessarily representative) tendency: questions and answers can be fairly complex, a task in design can be easy to solve and human tasks (like *Amazon Mechanical Turk*)[1] can actually include the entire spectrum from simple "click-working" to solving highly complex assignments.

This section focuses on scientific methods for Open Science via crowdsourcing, also including possibilities and risks for open innovation and crowdsourcing in the sciences. Two major aspects of online crowd creation via crowdsourcing are *firstly* being part of a crowd by contributing to a question raised on a crowdsourcing platform and *secondly* posing a question to be answered by a crowd.

Specialists, scientists in particular, are now the subject of closer inspection: how can scientists and scientific institutions in particular take part in open innovation and open up science projects, and how can they collaborate with companies?

## How Scientists Employ Crowdsourcing

The use of crowdsourcing not only makes it possible to pool and aggregate data but also to group and classify data. It would seem, however, that the more specific a task, the more important it becomes to filter specialists out of the participating mass.

Scientists can chose between four main forms of crowdsourcing:

---

[1] Amazon Mechanical Turk: https://www.mturk.com/mturk/welcome.

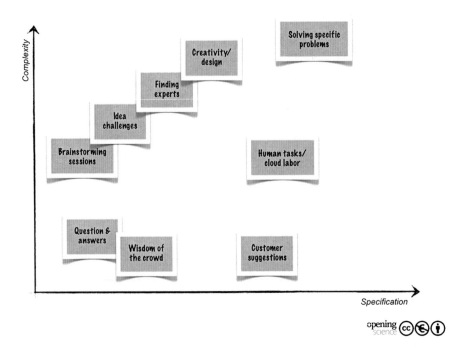

**Fig. 1** Crowdsourcing and open innovation

1. Scientists can connect to individuals and to interest communities in order to collate data or to run through one or a set of easy tasks, such as measurements.
2. Scientists can also use the Internet to communicate with other scientists or research labs with whom they can conduct research into scientific questions on equal terms.
3. The second option can also work the other way round: scientists or experts can contribute to scientific questions.
4. Options 2. and 3. are frequently chosen by firms and companies as a means of open innovation, often combined with monetary benefits for the participant.

We can conclude that the two major forms of open innovation and crowdsourcing in the sciences are: contributing towards a solution (perspective 1) and requesting a solution (perspective 2).

## Perspective 1: Contributing to a Crowdsourcing Process (Open Science)

One form of open innovation through crowdsourcing in the sciences is to contribute to research questions by setting out ideas—often free of charge. In sciences like mathematics and biology or medicine, in particular, Open Science is a well-known and much appreciated form of scientific collaboration.

One famous example is the U.S. "Human Genome Project",[2] which was coordinated by the U.S. Department of Energy and the National Institutes of Health. It was completed in 2003, two years ahead of schedule, due to rapid technological advances. The "Human Genome Project" was the first large scientific undertaking to address potential ethical, legal and social issues and implications arising from project data. Another important feature of the project was the federal government's long-standing dedication to the transfer of technology to the private sector. By granting private companies licences for technologies and awarding grants for innovative research, the project catalyzed the multibillion dollar U.S. biotechnology industry and fostered the development of new medical applications.[3] This project was so successful that the first, original project spawned a second one: the ENCODE project.[4] The National Human Genome Research Institute (NHGRI) launched a public research consortium named ENCODE, the Encyclopedia of DNA elements, in September 2003, to carry out a project for identifying all the functional elements in the human genome sequence.[5]

Another famous project was proposed by Tim Gowers, Royal Society Research Professor at the Department of Pure Mathematics and Mathematical Statistics at Cambridge University who set up the "polymath project",[6] a blog where he puts up tricky mathematical questions. Gowers invited his readers to participate in solving the problems. In the case of one problem, it so happened that, 37 days and over 800 posted comments later, Gowers was able to declare the problem as solved.

Collaborating online in the context of Open Science can be achieved using a multitude of various tools that work for scientists but also for any other researchers: such as a digital workbench, where users can collaborate by means of online tools (network.nature.com); They can also build open and closed communities or workshop groups consisting of worldwide peers by exchanging information and insights (DiagnosticSpeak.com, Openwetware.org); researchers can also establish social networks and pose questions and get them answered by colleagues from all over the world (ResearchGate.com).

---

[2] Human Genome Project Information: http://www.ornl.gov/sci/techresources/Human_Genome/home.shtml.

[3] Human Genome Project Information—About the Human Genome Project: http://www.ornl.gov/sci/techresources/Human_Genome/project/about.shtml.

[4] The Encyclopedia of DNA Elements (ENCODE) Consortium: http://genome.ucsc.edu/ENCODE.

[5] National Human Genome Research Institute: http://www.genome.gov/10005107.

[6] The polymath blog: http://polymathprojects.org.

# Perspective 2: Obtaining Support for One's Own Science (Citizen Science)

The other aforementioned aspect of open innovation through crowdsourcing in the sciences is to ask a community for help. This aspect refers to Luis von Ahn[7] and his approach to "human computation": numerous people carry out numerous small tasks (which cannot be solved by computers so far). To ask a community for help works in "citizen science", which, for the sake of simplicity, we can define as the inclusion of non-experts in a research process, whether it is a matter of data collection or specific problem-solving. Crowdsourcing is a well-known form of "citizen science". Here, as scientificamerican.com explains, "research often involves teams of scientists collaborating across continents. Now, using the power of the Internet, non-specialists are participating, too".[8]

There are various examples where scientists can operate in this manner and obtain solutions by asking the crowd. This form of crowdsourcing is also present in the media: scientific media bodies have established incorporated websites for citizen science projects like www.scientificamerican.com/citizen-science/ where projects are listed and readers are invited to take part. In view of the crowd-sourcing strategy "Ask the public for help", scientists can use these (social) media websites to appeal to the public for participation and help. A research area or assignment might be to make observations in the natural world to count species in the rain forest, underwater or pollinators visiting plants—especially sunflowers, as in "The Great Sunflower Project"[9]—or to solve puzzles to design proteins, such as in the "Fold It"[10] project. Citizens interested in this subject and scientists working in this field of knowledge can therefore be included as contributors.

A very vivid example is the "Galaxy Zoo"[11] project. Briefly, the task is to help classify galaxies. Volunteers are asked to help and it turned out that the classifications galaxyzoo.org provides are as good as those from professional astronomers. The results are also of use to a large number of researchers.

Another example of how to activate the crowd is ARTigo, a project from art history. A game has been created and each player helps to provide keywords or tags for images. The challenge here is to find more suitable tags—preferably hitherto unnamed ones—than a rivaling player in a given time. The Institute for Art History at the Ludwig Maximilian University in Munich was accordingly able to collect more than four million tags for its stock of more than 30,000 images.[12] Paying experts to perform this task would have been unaffordable.

---

[7] Luis von Ahn: http://www.cs.cmu.edu/~biglou/.

[8] Scientific American: http://www.scientificamerican.com/citizen-science/.

[9] The Great Sunflower Project: http://www.greatsunflower.org.

[10] Fold it: http://fold.it/portal/.

[11] Galaxy Zoo: http://www.galaxyzoo.org.

[12] ARTigo: http://www.artigo.org/about.html.

The following examples show how different platforms allow scientists and other experts to engage in open innovation, and how scientists and research departments can use these platforms for their own purposes.

| | Innocentive | Innoget | Solution-xchange | One billion minds | Presans | Inpama | Marblar |
|---|---|---|---|---|---|---|---|
| Country | USA | Spain | India | Germany | France | Germany | UK |
| Founded in | 2001 | 2007 | 2008 | 2009 | 2008 | 2012 | 2012 |
| Focus | Innovation challenges (initiated by companies/ organisations); community | Innovation challenges and presentation of new solutions | Innovation challenges; community | Scientific and social projects | Search for experts on specific issues | Completed ideas to date | Develop products based on new and existing technologies; gamification |

## Innocentive (www.innocentive.com)

Innocentive.com is the best known open innovation platform that allows companies and experts to interact (Wessel 2007). It was founded by the pharmaceutical company Eli Lilly. According to their own information, there are now more than 260,000 "problem solvers" from nearly 200 countries registered on Innocentive.com. Thanks to strategic (media) partnerships, however, more than 12 million "solvers" can be reached. Over $ 35 million were paid out to winners, with sums ranging between $ 500 and over $ 1 million, depending on the complexity of the task.

## *Forms of Challenges and Competitions*

Challenges can either be addressed to the external community, or they may be limited to certain groups of people, such as employees. There are also various forms of competitions: "Ideation Challenge", "Theoretical Challenge", "RTP Challenge" and "eRFP Challenge".

- "Ideation Challenges" are for the general brainstorming of ideas—relating to new products, creative solutions to technical problems or marketing ideas, for example. In this case, the solver grants the seeker the non-exclusive rights to his ideas.
- "Theoretical Challenges" represent the next level: ideas are worked out in detail, accompanied by all the information required to decide whether or not the idea can be turned into a finished product or solution. The period of processing is longer than for an "Ideation Challenge". The financial incentives are also

much higher. The solver is usually requested to transfer his intellectual property rights to the seeker.

- "RTP Challenge" calls for a further solution layout on how the solution, once it has been found, can be applied by the company that invited contributions. The "solvers" are accordingly given more time to elaborate the drafts they have submitted, while the reward rises simultaneously. Depending on how the challenge is put, either the intellectual property rights are transferred to the "seeker" or the "seeker" is at least given a licence to use.
- "eRFP Challenge" is the name of the last option to pose a challenge. Scientists in particular might be interested in this option: Normally, companies have already invented a new technology and are now looking for an experienced partner—like external consultants or suppliers—to finalize the developed technology. In this case, legal and financial stipulations are negotiated directly between the cooperating parties.

The site's "Challenge Center" feature provides an opportunity for interaction between the "seekers" and "solvers". Companies and institutions—the "seekers"—post their assignments, and the "solvers" select those that are of interest to them based on the discipline in which they work.

## *Registration, Profile and CV*

Anybody can register as a "solver", even anonymously, if they chose, but a valid email address is required. The profile, which is open to the public, can either be left blank or provide substantial personal information. It is possible to name one's own fields of expertise and interest. There is no strict format for the CV; academic degrees and a list of publications may be mentioned. External links, to one's own website, for example, or to a social network profile can be added. The "solver" can decide whether he or she wants to make his or her former participations in challenges public. "Solvers" can easily be classified on the basis of this information: the "seeker" obtains an immediate impression of how many "solvers" might have the potential to contribute a solution for the given task. It is also possible to recruit new "solvers". In this case the "seeker" can observe the activities of the "solvers" involved (under "referrals"). If a successful solution is submitted, the "solver" who recruited his colleague who actually solved the problem gets a premium. The recruitment takes place via a direct linkage to the challenge. This link can be published on an external website or in a social network. The "InnoCentive Anywhere" App creates an opportunity for the "solver" to keep up-to-date with regard to forthcoming challenges.

# Innoget (www.innoget.com)

Innoget focuses on linking up organizations that generate innovations with those that are in search of innovation, both having equal rights. Research institutions in particular are addressed as potential solution providers. Solution providers can put forward their proposals for a solution in return for ideas on creating a surplus which might be valuable to them. The basic difference between this and Innocentive.com is that, while Innocentive builds up a community—quite detailed profile information including expertise, subjects of interest and (scientific) background are called for—which makes it possible to form teams to find solutions for a challenge, Innoget.com merely asks for a minimum set of profile questions. It also has to be mentioned that offering solutions/technologies has to be paid for, so Innoget.com seems to be less interesting to individuals than to companies. Participating in and posing challenges is free of charge, although other options have to be remunerated: providing a company profile and starting an anonymous challenge, for instance. Offers and requests are both furnished with tags detailing the branch and knowledge field. You can also look for partners via the detailed search provided. You can choose categories like countries, nature of challenge (such as a collaboration, licensing or a research contract) or organization/institution (major enterprise, public sector, university etc.).

# SolutionXchange (www.solutionxchange.com)

SolutionXchange.com was founded by Genpact, an Indian provider of process and technology services that operates worldwide. A distinctive feature is that only Genpact-members and customers can submit challenges to the platform.

As mentioned in the previous examples, registration is easy and free to all experts and users. After naming the most basic information, such as primary domain and industry, it is possible to add detailed information on one's profile: education, career or social network links etc., but you can opt to dispense with that. As soon as you have registered, you can upload white papers or your own articles or write blog entries that you wish to be discussed. You can also join and found communities. At SolutionXchange.com you can also request to join the network as a pre-existing group or organization.

Ongoing challenges are initially listed according to your profile information; after using filter options, different challenges will be displayed on your profile page as well. Of special interest is the area called "IdeaXchange", where all the different communities, articles and blogs appear and—independent of the actual challenges—external experts meet Genpact members for discussion. Submitted articles are evaluated by Genpact experts or by the companies that set up the challenge. At the end of the challenge, Genpact has the opportunity to assign individual experts with the task of evolving an idea that was remunerated, depending on the importance or size of the project or the time spent on development.

# One Billion Minds (www.onebillionminds.com)

This platform calls itself "Human Innovation Network"; "openness" according to the open innovation principle is highlighted in particular.

Registration is simple, detailed information on one's profile cannot be named, but you can type in links to your profile located on an external social network.

Inviting contributions towards a given challenge is simple, too: after providing information on the challenger (whoever set up the challenge: company, non-profit organization, individual as well as the origin) only the challenge's title, a further description of it and a public LinkedIN-profile are required. Afterwards the challenger has to describe the aim of the challenge, possible forms of collaboration between initiator/challenger and participant, a deadline and a description of the rewards (not necessarily monetary rewards). It is also possible to pay for and charge Onebillionminds.com with moderating the submitted answers. At Onebillionminds.com social and scientific projects have equal rights to those that have an economical aim. The declared intention of Onebillionminds.com is "to change the world".[13]

# Presans (www.presans.com)

Presans.com follows a very different approach from those mentioned above: The company provides a search engine that—according to the platform's own description—browses through the whole data base that contains about one million experts looking for matching partners. Here Presans.com keeps a low profile when it comes to selection criteria: Nevertheless, it seems that publications and the assurance of the expert's availability are of value. This issue is based on the assumption that the solution-seeking company often does not know what kind of solution the company is actually looking for.

# Inpama (www.inpama.com)

Inpama.com enables inventors and scientists to present their solutions ready for licensing and accordingly ready to be put on the market. Inpama.com was founded by InventorHaus, a company that runs several inventors' businesses and inventor or patent platforms in the German-speaking countries. Companies that are looking for solutions can receive information on offers that fit their own business area, so they can easily get in touch with inventors. Impama.com offers inventors various possibilities via different media such as image, text, video or web links to describe

---

[13] One Billion Minds: http://www.onebillionminds.com/start/.

their products and patents. Tags mark the product's category. Also, Inpama.com offers further information and assistance with improving the product or invention by contacting test consumers or industrial property agents or by marketing the invention.

## Marblar (www.marblar.com)

Marblar.com adopts a very interesting approach. Assuming that a minimum of 95 % of the inventions that have been developed at universities are never realized, scientists are given a chance to present their inventions to potential financiers and to the public. The special aspect in this instance is for the presented inventions to be developed further through gamification: Players can earn points and can receive monetary rewards up to £10,000. In this way, Marblar.com helps to make inventions useful that would have been filed away. Marblar.com also helps to open up a further source of income to the research institutions.

## A Landscape of Today's Platforms: Summary

The crowdsourcing platforms often consist of creatives that participate either by submitting active content, such as contributions to a challenge, or by judging contributions to challenges. Referring to the platform Innocentive.com, where more than 200,000 "problem solvers" are registered, it is obvious that not every single member submits input for every single challenge. Due to the size of the group, however, there is a very great likelihood that a lot of valuable ideas will be put forward. Technically speaking, it is possible that every participant could take part in every challenge, but this is not true of all the platforms mentioned here. Nevertheless, Innocentive.com provides an opportunity of thinking "outside the box" because it allows the participants to name not only their own field of knowledge but also their field of personal interest. It is accordingly possible to generate new ways of solving complex problems. It seems obvious that either communication and interaction within a community or the building of new communities is of interest: the submitted ideas are frequently hidden. It is possible that lots of companies are not as "open" as open innovation suggests, but perhaps concealing ideas is not that absurd after all: these open innovation challenges do not interact with the masses like many other common crowdsourcing projects do. Many crowdsourcing platforms that work in the field of open innovation provide an opportunity for organizing challenges for closed groups or pre-existing communities whose members are either invited, belong to the company or other associated communities that are then sworn to secrecy.

   As shown above, scientists can choose between diverse platforms if they want to participate in open innovation. Usually you can register with detailed profiles. In most cases you can communicate with different experts within your fields of knowledge or interest. In this way, there are other advantages apart from the financial benefits in the event of winning a challenge: insights into a company's internal problems are given that might also fit in with a scientist's own range of duties.

It is apparent that there are a great many inspiring options and processes to be gained from the variety of platforms, which may play a substantial role in fostering the integration of and collaboration between scientists.

It will be exciting to watch and see how Marblar's gamification principle develops and to find out if financial incentives are to remain the most important aspect of open innovation. But how do individuals, companies, scientists and experts respond to platforms like Inpama.com or Presans.com: will challengers/inititators prefer to submit challenges to platforms like Innocentive.com or do they accept the possibility of search engines browsing through the data of submitted technologies?

The legal aspect remains of considerable importance: Innocentive.com outlines the point of the challenge fairly clearly when intellectual property changes ownership. But still, details of that have to be discussed between the "solver" and the "seeker".

## Risks in Crowdsourcing Science

It is clear that different risks have to be taken into account when using or applying the methods of crowdsourcing or open innovation. The crowd is not invincible, although often praised for clustered intelligence. A high number of participants does not guarantee the finding of an ideal solution.

But who actually makes the final decision about the quality of the contributions in the end? Does it make sense to integrate laymen, customers or individuals and researchers who work outside the problem field into these kind of creative processes in any case?

A detailed and unambiguous briefing by the platform host seems to be called for. This also applies to participants: ideas need to be short and formulated clearly in order to survive the evaluation process. It is one thing for a company to ask its target group about marketing problems but quite another to ask the target audience—where only a few are professionals in the problem field—to solve difficult and complex (research) questions. Nevertheless, human tasks of different but less complexity can be carried out by anonymous carriers, although the limits are still reached fairly quickly.

Another important factor is dealing with the high number of submitted ideas and proposed solutions. Who should and might actually be able to evaluate them all? How does one avoid overlooking the best ideas? Often crowdsourcing also means that the participants themselves evaluate their proposals—in this way a form of pre-selection takes place and points out ideas that should attract interest.

Nonetheless, manipulation may occur when networks or communities fuse to support certain ideas because they aim to win the prize, inflict damage on the initiator or for any other reasons. You can overcome this risk by backing up the crowdsourcing process with a jury of experts who monitor the process and can intervene and provide a final evaluation, where required.

There is always the risk of a participant losing his or her idea without getting paid for it. This might even happen without the initiator's appearance: it is possible that other participants or external viewers steal the idea. In this context we have to mention that it is frequently only the winner who gets rewarded for his or her input—all the other participants miss out although they might have contributed several days of dedicated effort for the purpose of the challenge.

For contestants, crowdsourcing and open innovation are a very debatable source of income. The safeguarding of a contestant's property is left to his or her own resources. Researchers should therefore check the agreement drawn up between them and the platform host to see whether intellectual property is covered properly. This can be ensured by documenting timestamps and with the help of a good community management through the platform host.

Of interest to both parties is the delicate question of profit participation: what happens if the participant receives 1,000 Euros for his or her idea but the company makes millions out of this idea? The question remains why a researcher or other collaborator should join in without any certainty that his or her contribution at any stage of the research/creation process is of value, whether it will be appreciated and adequately remunerated.

So, the initiator and participant have to take a careful look at legal protection. Actually, this can prove to be quite easy: The initiator can set up the rules and the participant can decide, after having studied the rules, whether he or she agrees and wants to participate or not. A situation under constraint, such as financial dependence, is often rejected a priori. Assigning intermediaries can often serve to adjust a mismatch. The more specialized the task, the more weight rests with the expert or "solver". Internet communication enables the solver to draw attention to unfair conditions: Both platform host and initiator are interested in retaining a good reputation; any possible future participants might be discouraged. Much depends on the question of how the Internet can be used to connect B2C or B2B companies, scientists or research institutions to target groups and how to receive desired opinions and ideas; but also how to integrate scientists in particular? How to ensure and achieve valid results? What legal, communicative, social factors need to be contemplated? And what further steps are there to mind after a crowdsourcing process? It would be unflattering if customers, scientists and creatives were motivated to participate but, after that, nothing happened or they weren't mentioned in reports on the crowdsourcing process. That would only cause or aggravate frustration and that is something nobody needs.

## Outlook: What the Future Might Bring

A possible future route for development might be hyper-specialization: "Breaking work previously done by one person into more specialized pieces done by several people" (Malone et al. 2011). This means that assignments that are normally carried out by one or only a few people can be divided into small sections by accessing a huge "crowd" of experts including researchers from all knowledge fields and task areas.

There is usually an inadequate number of hyper-specialists working for a company. Provided the transition between different steps of a working process is smooth, the final result might be of a higher quality. Here the following question arises: at what point would "stupid tasks" start to replace the highly specialized work, i.e. where experts are reduced to the level of a mental worker on the assembly line?

One possible result of open innovation's success might also be the decline or disappearance of research and development departments or whole companies: to begin with, staff members would only be recruited from the crowd and only then for work on individual projects.

Another outcome might also be that the social media principle of user generated content could be transferred to the area of media products: normal companies could be made redundant if the crowd develops products via crowdsourcing and produces and finances them via crowdfunding.

A further conceivable consequence might be the global spread of the patent right's reform: new solutions might not get off the ground if they violated still existing patents. The more the crowd prospers in creating inventions, developments and ideas, the more difficult is becomes to keep track and avoid duplicates in inventions. This raises the question of authorship: what happens to authorship if the submitted idea was created by modifying ideas put forward by the crowd's comments? When does the individual become obsolete so that only the collective prevails? Do we begin to recognize the emergence of a future model where individuals are grouped and rearranged according to the ideas being shared and the resulting benefits? And to what extent will the open source trend increase or find its own level?

## References

Baldwin, C. Y. (2010). *When open architecture beats closed: The entrepreneurial use of architectural knowledge*. Massachusetts: Harvard Business School.

Chesbrough, H. W. (2003). *Open innovation: The new imperative for creating and profiting from technology*. Boston: Harvard Business School Press.

Cooper, R. G., & Kleinschmidt, E. J. (1994). Perpektive. Third generation new product process. *Journal of Product Innovation Management, 11*, 3–14.

Dougherty, D., & Dunne, D. D. (2011). Digital science and knowledge boundaries in complex innovation. *Organization Science, 23*(5), 1467–1484. doi:10.1287/orsc.1110.0700.

Ehn, P., & Kyng, M. (1987). The collective resource approach to systems design. In G. Bjerknes, P. Ehn, & M. Kyng (Eds.), *Computers and democracy* (pp. 17–58). Aldershot: Avebury.

Enkel, E., Gassmann, O., & Chesbrough, H. (2009). Open R&D and open innovation: Exploring the phenomenon. *R&D Management, 39*(4), 311–316.

Friesike, S., Send, H., & Zuch, A. N., (2013). Participation in Online Co-Creation: Assessment and Review of Motivations. Conference Paper. Unpublished work.

Gassmann, O. (2006). Opening up the innovation process: Towards an agenda. *R&D Management, 36*(3), 223–228.

von Hippel, E. (2005). Democratizing innovation. The evolving phenomenon of user innovation. *Journal für Betriebswirtschaft, 55*(1), 63–78.

von Hippel, E., & von Krogh, G. (2003). Open source software and the "private-collective" innovation model: Issues for organization science. *Organization Science, 14*(2), 209–223. doi:10.1287/orsc.14.2.209.14992.

Howe, J. (2008). *Crowdsourcing: Why the power of the crowd is driving the future of business* (1st ed.). New York: Crown Business.

Kline, S. J., & Rosenberg, N. (1986). An overview of innovation. In R. Landau (Ed.), *The positive sum strategy* (pp. 275–305). Washington: National Academy of Sciences.

Lakhani, K.R. (2006). *The core and the periphery in distributed and self-organizing innovation systems*. Doctor's Thesis. Cambridge: MIT Sloan School of Management.

Lakhani, K. R. et al. (2007). *The value of openness in scientific problem*. In working paper. Boston: Harvard Business School.

Laursen, K., & Salter, A. (2006). Open for innovation: The role of openness in explaining innovation performance among U.K. manufacturing firms. *Strategic Management Journal, 27*, 131–150.

Lichtenthaler, U., & Lichtenthaler, E. (2009). A capability-based framework for open innovation: Complementing absorptive capacity. *Journal of Management Studies, 46*(8), 1315–1338.

Malone, T. W., Laubacher, R. J., & Johns, T. (2011). The big idea: The age of hyperspecialization. *Harvard Business Review*, July–August 2011. Available at: http://hbr.org/2011/07/the-big-idea-the-age-of-hyperspecialization/ar/1.

Murray, F., & O'Mahony, S. (2007). Exploring the foundations of cumulative innovation: implications for organization science. *Organization Science, 18*(6), 1006–1021. doi:10.1287/orsc.1070.0325.

Schuler, D., & Namioka, A. (1993). *Participatory design: Principles and practices*. Hillsdale: L. Erlbaum Associates.

Tapscott, D., & Williams, A. D. (2006). *Wikinomics: How mass collaboration changes everything*. New York: Portfolio.

Wessel, D. (2007). Prizes for solutions to problems play valuable role in innovation. *The Wall Street Journal*. Available at: http://online.wsj.com/public/article/SB116968486074286927-7z_a6JoHM_hf4kdePUFZEdJpAMI_20070201.html.

# The Social Factor of Open Science

Tobias Fries

**Abstract** Increasing visibility in the Internet is a key success factor for all stakeholders in the online world. Sky rocketing online marketing spending of companies as well as increasing personal resources in systematic "self-marketing" of private people are a consequence of this. Similar holds true for the science and knowledge creation world—here, visibility is also a key success factor and we are currently witnessing the systematic exploitation of online marketing channels by scientists and research institutes. A theoretical base for this novel interest in science marketing is herein provided by transferring concepts from the non-science online marketing world to the special situation of science marketing. The article gives hints towards most promising, practical approaches. The theoretical base is derived from considerations in the field of scale-free networks in which quality is not necessarily a predominant success factor, but the connectivity.

## Introduction

New aspects of Web 2.0, together with those that are already familiar, are about to completely revolutionize the world of academic publishing. The gradual removal of access barriers to publications—like logins or unavailability in libraries—will increase the transparency and accordingly the use of Web 2.0 elements. We can envisage evaluation and suggestion systems for literature based on such factors as relevance and reputation along similar lines to search engines. Conversely, while it is conceivable that networking systems and search engine technology will consequently become increasingly prone to manipulation, this will at the same time be preventable up to a certain point.

T. Fries (✉)
Witten/Herdecke University, Witten, Germany
e-mail: Tobias.Fries@gmx.de

S. Bartling and S. Friesike (eds.), *Opening Science*,
DOI: 10.1007/978-3-319-00026-8_18, © The Author(s) 2014

# The Transition from Science to Open Science

Admittedly some way behind the consumer sector, the field of science is now beginning to grow accustomed to the Internet. Certain ingrained dogmas that previously stood in the way, like a general sense of apprehension on the grounds of it being "unscientific" are being cast aside—slowly but surely—to reveal the innovative concepts, even though this is proving to be a slightly hesitant process. Just how hesitant becomes clear when we take a look at the use of Wikipedia, by way of an example. Wikipedia is admittedly not a primary source of information and calls for considerable caution when quoting, but this doesn't make it apply any less to the seemingly objective conventional science. This is not meant as a disparaging remark or an insult to the significance of scientific relevance but merely serves to point out comparable dangers. We cannot judge the objectivity of unofficial editors who contribute to the Social Internet on a voluntary basis any more than we can assess the source of funds used to sponsor an academic study. It is in any event wise to exercise basic level of caution when employing it for any objective purpose.

Anyone—including scientists—who acquainted himself/herself with the new media early on is already at a great advantage, even now. The earliest pioneers were able to send the treatises to and from much more frequently via email than with the traditional postal system, and this in turn considerably shortened editing cycles, and whoever dared to blow caution to the wind and post his/her text on the Internet, despite any fears of data theft, was rewarded with tangibly higher citation rates. The reasons for this are intuitively plausible to anyone who has ever carried out research work him- or herself: we only quote what we find. No matter how brilliant an unavailable text may be, if it is unknown, nobody will cite it. This conclusion can be drawn by taking into account the work of de Solla Price (1976), who analyzed Cumulative Advantage Processes on the example of paper citations. By showing that the Science Citation Index only used to consider 1573 sources out of 26000 journals of interest, he calculated a possible total reach of 72 % by having access to only the first 6 % of journals. He also found out that a longer presence in the archives increased citation rates as a result of higher potential availability. To transform de Solla Prices findings into other words, it is not the content alone that leads to its subsequent utilization in academic circles but also the extent of its reach. This correlation can also be expressed in the form of an citation conversion equation, by dividing the number of quotes (k) by the number of times a text is read (n):

$$k_{Cit} / n_{Read} = C \tag{1}$$

Factor C is used here to denote the citation conversion rate, a coefficient already familiar from conventional web analysis. The conversion rate refers to the ratio between the number of orders placed with online shops and the overall amount of web traffic or the number of baskets/shopping carts filled without proceeding to the check-out. It serves as an indication of the quality of the website which, by deduction, can also provide a straightforward analogy to the quality of the academic publication. Although the concept of the quality of academic publications has been around for decades, a reliable evaluation has yet to be realized, because no-one so far has managed to track the frequency with which they are read. State-of-the-art performance assessment of academic articles is largely restricted to the quantitative number of citations and, very occasionally, the publication location and the circulation of the journals and books can, with considerable limitations, provide some clues as to the distribution. Acceptance for publication is, however, much more subjective than academia would like to admit. Publication frequently depends on personal contacts, political considerations or the scientific expertise of small editing committees, who may not necessarily fully recognize the significance of a treatise that is indeed new from an academic point of view.

By contrast, academics who post their publications on the Internet in an open, search-friendly format, stand a better chance of being quoted which, given the specific rationale of de Solla Price findings, consequently creates a self-perpetuating effect with every additional citation. Anyone who can be accessed is absolutely bound to be read more frequently, and even where the quality is inferior, may well be quoted less often (in relative terms) but more frequently from the point of view of the absolutely greater number of readers. Since the absolute citation rate in the current status quo is one of the key indicators of quality, a citation volume derived from the high statistical figures leads to a real perception of quality, possibly even when there are better articles on the same topic.

In their own interests, anyone who has grasped this concept is hardly likely to hide the treatises they have written behind the log-ins of a personal homepage, for which there may be a charge, or the internal domains of publishing companies' websites. Academic publications are not a mass product, and anyone who wants to earn money on the basis of the print run would be better off with books dealing with sexuality, entertainment or automotive topics, as these subjects regularly attain a publication run of a million copies or more. In so far as academics are ever involved in their field of interest for money, this is earned indirectly through lectures, consultation fees or application products derived from scientific research, to which the publication itself only contributes the legitimizing reputation. Browsing the Internet with the help of Google Scholar, Google Books or any other search engine while restricting one's search to documents with the ending.pdf will nowadays turn up a large number of academic publications whose full text is extremely specific and its perusal accordingly highly productive for one's own publications. Some publishers and authors even go as far as placing long passages of their books verbatim on online book portals like Amazon, specifically for search purposes, which a good many academics employ for the inclusion of such books that might not otherwise have been selected for citation. There is undoubtedly a conflict of goals and it is proving to be a problem for quite a number of researchers today: the more pages of a book or publication are read in a public domain, the fewer copies are going to be sold. If we regard the turnover achieved with the product and the number of book sales as a yardstick for measuring success, then this viewpoint is justified. If we go one step further, however, to the level of reach or prominence they gain, the number of sales is of absolutely secondary importance.

Barabási/Albert provide a next level of scientific explanation for this correlation with their analysis of networks, which can be regarded as the indisputable standard in network research—at least in terms of the number of recorded citations (cf. Barabási and Albert 1999). At the time of writing this article, Barabási had been quoted by more than 12,000 other scientists, according to Google Scholar. The content of the article deals with the clustering behavior of nodes in scale-free networks. This designation refers to graphs displaying structures that resemble their own but on a different scale: in other words, their structures look similar when enlarged or decreased in size. Another feature of scale-free networks is an exponential function in the number of clusters. Conventional random networks typically display a bell-shaped curve in their distribution function, according to which most nodes have a similar number of links and, in the boundary areas of the bell-shaped curve, tend to be those that deviate from this mean (cf. Erdős and Rényi 1960). Examples of conventional random networks include transport or electricity networks, as depicted in Figs. 1 and 2 for the European high-speed railway network.

During their investigation, Barabási and Albert (1999) looked at Internet links and initially assumed a random network of the kind introduced by Erdös and Rényi (1960). They were, however, surprised to discover an exponential distribution function rather than a bell-shaped curve. This contained a small number of websites (nodes) which were linked to an extremely large number of other

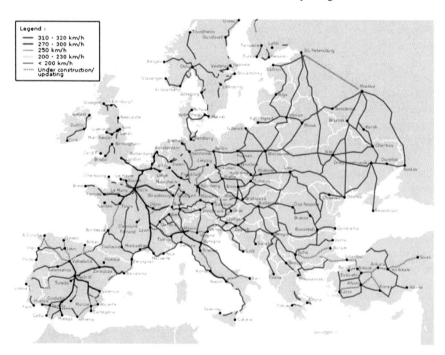

**Fig. 1** The high-speed railway network in Europe. It represents a random network as proposed by Erdős and Rényi. (*Source and copyright of the diagram* Akwa and Bernese media and BIL under a creative commons licence)

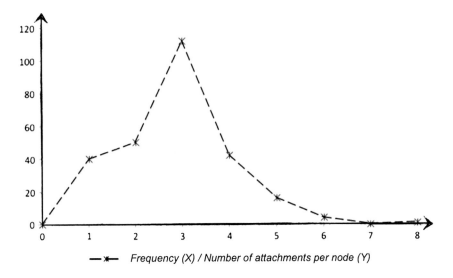

**Fig. 2** The frequency distribution of the links between the nodes of the European high-speed railway network. The density function superimposed on the *dots* illustrates the underlying Poisson distribution

websites and an extremely large number of websites to which just a very few other sites pointed. Taking their research further, they came across a probability mass function in other scale-free networks, with the help of which it was easier to find well-attached nodes, so they were linked up more often. They called this phenomenon "Preferential Attachment" and succeeded in proving that clustering dynamics of this kind give rise to ever-increasing imbalances in the network system over a longer period of time, so that well-attached nodes accumulate further links whereas less well-attached nodes attract even fewer new links. Barabási later coined the very apt designation "The Rich get Richer Phenomenon" to describe this effect (cf. Barabási and Bonabeau 2003, p. 64f).

Applying this investigation to science, it confirms the hypothesis proposed at the beginning of this treatise that reach, rather than quality, can lead to truth—particularly in the case of low visibility and accordingly less likelihood of the better essay being linked. Both de Solla Price and Barabasi/Albert identified exponential distribution functions in scientific citation, one called the phenomenon "Cumulative Advantage Processes", the other one "Preferential Attachment".

There are nevertheless far-reaching discussions currently in progress in academic circles regarding free access to publications, intellectual property rights and the supposed protection of scientific independence. The conflicting goals of scientists and publishers might be interpreted as the reason behind these discussions. Scientific advancement does not necessarily have to be the main priority of the publishing companies, seeing as they are financing an infrastructure and pay its owners dividends. They themselves do not have a share in the indirect income raised through the reputation of the scientist concerned, so the publishers' main interest must lie in the direct generation of revenue, while intellectual property rights and limited access safeguard their influence. By contrast, if we take a closer look, the researcher has an interest in barrier-free accessibility and is therefore trying to break free of the publishers' sphere of influence, although they give him the benefit of the Open Science network. The fact that discussions of this nature are already in progress could be construed as friction due to a change of paradigms, because science could become more objective, more transparent and consequently more democratic, offering impartial benefits to researchers and research outcomes alike, if it were organized properly and supported by the rigorous use of certain aspects of the social web. To ensure that publishers don't come away empty-handed from a turn-around of this kind, they would be well advised to grasp the mechanisms behind this trend—the sooner, the better—and help to shape the framework in which science will be operating in the future through timely investments in the infrastructure for this Science Web 2.0. The fact that those who get noticed early on benefit from long-term reach applies to publishers as well, because a publishing company's reputation—and accordingly being published within its infrastructure—already attracts the better scientists; an innovative form of publication will make no difference to the fundamental research results achieved by de Solla Price and Barabási/Albert. The early bird catches the worm, regardless of whether that bird is a publisher or a researcher.

## The Importance of Network Science for Research Relevance

There are only a few research results that can be described as "objectively good". It is usually those publications about which enough other people speak favorably in terms of that particular topic that are perceived as being "good". The few contributions to research that are objectively and indisputably good receive favorable feedback anyway, due to the excellent quality of their work, provided they attract a sufficiently wide audience. More often than not, however, work that is merely mediocre receives positive feedback because its stands out from the rest or because the author already enjoys a good reputation. The most obvious forms of favorable feedback in academic circles are citations and references. And the higher the number, the greater the likelihood of being quoted again in the future, since it is easier to find a frequently cited article than one that has been cited less often. So the "Rich get Richer" phenomenon applies to researchers, too. On a practical level, this explains why it is much easier for a professor who has been publishing articles for many years to get his next paper published in an acclaimed journal than a young person, even though he might be the more brilliant of the two, who is trying to make his debut with an outstanding first work. At the same time it becomes clear why it may be of an advantage for the brilliant young individual to ask the professor for his support in publishing his first article, as this would allow the young author to establish his first links via the science network while the older research might profit a little from the spillover effect of the excellent debut article.

Seen as a whole, this section serves to explain why publishing scientists have an interest in being quoted as frequently as possible. It is equally conceivable that there are sufficient reasons for manipulating citations, always with the aim of being cited more often by others. A number of scientists managed to solve this problem in the past by means of citation cartels, and in case this is controversial, let it be said that it definitely applies to some operators of websites at least, because it constituted a problem for search machines for a long time.

The following section addresses feasible aspects of the Social Internet for Open Science, always against the backdrop of possible manipulation and the ensuing consequences in practice. This list, like the whole book, is an incomplete preview of a topic that is still under development but will revolutionize science.

## Aspects of the Social Web in Open Science

Users particularly welcome innovations when they hold the promise of an advantage of some kind. Individual features embedded in otherwise linear platforms will be just as unsuccessful as those that regularly fail nowadays in consumer applications. The intelligent consolidation of information to create an outcome that is of broad use to all stakeholders involved will assert itself unless an inferior, but high-reach solution achieves exclusive prominence in the eyes of the users. For this reason, the aspects set out below can only realize a fraction of their collective, self-multiplying effect. They are nevertheless being included individually for the sake of maintaining the linear structure of the text.

## *The Basic Principles of Search Engines: Relevance and Reputation*

The purpose of search engines is to present results of relevant Internet searches, arranged according to their reputation. Relevance is assessed by subjecting the available contents and the contents of other referring websites to a special quantification process, while the reputation is determined from a wide range of other aspects, beginning with the number of referring websites and including users' appraisals and the surfing patterns of people visiting the websites. Due to the widespread manipulation of search results, search engines have long since moved away from metrics based solely on the number of inbound links—a practice which, despite similar manipulation incentives, has not yet caught on in the field of science, where the number of citations still prevails as the standard benchmark.

The operators of Open Science platforms accordingly have a similar responsibility to that of search engines. In present-day research, scientists already have to select from the literature pertaining to their specific sphere of research. Purely determining the topical relevance is the simplest task; assessing the technical relevance is much more difficult. In cases of uncertainty or other causes of hesitation, the researcher will also take the reputation of a scientist into account when contemplating who to quote. Each and every piece of research is restricted by the subjective field of vision of that which the scientist finds. Publications that escape his or her notice due to a language or access barrier will not be included in the shortlist.

The challenge in setting up Open Science is to achieve as comprehensive a selection of scientific texts as possible with the lowest possible access barrier, to enable publishing scientists to obtain the desired level of relevance and reputation with the help of publication platforms. Merely widening the field of vision for researchers is the easiest task: increasing objectivity and transparency in the assessment of reputation will prove to be a challenge. Bearing the evolution of search engines in mind, we anticipate a highly dynamic advancement and permanent alignment of the algorithms employed.

## Identification of the Protagonists

The fact that there are sometimes two or more scientists with the same name can be misleading, but this is not so serious that it renders research impossible, although common names do make it more difficult to identify which researcher is meant, especially when they are both active in the same field. With the Open Science Web approach, every scientist can be allocated an unambiguous profile, complete with photo, a brief CV, main research focus and, in particular, a specific ID number. Existing Science Communities like ResearchGate,[1] which already provide a representative picture, seem to be particularly suitable. Profiles with an open platform identification number enable an integrated use of Open Science features, as introduced below. The open-platform architecture is of particular importance. A platform such as ResearchGate, for instance, will gain a strategic lead as far as reach is concerned, along similar principles to those presented above, if it makes its own researcher ID available on the Internet for other academic purposes free of charge and without any barriers. The permanent core reference to this platform will lead every researcher back to the original community—a long-term benefit in terms of influence and reputation cannot actually be foreseen at the moment, due to the growing number of members, but it is highly probable when we consider the dynamic evolution of scale-free networks.

## Ascertaining a Quality Factor from Likes, Dislikes, Assessments and Comments

One of the most straightforward uses of the Social Web 2.0 for Open Science is the ability to transfer positive and negative ratings and comments. These features

---

[1] www.researchgate.com.

are not new by any means, the most prominent among them being those employed by Facebook, but even there they were not new, owing to their simplicity. Blogs, online book marketplaces and bidding platforms recognized the principle of assessment for boosting one's reputation at a much earlier stage and used it to their own advantage. It can basically be divided into simple expressions of approval or disapproval (like or dislike), an interesting aspect being that Facebook only allows the affirmative "like" vote which, judging by the demographic structure of its users, may be of inestimable value in protecting the psychological development of school-children/minors, seeing as countless cases of cybermobbing have been heard of even when the voting is limited to favorable "thumbs up" ratings. Although science ought to be regarded as objective and rational, it would be wrong to underestimate the interests that lie behind research results, and which might play a role in influencing the assessment of publications beyond the limits of objectiveness. Only a process of experimentation and subsequent evaluation can determine whether the accumulation of negative votes leads to an objective improvement in assessment or encourages the intentional underrating of undesirable research results. In the interests of transparency, however, it would probably make sense to show features of this kind with a clear, publicly visible reference to the originator. In this way, likes, dislikes, assessments and comments would reflect straight back on the reputation of the person passing the criticism and would consequently be better thought-out than anonymous comments. This contrasts starkly with the fear of uncomfortable, but justified truths which are more easily expressed anonymously. It might be possible to experiment with both forms in order to ascertain a quantified quality factor that would also be taken into consideration in evaluating the reputation of an article or researcher.

## Crowd Editing

The possibility of crowd editing is a completely new, feasible feature in the Open Science web. Strictly speaking, it amounts to the steadfast further development of joint publications. While the ideal number of academics working on a treatise is limited to two, three or occasionally four scientists, crowd editing opens up a publication on a general level. As introduced earlier on in this book (see chapter Dynamic Publication Formats and Collaborative Authoring), anyone reading the article can contribute voluntarily to it provided he/she has something relevant to add. Old versions can remain stored in archives, as is the case with Wikipedia articles, and subject-related changes can be either approved or rejected by a group of editors before an official new version of the article is published. It is conceivable that the relevant subversion could be cited—not really a new procedure—but the principle of crowd editing might increase the frequency of amendments.

## *Suggestion Systems for Articles During the Writing Process*

The potentiality of suggestion systems is, however, really new. Whereas authors today actively look for literary sources in conventional and digital libraries, innovative technologies enable smart suggestion systems. The insertion of context-based Internet advertising is a long-established practice, whilst its academic counterpart is still in its infancy. Only Google, in its capacity as trailblazer of search-engine technology, already proposes search-related topics and authors, thus paving the way for the intelligent linking of academics and their publications.

It starts to become exciting when suggestions for potentially interesting, subject-related articles are put forward during the actual writing process. This might to a certain extent release researchers from the somewhat less intellectual task of merely compiling information while simultaneously providing them with additional sources, which they might not have found so easily on their own, since they are only indirectly linked to the topic in question via another association, for instance. Special attention should be paid, when developing the relevant technologies, however, to the selection algorithm, which harbors the risk of tempting the researcher into a convenience trap. The mental blanking out of other sources might represent one aspect of a trap of this kind—a phenomenon that is likewise rooted in the network theory. In this case, the sources that attract most attention are those that are closest to the interests of the researcher in question and are already most visible (cf. Barabási and Albert 1999). The predefined ranking of pop-up results is another hazard. There are countless analyses of the recorded click rate for search results using the Google search engine. Various analysis in Google Analytics reports conducted over several years have repeatedly provided a similar picture—about 80 % of all clicks landed on the first five search results that appeared on the screen, 18 % on the remaining ones on the first page and only 2 % on the second page. This data has been retrieved by comparing search statistics with click statistics. Due to their previous experience and working routines, one can assume that academics conduct their research more thoroughly than general consumers. Nevertheless, such attributes as convenience and circumstances like being in a hurry are only human and also apply to a certain extent to researchers, which bodes quite well for the first secondary sources in the list, at least.

Against this backdrop it emerges what a high priority status the algorithm will have with regard to the presentation of suitable secondary literature. Due to the great resemblance in structure, we assume that this feature will operate along much the same lines as search engines, so it is likely to face similar challenges and problems. We will revert to this topic further down, in the section dealing with the presentation of results.

Once these technical problems have been solved satisfactorily, we can envisage a completely new form of academic writing, along the lines of the example outlined briefly below:

## *Example of Academic Writing*

A researcher has an idea for an article and already possesses some previous knowledge of the subject-matter, which allows him to put his idea into words straight away. So, using a web application designed specifically for academic writing, he begins to type his idea into the space provided. Since he is logged in, the platform is not only able to create direct references to his previous work and topics processed on the platform but can also read his current input and compare it with texts contributed by other scientists. While he is writing, the researcher can now view context-related excerpts on the screen next to his own text, which might be of interest for the passage he is writing. Other, more general articles dealing with the subject concerned, which might be of relevance to this treatise, appear elsewhere. Based on the topics and contributions evaluated on the platform, the researcher in this particular example also receives suggestions as to which other scientists he should contact for the purpose of exchanging information and views.

This case illustrates a scenario of higher transparency on several levels. Besides those relating to texts, the researcher also receives suggestions relating to people who might prove to be an interesting point of contact. This might conceivably be extended to announcements for specialist conferences, other relevant events or items that match the theme.

## Parallels to Search Engines

Expressed in simplified terms, search engines consist of a crawler and an indexer. The crawler visits websites, records the contents and proceeds to the next website via the links provided. There is also a so-called scheduler designed to determine the order in which the next sites will be visited by arranging the links according to priority. The indexer orders the recorded contents and allots them priority for displaying in the lists of results. The precise technical principle is of secondary importance in this context, but a general outline of the analogical derivation process is no doubt useful. To sum up, a search engine arranges results according to their relevance and reputation. It is this principle that will be crucial for a suggestion system in Open Science, too; other technical features that will also be essential for a suggestion system include a crawler, an indexer and a scheduler, thus displaying numerous parallels between search engines and social science in the Open Web.

The background is that, even where the content is of equal relevance, one or more additional coefficients are needed to determine which results appear at the top of the list. These might be such dimensions as frequency of citation, the number of favorable comments and maybe even comments posted by other highly rated scientists. These other dimensions may be varied and, in the interests of maintaining a high standard of output, subject to dynamic change. This is due to the high probability of leading, and implicitly more relevant, search results being used more often for quoting, so scientists strive to optimize their own input.

## Similar Problems to Those of Search Engines

The history of search engines is dotted with attempts to influence this process—initially through the frequent repetition of keywords taken from the body of the text. Since this was easy for the author himself to manipulate, the quality of an assessment based primarily on this factor was fairly meaningless. For this reason, external criteria such as the number of links from other websites were added, but they were also easily influenced by means of self-developed networks. We have observed a kind of cat and mouse game between search engines and so-called search engine optimizers over the past 15 years. These SEOs began by inserting a large number of keywords on their websites, which led to the search engines introducing a kind of maximum quota. Everything over and above that quota was classified as spam and greater importance was ascribed to the number of incoming links. So the SEOs began devising their own website structures that pointed to the target sites to be optimized. Search engines consequently began to evaluate the number of different IP numbers as well, so the SEOs retaliated by setting up different servers, whose sites highlighted the target sites in the shape of a star or a circle. And we could add many more examples to his list. Similar developments are to be expected in the scientific sphere, particularly as the setting up of citation networks is nothing unusual even in traditional academia. What does need to be solved is the problem of avoiding cartels of this kind and it is essential that we learn as much as possible from past experience with search engine optimization.

## Similar Solutions to Those of Search Engines

Solutions in the field of search engine technology are increasingly permeating the domain of network science. Analyzing typical and atypical linkages has now advanced so far that it can determine with reasonable probability whether a more or less naturally evolved linking network is behind a certain website or whether there are numerous links bred on search engine optimizers' own farms. The solution is not yet complete but the number of very crude manipulations has receded noticeably during the past few years, as Google and other search engines were evaluating search engine positions for those detected. Similar occurrences are to be anticipated in the academic sphere of Open Science. In such areas where network references are unmistakably concentrated in denser clusters than the extent of the subject-matter would normally justify, an algorithm will be employed to reduce the reputation factor to a natural size. Search engines meanwhile go one step further and remove excessively optimized sites completely from the index, a move that can only be reversed by dismantling the linkage cartel or stopping the manipulations. Whilst the hitherto anonymously functioning search engines are only just beginning to identify users in the registered domains and to incorporate their search and surf patterns in the reputation assessment process, this has been common practice in the publication of scientific treatises on the social web right from the start due to the clear authentication system described above. This has the added advantage of being able to include commenting and rating behavior, and possibly even the amount of time spent on a page of a treatise, in the reputation assessment of an article. It is not possible to forecast the entire range of potential manipulations as yet, and a certain amount of reciprocal technological upgrading is also to be anticipated in academic circles—in the interests of unbiased, relevant results on the one hand and motivated by a desire for upfront placements, which hold the promise of additional citations, on the other.

# References

Barabási, A.-L., & Albert, R. (1999). Emergence of scaling in random networks. *Science, 286*(5439), 509–512.

Barabási, A.-L., & Bonabeau, E. (2003). Scale free networks. *Scientific American* 60–69.

Erdös, P., & Rényi, A. (1960). On the evolution of random graphs. *Publications of the Mathematical Institute of the Hungarian Academy of Sciences, 5*, 17–61.

de Solla Price, D. (1976). A general theory of bibliometric and other cumulative advantage processes. *Journal of the American Society for Information Science, 27*(5–6), 292–306

# Part IV
# Cases, Recipes and How-Tos

# Creative Commons Licences

Sascha Friesike

**Abstract** Licences are a topic many researchers shy away from. And it is common behavior that property rights are unknowingly signed away. In this little section we would like to present the different creative commons licences one is oftentimes confronted with. This book for instance is published under a creative commons license. They are widely used and especially popular online and it is helpful to any researcher to understand what they mean.

**Attribution CC BY**

This license lets others distribute, remix, tweak, and build upon your work, even commercially, as long as they credit you for the original creation. This is the most accommodating of licenses offered. Recommended for maximum dissemination and use of licensed materials

**Attribution-NoDerivs CC BY-ND**

This license allows for redistribution, commercial and non-commercial, as long as it is passed along unchanged and in whole, with credit to you

(continued)

S. Friesike (✉)
Alexander von Humboldt Institute for Internet and Society, Berlin, Germany
e-mail: friesike@hiig.de

S. Bartling and S. Friesike (eds.), *Opening Science*,
DOI: 10.1007/978-3-319-00026-8_19, © The Author(s) 2014

(continued)

**Attribution-ShareAlike CC BY-SA**

This license lets others remix, tweak, and build upon your work even for commercial purposes, as long as they credit you and license their new creations under the identical terms. This license is often compared to "copyleft" free and open source software licenses. All new works based on yours will carry the same license, so any derivatives will also allow commercial use.

This is the license used by Wikipedia, and it is recommended for materials that would benefit from incorporating content from Wikipedia and similarly licensed projects

**Attribution-NonCommercial CC BY-NC**

This license lets others remix, tweak, and build upon your work non-commercially, and although their new works must also acknowledge you and be non-commercial, they don't have to license their derivative works on the same terms

**Attribution-NonCommercial-ShareAlike CC BY-NC-SA**

This license lets others remix, tweak, and build upon your work non-commercially, as long as they credit you and license their new creations under the identical terms

**Attribution-NonCommercial-NoDerivs CC BY-NC-ND**

This license is the most restrictive of our six main licenses, only allowing others to download your works and share them with others as long as they credit you, but they can't change them in any way or use them commercially

**No Copyright: Public Domain CC0**

The person who associated a work with this deed has dedicated the work to the public domain by waiving all of his or her rights to the work worldwide under copyright law, including all related and neighboring rights, to the extent allowed by law. You can copy, modify, distribute and perform the work, even for commercial purposes, all without asking permission

You can find more information on the well curated website of www.creativecommons.org where all the licences descriptions stem from. And here: http://www.nejm.org/doi/full/10.1056/NEJMp1300040.

# Organizing Collaboration on Scientific Publications: From Email Lists to Cloud Services

**Sönke Bartling**

Scientific publications—ranging from full papers, abstracts, and presentations to posters, including grant applications and blog posts—are usually written by one or a few authors and then corrected and reviewed by many authors. Collaboration on scientific publications is a cornerstone of science. Many novel tools exist that can be integrated and facilitate this process. However, novel disadvantages come with the changes of the workflow—the future will tell as to which way to work on documents will be the most efficient one.

Here we will discuss several ways of organizing collaboration and discuss the advantages and disadvantages.

The **1.0 way** of organizing collaboration:

- Sending out emails with texts, presentations and manual tracking of the version number
- Using the track change or compare documents functionality of word processing tools
- Using data transfer protocols, such as shared local networks or FTP to transfer larger files
- Manual tracking of versions, backups, etc.

Advantage:

- Current state of the art
- Full data control—the process can be organized, so that only known and trusted parties gain access to the content
- Politics—authors and co-authors can decide who sees which version and when

S. Bartling (✉)
German Cancer Research Center, Heidelberg, Germany
e-mail: soenkebartling@gmx.de

S. Bartling
Institute for Clinical Radiology and Nuclear Medicine, Mannheim University Medical Center, Heidelberg University, Mannheim, Germany

S. Bartling and S. Friesike (eds.), *Opening Science*,
DOI: 10.1007/978-3-319-00026-8_20, © The Author(s) 2014

- Free and open source solutions available

  Disadvantage:

- Can be hard to keep track of edits and to integrate changes into a summarized version
- Many "local cultures of keeping track of versions"
- Simultaneous work needs central organization (leading author?) and might create high workload to keep versions in sync

  Solutions:

- Standard Email and document processor software packages, FTP, network file systems
- MS Office solutions
- Open Office
- Text editors, LaTex

The **cloud way** of organizing collaboration:

- Using cloud tools that synchronize folders within the work group and create a version history/backup of old files
- Using collaborative authoring tools to work simultaneously on documents

  Advantage:

- Simultaneous work
- No out-of-sync version of documents
- Complete history
- No work load overhead for version synchronization and file transfer management

  Disadvantages:

- Only 97 % compatibility with current standard word or presentation software solutions
- Third party companies gain access to data and texts, therefore have to be trusted
- Most free solutions are high-maintenance and need high amount of training, local cloud solutions may lack features
- Scepticism regarding novel concepts with both good and bad arguments (the old fashioned way is usually perceived as secure and well established, while disadvantages of novel concepts are over-perceived)
- Collaborative authoring tools do not relieve authors from recursively checking the internal integrity of the documents—low threshold to submit changes may decrease the diligence of contributors

Solutions (examples):

- Dropbox
- Google documents/drive
- Zotero
- other Concurrent version systems (social coding!) with front ends to focus on collaborative text editing

# Unique Identifiers for Researchers

**Martin Fenner and Laure Haak**

**Abstract** Two large challenges that researchers face today are discovery and evaluation. We are overwhelmed by the volume of new research works, and traditional discovery tools are no longer sufficient. We are spending considerable amounts of time optimizing the impact—and discoverability—of our research work so as to support grant applications and promotions, and the traditional measures for this are not enough.

## The Problem

Two large challenges that researchers face today are discovery and evaluation. We are overwhelmed by the volume of new research works, and traditional discovery tools are no longer sufficient. We are spending considerable amounts of time optimizing the impact—and discoverability—of our research work so as to support grant applications and promotions, and the traditional measures for this are not enough.

Research is increasingly global and many interactions do not happen at a personal level anymore, but rather through online tools, from email to videoconferencing and online databases. Researchers have traditionally been identified by their names, but this has never worked reliably because of confusions between popular names (John Smith or Kim Lee), errors in transliteration (e.g. Müller becomes Mueller or Muller), and name changes through marriage. These name issues present an even greater challenge when we try to find out more about

M. Fenner (✉)
Public Library of Science, San Francisco, CA, USA
e-mail: mfenner@plos.org

L. Haak
ORCID, Bethesda, MD, USA
e-mail: l.haak@orcid.org

S. Bartling and S. Friesike (eds.), *Opening Science,*
DOI: 10.1007/978-3-319-00026-8_21, © The Author(s) 2014

researchers who we do not know personally, for example an author of a paper we find interesting or an interesting speaker at a conference, or about the research going on in an institution where we have applied for a job.

## Unique Identifiers as a Solution

The only way to uniquely identify a researcher is through an identifier rather than a name. We, of course, use unique identifiers already with usernames for email, social media accounts, institutional accounts, and more. What is missing is a standard unique researcher identifier that is widely used by academic institutions, funders, publishers, and online tools and services for researchers that is embedded in research workflows and that automates the process of connecting researchers and their research. The existing researcher identifier services and social networks for scientists do not fill that gap. Many of the existing solutions are limited to a geographic region or discipline, many researchers and institutions are reluctant to use a commercial service, and some of the open solutions do not have the wide support from the community needed to reach critical mass.

Open Researcher & Contributor ID (ORCID)[1] is an international, interdisciplinary, open and not-for-profit organization created to solve the researcher name ambiguity problem for the benefit of all stakeholders. ORCID was built with the goal of becoming the universally accepted unique identifier for researchers:

1. ORCID is a community-driven organization
2. ORCID is not limited by discipline, institution, or geography
3. ORCID is an inclusive and transparently governed not-for profit organization
4. ORCID data and source code are available under recognized open licenses
5. the ORCID iD is part of institutional, publisher, and funding agency infrastructures.

Furthermore, ORCID recognizes that existing researcher and identifier schemes serve specific communities, and is working to link with, rather than replace, existing infrastructures.

## ORCID Registry

The ORCID Registry launched in October 2012, and as of July 2013 more than 200,000 researchers have registered. Use of the Registry is free: individuals may create, edit, and share their ORCID record. ORCID staff, infrastructure, and software development is supported by member fees for organizations embedding the iD into systems.

---

[1] ORCID: http://orcid.org/.

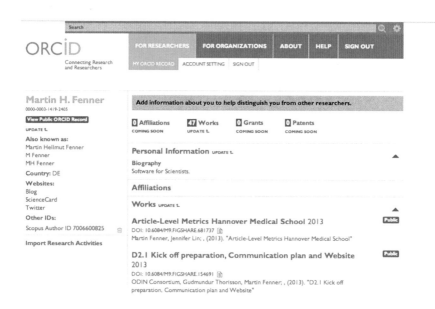

Many organizations have started to integrate ORCID identifiers into their infrastructure. In early 2013, this includes manuscript submission systems from several publishers (Nature Publishing Group, Copernicus, Hindawi, and others), linkage with other identifier schemes (Scopus, ResearcherID, Faculty of 1,000), and integration with research works databases such as CrossRef and Figshare. The first services building on top of the Registry have also emerged, including altmetrics (see chapter Altmetrics and Other Novel Measures for Scientific Impact) tools to track the impact of all research outputs linked to a particular ORCID identifier.

## Outlook

One of the stated goals of the ORCID initiative is to facilitate linkage with all research outputs: papers, monographs, books, datasets, software, peer review, clinical trials, patents, grants, etc. By providing a switchboard for this information, ORCID can help raise awareness of—and credit for—important research and scholarly activities and help the research community develop tools and metrics to better understand and evaluate impact. By embedding the ORCID iD in research workflows, ORCID can also help to reduce the time researchers spend on administrative and reporting activities, including publication lists for institutions and funders, submissions to the institutional repository, and more. Unique identifiers for researchers and research outputs can automate much of this reporting, giving researchers more time to do actual research. Widespread adoption of unique researcher identifiers will foster the development of exciting new tools and services for researchers which will make science more collaborative, productive, and interesting.

# Challenges of Open Data in Medical Research

**Ralf Floca**

**Abstract** The success of modern, evidence based and personalized medical research is highly dependent on the availability of a sufficient data basis in terms of quantity and quality. This often also implies topics like exchange and consolidation of data. In the area of conflict between data privacy, institutional structures and research interests, several technical, organizational and legal challenges emerge. Coping with these challenges is one of the main tasks of information management in medical research. Using the example of cancer research, this case study points out the marginal conditions, requirements and peculiarities of handling research data in the context of medical research.

## Introduction

First the general importance of data exchange and consolidation will be discussed. In the second section, the important role of the patient in medical research will be addressed and how it affects the handling of data. The third section focuses on the question what the role of open data could be in this context. Finally, the fourth section tackles the topic of challenges of open data in the context of medical (research) data. It tries to illustrate why it is a problem and what the obstacles are.

R. Floca (✉)
German Cancer Research Center, Heidelberg, Germany
e-mail: r.floca@dkfz.de

S. Bartling and S. Friesike (eds.), *Opening Science*,
DOI: 10.1007/978-3-319-00026-8_22, © The Author(s) 2014

# Importance of Data Exchange and Consolidation

With oncology striving after personalized medicine and individualized therapy, stratification becomes a major topic in cancer research. The stratification of tumor biology and patients is important to provide individual therapies with maximum tumor control (optimally total remission) and minimal side effects and risks for the patient. Therefore, the search for diagnostic markers, e.g. diagnostic imaging, antibody tests or genome analysis, as well as for adequate treatments with respect to specific markers is constantly intensified.

Looking at research results, it becomes obvious that cancer diseases (e.g. prostate cancer or breast cancer) are more like disease families with a multitude of sub-types and that the anatomical classification of tumors might be misleading and a classification according to the pathological change of signaling pathways on the cellular level is more adequate. This differentiation is very relevant because for one patient a certain treatment may be effective and absolutely relevant while it has no positive impact on tumor control for other patients with the "same" cancer and only bears side effects.

In order to have an evidence-based medicine with a sound statistical basis, the amount and quality of available data becomes very important. The required amount of data increases with the number of relevant factors. Looking at the current cancer research, one has a vast array of factors and information—and it is still increasing. One has for example the patient and tumor biology (e.g. a multitude of diagnostic images; analysis of the genome, proteome etc.; lab results; cell pathologies; ...); way of living before and after the diagnose/therapy; environmental factors and chosen individual therapy.

The current situation can therefore be characterized as too few cases for too many factors. The size of sample sets even large institutions can collect is too small for evidence-based and highly stratified medicine. John Wilbanks, the chief commons officer of Sage Bionetworks,[1] put this fact more bluntly:

> [...] neither Google nor Facebook would make a change to an advertising algorithm with a sample set as small as that used in a Phase III clinical trial.
> John Wilbanks, Sage Bionetworks
> Kotz, J.; *SciBX* 5(25); 2012

One strategy to tackle these shortcomings is to build up networks and initiatives and pool the data to acquire sufficient sample sets[2]. This is not a trivial task because of the heterogeneity of the public health sector that has to be managed.

---

[1] Sage Bionetworks is the name of a research institute which promotes biotechnology by practicing and encouraging Open Science. It is founded with a donation of the pharmaceutical services company Quinitles. cf. http://en.wikipedia.org/wiki/Sage_Bionetworks.

[2] An Example is the German Consortium for Translational Cancer Research (Deutsches Konsortium für Translationale Krebsforschung, DKTK; http://www.dkfz.de/de/dktk/index.html). One objective in the DKTK is the establishement of a clinical communication platform. This platform aims amongst others to better coordinate and standardize multi centric studies.

You have got several stakeholders, heterogeneous documentation of information (different in style, recorded data, formats, storage media) and different operational procedures (time and context of data acquisition).

Thus, it is inevitable to cope with this heterogeneity and to build large study bases by sharing and pooling medical research data in order to realize evidence-based personalized medicine. One way to achieve this goal could be the adaption of ideas and concepts of open research data (see below).

## Role of the Patient and its Data

As described in the previous section, data is of high importance. This data cannot be collected without patients and their cooperation is crucial on several levels. This leads to a very central role for the patient and, in addition, to a special nature of medical data and its acquisition compared to other research data.

1. *Medical data is personal data*

By default medical data is always personal data. The implications that derive from this fact may vary according to the legal framework of a country (e.g. USA: Health Insurance Portability and Accountability Act (HIPAA); Germany: right to informational self-determination/personal rights), but it has almost always an impact on how medical data may be acquired, stored and used. In Germany, for instance, an individual (in this context a patient) must always be able to query which personal information is stored, where the information is stored and for which purpose this information is used. The information may only be altered, transferred, used, stored or deleted with according permission and sufficient traceability guaranteed.

2. *Ethics*

Having an experimental setup that allows the acquisition of data suitable for verifying or falsifying the scientific hypothesis goes without saying. But in the context of human research it is also mandatory to ensure that ethical principles are regarded. These principles are often derived from the Declaration of Helsinki[3] and implemented by national regulations (e.g. USA: institutional review boards; Germany: Ethikkommision). Thus every study design is reviewed and needs ethic approval. This may lead to situations where experimental setups are optimal from a technocratic research perspective but cannot be approved ethically and therefore must be altered or not conducted.

---

[3] The Declaration was originally adopted in June 1964 in Helsinki, Finland. The Declaration is an important document in the history of research ethics as the first significant effort of the medical community to regulate research itself, and forms the basis of most subsequent documents.

### 3. *Lack of predictability and limits of measurements*

Most research-relevant incidents (e.g. (re)occurrence of an illness, adverse reactions) are not predictable and not projectable (fortunately; see "Ethics"). Therefore, you have to wait until enough natural incidents have happened and are monitored. The latter can be complicated, because not every measurement technique can be used arbitrarily frequent due to technical, ethical[4] or compliance[5] reasons. Without the possibilities to repeat[6] "measurements" and in conjunction with the heterogeneity explained in the previous section, getting a sufficient number of cases is a nontrivial task.

### 4. *Long "field" observation periods*

In order to derive conclusions that really matter for patients, like "improved survival"or "improved quality of life" you need observation periods of 10 and more years. In this time, the individuals will move around in the distributed public health system (e.g. by changing their place of residence, choosing new general practitioners). Data will be accumulated, but is not centrally available because of the heterogeneous nature of the system. Therefore, keeping track on a study participant and assembling a non-biased, non-filtered view on study relevant data[7] can be very complicated.

### 5. *Compliance*

Besides all the explained technical and organizational problems, the key stakeholder is the study participant/patient and its compliance to the study and the therapy. If the participant is not compliant to the study, he drops out, which results in missing data. This missing data can lead to a selection bias and must be handled with expertise in order to make a reliable assessment of the trial's result. The dropout rates vary and depend on the study; rates around 20 % are not unusual, also rates up to 50 % have been reported.

Participants that are not therapy compliant alter the therapy or skip it totally (e.g. changing medication; skipping exercises; taking additional drugs). According to a report (WHO 2003) of the World Health Organization up to 50 % of the patients are not therapy compliant. An unnoticed lack of therapy compliance may introduce a bias towards the trial results.

---

[4] e.g.: you cannot repeat an x-ray based imaging arbitrarily often, due to radiation exposition; you cannot expect a person suffering from cancer to daily lie in an MRI scanner for an hour.

[5] e.g.: The payload for an imaging study can easily double the duration of an examination. This may lead to more stress for the participant and decreasing compliance.

[6] Single measurements can be repeated (but this implies stress and leads to decreasing compliance; or is not ethically not compliant). But the complete course of treatment cannot be repeated; if a treatment event is missed, it is missed.

[7] This could be a lot of (different) data. See for example the relevant factors from section Importance of Data Exchange and Consolidation.

## 6. *Consent*

The patient has to consent[8] on three levels before he can be part of a medical trial. First, he must consent to a therapy that is relevant for the trial. Second, if all inclusion criteria and no exclusion criteria for the trial are met, the patient must consent to be part of the trial. Third, the patient must consent to the usage of the data. The third consent exists in different types, namely: specific, extended, unspecific/broad. The specific consent limits the usage to the very trial it was made for. In the context of open data this type of consent is not useful and is considered as limiting by many researchers (see challenges). The extended consent often allows the usage for other questions in the same field as the original trial (e.g. usage for cancer research). If it is extended to a level where any research is allowed, it is an unspecific consent. An example for this type of consent is the Portable Legal Consent devised by the project "Consent to Research".[9]

You may find each aspect in other types of research data, but the combination of all six aspects is very distinctive for medical research data and makes special handling necessary.

# Role of Open Research Data

The chapter "Open Research Data: From Vision to Practice" in this book gives an overview over the benefits open data is supposed to bring. Websites like "Open Access success stories"[10] try to document these benefits arising from Open Access/Open Science. Also in the broad field of medical research, many groups advocate a different handling of data (often in terms of open data).

One main reason is the requirement of transparency and validation of results and methods. For example in the domain of medical image processing the research data (test data, references and clinical meta data) is often not published. This renders the independent testing and verification of published results, as well as the translation into practice very difficult. Thus initiatives like the concept of Deserno

---

[8] The necessity for an informed consent of the patient can be derived from legal (see point 1) and ethical (see point 2) requirements. It is explained in detail here to characterize the different types of consent.

[9] "Consent to Research"/WeConsent.us, is an initiative by John Wilbanks/Sage Bionetwirks with the goal to create an open, massive, mine-able database of data about health and genomics. One step is the Portable Legal Consent as a broad consent for the usage of data in research. Another step is the We the People petition lead by Wilbanks and signed by 65,000 people. February 2013 the US Government replied and announced a plan to open up taxpayer-funded research data and make it available for free.

[10] http://www.oastories.org: The site is provided by the initiative knowledge-exchange.info which is supported by Denmark's Electronic Research Library (DEFF, Denmark), the German Research Foundation (DFG, Germany), the Joint Information Systems Committee (JISC; UK) und SURF (Netherlands).

et al. (2012) try to build up open data repositories. Another example would be the article of Begley and Ellis (2012), which discusses current problems in preclinical cancer research. Amongst others, it recommends a publishing of positive and negative result data in order to achieve more transparency and reliability of research.

Besides this, several groups (e.g. the Genetic Alliance[11] or the former mentioned project Consent to Research) see Open Access to data as the only sensible alternative to the ongoing privatization of Science data and results. For instance the company 23 and Me offers genome sequencing for $99.[12] In addition to the offered service the company builds up a private database for research and the customers consent that this data may be used by the company to develop intellectual property and commercialize products.[13]

Another topic where the research community could benefit from the implementation of open data publishing is the heterogeneity of data (see next section: challenges). Making data available means, that it is:

• open (in terms of at least one public proceeding to get access)
• normed (content of data and semantics are well defined)
• machine readable
• in standardized format.

Having this quality of data would be beneficial, for instance, for radiology, whose "[…] images contain a wealth of information, such as anatomy and pathology, which is often not explicit and computationally accessible […]", as stated by Rubin et al. (2008). Thus, implementing open data could be an opportunity to tackle this problem as well.

## Challenges

The previous sections have discussed the need for data consolidation, the peculiarities of medical research data and how medical research is or could be (positively) affected by concepts of open research data. It is irrelevant which approach is taken in order to exchange and consolidate data, you will always face challenges and barriers on different levels: regulatory, organizational and technical.

The general issues and barriers are discussed in detail by Pampel and Dallmeier-Tiessen (see chapter Open Research Data: From Vision to Practice). This section adds some aspects to this topic from the perspective of medical research data.

---

[11] http://www.geneticalliance.org.

[12] https://www.23andme.com/about/press/12_11_2012/.

[13] The article of Hayden (2012a) discusses the topic of commercial usage on the occasion of the first patent (a patented gen sequence) of the company 23 and me.

Regulatory constraints for medical (research) data derive from the necessity of ethic approval and legal compliance when handling personal data (see section Role of the Patient and Its Data, point 1 and 2). There are still open discussions and work for the legislative bodies to provide an adequate frame. The article of Hayden (2012a) depicts the informed consent as a broken contract and illustrates how today on one hand participants feel confused by the need of "reading between the lines", on the other hand researchers cannot pool data due to specific consents and regulatory issues.

Although there are open issues on the regulatory level, ultimately it will be the obstacles on the organizational and technical level—which may derive from regulatory decisions—which determine if and how open data may improve medical research. Therefore, two of these issues will be discussed in more detail.

## Pooling the Data

Given that the requirements are met and you are allowed to pool the data of different sources for your medical research, you have to deal with two obstacles: mapping the patient and data heterogeneity.

As previously noted, patients move within the public health system and therefore medical records are created in various locations. In order to pool the data correctly, you must ensure that all records originated with an individual are mapped towards it but no other records. Errors in this pooling process lead either to "patients" consisting of data from several individuals or the splitting of one individual in several "patients". Preventing these errors from happening can be hard to implement because prevention strategies are somehow competing (e.g. if you have very strict mapping criteria, you minimize the occurrence of multi-individual-patients but have a higher change of split individuals due to typing errors in the patient name).

In the case that you have successfully pooled the data and handled the mapping of patients, the issue of heterogeneity remains. This difference of data coverage, structure and semantics between institutions (which data they store, how the data is stored and interpreted) makes it difficult to guarantee comparability of pooled data and to avoid any kind of selection bias (e.g.: Is an event really absent or just not classified appropriately by a pooled study protocol).

## Anonymization, Pseudonymization and Reidentification

Individuals must be protected from (re)identification via their personal data used for research. German privacy laws, for instance, define anonymization and pseudonymization as sufficient, if they prohibit reidentification or reidentification is only possible with a disproportional large expenditure of time, money and workforce.[14]

---

[14]  see § 3 (6) Federal Data Protection Act or corresponding federal state law.

Ensuring this requirement becomes increasingly harder due to technical progress, growing computational power and—ironically—more open data.

Reidentification can be done via data-mining of accessible data and so-called quasi-identifiers, a set of (common) properties that are—in their combination—so specific that they can be used to identify. A modern everyday life example would be Panopticlick.[15] It is a website of the Electronic Frontier Foundation that demonstrates the uniqueness of a browser (Eckersley 2010) which serves as a quasi-identifier. Therefore, a set of "harmless" properties is used, like screen resolution, time zone or installed system fonts.

The following examples illustrate possibilities and incidents of reidentification:

a. *Simple demographics*: The publications of Sweeney (2000) and Golle (2006) indicate that for 63–87 % of the U.S. citizens the set of birth date, sex and postal code is unique and a quasi-identifier.
b. *ICD codes*: Loukides et al. (2010) assume that 96.5 % of the patients can be identified by their set of ICD9[16] diagnoses codes. For their research the Vanderbilt Native Electrical Conduction (VNEC) dataset was used. The data set was compiled and published for an NIH[17] funded genome-wide association study.
c. *AOL search data*: AOL put anonymized Internet search data (including health-related searches) on its web site. New York Times reporters (Barbaro et al. 2006) were able to re-identify an individual from her search records within a few days.
d. *Chicago homicide database*: Students (Ochoa et al. 2001) were able to re-identify a 35 % of individuals in the Chicago homicide database by linking it with the social security death index.
e. *Netflix movie recommendations*[18]: Individuals in an anonymized publicly available database of customer movie recommendations from Netflix are re-identified by linking their ratings with ratings in a publicly available Internet movie rating web site.
f. *Re-identification of the medical record of the governor of Massachusetts*: Data from the Group Insurance Commission, which purchases health insurance for state employees, was matched against the voter list for Cambridge, re-identifying the governor's health insurance records (Sweeney 2002).

---

[15] see https://panopticlick.eff.org/

[16] ICD: International Classification of Diseases. It is a health care classification system that provides codes to classify diseases as well as a symptoms, abnormal findings, social circumstances and external causes for injury or disease. It is published by the World Health Organization and is used worldwide; amongst others for morbidity statistics and reimbursement systems.

[17] National Institutes of Health; USA.

[18] See http://www.wired.com/threatlevel/2009/12/netflix-privacy-lawsuit and http://www.wired.com/science/discoveries/news/2007/03/72963.

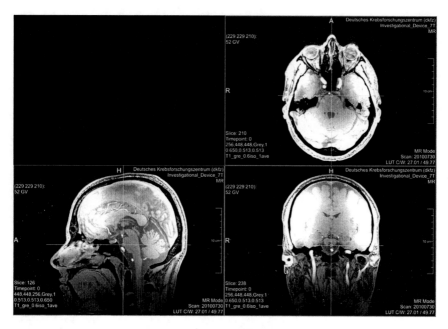

**Fig. 1** Example for a magnetic resonance head image (*MRI*). The *upper* MRI shows an original layer of data set of an study participant (axial view, parallel to the feet). The MRIs below are reconstructions of the original data in sagittal view (*left*) and coronal view (*right*). The sagittal view is similar to a head silhouette and therefore more familiar

The examples illustrate the increasing risk of reidentification and the boundary is constantly pushed further. If you look for example at the development of miniaturised DNA sequenzing systems[19] (planned costs of US$1,000 per device), sequencing DNA (and using it as data) will presumably not stay limited to institutions and organisations who can afford currently expensive sequencing technologies.

Thus proceedings that are compliant to current privacy laws and the common understanding of privacy are only feasible if data is dropped or generalized (e.g. age bands instead of birth date or only the first two digits of postal codes). This could be done for example by not granting direct access to the research data but offering a view tailored for the specific research aims. Each view ponders the necessity and usefulness of each data element (or possible generalizations) against the risk of reidentification.

Even if an infrastructure is provided that enables the filtering of data described above, you will always have medical data that is easily reidentifiable and at least hard to be pseudonymized. Good examples are radiological head or whole body

---

[19] e.g. the MinION™ device from Oxford Nanopore Technologies (http://www.nanoporetech.com). See also (Hayden 2012b).

**Fig. 2** Volumetric rendering
of the data set shown in
Fig. 1. The possibility to
reidentify is now strikingly
obvious. Volumetric
rendering can easily be done
with software tools publically
available

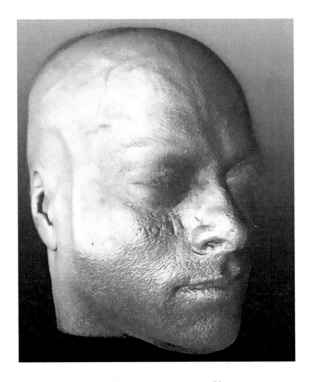

images. Figure 1 shows head images from a study participant.[20] The original
perspective of the image (axial view) and the other medical perspectives (sagittal
and coronal view) may not be suitable for reidentification by everyman. But a
simple volume rendering of the data (Fig. 2) allows easy reidentification. Starting
from this point with modern technologies several scenarios are not too far-fetched.
An artificial picture, for instance, could be reconstructed and used with available
face recognition APIs[21] or you could take the volume data convert it into a 3D
model and print it via a 3D-printer.[22]

---

[20] The data shown in Figs. 1 and 2 are provided by courtesy of Markus Graf (German Cancer
Research Center).

[21] One example would be web API offered by face.com (http://en.wikipedia.org/wiki/Face.com).

[22] In order to print 3D-Models you can use services like www.shapeways.com or http://
i.materialise.com.

# References

Barbaro, M., et al. (2006). A face is exposed for AOL searcher no. 4417749. *NY Times*.

Begley, C. G., & Ellis, L. M. (2012). Drug development: Raise standards for preclinical cancer research. *Nature, 483*(7391), 531–533. doi:10.1038/483531a.

Deserno, T. M., Welter, P., & Horsch, A. (2012). Towards a repository for standardized medical image and signal case data annotated with ground truth. *Journal of Digital Imaging, 25*(2), 213–226. doi:10.1007/s10278-011-9428-4.

Eckersley, P. (2010). *How unique is your browser? In Proceedings of the Privacy Enhancing Technologies Symposium (PETS 2010). Springer Lecture Notes in Computer Science*.

Golle, P. (2006). *Revisiting the uniqueness of simple demographics in the US population. In WPES 2006 Proceedings of the 5th ACM workshop on Privacy in electronic society* (pp. 77–80). New York: ACM.

Hayden, E. C. (2012a). Informed consent: A broken contract. *Nature, 486*(7403), 312–314. doi:10.1038/486312a.

Hayden, E. C. (2012b). Nanopore genome sequencer makes its debut. *Nature,*. doi:10.1038/nature.2012.10051.

Loukides, G., Denny, J. C., & Malin, B. (2010). The disclosure of diagnosis codes can breach research participants' privacy. *Journal of the American Medical Informatics Association, 17*, 322–327.

Ochoa, S., et al. (2001). *Reidentification of individuals in Chicago's homicide database: A technical and legal study*. Massachusetts: Massachusetts Institute of Technology.

Rubin, D. L., et al. (2008). *iPad: Semantic annotation and markup of radiological images. In Proceedings of AMIA Annual Symposium* (pp. 626–630).

Sweeney, L. (2000). *Uniqueness of simple demographics in the U.S. poopulation, LIDAPWP4. In* Pittsburgh: Carnegie Mellon University, Laboratory for International Data Privacy.

Sweeney, L. (2002). k-Anonymity: A model for protecting privacy. *International Journal of Uncertainty, Fuzziness and Knowledge-Based Systems, 10*(05), 557–570. doi:10.1142/S0218488502001648.

WHO. 2003. *Report. Adherence to long-term therapies: evidence for action*, Available at: http://www.who.int/chp/knowledge/publications/adherence_report/en/.

# On the Sociology of Science 2.0

Vladimir B. Teif

> The difference between technology and slavery is that slaves
> are fully aware that they are not free
> —Nassim Nicholas Taleb

**Abstract** While the previous chapters of this book reveal some technical principles of Science 2.0, here we look at the psychological and sociological motives of researchers using these novel tools. In this chapter we will see how and why the main drivers of scientists in the Internet are different from usual "offline" scientists. We consider here an Internet-geek (driven by the psychological principles described below), assuming that he/she is also a scientist (the potential audience of Science 2.0). So how would such a person behave?

While the previous chapters of this book reveal some technical principles of Science 2.0, here we look at the psychological and sociological motives of researchers using these novel tools. In this chapter we will see how and why the main drivers of scientists in the Internet are different from usual "offline" scientists. We consider here an Internet-geek (driven by the psychological principles described below), assuming that he/she is also a scientist (the potential audience of Science 2.0). So how would such a person behave?

Let us first outline the classical understanding of the usual "offline" scientist. About 70 years ago Merton (1942) summarized some of the basic sociological principles that drive scientists, the Mertonian norms of science, often referred to by the acronym "CUDOS". These include *communalism*—the common ownership of scientific discoveries, according to which scientists give up intellectual property in exchange for recognition and esteem; *universalism*—according to which claims to truth are evaluated in terms of universal or impersonal criteria, and not on the basis of race, class, gender, religion, or nationality; *disinterestedness*—according to which scientists are rewarded for acting in ways that outwardly appear to be selfless; *organized skepticism*—all ideas must be tested and are subject to rigorous, structured community scrutiny.

V. B. Teif (✉)
German Cancer Research Center (DKFZ), Heidelberg, Germany
e-mail: v.teif@dkfz-heidelberg.de

S. Bartling and S. Friesike (eds.), *Opening Science*,
DOI: 10.1007/978-3-319-00026-8_23, © The Author(s) 2014

In addition to the Mertonian principles, western scientists are also governed by the economic principles outlined in the "Republic of Science" by Polanyi (1962) about half a century ago. These economic principles have become extremely important now, when the era of "scientific Eldorado" has finished and scientists have to make efforts just to remain in science. Economic pressure dictates that scientists are rewarded for being productive, competitive, and successful. Scientists need to publish as much as possible, as often as possible, and do their best to advertise their work through all types of media so as to attract citations, funding, and recognition. Sociologically, all of the forces mentioned above, whether they are egoistic or altruistic, are job-centric. This is true for conventional "offline" scientists. Is it still true for Science 2.0?

To address this question, the author has conducted a survey online. 50 most active users of one of the leading scientific online communities, professional life scientists with Ph.D. degree, were asked the following question: "What are you doing here?" The respondents were given several choices and were asked to choose *only one* answer, most closely resembling their feelings. Below is a summary of received answers:

| | |
|---|---:|
| I am having here a nice time **and** it is useful for my work ($\sim$ 50/50) | 40 % |
| I am having here a nice time, relaxing after work | 19 % |
| I am polishing my scientific arguments in online discussions | 12 % |
| I am addicted to Internet. I would like to leave this resource but can not | 10 % |
| I am getting here some useful information for my work | 5 % |
| I am popularizing my scientific ideas/publications | 5 % |
| I am advertising my products/services | 5 % |
| I am helping other members, and I like it | 2 % |
| I am maintaining contacts with my colleagues here | 2 % |
| I am here mainly to exchange PDF articles free of charge | 0 % |

This survey presents quite surprising results for the advocates of Science 2.0. Firstly, we see that the overstated need for free access to scientific publications is not the driving force at all (none of the 50 respondents was using social tools to exchange PDFs of articles behind subscriptions). Secondly, the "facebook-type" activity of maintaining contacts with "friends" is negligible (just 2 % of respondents use Science 2.0 tools to maintain contacts with colleagues). As expected, few people use social media to sell/buy/advertise something scientific (5 % for each of these categories). Now we come to the largest shares. 10 % of scientists openly say in this anonymous survey that they are simply addicted to the Internet (in the negative sense). 12 % use scientific tools online to polish their arguments (probably before publication). 19 % enjoy Science 2.0 tools just for fun. Finally, 40 % of scientists combine fun and usefulness for work. (Compare with just 5 % of scientists who answered that they are using Science 2.0 tools primarily to get something useful to work). Taken together, these data explain why scientific social media has failed to attract the majority of usual "offline" scientists. Just the basic motivation behind most Science 2.0 systems offering services other than the top three lines of this survey is wrong. Nothing is wrong with scientists. Something is wrong with Science 2.0, which needs to be more flexible. Acknowledging the huge progress reached by Science 2.0, we have to admit that it still requires large changes, and the next wave of science, Science 3.0, is yet to come (Teif 2013, 2009).

# References

Merton, R. K. (1942). *The sociology of science: Theoretical and empirical investigations.* Chicago: University of Chicago Press.

Polanyi, M. (1962). The republic of science: Its political and economic theory. *Minerva, 1,* 54–74.

Teif, V. B. (2009). Science 3.0: The future of science in the Internet. Available at: http://generegulation.info/index.php/science-30.

Teif, V. B. (2013). Science 3.0: Corrections to the Science 2.0 paradigm. Available at: ArXiv:1301.2522.

# How This Book was Created Using Collaborative Authoring and Cloud Tools

Sönke Bartling

**Abstract** This book about novel publishing and collaboration methods of scholarly knowledge was itself created using novel and collaborative authoring tools. Google Docs as a collaborative authoring and text editing tool and Dropbox as a cloud storage solution were used. Our experience was a positive one and we think that it saved us a lot of organisational emails and hundreds of work hours. Here we describe the workflow process in detail so that the interested author might benefit from what we learnt.

## How this Book was Created

The creation process can be divided in several phases in regard to the online tools which were used.

**Phase I:** Potential content was collected and authors were invited to participate. Shortly afterwards, a table in Google Docs was collaboratively maintained by both editors. For each chapter, the title and possible authors were discussed, emails to authors were sent, and feedback was added. Chapters were divided among both editors, so that one contact person was responsible for each chapter. In jour-fixe Skype sessions the status of the work in progress was discussed.

**Phase II:** A table of contents was created as a text document in Google Docs. The returning abstracts were uploaded to Google Docs and the links were created to the abstracts. The table of contents file served as the central document (Fig. 1).

S. Bartling (✉)
German Cancer Research Center, Heidelberg, Germany
e-mail: soenkebartling@gmx.de

S. Bartling
Institute for Clinical Radiology and Nuclear Medicine, Mannheim University Medical
Center, Heidelberg University, Mannheim, Germany

S. Bartling and S. Friesike (eds.), *Opening Science*,
DOI: 10.1007/978-3-319-00026-8_24, © The Author(s) 2014

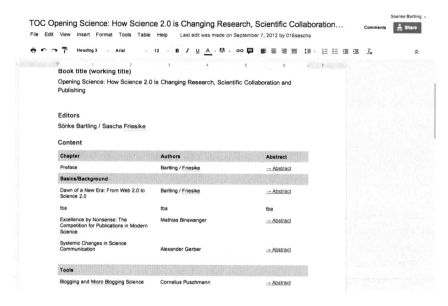

**Fig. 1** The table of contents was the central workplace for the editors in the early phase of this book project

**Phase III:** Returning articles were uploaded to Google Docs and the authors were invited to participate with 'editing' privileges (Fig. 2). Articles were also linked to the TOC. Authors and editors worked iteratively on the Google documents. Commenting functionality was used to discuss points of controversy. Images were designed in Apple Keynote and the image files and other files were shared using Dropbox.

**Phase IV:** An internal review started once almost final versions of the chapters existed. All authors received a TOC with links to every chapter—all authors possessed commenting privileges for all other chapters. Only the chapter authors and editors had the right to change text. The internal references within the book were set in this phase and consistency among the chapters was assured. Citations were added using the Harvard author-date style, omitting the necessity of changing in-text references if novel references were added. Since Google Docs lacks integration with a reference management system, Zotero was used to import the references from databases. The bibliographies for each chapter were generated from

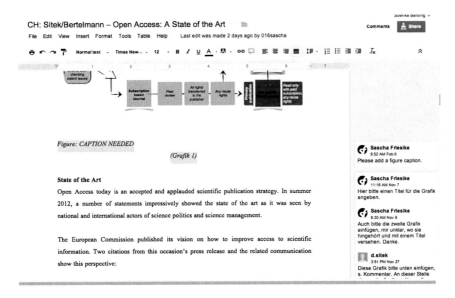

**Fig. 2** During the editing process of the chapters, the authors and editors changed the chapters with editing privileges, while all others authors were invited to comment—serving as a form of internal peer-review

shared Zotero databases (one for each chapter) and manually inserted into the documents. URLs were included as footnotes.

**Phase V:** After reviewing changes and undertaking final proofreading, a finalized table of contents with embedded links was sent to the publisher.

**Phase VI (now):** The book is now available as Open Access printed book and its content can be downloaded from www.openingscience.org. Here the content can also be edited.

# History II.O

**Luka Orešković**

**Abstract**  Science 2.0 is a concept of immense potential for the historical discipline. Throughout the world, researchers are undertaking different projects that attempt to harness the benefits of research efforts employing a wider community, be it fellow historians or the general public, and have reached different conclusions and results. Yet, most of these projects point to a clear direction in historical research of increasingly relying on the tremendous benefits that digital, and at times, Open Access to both scholarly work and primary sources has given them. While the idea of using Science 2.0 and crowd sourcing for historical research has produced a number of projects of great potential, Open Science and ideas of open publishing remain largely underutilized and avoided by the academic community of historians.

## Introduction: Issues and Opportunities of Open History and 2.0

Science 2.0 is a concept of immense potential for the historical discipline. Throughout the world, researchers are undertaking different projects that attempt to harness the benefits of research efforts employing a wider community, be it fellow historians or the general public, and have reached different conclusions and results. Yet, most of these projects point to a clear direction in historical research of increasingly relying on the tremendous benefits that digital, and at times, Open Access to both scholarly work and primary sources has given them. While the idea of using Science 2.0 and crowd sourcing for historical research has produced a number of projects of great potential, Open Science and ideas of open publishing remain largely underutilized and avoided by the academic community of historians. Many issues arise between using Science 2.0 in historical research and becoming an

L. Orešković (✉)
Harvard University, Cambridge, USA
e-mail: luka.oreskovic@gmail.com

S. Bartling and S. Friesike (eds.), *Opening Science*,
DOI: 10.1007/978-3-319-00026-8_25, © The Author(s) 2014

"Open Science" for history as an academic discipline, as opening academic history and research to Open Access, digital publication is both challenging and alarming for historians. It is challenging in terms of opening the field and competition in publishing historical work to a series of authors who might previously be disqualified due to lack of academic status such as scholarly success and track record as well as institutionally recognized intellectual credibility derived from a Ph.D. It is alarming in terms of economic constraints professional historians face today as institutions and fellow academics are unlikely to recognize scholarship published as Open Science, thus limiting career advancement possibilities in academia. While academic history increasingly comes to rely on open research platforms and Science 2.0 methods of historical research, it is likely that historical publishing, even though numerous new open publication platforms are developed, will remain largely limited to print or access-limiting journals and books.

## History 2.0: Developments, Directions and Conclusions

A number of noteworthy projects either offering Open Access to historical sources or relying on crowd sourcing and online research contribution platforms that are open to a wider professional community or even the general public have come into being over the past years. While numerous platforms offer the general public Open Access to historical databases, projects that also involve contributors in the research effort are fewer.[1] Still, several projects that pool research from a wide array of contributors, ranging from professional historians to the interested general public, have gained traction and achieved noteworthiness. Projects like University College London's *Transcribe Bentham,*[2] National Geographic's *Field Expedition: Mongolia,*[3] *Founders and Survivors*[4] on Tasmanian convicts and University of Oxford's *Ancient Lives* and *The project Woruldhord*[5] have achieved very successful collaboration among its members, and offer insight into successful practices for crowd sourcing historical research.[6] Each of these projects in particular holds a valuable lesson on how crowd sourcing in historical research should be approached and raises both conceptual and practical questions about the nature of the practice.

---

[1] Diaspora: http://www.diaspora.illinois.edu/newsletter.html; Old Biley Online: http://www.oldbaileyonline.org/

[2] see Causer 2013

[3] National Geographic: http://exploration.nationalgeographic.com/mongolia

[4] Founders and Survivors: http://foundersandsurvivors.org

[5] Woruldhord: http://projects.oucs.ox.ac.uk/woruldhord/

[6] Ancient Lives: http://www.ancientlives.org

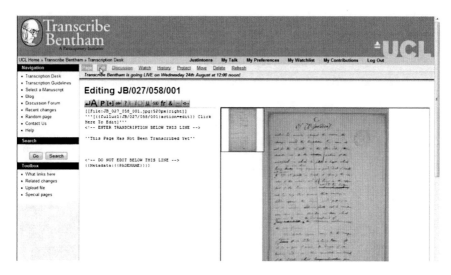

**Fig. 1** Transcribe Bentham, University College London, Screenshot, February 26, 2013

## Types of Collaboration in Research Crowd Sourcing Projects

*Transcribing platforms*—The University College London project *Transcribe Bentham* presents the most elementary of models for employing crowd sourcing in historical research.[7] The project, as its name aptly describes, uses its members who join the platform from the wider public for transcribing original and unstudied manuscripts and documents written by the philosopher Jeremy Bentham with the aim of assembling an online database of all of Bentham's writing in unedited form. The elementary nature of this project is in the type of contribution it seeks from its members, using them as a free resource for manuscript transcription. Any content-level contribution is not possible in *Transcribe Bentham* yet its very nature and goal of completing an online database of Bentham's writings limits the level and type of members' contribution. The project attracted great attention and won the Prix Ars Electronica prize for Distinction in the Digital Communities (Fig. 1).

A very similar model is also employed by University of Oxford's *Ancient Lives* platform that allows users to transcribe the Oxyrhynchus Papyri through an online tool with specific symbols and scanned papyri. The tool allows anyone interested to contribute in the physical work of transcribing ancient manuscripts while the contributions are then analyzed, evaluated for accuracy by historians curating the project and and translated into English by professional translators. The historians, papyrologists and researchers providing curatorial oversight of contributions by

---

[7]  http://www.transcribe-bentham.da.ulcc.ac.uk/td/Transcribe_Bentham

**Fig. 2** Greek papyrus in the web interface for online transcription. Courtesy of Ancient Lives Project, Oxford

the participating public in the crowd sourcing project allows for academic accuracy and credibility, thus enabling more reliable usage of the material transcribed in the project (Fig. 2).

Projects that employ the crowd for transcribing and information pooling from the already existing resources, such as the *Ancient Lives, Transcribe Bentham* and others also implemented possibilities for crowd contributions such as forms for additional information on transcribed documents, indexing tools for transcribed documents or applications that provide a space for interaction and commentary among various contributors to the project about their work. While the first two additional contribution modes are of questionable applicability as they often require some degree of professional knowledge, the possibility of exchanging comments and experiences, coupled with the possibility of moderating such discussions for the purpose of establishing and sharing best transcription practices could be beneficial.

***Content platforms***—More demanding platform for participant collaboration in historical research was implemented by National Geographic's *Field Expedition: Mongolia, The Founders and Survivors* Project and University of Oxford's *The project Woruldhord.*

National Geographic's project might be the least beneficial one in terms of actual contributions to historical research, yet it represents an idea in the right direction that opens existing sources such as transcripts, documents or maps, for analysis by the general public, the results of which are then reviewed, curated and applied by professionals. The *Field Expedition: Mongolia* platform is based on an actual historical and archaeological project of search for Genghis Khan's tomb. The platform enables users, of whom there are an astounding 31,591 registered at the moment of writing this review, to review satellite imagery and tag it for objects and landmarks that researchers on the ground can then potentially utilize for their professional work. While the platform's aim is primarily to increase awareness of Mongolia's rich historical heritage than actually contributing to research on the ground, the idea of using crowd sourcing for more advanced research tasks that still demand substantial manpower and thus limit the number of professionals doing the work shows great promise.

*Founders and Survivors* project and University of Oxford's *The project Woruldhord* elevate collaboration of the participating public to a new level. Rather than relying on non-expert users for working or reviewing already existing sources, these two projects aim to build and assemble databases of historical primary sources submitted by users, thus relying on users for actual content building. *Founders and Survivors* isa study of the 73,000convicts transported to Tasmania between 1803and 1853, aiming toassemble a record systemof these convicts and buildupon this with data suchas health records,demographics andpersonal information. The project, in the words of its founders, aims to "combine professional expertise with the enthusiasm of volunteers." Some types of documents submitted by registered users in the project include conduct records, surgeons' journals, newspaper reports, births, deaths and marriages, parish records, family histories, memories and legends as well as formal sources like records from the convict system, trial and conviction documents and tickets of leave. Volunteers included genealogists and family historians, librarians, members of the wider public whose personal or family histories relate to the Tasmanian convicts and other researchers interested in the field. The submitted data is reviewed and organized by IT specialists and professional historians and published in the database (Fig. 3).

The applications of such a database are best exhibited in the number of research projects that arose from the *Founders and Survivors* project—these include a study of Morbidity and mortality on the voyage to Australia, Crime and convicts in Tasmania, 1853–1900, Fertility decline in late C19 Tasmania, Prostitution and female convicts and Tracing convicts' descendants who served in WWI. The success of the projectcan largely be attributedto relying on a largenumber of public users forresearch while navigatingand moderating theirresearch through bothprepopulated forms thatlimit the type of data andinformation users can submit as well asprofessional curation byhistorians and otherspecialists (Fig. 4).

A very similar model is used by University of Oxford's *The project Woruldhord* that collects a database of photographs, documents and presentations relating to Anglo-Saxon centered English History and Old English literature and language. The materials in *The project Woruldhord* were collected from both members of the public, free to submit any documents related to the period and field of *Woruldhord* as well as museums, libraries, academics and scientific societies and resulted in a

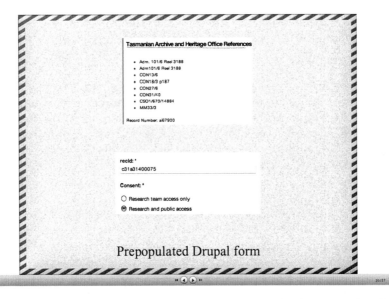

**Fig. 3** Prepopulated Form, Crowdsourced project structure, instructional process and workflow designed by Professor Janet McCalman, Centre for Health & Society, University of Melbourne, with technical assistance from Sandra Silcot and Claudine Chionh. Funded by the Australian Research Council

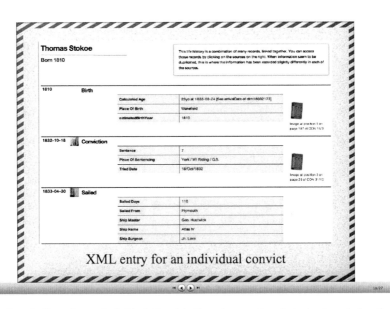

**Fig. 4** Sample Entry for an Individual Convict, Crowd sourced project structure, instructional process and workflow designed by Professor Janet McCalman, Centre for Health & Society, University of Melbourne, with technical assistance from Sandra Silcot and Claudine Chionh. Funded by the Australian Research Council

**Fig. 5** Project Woruldhord, University of Oxford, February 27, 2013

collection of approximately 4,500 various digital objects. *Woruldhord's* own description appropriately terms the project a community collection open to access of everyone interested in the field (Fig. 5).

Projects like *Founders and Survivors* and *Project Woruldhord* exemplify the frontier of crowd sourcing practices for historical research that employ the general public for content contribution and aggregate databases of primary sources that are broader in scope than many projects have achieved in spite of having a larger professional staff and more funding.

## Conceptual Questions and Challenges

Edward L. Ayers, currently the President of University of Richmond, argued in 1999 in his seminal essay on "The Pasts and Futures of Digital History" that history as an academic discipline underwent "democratization" while meaningful "democratization of the audience" was lacking at that time (Ayers 1999). His hope was that the "digital world" might be able to, once again, spur innovation in academic history and it is possible that this time has arrived. History as a 2.0 Scienceand eventually, an OpenScience, has the potentialto involve professional historians globally moreclosely than ever before,creating platforms for collaborations across disciplines of academichistory. Although historians are increasingly relying on collaborative and crowd sourcing platforms for their research, the methods also give rise to questions of the role of historians in the research process. Shawn Graham, Assistant Professor of Digital Humanities in the Department of History at Carleton University, together with two students at Carlton, wrote a Case

Study on a crowd sourcing project they administered (Graham et al. 2012). In this case, they raise questions of what the role of historians in projects relying on crowd sourcing for historical research is as well as claims over authorship of the work of history that results from crowd sourcing research. Namely, is the research produced this way primarily historian's or the crowd's? In answering this and similar questions, it is important to keep in mind that all the aforementioned projects were curated and led by professional historians. The established processes of source review and criticism in history demand professional expertise and thus, any crowd research efforts or community contributed content (CCC) projects still closely rely on guidance and review processes by professional historians (cf. Howell and Prevenier 2001).

## Conclusions

Crowd sourcing and Science 2.0 in academic history holds the potential of unparalleled access to research resources for historians focusing on a range of fields, from "big history" to "microhistory" as well as everything in between. Access to the plethora of perspectives, personal data and documents from individual repositories of the past, family histories and communal archives is already attracting numerous historians, with future trends set to continue in this direction. Yet there is still a big gap between utilizing Science 2.0 (online resources) for research and making history an Open Science in terms of publishing practices. Economic constraints such as a shrinking market for academic appointments in history are among the most often mentioned reasons for historians' shying away from open publishing as academic institutions that recognize such publications are rare. Hesitance to recognize "Open Science" publishing as reference for academic track record is understandable, and the hesitance is not only on the part of academic institutions. The Open Source knowledge and publishing processes already have considerable drafting and review procedures in place, but there is space for improvement. While the transparency of review processes that are noticeable in the "Open Science" are laudable, the critical review of submissions can still be improved and in accordance with the principles of Open Science, it will likely keep improving (forever?). As Open Science publishing practices reach the level of high-quality peer review and editorial processes that traditional academic publications exhibit, it will be upon academic institutions to begin recognizing open source knowledge and publications as contributing to the scholarly success and track record of its faculty. The widely covered "Memorandum on Journal Pricing" published by Harvard Library's Faculty Advisory Council in April of 2012 calls on all Harvard Faculty Members in all Schools, Faculties, and Units to, among other things, make sure their papers are accessible by submitting them to Harvard's DASH Open-Access repository as well as consider "submitting articles to Open-Access journals, or to ones that have reasonable, sustainable subscription costs; move prestige to Open Access". The Council also asked scientists to sway journals that restrict access to their content to become more open.[8] If impossible to make these journals Open Access, the members of Harvard Library's Faculty Advisory Council recommend to their Harvard peers to consider resigning such journals' advisory boards. While calls from Harvard's Library have been welcomed in numerous publications worldwide, the memorandum also raises questions on the issue of peer and institutional recognition of open source publishing as relevant to scholarly track record. Many headlines cited "Memorandum on Journal Pricing" as ultimate proof that current publishing pricing practices are economically impossible since Harvard, the wealthiest of academic institutions globally, could not afford them. As Open Science platforms continue to grow in prominence, Harvard should take the first step in encouraging research published as Open Science to be weighted more equally compared with more traditional publishing platforms.

# References

Ayers, E.L. (1999). The pasts and futures of digital history. Available at: http://www.vcdh.virginia.edu/PastsFutures.html.

Causer, T. (2013). Welcome to transcribe bentham. *Transcribe Bentham*. Available at: http://blogs.ucl.ac.uk/transcribe-bentham/.

Graham, S., Massie, G., & Feurherm, N. (2012). The heritage crowd project: A case study in crowd sourcing public history (Spring 2012 version). Available at: http://writinghistory.trincoll.edu/.

Howell, M. C., & Prevenier, W. (2001). *From reliable sources: an introduction to historical methods*. Ithaca, New York: Cornell University Press.

---

[8] Faculty Advisory Council Memorandum on Journal Pricing: http://isites.harvard.edu/icb

# Making Data Citeable: DataCite

**Jan Brase**

**Abstract** In 2005 the German National Library of Science and Technology started assigning DOI names to datasets to allow stabile linking between articles and data. In 2009 this work lead to the funding of DataCite, a global consortium of libraries and information institutions with the aim to enable scientists to use datasets as independently published records that can be shared, referenced and cited.

Data integration with text is an important aspect of scientific collaboration. It allows verification of scientific results and joint research activities on various aspects of the same problem. Only a very small proportion of the original data is published in conventional scientific journals. Existing policies on data archiving notwithstanding, in today's practice data are primarily stored in private files, not in secure institutional repositories, and effectively are lost to the public. This lack of access to scientific data is an obstacle to international research. It causes unnecessary duplication of research efforts, and the verification of results becomes difficult, if not impossible. Large amounts of research funds are spent every year to recreate already existing data.

Handling datasets as persistently identified, independently published items is a key element for allowing citation and long term integration of datasets into text as well as supporting a variety of data management activities. It would be an incentive to the author if a data publication had the rank of a citeable publication, adding to their reputation and ranking among their peers.

The German National Library of Science and Technology (TIB) developed and promotes the use of Digital Object Identifiers (DOI) for datasets. A DOI name is used to cite and link to electronic resources (text as well as research data and other types of content). The DOI System differs from other reference systems commonly used on the Internet, such as the URL, since it is permanently linked to the object

J. Brase (✉)

National Library of Science and Technology (TIB), Hanover, Germany

e-mail: Jan.Brase@tib.uni-hannover.de

S. Bartling and S. Friesike (eds.), *Opening Science*,

DOI: 10.1007/978-3-319-00026-8_26, © The Author(s) 2014

itself, not just to the place in which the object is located. As a major advantage, the use of the DOI system for registration permits the scientists and the publishers to use the same syntax and technical infrastructure for the referencing of datasets that are already established for the referencing of articles. The DOI system offers persistent links as stable references to scientific content and an easy way to connect the article with the underlying data. For example:

The dataset:

G.Yancheva, N. R. Nowaczyk et al. (2007)

Rock magnetism and X-ray flourescence spectrometry analyses on sediment cores of the Lake Huguang Maar, Southeast China, PANGAEA
   doi:10.1594/PANGAEA.587840 (http://dx.doi.org/10.1594/PANGAEA.587840)

Is a supplement to the article:

G. Ycheva, N. R. Nowaczyk et al. (2007)
Influence of the intertropical convergence zone on the East Asian monsoon
Nature 445, 74-77
doi:10.1038/nature05431 (http://dx.doi.org/10.1038/nature05431)

Since 2005, TIB has been an official DOI Registration Agency with a focus on the registration of research data. The role of TIB is that of the actual DOI registration and the storage of the relevant metadata of the dataset. The research data themselves are not stored at TIB. The registration always takes place in cooperation with data centers or other trustworthy institutions that are responsible for quality assurance, storage and accessibility of the research data and the creation of metadata.

Access to research data is nowadays defined as part of the national responsibilities and in recent years most national science organisations have addressed the need to increase the awareness of, and the accessibility to, research data.

Nevertheless science itself is international; scientists are involved in global unions and projects, they share their scientific information with colleagues all over the world, they use national as well as foreign information providers.

When facing the challenge of increasing access to research data, a possible approach should be global cooperation for data access via national representatives.

– a global cooperation, because scientist work globally, scientific data are created and accessed globally.
– with national representatives, because most scientists are embedded in their national funding structures and research organisations .

The key point of this approach is the establishment of a Global DOI Registration agency for scientific content that will offer to all researchers dataset registration and cataloguing services. DataCite was officially launched on December 1st 2009 in London to offer worldwide DOI-registration of scientific data to actively offer scientists the possibility to publish their data as an independent citable object. Currently DataCite has 17 members from 12 countries:

The German National Library of Science and Technology (TIB), the German National Library of Medicine (ZB MED), the German National Library of Economics (ZBW) and the German GESIS—Leibniz Institute for the Social Sciences. Additional European members are: The Library of the ETH Zürich in Switzerland, the Library of TU Delft, from the Netherlands, the L'Institut de l'Information Scientifique et Technique (INIST) from France, The technical Information Center of Denmark, The British Library, the Sedish National Data Service (SND), the Conferenza dei Rettori delle Università Italiane (CRUI) from Italy. North America is represented through: the California Digital Library, the Office of Scientific and Technical Information (OSTI), the Purdue University and the Canada Institute for Scientific and Technical Information (CISTI). Furthermore the Australian National Data Service (ANDS) and the National Research Council of Thailand (NRCT) are members.

DataCite offers through its members DOI registration for data centers, currently over 1.7 million objects have been registered with a DOI name and are available through a central search portal at DataCite.[1]

Based on the DOI registration DataCite offers a variety of services such as a detailed statistic portal of the number of DOI names registered and resolved.[2] In cooperation with CrossRef, the major DOI registration agency for scholarly articles a content negotiation service has been established that allows persistent resolution of all DOI names directly to their metadata in XML or RDF format.[3]

In June 2012 DataCite and the STM association[4] signed a joint statement to encourage publishers and data centers to link articles and underlying data.[5]

---

[1]  DataCite Metadata Search: http://search.datacite.org/ui

[2]  DataCite Statistics: http://stats.datacite.org

[3]  DOI Content Negotiation: http://www.crosscite.org/cn

[4]  STM Association: http://www.stm-assoc.org

[5]  Joint statement from STM and DataCite: http://www.datacite.org/node/65

# About the Authors

**Sönke Bartling**

PD Dr. med. Sönke Bartling is a researcher in medical imaging sciences (CT/X-ray) at the German Cancer Research Center in Heidelberg and a board certified radiologist at the University Medical Center in Mannheim, both in Germany. His interest in Open Science grew over the last few years, when he realized that several things aren't the way they could be. The transition towards More Open Science is an opportunity for profound changes within the world of research, if driven by knowledgeable and opinionated researchers. *email: soenkebartling@gmx.de.*

**Roland Bertelmann**

Roland Bertelmann is head of the Library "Wissenschaftspark Albert Einstein", Potsdam, a joint library of several research institutions (GFZ German Research Centre for Geosciences, PIK Potsdam Institute for Climate Impact Research, Potsdam branch of Alfred Wegener Institute and IASS Institute for Advanced Sustainability Studies). He is responsible for Helmholtz Association's Open Access Coordination Office and is a member of the working group 'Open Access' in the Priority Initiative "Digital Information" of the German Alliance of Science Organisations. *email: roland.bertelmann@gfz-potsdam.de*

**Peter Binfield**

Peter Binfield is Co-Founder and Publisher of PeerJ, a recently launched open access publisher of *PeerJ* (a peer-reviewed journal for the biological and medical sciences) and *PeerJ PrePrints* (a preprint server). PeerJ aims to make high quality publication open and affordable to all, and it incorporates several innovations in regard to open peer review, cutting edge functionality, and new business models. Prior to founding PeerJ, Pete ran PLOS ONE for 4 years and before that worked at IoPP, Kluwer Academic, Springer, and SAGE. Pete has a PhD in underwater holography, which sounds much more interesting than it actually is. *email: pete@peerj.com*

S. Bartling and S. Friesike (eds.), *Opening Science,*
DOI: 10.1007/978-3-319-00026-8, © The Author(s) 2014

## Mathias Binswanger

Mathias Binswanger is professor for economics at the University of Applied Sciences Nordwestschweiz in Olten and lecturer at the University of St.Gallen, Switzerland. He was also visiting professor at the Technical University Freiberg in Germany, at the Qingdao Technological University in China, and the Banking University in Saigon (Vietnam). Mathias Binswanger is author of numerous books and articles in professional journals as well as in the press. His research foci are in the areas of macroeconomics, financial market theories, environmental economics, and also in exploring the relation between happiness and income. Mathias Binswanger is also the author of the book *"Die Tretmühlen des Glücks" (Treadmills of Luck)*, published in 2006, which became a bestseller in Switzerland. In 2010, his most recent book *"Sinnlose Wettbewerbe - Warum wir immer mehr Unsinn produzieren" (Pointless Competitions – Why we keep on producing more and more Nonsense)* was published.

## Jan Brase

Jan has a degree in Mathematics and a PhD in Computer science. His research background is in metadata, ontologies, and digital libraries. From 2005 to 2012 he was head of the DOI-registration agency for research data at the German National Library of Science and Technology (TIB). Since 2009 he has furthermore been Managing Agent of DataCite, an international consortium with 17 members from 12 countries. DataCite was founded in December 2009 and has set itself the goal of making the online access to research data for scientists easier by promoting the acceptance of research data as individual, citable scientific objects. Jan is Chair of the International DOI foundation (IDF), Vice-President of the International Council for Scientific and Technical Information (ICSTI), and Co-Chair of the recently established CODATA Data Citation task group. He is the author of several articles and conference papers on the citation of data sets and the new challenges for libraries in dealing with such non-textual information objects.

## Sünje Dallmeier-Tiessen

Sünje is currently working as a postdoctoral fellow in the Scientific Information Service at CERN (www.cern.ch). She came to CERN the end of 2009. Her research focuses on innovations in digital scholarly communication, i.e. the integration of research data. She is also particularly interested in the engagement of research communities in Open Science and possible support solutions. Beforehand, she worked for the Helmholtz Association's Open Access Coordination Office. *email: sunje.dallmeier-tiessen@cern.ch*

## Jörg Eisfeld-Reschke

Jörg Eisfeld-Reschke is a founder of ikosom - "Institut für Kommunikation in sozialen Medien". ikosom has been researching trends like Crowdfunding, Crowdinvesting, and Crowdsourcing through several publications and studies. The first Crowdsourcing Report for Germany and several studies on Crowdfunding in the creative industries has been published by ikosom. Jörg Eisfeld-Reschke is head of the working group "Digital Fundraising" of the German Fundraising Association and an alumnus of the Humboldt-Viadrina School of Governance.

## Benedikt Fecher

Benedikt Fecher is a doctoral researcher at the Humboldt Institute for Internet and Society in Berlin, Germany. The focus of his dissertation is on commons-based peer production in science and motivational aspects of participation in Open Science.

## Martin Fenner

Martin Fenner is a software developer for the publisher Public Library of Science (PLOS). Before joining PLOS in 2012, he worked as medical doctor and clinical cancer researcher at Hannover Medical School. He regularly writes about Science 2.0 in his blog *"Gobbledygook"*.

## Ralf Floca

Dr. Ralf Floca is a researcher in the fields of medical informatics and image processing, as well as group leader at the German Cancer Research Center in Heidelberg, Germany. His group, "Software Development for integrated Diagnostic and Therapy", facilitates translation within the research program "Imaging and Radiooncology" of the German Cancer Research Center. Ultimately the goal is to build bridges in order to overcome the gaps between state-of-the-art research and clinical application, therefore supporting a more personalized, more effective treatment of cancer. One important step towards this goal is the correlation and analysis of different data sources in terms of data intensive science. This is one of many connection points with topics within Open Science that motivated his contribution to this book. *email: r.floca@dkfz.de*

## Tobias Fries

While studying business and economics and writing his doctoral dissertation at Witten/Herdecke University in Germany, Tobias Fries was already building up various different internet companies. Living many years abroad in places like Buenos Aires and Geneva and working in the internet industry, he became interested in the field of scale free networks. His current startup companies all include some elements of scale free network thinking, from when his contribution is derived.

## Sascha Friesike

Dr. Sascha Friesike works as a postdoctoral researcher at the Alexander von Humboldt Institute for Internet and Society in Berlin, Germany. There he is in

charge of the research group "Open Science". He holds an engineering degree
from the Technical University in Berlin and a Ph.D. from the University of
St.Gallen. Prior to his engagement in Berlin, he worked as a researcher at the
Center for Design Research at Stanford University.

**Alexander Gerber**

Managing Director of the German Research Center for Science and Innovation
Communication, Alexander Gerber teaches science marketing (Technical
University Berlin), science communication (Rhine-Waal University), and
science policy (Rhine Sieg University). He is an elected member of the
Governing Board of Euroscience, and the ESOF Supervisory Board. He chairs
the Editorial Board of *Euroscientist* and the Stakeholders Assembly of the EU
science communication network *PLACES* (FP7). Mr. Gerber is also Secretary
General of the German Society for Science & Technical Publishing (TELI).

As an information scientist, he primarily focuses his research and consulting on
interactive media, citizen involvement, communication impact measurements, and
market insight in science and innovation. Before that, he was head of Marketing &
Communications at Fraunhofer ICT Group for 7 years, and editor of *InnoVisions*
Magazine for 5 years.

**Laure Haak**

Laurel L. Haak (http://orcid.org/0000-0001-5109-3700) is the Executive Director
of ORCID. She has experience in research evaluation, science policy, editing, and
IT systems development, with positions at Science Magazine, The US National
Academies, Discovery Logic, and Thomson Reuters. Dr. Haak was awarded a PhD
in Neuroscience by Stanford University Medical School, and performed
postdoctoral work at the US National Institutes of Health.

**Lambert Heller**

Lambert Heller is a librarian (LIS master degree from Humboldt University Berlin)
and social scientist. He heads the "Open Science Lab" team at TIB Hannover, the
German National Library of Science and Technology. Before that he worked for
DFG funded projects on information management and libraries. He then worked as
a subject librarian in Hannover, introducing reference management, publishing, and
social media related services at the TIB. He publishes and teaches about open
knowledge production, (scholarly) communication on the Internet, and library 2.0.

**Ulrich Herb**

Ulrich Herb holds a diploma in Sociology and is a PhD candidate in Information
Science at Saarland University. He is the Open Access expert at Saarland
University and the project manager at Saarland University and State Library for
projects in the realm of Electronic Publishing and Open Access. He also acts as a
freelance science consultant and science journalist. In 2012 he edited the

anthology *"Open Initiatives: Offenheit in der digitalen Welt und Wissenschaft"* which describes and analyzes claims and initiatives for Openness in scientific and non-scientific contexts as in, e.g. Open Access, Open Metrics, Open Data or Open Research Data.

## Michael Nentwich

The lawyer and science and technology scholar Michael Nentwich has worked and studied in Vienna, Bruges, Cologne, Warwick, and Colchester. Since 2006 he has been the director of the Institute of Technology Assessment (ITA) of the Austrian Academy of Sciences. In 2003, he published the volume *"Cyberscience. Research in the Age of the Internet"*, and, in 2012, together with René König, *"Cyberscience 2.0. Research in the Age of Digital Social Networks"*.

## René König

René König has studied sociology in Bielefeld (Germany) and Linköping (Sweden). He is currently working on his PhD thesis at Karlsruhe Institute of Technology's Institute for Technology Assessment and Systems Analysis (ITAS), focusing on online search behavior in the context of scientific controversies. Before this, he was a researcher at the Austrian Academy of Sciences in Vienna and published the book *"Cyberscience 2.0: Research in the Age of Digital Social Networks"* (2012) together with Michael Nentwich.

## James MacGregor

Formerly of the Electronic Text Centre at the University of New Brunswick, James has been a PKP system developer and community coordinator since 2007. He is involved in various components of the Project, including translation, testing, documentation, teaching, research, and even some code development occasionally. Ongoing areas of interest include alternative research metrics, community outreach and organization, and the ongoing and worldwide push for open access to scholarly research.

## Luka Oreskovic

Luka is a historian, publicist, and political analyst. At Harvard, he studies modern European political and economic history and is currently working on research of diplomatic and political history between the US and Yugoslavia for a biography of Henry Kissinger. He is a columnist for The Moscow Times and his writing has appeared in the Financial Times, LSE's EUROPP, UN Chronicle, Acque&Terre, and others. He advises leading geopolitical risk research and consulting companies on economic reform and policy.

## Heinz Pampel

Heinz Pampel studied library and information management at Stuttgart Media University (HdM). Since 2007 he has worked for the Helmholtz Association's Open Access Coordination Office at GFZ German Research Centre for Geosciences, and the Alfred Wegener Institute for Polar and Marine Research (AWI). He is a member of several work groups on the permanent access to scientific information. He is currently working on a doctoral dissertation at the Berlin School of Library and Information Science at Humboldt-Universität zu Berlin.

## Cornelius Puschmann

Dr. Cornelius Puschmann is a postdoctoral researcher at Humboldt University Berlin's School of Library and Information Science, a research associate at the Alexander von Humboldt Institute for Internet and Society, and a visiting fellow at the Oxford Internet Institute. Cornelius studies computer-mediated communication and the Internet's impact upon society, especially upon science and scholarship. He is also interested in the role of digital data for various different stakeholders (platform providers, data scientists, end users).

## Kaja Scheliga

Kaja Scheliga studied English and Drama (BA) at Royal Holloway, University of London, and Computer Science (MSc) at University College London. At the Humboldt Institute for Internet and Society, she is currently a doctoral researcher in the field of Open Science.

## Thomas Schildhauer

Since April 1999, Prof. Schildhauer has been the founder and director of the Institute of Electronic Business – the first affiliated institute of the University of Arts Berlin. In May 2007, he was appointed executive director of the Berlin Career College at the University of Arts, Berlin.

Since 2012 Prof. Schildhauer has been one of the executive directors of the Alexander von Humboldt Institute for Internet and Society gGmbH, where he is responsible for the research topic "Internet based innovation".

Since October 2012, he has served as the scientific director of the digital consultancy iDeers Consulting GmbH, founded by IEB and Hirschen Group GmbH.

## Michelle Sidler

Michelle Sidler is an Associate Professor of writing studies at Auburn University, Alabama, USA where she teaches classes in the rhetoric of science and technology, professional and technical communication, and English composition. Her research interests include writing, technology, science, and medicine. She has published multiple journal articles and chapters in edited collections, and her co-edited anthology, Computers in the *Composition Classroom*, won the 2008 Distinguished Book Award from the Computers and Composition community.

## Dagmar Sitek

Dagmar is head of the library at the German Cancer Research Center in Heidelberg, Germany. She is a member of the working group "Research Data" in the Priority Initiative "Digital Information" from the Alliance of German Science Organisations. *email: d.sitek@dkfz.de*

## Victoria Stodden

Victoria is an assistant professor of Statistics at Columbia University, and affiliated with the Columbia University Institute for Data Sciences and Engineering. She completed both her PhD in statistics and her law degree at Stanford University. Her research centers on the multifaceted problem of enabling reproducibility in computational science. This includes studying adequacy and robustness in replicated results, designing and implementing validation systems, developing standards of openness for data and code sharing, and resolving legal and policy barriers in disseminating reproducible research. She is the developer of the award winning "Reproducible Research Standard", a suite of open licensing recommendations for the dissemination of computational results. She is a co-founder of http://www.RunMyCode.org, an open platform for disseminating the code and data associated with published results, and enabling independent and public cloud-based verification of methods and findings. She is the creator and curator of SparseLab, a collaborative platform for reproducible computational research in underdetermined systems.

She was awarded the NSF EAGER grant "Policy Design for Reproducibility and Data Sharing in Computational Science." She serves as a member of the National Science Foundation's Advisory Committee on Cyberinfrastructure (ACCI), the Mathematics and Physical Sciences Directorate Subcommittee on "Support for the Statistical Sciences at NSF",and the National Academies of Science Committee on "Responsible Science: Ensuring the Integrity of the Research Process." She is also on several committees in the American Statistical Association: The Committee on Privacy and Confidentiality, the Committee on Data Sharing and Reproducibility, and the Presidential Strategic Initiative "Developing a Prototype Statistics Portal". She also serves on the Columbia University's Senate Information Technologies Committee.
*email: victoria@stodden.net*

## Kevin Stranack

Kevin is a Learning & Development Consultant with the Public Knowledge Project at the Simon Fraser University Library. Kevin received his Master of Library and Information Studies from the University of British Columbia in 2002, and his Master of Adult Education from the University of Regina in 2013.

## Vladimir Teif

Dr. Vladimir B. Teif works at the German Cancer Research Center (DKFZ). His current professional interests include quantitative modeling of gene regulation processes in chromatin. His research in this field was reported in "classical-style" peer-reviewed publications and highlighted by prestigious young scientist awards and fellowships. As a hobby, he is also an administrator or moderator for several scientific internet projects. In his manuscript, *"Science 3.0: The future of science in the Internet"*, he has critically evaluated current business models behind Science 2.0 and proposed alternatives that aim to make what he calls "Science 3.0" a more democratic and more effective solution, both for individual scientists and society.

## Ronald The

Ronald The is a designer, information architect, and concept developer. He holds a Graphic Design Diploma from the Karlsruhe University of Arts and Design and a Master of Arts in Communication, Planning, and Design from the University of Design, Schwäbisch Gmünd. Ronald founded the user experience consultancy company *infotectures*, based in Heidelberg, Germany. He specializes in user interface design, web-design/mobile design, and presentations. His involvement in research and Open Science was stimulated by his position as a guest lecturer at the Popakademie Mannheim and the University of Design Schwäbisch Gmünd.

## Hilger Voss

Consultant at iDeers Consulting, a joint venture between the Hirschen Group and the Institute of Electronic Business (affiliated institute of the University of Arts Berlin), where he used to be a member of the research staff. He studied Media Consulting at TU Berlin.

## Karsten Wenzlaff

Karsten Wenzlaff is the CEO and a founder of ikosom - "Institut für Kommunikation in sozialen Medien". ikosom has been researching trends like Crowdfunding, Crowdinvesting, and Crowdsourcing through several publications and studies. The first Crowdsourcing Report for Germany and several studies on Crowdfunding in the creative industries has been published by ikosom. Karsten Wenzlaff is an alumnus of the University of Cambridge and the University of Bayreuth.

## John Willinsky

John Willinsky is the Khosla Family Professor of Education at Stanford University and Professor (Limited Term) of Publishing Studies at Simon Fraser University, where he directs the Public Knowledge Project, which conducts research and develops scholarly publishing software intended to extend the reach and effectiveness of scholarly communication. His books include the *"Empire of Words: The Reign of the OED"* (Princeton, 1994); *"Learning to Divide the World: Education at Empire's End"* (Minnesota, 1998); *"Technologies of Knowing"* (Beacon 2000); and *"The Access Principle: The Case for Open Access to Research and Scholarship"* (MIT Press, 2006).